CONTEMPORARY

The Irwin Series in Marketing

Alreck and Settle
The Survey Research Handbook
Second Edition

Arens
Contemporary Advertising
Sixth Edition

Belch and Belch
*Introduction to Advertising and Promotion:
An Integrated Marketing Communications
Approach*
Third Edition

Bearden, Ingram, and LaForge
Marketing: Principles and Perspectives
First Edition

Bernhardt and Kinnear
Cases in Marketing Management
Sixth Edition

Berkowitz, Kerin, Hartley, and Rudelius
Marketing
Fourth Edition

Boyd, Walker, and Larréché
*Marketing Management: A Strategic
Approach, with a Global Orientation*
Second Edition

Cateora
International Marketing
Ninth Edition

Churchill, Ford, and Walker
Sales Force Management
Fourth Edition

Cole and Mishler
Consumer and Business Credit Management
Tenth Edition

Cravens
Strategic Marketing
Fourth Edition

Cravens, Lamb, and Crittenden
Strategic Marketing Management Cases
Fifth Edition

Crawford
New Products Management
Fourth Edition

Dillon, Madden, and Firtle
Essentials of Marketing Research
First Edition

Dillon, Madden, and Firtle
*Marketing Research in a Marketing
Environment*
Third Edition

Engel, Warshaw, and Kinnear
Promotional Strategy
Eighth Edition

Faria, Nulsen, and Roussos
Compete
Fourth Edition

Futrell
ABC's of Selling
Fourth Edition

Futrell
Fundamentals of Selling
Fifth Edition

Hawkins, Best, and Coney
Consumer Behavior
Sixth Edition

Lambert and Stock
Strategic Logistics Management
Third Edition

Lehmann and Winer
Product Management
First Edition

Levy and Weitz
Retailing Management
Second Edition

Levy and Weitz
Essentials of Retailing
First Edition

Mason, Mayer, and Ezell
Retailing
Fifth Edition

Mason and Perreault
The Marketing Game!
Second Edition

McCarthy and Perreault
*Essentials of Marketing: A Global-Managerial
Approach*
Sixth Edition

Meloan and Graham
*International and Global Marketing Concepts
and Cases*
First Edition

Patton
*Sales Force: A Sales Management Simulation
Game*
First Edition

Perreault and McCarthy
*Basic Marketing: A Global-Managerial
Approach*
Twelfth Edition

Peter and Donnelly
A Preface to Marketing Management
Sixth Edition

Peter and Donnelly
*Marketing Management: Knowledge and
Skills*
Fourth Edition

Peter and Olson
Consumer Behavior and Marketing Strategy
Fourth Edition

Peter and Olson
Understanding Consumer Behavior
First Edition

Quelch
Cases in Product Consumer Behavior
First Edition

Quelch, Dolan, and Kosnik
Marketing Management: Text and Cases
First Edition

Quelch and Farris
*Cases in Advertising and Promotion
Management*
Fourth Edition

Quelch, Kashani, and Vandermerwe
European Cases in Marketing Management
First Edition

Rangan
*Business Marketing Strategy: Cases, Concepts,
and Applications*
First Edition

Rangan
*Business Marketing Strategy: Concepts and
Applications*
First Edition

Smith and Quelch
Ethics in Marketing
First Edition

Stanton, Buskirk, and Spiro
Management of a Sales Force
Ninth Edition

Thompson and Stappenbeck
The Marketing Strategy Game
First Edition

Walker, Boyd, and Larréché
*Marketing Strategy: Planning and
Implementation*
Second Edition

Weitz, Castleberry, and Tanner
Selling: Building Partnerships
Second Edition

CONTEMPORARY

Advertising

SIXTH EDITION

WILLIAM F. ARENS
with the editorial collaboration of Jack J. Whidden

IRWIN
Chicago • Bogotá • Boston • Buenos Aires • Caracas
London • Madrid • Mexico City • Sydney • Toronto

Senior sponsoring editor: *Stephen M. Patterson*
Managing development editor: *Eleanore Snow*
Marketing manager: *Colleen Suljic*
Production supervisor: *Bob Lange*
Project editor: *Susan Trentacosti*
Assistant manager, desktop services: *Jon Christopher*
Interior designer: *Michael Warrell*
Art studio: *Precision Graphic Services, Inc.*
Cover designer: *AM Design/Michael Warrell*
Cover photographer: *Sharon Hoogstraten*
Coordinator, graphics & desktop services: *Keri Kunst*
Photo researcher: *Michael J. Hruby*
Compositor: *Precision Graphic Services, Inc.*
Typeface: *10/12 ITC Garamond Light*
Printer: *Von Hoffmann Press, Inc.*

Library of Congress Cataloging-in-Publication Data

Arens, William F.
     Contemporary advertising / William F. Arens with the editorial
collaboration of Jack J. Whidden. — 6th ed.
          p.   cm.
     Incudes bibliographical references and index.
     ISBN 0-256-18257-4
     1. Advertising,   I. Whidden, Jack J.   II. Title.
HF5821.B62   1996
659.1—dc20   95–33468

Printed in the United States of America
1 2 3 4 5 6 7 8 9 0 VH 2 1 0 9 8 7 6 5

To John E. and Ruth H. Arens
and to Jack D. and Francis E. Whidden

With love and appreciation for your
unwavering encouragement and support

Preface

veryone living and working in the modern world today is influenced by advertising. In fact, at some time in their lives, most people become creators of advertising—whether they design a flier for a school car wash, write classified ads for a garage sale, or develop a whole campaign for a business, charity, or political endeavor.

While advertising may have been viewed as a particularly American institution in the first half of the 20th century, that is certainly no longer the case. In fact, as the cover of this book illustrates, as early as 1917, British novelist Norman Douglas affirmed the global significance of advertising when he remarked, "You can tell the ideals of a nation by its advertisements." That was before radio and television. Today, our voices are no longer limited by the scope of 20th-century media. Thanks to the Internet and a variety of online database services, people and organizations can now send advertising messages to millions of people around the world—instantly. Advertising is undergoing a transformation of historic dimensions—from a monopolistic corporate monolog to a totally democratic dialog. Suddenly everybody has a voice.

That makes the study of advertising more important today than ever before, not only for students of business or journalism—who may be contemplating a career in the field—but also for students of sociology, psychology, political science, economics, history, language, science, or the arts. Most of these people will become users of advertising; all will be lifetime consumers of it.

The study of advertising gives students, regardless of their major, many valuable tools to use in any subsequent profession. For example, it helps them learn to:

- Plan and think strategically.
- Gather and analyze primary and secondary research data.
- Compute and evaluate the potential of alternative courses of action.
- Cooperate with a team in developing creative solutions to a problem.
- Analyze competitive proposals.
- Understand why people behave the way they do.
- Express themselves and their ideas with clarity and simplicity.
- Persuade others to their point of view.
- Appreciate and assess the quality of different creative endeavors.
- Use data to speak with knowledge, confidence, and conviction.

In addition, students of business and journalism gain several specific benefits from studying advertising. For example, it can help them:

- Discern the real social and cultural role of advertising and, conversely, the impact of a society's values on advertising.
- Understand how advertising supports the profession of journalism and relates to the whole field of communications.
- Appreciate the important, global effect of marketing and advertising on business, industry, and national economies.
- Comprehend the strategic function of advertising within the broader context of business and marketing.

- Evaluate and appreciate the impressive artistic creativity and technical expertise required in advertising.
- Discover what people in advertising and related disciplines do, how they do it, and the expanding career opportunities these fields now offer.

In previous editions of *Contemporary Advertising,* our mission was to present advertising as it is actually practiced—to put flesh on the bones of academic theory—with clarity and verve. As we approach the 21st century, our purpose remains the same. Advertising should be taught as it really is—as a business, as a marketing tool, as a creative process, and as a dynamic, hybrid discipline that employs various elements of the arts and sciences. We also believe advertising should be taught in an intelligible manner and lively style relevant to today's student.

For these reasons, *Contemporary Advertising* provides a number of exclusive student-oriented features.

STUDENT-ORIENTED FEATURES FOR THE 21ST CENTURY

Award-Winning Graphic Design

Contemporary Advertising has always been distinguished by its elegant, coffee-table-book feel and award-winning graphic design—an important feature for a book that has the responsibility of educating students about high quality in advertising art and production. The open, airy look—reinforced by the book's high-quality, non-see-through, clay-coated paper stock—contributes to learning by making the text material colorful, inviting, and accessible to the widest range of students. In the Sixth Edition, the elegance of this design is further enhanced with beautiful new part and chapter openers and a redesign of all the technical illustrations for greater clarity and simplicity. The text material is made reader-friendly with part and chapter overviews and chapter learning objectives.

Chapter-Opening Vignettes

To capture and hold student interest, each chapter begins—not with a case—but with a story. Written in a warm, narrative style, each vignette depicts an actual situation that illustrates a basic concept in the study of advertising. Wherever possible, the opening story is then woven through the chapter to demonstrate how textbook concepts actually come to life in real-world situations. For example, throughout Chapter 1, we use the history of the world's first branded commodity—Sunkist—to trace the development and growth of modern advertising and to demonstrate its marketing and economic functions. In Chapter 6, we use the launch of Claritin (already number-one in the Canadian over-the-counter antihistamine market) to illustrate the depth and complexity of marketing and advertising research. And in Chapter 9, we've wrapped the whole subject of creativity and the creative process around the story of how the Vitro/Robertson agency developed its magnificent, award-winning campaign for Taylor Guitars.

Extensive Illustration Program

The best way to teach is to set a good example. So each of the 17 chapters features beautiful full-color illustrations of currently running, award-winning ads, commercials, and campaigns that demonstrate the best in the business from the last three years. In fact, *Contemporary Advertising* may be the most heavily illustrated textbook on the market, representing all the major media—print, electronic, outdoor—in a balanced manner. We carefully selected the examples and illustrations for both their quality and their relevance to students.

Furthermore, we included a mix of local, national, and international ads from both business-to-business and consumer campaigns. In-depth captions tell the stories behind many of the ads and explain how the ads demonstrate the concepts discussed in the text.

We illustrated the book liberally with models, charts, graphs, and tables. Some of these encapsulate useful information on advertising concepts or the advertising industry. Others depict the processes employed in account management, research, media planning, and production.

Full-Color Portfolios

In addition to the individual print ads and actual frames from TV commercials, the book contains several multipage portfolios of outstanding creative work. These include "Strategic Use of the Creative Mix," "Out-of-Home Advertising: A 20th Century Art Form," "Portfolio of Award-Winning Magazine Advertising," and others.

Creative Department

The "Creative Department" is a special section in Chapter 11 that describes how an interesting print ad and TV commercial were produced from beginning to end. A full-color print ad for Adidas features an actual acetate color key (called a *transvision*)—a first in advertising texts. And the TV commercial for Adidas' new Predator model features its highly successful and popular World Cup spot—"This shoe sucks!"

Advertising Laboratories

Active participation enhances learning, so we incorporated "Advertising Laboratories" into every chapter. These unique sidebars to the world of advertising introduce students to topics of current interest or controversy and then involve them in the subject by posing questions that stimulate critical thinking. Some of the many topics presented in Ad Labs include government regulation, bottom-up marketing, creativity, "green" marketing, and direct-mail advertising.

Ethical Issues in Advertising

Today's students will be 21st century practitioners. They will face new and challenging ethical issues, and they will need to exercise greater sensitivity than their 20th century counterparts. Therefore, in *every* chapter of the book, we introduced a current Ethical Issue in advertising—to focus attention on the most critical social questions facing advertisers today. These include puffery, advertising to children, targeting ethnic minorities, privacy, negative political advertising, visual and statistical manipulation, and others.

Practical Checklists

Advertising is a broad subject encompassing many disciplines, and one dilemma both advertising students and practitioners face is how to handle and organize large volumes of information and then creatively convert this data into effective advertising. For this reason, students truly appreciate the numerous, handy Checklists that appear regularly throughout the text. The Checklists can stimulate memory, organize thinking, and reinforce important concepts. Some of these include Checklist for Writing Effective Copy; Checklist for International Media Planning; Checklist for Creating Effective TV Commercials; Checklist for Writing a News Release; and Checklist for Developing Local Advertising Budgets, to mention just a few. In the years that follow, students will find the Checklists an invaluable, practical career resource for developing marketing and advertising plans, writing and designing effective ads and commercials, selecting and scheduling media, evaluating advertising work, and making advertising decisions.

Reference Library

In keeping with our desire to build long-term value into the book (without adding text length), we introduced the Reference Library as a new feature in the Sixth Edition. Located at the end of the book immediately following Chapter 17, the Reference Library contains a wealth of supplementary exhibits, checklists, tables, and models for students or professors who seek additional information or greater detail on a subject of interest. The exhibits in the Reference Library are numbered to correspond to relevant chapters. Professors can assign this material or not, depending on their course objectives. But students will find the Reference Library a valuable, long-term handbook for their future careers and lives. Some exhibits in the Reference Library include Advertising Regulations in Western Europe; Using Marketing Research for New Product Development; Checklist of Product Marketing Facts for Creatives; Young's Techniques for Producing Ideas; Detailed Explanation of Duncan's IMC Model; Trade Show Budgeting Checklist; and many, many others.

Additional Learning Aids

Each chapter concludes with a summary followed by questions for review and discussion. These pedagogical aids are designed to help students review chapter contents and assimilate what they have learned. Throughout the text, key ideas and terms are highlighted with boldface type and defined when introduced. The definitions of all these terms are collected at the end of the book in the most thorough and extensive Glossary in the field.

Our continuing goal has been to bring clarity to the often-murky subject of advertising. Our method has been to personally involve students as much as possible in the practical experiences of advertising while simultaneously giving them a clear understanding of advertising's dynamic role in both marketing management and the human communication process. In the pursuit of this objective, we instituted an immense number of modifications and improvements in the Sixth Edition of *Contemporary Advertising,* making this the most extensive revision in the book's history.

Because of the inclusion of chapters focused on marketing and advertising research, the creative process, relationship marketing, IMC, direct marketing and sales promotion, public relations and corporate advertising, and local and noncommercial advertising, *Contemporary Advertising* remains the most comprehensive and current text on the market.

Up to Date and Concise

In this revision, our first effort was to update all statistics and tables and to document the most recent academic and professional source material to give *Contemporary Advertising* the most current and relevant compendium of academic and trade citations in the field. We referenced important recent research on topics ranging from the effects of advertising and sales promotion on brand-building to relationship marketing, integrated communications, and international advertising law. And we introduced or redesigned the building-block models that facilitate student comprehension of the often-complex processes involved in human communication, consumer behavior, marketing research, and IMC.

Second, we prudently governed the length of the text material. We integrated new material on the creative process and interactive media while eliminating an entire

FOR THE PROFESSOR: THE SIXTH EDITION HAS BEEN EXTENSIVELY REVISED

chapter from the book. The main body of text measures only 340 pages. The remaining 300 pages are devoted to illustrations, graphics, sidebar information, and design, all of which keep the text open, airy, and inviting while sharpening *clarity*—the hallmark of *Contemporary Advertising*.

Compared to the true length of other comprehensive course books—some of which have masked almost 25 percent more body text by the clever compression of type—*Contemporary Advertising* is now the most efficient textbook in the field.

Fresh, Contemporary, Relevant Examples

We added many new, real-world examples, selected for their currency and their relevance to students. Likewise, most of the chapter-opening stories are new, such as the advertising success stories of Sunkist, *Jurassic Park,* United Parcel Service, Prodigy, Snapple, and the *Village Voice.* Others document communication misfires such as *Last Action Hero* and Intel. All the Ad Labs, Checklists, and full-color portfolios have been updated, expanded, or replaced with more recent examples.

Global Orientation Integrated Throughout

In light of the increasing globalization of business, we added more examples of international advertising throughout the book. All the international data has been extensively revised and updated to reflect the increased importance of advertising in the new economic and marketing realities of Europe. Throughout the text, a new global icon flags international examples or data.

Focus on Technology and Integrated Marketing Communications

In recent years, the technology of advertising has changed dramatically. For example, in just the last five years, the computer revolutionized the way advertising is planned, designed, produced, and scheduled. And the introduction of the new digital, interactive media is sparking another creative revolution in advertising. The Sixth Edition of *Contemporary Advertising* chronicles the advent of this revolution in numerous chapters.

One result of this exploding technology—and consequent market fragmentation—has been a growing realization by major advertisers and agencies of the importance of relationship marketing and integrated marketing communications. In response to this, we wove the IMC perspective throughout the text, introduced the concept of IMC early in the book, explained the impact of IMC on marketing, advertising, and media planning, and focused the entire last part of the book on the details of relationship marketing and IMC, with references to the most recent important research on these topics.

NEW: Complete Campaign

So that students can see how many of the principles taught in the text come together in the real world, we have included (in Appendix C) the complete story of the currently running, highly successful advertising campaign for Mountain Dew created by BBDO New York. We are indebted to both BBDO and PepsiCo for authorizing us to share the details of this entertaining, student-relevant campaign.

Local and Business-to-Business Advertising Coverage

Throughout the book, *Contemporary Advertising* addresses the needs of both small and large consumer and business-to-business advertisers with its many examples, case histories, Ad Labs, Checklists, and advertisements. Moreover, this is one of the few texts to devote adequate attention to the needs of the small retail advertiser by discussing how local advertisers can integrate their marketing communications.

Canadian Examples

Most U.S. students do not realize that Canada is by far the largest trading partner of the U.S., and it's only going to become larger in light of the North American Free Trade Agreement. We feel it's very worthwhile for these students to develop some familiarity with the importance of our closest neighbor.

Contemporary Advertising is widely used in Canada. Likewise, many academic and trade references for the text emanate from Canadian journals and trade publications. Therefore, we have included a variety of high-quality Canadian advertisements throughout the book—in both English and French—with which Canadian students and professors will be familiar. And wherever differences exist between Canadian and U.S. advertising, we have attempted to point this out.

Highlights of This Revision

While all chapters have been edited and updated, other specific highlights of the Sixth Edition revision include the following:

Chapter 1: "The Dimensions of Advertising." A new chapter-opening vignette—the story of the Sunkist brand—kicks off the Sixth Edition. The communication process (previously discussed in Chapter 4) moved up to Chapter 1. We present it, along with Stern's new advertising communication model, immediately following the definition of advertising. We augmented the history section with a thorough discussion of the impact of new technology and laid the groundwork for the creative revolution on the horizon. A new Ethical Issue discusses the difference between an ethical dilemma and an ethical lapse.

Chapter 2: "The Social, Legal, and Ethical Aspects of Advertising." This chapter opens with a new story—the incredible success of the movie *Jurassic Park* and the role advertising played in protecting the film's trademark rights for the studio's worldwide merchandising efforts. This chapter offers a more balanced presentation of what's right and wrong about advertising, acknowledging the profession's shortcomings—for instance, in the area of sexual and ethnic stereotyping. The discussion of deception in advertising has been updated, referencing the recent work by Ivan Preston. We treat the subject of ethics in advertising in the text, and we introduce a new model explaining the levels of ethical responsibility. Further, the Ethical Issue in this chapter explains in detail the subject of puffery. The detailed process charts from the previous edition have moved to the Reference Library.

Chapter 3: "The Advertising Business: Agencies, Clients, Media, and Suppliers." This chapter also features a new opening story: how a top American ethnic-specialty agency, Muse Cordero Chen, developed a mundane job into an outstanding ethnic-oriented dealer advertising kit for Honda. The story is woven throughout the chapter to demonstrate what agency people do and how they work. We introduced new material on the hottest new agency discipline—account planning. And we incorporated new material on the media and suppliers in order to present a balanced view of all the participants in the advertising industry. The Ethical Issue deals with client-agency etiquette in account reviews.

Chapter 4: "Marketing and Consumer Behavior: The Foundations of Advertising." The marketing misfire of Arnold Schwarzenegger's *Last Action Hero* film introduces this chapter and demonstrates the important role marketing plays in advertising success. The discussion of the communication process moved to Chapter 1; careful editing cut this chapter's length by six pages. The Ethical Issue deals with the subject of marketing and advertising exploitation.

Chapter 5: "Using Marketing and Advertising to Link Products to Markets." To enhance this chapter, we expanded coverage of international markets, introduced the concept of occasion-based segmentation, extended the discussion of product user status, offered greater detail on segmenting business markets, and focused more attention on the role of branding. We describe the elements of the marketing mix as product, price, distribution, and communication, referring to the 4Ps as a convenient mnemonic device for remembering these elements. The Ethical Issue deals with the morality of targeting ethnic markets.

Chapter 6: "Marketing and Advertising Research: Inputs to the Planning Process." The successful introduction of Claritin by Schering Canada to the over-the-counter antihistamine market is recounted in the chapter-opening story and used to demonstrate the basic steps in the research process. We describe the role of marketing research in helping companies develop marketing mixes committed to the three Rs of marketing: recruiting, retaining, and regaining customers. We reorganized elements within the chapter, clarified the categories of advertising research, and expanded the section on doing research in international markets. The Ethical Issue deals with the use of statistical manipulation to sell an idea or a product or to fulfill a predetermined agenda.

Chapter 7: "Marketing and Advertising Planning: Top-Down, Bottom-Up, and IMC." This chapter has been extensively revised. We present the three models for marketing planning in use today: top-down, bottom-up, and integrated marketing communications (IMC). The Saturn story, highlighted with many illustrations and specific examples, demonstrates the importance of IMC and serves as an apt case for introducing this popular new concept and process. We also show how the accepted concept of advertising effects is changing in light of new research. In the section on the creative mix, we present the new Kim-Lord Grid, an improvement over the old FCB Grid, to further clarify the product concept element for students. A new Ethical Issue discusses the controversy surrounding comparative advertising.

Chapter 8: "Planning Media Strategy: Finding Links to the Market." We moved the chapter on media planning forward to assemble all the planning chapters in the same part and introduce them in a more logical order preceding the creative section. The chapter begins with a new story—how a young media director at J. Walter Thompson used modern technology to put together an award-winning, cutting-edge media plan for Prodigy on a very limited budget. We updated the discussion of effective reach and frequency with new research; and the elements of the media mix have expanded to include 5Ms—markets, money, media, mechanics, and methodology. The chapter also features expanded coverage of global media and a new Ethical Issue discussion of gifts and commissions.

Chapter 9: "Creative Strategy and the Creative Process." This chapter is new to the Sixth Edition. It examines the nature of creativity, styles of thinking, the importance of creativity to advertising, and the role of the agency creative team. We even included a creative gymnasium in the chapter to give students the fun of exploring their creative side. The chapter-opening story concerns a highly creative campaign for Taylor Guitars; and a new Ethical Issue discusses a controversial topic in advertising creativity—the use of sex appeal in advertising appeals.

Chapter 10: "Creative Execution: Art and Copy." This chapter responds to many requests by combining material from old chapters 8 and 9 to create a new single chapter on art and copy in advertising. The elegant Timberland story introduces the chapter as an exceptional example of the best in advertising copywriting and art direction. We balanced our treatment of ads for both print and electronic media in this chapter and expanded the discussion of art in international markets. A completely new illustration program is included, and the art director's portfolio contains current, student-relevant ads to enliven the text matter. A new Ethical Issue discusses the morality of using high-tech methods to make changes to other people's artistic work.

Chapter 11: "Producing Ads for Print, Electronic, and Digital Media." Chapter 11 is a combination of old chapters 10 and 11, plus new material on producing ads for the digital interactive media. A new opening story on Kraft Systems demonstrates the intricacy of producing an ad from initiation to completion. In response to professor requests, much of the detail on production has moved to the Reference Library. The chapter was carefully edited throughout to ensure that students gain the most practical information possible on how to produce quality print and broadcast media materials. A new Creative Department shows how a print ad and a TV commercial were produced for Adidas. And a new Ethical Issue focuses on the employee medical problems that may arise in the absence of ethical decisions about the workplace environment.

Chapter 12: "Buying Print Media." A dramatic, award-winning, business-to-business advertising campaign for United Parcel Service provides a fresh opening for the magazine section of this chapter; and an amusing story about the irreverent campaign for the *Village Voice* newspaper kicks off the newspaper section. A new section on Print Media and New Technologies has been added, and we carefully edited the chapter for currency, efficiency, and clarity. A new Ethical Issue discusses plagiarism and shows how close borrowing can come to stealing.

Chapter 13: "Buying Electronic and Digital Interactive Media." A new chapter-opening story on Duracell features the phantasmic Putterman family created by Ogilvy & Mather and demonstrates state-of-the-art commercial technology and special effects. The discussion on TV audience trends is shorter and updated, and we added greater clarity to the section on audience measurement. The story of Snapple's incredible success opens the radio section of the chapter and helps introduce a new concept—*imagery transfer.* A completely new section in this chapter discusses digital interactive media: PCs, online databases, the Internet, CD-ROM, electronic kiosks, and interactive TV. The Ethical Issue in this chapter focuses on advertising to and through children.

Chapter 14: "Buying Out-of-Home, Exhibitive, and Supplementary Media." We completely reorganized this chapter. We updated and streamlined the information on outdoor and transit advertising. The next section introduces the concept of *exhibitive media*—media designed to bring customers eyeball-to-eyeball with the product. These include product packaging, point-of-purchase, and trade show booths and exhibits. The supplementary media section features an expanded discussion of Yellow Pages advertising, which is often the primary medium for small local businesses. A new Ethical Issue discusses the effect of spillover media on unintended audiences such as children.

Chapter 15: "Relationship Building: IMC, Direct Marketing, Direct Mail, and Sales Promotion." The key to building brand equity in the 90s and beyond will be for companies to develop mutually beneficial relationships with their customers and other stakeholders. This premise guided our treatment of the last three chapters in *Contemporary Advertising.* We present new material on relationship marketing and demonstrate that, because communication is the key to any relationship, integrated marketing communications is the best way for companies to manage their relationship marketing efforts. We introduce Duncan's new IMC Macro Model, but save the detailed description of the model for the Reference Library. The chapter then discusses the important role of direct marketing and direct-mail advertising in the IMC process. Finally, sales promotion is presented as an important IMC tactic. The Ethical Issue discusses privacy—the individual's rights versus the rights of the public.

Chapter 16: "Relationship Building: Public Relations and Corporate Advertising." The recent public relations gaffe over the Pentium chip that tarnished Intel's stellar image leads off this chapter and demonstrates the importance of effective public relations management in any IMC program. We introduce the term *marketing public relations (MPR)* to refer to PR activities used for marketing purposes. We also discuss the current interest in *reputation management* as a major division of PR activities. The Ethical Issue debates the controversy surrounding advertorials.

Chapter 17: "Relationship Building: Local and Noncommercial Advertising." The subject of integrated marketing communications concludes with a discussion of how local and noncommercial advertisers, who typically lack the funding of large national advertisers, can employ IMC to achieve their marketing objectives. We added new material on signage and displays in the retail environment. A short story about Maisonette Restaurant in Cincinnati demonstrates how a sophisticated local marketer integrates all its activities. Discussion of the Ad Council has been expanded and updated to include its new commitment to the health and welfare of children. The Ethical Issue in this chapter debates the morality of negative political advertising.

Appendix C: "The Complete Campaign—Creating a Splash for Mountain Dew." The incredibly successful Mountain Dew campaign from BBDO describes in detail how all the concepts taught in the text come together in real life. A video supplement to the text includes the commercials in the campaign.

Appendix D: "Career Planning in Advertising." This section has been completely updated with many helpful hints for students about to launch their careers. It includes salary figures for entry-level employees in a variety of advertising-related positions.

Appendix E: "Industry Resources." This new appendix organizes a great deal of practical information students can use to perform further research in areas of interest or to advance their careers by joining an organization focused on their specialty.

SUPPLEMENTARY MATERIALS

While the text itself is a complete introduction to the field of advertising, it is accompanied by a number of valuable supplemental materials designed to assist the instructor.

Instructor's Manual

With the assistance of Bonnie Dowd of Palomar College, we greatly expanded the Instructor's Manual to include a wealth of new material and suggestions for classroom lectures and discussions. It includes a lecture outline for each chapter, answers to all discussion questions, suggested workshops, projects, and debates, and additional material for reading or project assigments.

Video Supplements

To illustrate how the principles discussed in the text have actually been applied in business, the book is supplemented by two special video programs and a video instructor's guide. One video was produced exclusively for *Contemporary Advertising* by the Author for instructor use in the classroom. It includes a wide variety of domestic and international commercials specially referenced with voice-over introductions to specific chapters. This video is not only text-specific in subject matter, it also includes many of the commercials discussed in the text—such as the Mountain Dew campaign from Appendix C, the Claritin campaign discussed in Chapter 6, the Saturn campaign from Chapter 7, and the Adidas and Gotcha campaigns from Chapter 11—to mention just a few.

The second video was produced by the Advertising Educational Foundation, to whom we express our deep gratitude and appreciation. It includes a behind-the-scenes look at advertising research at work. The video, entitled "Good-bye Guesswork: How Research Guides Today's Advertisers," includes case studies for V8 Juice, Maidenform, and AT&T's "800" Service, and shows how research is used to develop new ads, to refine ad campaigns, to decide the best place to advertise, and to evaluate current ads.

Offered at no charge to adopters of *Contemporary Advertising*, these video supplements are designed to help the instructor teach real-world decision making and demonstrate some of the best current examples of television advertising from around the world.

Color Transparencies

Also available to instructors is a high-quality selection of overhead transparencies. These include over 50 of the important models and graphs presented in the text and over 70 ads not found in the text—all produced in full color. The ads are accompanied by Teaching Notes that tie them specifically to their relevant chapter concepts.

Testing Systems

An extensive bank of objective test questions prepared by Tom Pritchett and Betty Pritchett of Kennesaw State University was carefully designed to provide a fair, structured program of evaluation. The testing system is available in several formats:

- Irwin Computerized Test Generator System—a convenient and flexible question retrieval device for mainframe systems, providing an extensive bank of questions to use as is or with additional questions of your own.
- COMPUTEST—a microcomputer testing system that provides convenient and flexible retrieval from an extensive bank of questions to use as is or with additional questions of your own.
- COMPUGRADE—a microcomputer gradebook that stores and prints all grades by name or ID number. Capable of weighting and averaging grades.
- Teletest—a toll-free phone-in service to request customized exams prepared for classroom use.

USES FOR THIS TEXT

Contemporary Advertising was written for the undergraduate student in liberal arts, journalism, and business schools. However, because of its practical, hands-on approach, depth of coverage, and marketing management emphasis, it is also widely used in independent schools, university extension courses, and courses on advertising management. The wealth of award-winning advertisements also makes it a resource guide to the best work in the field for students in art and graphic design courses and for professionals in the field.

Many of the stories, materials, and techniques included in this text come from the Author's personal experience as a full-time marketing communications executive and adjunct professor at San Diego State University and the University of California—San Diego. Others come from the experiences of friends and colleagues in the business. We believe this book will be a valuable resource guide, not only in the study of advertising but later in the practice of it as well. In all cases, we hope readers will experience the feel and the humanness of the advertising world—whether they intend to become professionals in the business, to work with practitioners, or simply to become more sophisticated consumers.

Acknowledgments

 e are deeply indebted to many individuals in advertising and related fields for their personal encouragement and professional assistance. These include, but are not limited to: Joyce Harrington at the American Association of Advertising Agencies; Rena Spangler and Linda McCreight at the Advertising Educational Foundation; Ed Erhardt and Priscilla Garsten at *Advertising Age;* Paul Alvarez at Ketchum Communications; Sean Hardwick at Team One; Bob Pritikin at the Mansion, San Francisco; Vonda LePage at FCB/Leber Katz; David Kreinick at Creative Media, Inc.; Keith Reinhard and Lou Tripodi at DDB Needham; Phillippe Krakowski and Kathleen Rouane at BBDO; Gary Hemphil at PepsiCo; Peter Farago at Farago Advertising; Hank Seiden at the Seiden Group; Larry Jones, Nicoletta Poloynis, and Andrew Gold at Foote, Cone & Belding, Los Angeles; Russ Hanlin and Gee Winands at Sunkist Growers; Barbara Callihan and Stephanie King Canter at Goldsmith Jeffrey, New York; P.J. Santro at Levi Strauss & Co.; Tom Robbins at Foote, Cone & Belding, San Francisco; David Mucha at Hal Riney & Partners; Vicki Holman and Steve Shannon at Saturn Corporation; Holly Petitjean at Johnson Ukropina Creative Marketing; Trevor Beattie and Steve Chetham at TBWA Holmes Knight Ritchie, London; Mike Salisbury at Salisbury Communications; Tom Drese at McCann Erickson, San Francisco; Larry Light of the Coalition for Brand Equity; Ella Strubel, Wally Petersen, Joe Silberman, and Mark Hart at Leo Burnett; Jo Muse, Mavis Cordero, David Chen, Mike Whitlow, and Lisa Wright at Muse Cordero Chen; Gerry Rubin at Rubin Postaer; Scott Bedbury at Nike; Cindy Becker and Alan Bonine at VitroRobertson, San Diego; Nick Cohen at Mad Dogs & Englishmen, New York; Kathryn Davis at Cole & Weber, Seattle; Robert Unmacht at M Street Directory; Maureen Sweeney at Sweeney Media; Douglas Atkin at Wells, Rich, Greene/BDDP; Diana Adachi at ViewZ; John Garrett at SRI International; Duncan Milner at Chiat Day, Los Angeles; Raphaele at Raphaele Digital Transparencies; and Paula Veale at the Ad Council.

For their warm, open and gracious contributions of time, counsel, and materials, we extend our appreciation, *avec tous nos remerciements,* to all our Canadian friends, especially Joe Mullie at the Association des Agences de Publicité du Quebec; Chuck McDonald and Robert West at Schering Canada; Francois Duffar, Daniel Rabinowicz, Pierre Delagrave, Nicole Lapierre, Normand Chiasson, Ian Saville, Jocelyn Laverdure, and Manon Caza at Cossette Communication-Marketing; Marcel Barthe at Optimum; Francois Descarie at Impact Research; Yves Gougoux, Caroline Jarvis, and Sylvie Thauvette at BCP Strategie Creátivité; Jacques LeFebvre at MacLaren LINTAS, Montreal; Andre Morrow at Marketel; Andre Beauchesne at Bos; Patrick Pierra at *InfoPress;* J. Richard Genin at the Television Bureau of Canada; Paul Lavoie at Taxi; Jane Williams and Andre Desmorais at Young & Rubicam, Montreal; Marcel Gilbert and Patrice Lafleur at the Quebec government office in Los Angeles; Jean Pelletier, formerly at the Publicité-Club de Montreal; Normand Grenier at Communications Grenier; and Elisabeth Cohen at the Biodome, Montreal.

For helping us navigate the Canadian legal waters, we greatly appreciate the generous contributions of Eric Gross of Gowling and Henderson, Toronto; Bryan Fraser of Hooey-Remus, Toronto; and Robert Legault of Legault & Joly, Montreal. And for great support and assistance, we are indebted to the Canadian Consulate General in Los Angeles, especially Pamela Johnson and Rosalind Wolfe.

Special thanks go to several longtime friends whose contributions, continuous support, and wise counsel we value and appreciate immeasurably: Al Ries at Ries & Ries; Susan Irwin at McCann-Erickson; Victoria Horstmann at Ketchum Advertising; Jan Sneed at Wells, Rich, Green/BDDP; Rance Crain at *Advertising Age;* Larry Londre at the University of Southern California; Randy Grimm at National Decision Systems; Gary Corolis at MacLaren LINTAS/Toronto; Cecil Scaglione at Scaglione Communications; Robert Baxter at McGill University; Jack Trout at Trout and Partners; and Brad Lynch formerly of the Ad Council.

In addition, we are appreciative of the moral support, encouragement, generous assistance, and friendship of Tom and Dena Michael, Brannon Wait, Dan Weinberg, Sid Stein, Alayne Harris, Kelly Segraves, Professor E. L. Deckinger, Larry Mattera, Suzie Toutant, Rob Settle, Pam Alreck, Bruce Henderson, Jann Pasler, Mary Beth McCabe, Barnard and Sylvia Thompson, Don and Ann Ritchey, Carlos and Yolanda Cortez, Susan Harding, Gene Theriault, Jim and LeAnna Zevely, Fred and Brenda Bern, Bill and Olivia Werner, Alan and Rita Moller, and—for giving so much to so many for so long—Stanley D. Woodworth, Sid Bernstein, and John O'Toole, gone from our midst but never forgotten.

We appreciate the understanding and support of our far-flung families, all the Arenses and Whiddens, and most especially Olivia, for her unwavering love and support.

A special thank you to Margene Pyeatte and Zahna Caillat, for their specialized knowledge and expert assistance. Likewise, great appreciation to Janne Flora for her enthusiastic mothering and total dedication to keeping us all organized; and to Brannon Wait, Matthew Spellman, and Brandy Constantino for timely editorial help and for being there when we needed them most. Our thanks to Tom and Betty Pritchett of Kennesaw State University, who worked against incredible deadlines to prepare the Manual of Tests. We are particularly thankful for the skill and expertise of our video mavens Kelly and Jake Segraves. Finally, special recognition goes to Bonnie Dowd of Palomar College for her inspired editorial assistance on the Instructor's Manual and her uncanny ability to do everything, now.

We are blessed with what must no doubt be the best editorial team in the business. Led by Steve Patterson, Eleanore Snow, and Michael Warrell, the Irwin A-team included Susan Trentacosti, Mike Hruby, Harriet Stockanes, Jon Christopher, Bob Lange, Colleen Suljic, and Irene Sotiroff. Special thanks also to the suits: John Black, Rob Zwettler, and Jerry Saykes. In the effort to make this the most timely and current book on the market, you all invariably found a way to do the impossible. We appreciate your dedication to excellence and your friendship more than you will ever know.

We also wish to recognize and thank the American Association for Education in Journalism and Mass Communications, the American Marketing Association, and the American Academy of Advertising, three organizations whose publications and meetings provide a valuable forum for the exchange of ideas and for professional growth.

We are deeply grateful to the many instructors, professors, practitioners, and academic reviewers whose ideas, critical insights, and suggestions were invaluable in the preparation of this edition. These include, but are certainly not limited to, the following individuals: Dan Stout, Brigham Young University; Robert H. Davis, University of Central Florida; Ivan L. Preston, University of Wisconsin–Madison; James W. Taylor, Shay Sayre, and J. Nicholas De Bonis, California State University–Fullerton; Kevin Hall and Patricia Rose, Florida International University; Marilyn Kern-Foxworth, Texas A&M University; Joel Dubow, St. Joseph's University; Tom Duncan, University of Colorado–Boulder; James Hunt, University of North Carolina–Wilmington; Marlene Kahla, Stephen F. Austin University; Priscilla LaBarbera, New York University; Marla Stafford, University of North Texas; Jan LeBlanc Wicks, Indiana University; Kurt Wildermuth, University of Missouri–Columbia; and Bern Wisner, Central Oregon Community College.

Survey respondents—those listed below and others who prefer to remain anonymous—merit our thanks for helping us get started on the sixth edition: Kevin Celuch,

Illinois State University; David Claire, Johnson and Wales University; Marjorie Cooper, Baylor University; James Cox, Jefferson Community College; Checkitan Dev, Cornell University; Kathleen Donnelly, Point Park College; Joel Dubow, St. Joseph's University; Alfred Fabian, Ivy Tech State College; Scott Follows, Acadia University; William Fudge, University of South Florida; Larry Haase, Central Missouri State University; Kelly Parker Hanna, Pittsburgh Technical Institute; David Heckenlively, San Francisco State University; Walter Henry, University of California–Riverside; Catherine Howard, Ball State University; Michael Johnson, Delaware County Community College; Regan Kania, Michigan State University; Donald Magly, Owens Community College; Henry Nash, Mississippi State University; J.R. Ogden, Kutztown University; James Parker, Hofstra University; Joe Ries, San Francisco State University; Nick Sarantakes, Austin Community College; Shay Sayre, California State University–Fullerton; Dennis Schneider, Fresno City College; Victoria Seitz, California State University–San Bernardino; Kenneth Shamley, Sinclair College; Ronald Taylor, Mississippi State; Emelda Williams, Arkansas State University; Molly Catherine Ziske, Michigan State University.

To all of you, thank you. Without you, it wouldn't happen.

W. F. A.

About the Cover

"You can tell the ideals of a nation by its advertising."—Norman Douglas, 1917

. . . And soon we will be able to tell the ideals of the <u>world</u>. Our cover shows the principles that must be followed to achieve this end. A tranquil mountain scene represents the clear goals and thinking one needs in all steps of advertising. The lap-top computer shows the effect of the emerging technology on advertising and production that will continue into the foreseeable future. The impressionist painting on the computer screen and the two pieces of chalk at the right of the collage emphasize the contribution of beauty and creativity to the "art" of advertising. The importance of originality is shown through the unique balance of the apple and the globe, which also remind us of the continuing globalization of business and its impact on advertising.

Contents in Brief

V

BUILDING RELATIONSHIPS THROUGH INTEGRATED MARKETING COMMUNICATIONS (IMC)

Contents

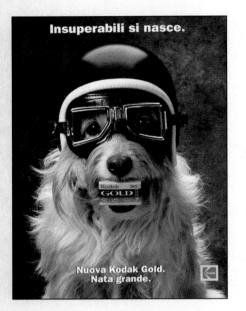

While you don't necessarily dress for men, it doesn't hurt, on occasion, to see one drool like the pathetic dog that he is.

BODYSLIMMERS™ by NANCY GANZ

II
CRAFTING MARKETING AND ADVERTISING STRATEGIES

4   **Marketing and Consumer Behavior: The Foundations of Advertising   104**

The Assumption Syndrome, 106

The Importance of Marketing to Advertising 106

What Is Marketing? 107
Customer Needs and Product Utility, 107   Perception, Exchanges, and Satisfaction, 109

The Key Participants in the Marketing Process 109
Customers, 110   Markets, 110   Marketers, 112

The Importance of Knowing the Consumer 112

Consumer Behavior from the Advertiser's Perspective 112

Personal Processes in Consumer Behavior 113
*The Consumer Perception Process, 113   The Consumer Learning Process, 117
The Consumer Motivation Process, 119*

Interpersonal Influences on Consumer Behavior 122
Family Influence, 122   Society's Influence, 122   The Influence of Culture and Subculture, 124

Nonpersonal Influences on Consumer Behavior 126
*Time, 126   Place, 126   Environment, 126
International Environments, 126*

The Purchase Decision and Postpurchase Evaluation 128

• Ad Lab 4–A: Understanding Needs and Utility 108

• Ethical Issue: Is It Marketing or Is It Exploitation? 120

• Ad Lab 4–B: Applying Consumer Behavior Principles to Ad Making 130

5   **Using Marketing and Advertising to Link Products to Markets   132**

The Market Segmentation Process 134
Segmenting the Consumer Market: Finding the Right Niche, 134   Segmenting Business and Government Markets: Understanding Organizational Buying Behavior, 141   Aggregating Market Segments, 144

The Target Marketing Process 146
Target Market Selection, 146   The Marketing Mix: A Strategy for Matching Products to Markets, 146

Advertising and the Product Element 147
Product Life Cycle, 147   Product Classifications, 150   Product Positioning, 150   Product Differentiation, 151   Product Branding, 152   Product Packaging, 154

Advertising and the Price Element 155
Key Factors Influencing Price, 155

Advertising and the Distribution (Place) Element 157
Direct Distribution, 157   Indirect Distribution, 158   Vertical Marketing Systems: The Growth of Franchising, 159

Minnesota celebrates Matisse.
An exhibit of selected works of Henri Matisse pulled entirely from collections within Minnesota. October 10th through January 9th.
THE MINNEAPOLIS INSTITUTE OF ARTS

III
CREATING ADVERTISEMENTS AND COMMERCIALS

IV

BUYING MEDIA SPACE AND TIME

V

BUILDING RELATIONSHIPS THROUGH INTEGRATED MARKETING COMMUNICATIONS (IMC)

CONTEMPORARY

Advertising

Part

I

ADVERTISING PERSPECTIVES

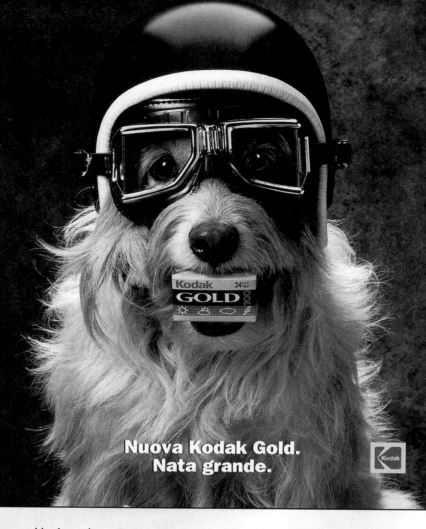

There are many ways to look at advertising—as a business, a creative communication process, a social phenomenon, and a fundamental ingredient of the free enterprise system. The first part of this text defines advertising, outlines its functions and scope, examines how it affects the economy, considers its social and legal ramifications, and looks at the major participants in the advertising business, not just in North America but around the world. • *Chapter 1,* "The Dimensions of Advertising," gives an overview of the profession. It defines advertising, examines its role in the communication process, and discusses its various functions and classifications. The chapter focuses on how technology has affected the evolution of advertising and discusses advertising's impact on the free enterprise system around the world. • *Chapter 2,* "The Social, Legal, and Ethical Aspects of Advertising," discusses some of the common criticisms of advertising and debates the ethical and social responsibilities of companies that advertise. It describes the roles played by government, industry, and consumer groups in regulating advertising. Finally, it compares important laws governing the practice of advertising in the United States and Canada with those in foreign countries. • *Chapter 3,* "The Advertising Business: Agencies, Clients, Media, and Suppliers," shows how people and groups organize themselves—as advertisers, agencies, media, and suppliers—to create, produce, and run advertising. The chapter describes the role of each of these organizations and discusses critical factors that affect the client-agency relationship.

1

The Dimensions of Advertising

Objective: To define advertising and introduce the profession. You'll learn the fundamental role of advertising in the communication process; basic terminology used; the many ways advertising is classified; how it works as a communication process; the evolution of advertising technology and strategic thinking; the functions and effects of advertising; and advertising's overall impact on the economy. These basics set the framework for the more detailed study to follow.

After studying this chapter, you will be able to:

- Define advertising and differentiate it from public relations.

- Understand and describe advertising's role in the marketing communication process.

- Enumerate the different classifications of advertising.

- Discuss milestones in the evolution of advertising.

- Explain the significance of marketing warfare to contemporary advertising.

- Debate the effect of advertising on the value and price of products.

- Explore the impact of advertising on competition and consumer choice.

The advertisement image in the center shows:

THE SHAPE *of* THINGS *to* COME.

When the worried band of small, independent citrus growers from Southern California gathered at the Chamber of Commerce building in downtown Los Angeles, they had no idea that their little organization would one day become a billion-dollar business, marketing one of the best-known and respected brands in the world. The date was August 29, 1893.

Farmers across the U.S. had difficult times that year. California's citrus farmers faced problems made even worse by the distance that separated them from their Eastern markets. Crops that left the orchard had no guarantee of a sale. They were at the mercy of often unscrupulous commission agents who took their fruit on consignment and paid them only after a sale.

So, led by T. H. B. Chamblin, an earnest, persuasive, 60-year-old Ohio-born man, they formed a nonprofit farmers' cooperative, the Southern California Fruit Exchange, to manage and control the packing and marketing of high-quality fresh citrus products from Southern California.

So desperate were the region's farmers and so persuasive were Chamblin's arguments that growers signed up in droves. In its first season, the Exchange represented 80 percent of the growers of Southern California. It shipped 6,000 of the state's 7,000 total carloads. (Three hundred boxes of fruit constituted a carload.) By regulating shipments, the Exchange enabled the farmers to net about $1 per box—four times what they would have gotten from commission agents.

Rocky times lay ahead, but the Exchange weathered them all and eventually added lemons and grapefruit to its product line. In 1904 the Exchange expanded and began to actively convince retailers and wholesalers to handle its fruit exclusively. In 1905 it invited northern growers to participate and changed its name to the California Fruit Growers Exchange.

By 1907 orange shipments increased fivefold, to nearly 30,000 carloads. But this increase brought other problems, namely oversaturation of the market for this "luxury" product. Management realized consumption must increase. With some trepidation, it budgeted $10,000 for its first advertising effort—the best investment it ever made. It was the first time a perishable product had ever been advertised.

With the Lord & Thomas advertising agency (now Foote, Cone & Belding), the Exchange developed a three-color newspaper ad to promote its oranges. The campaign, launched in the *Des Moines Register,* declared the first week in March "Orange Week in Iowa." The ad announced that Des Moines would receive "direct from the beautiful groves of California hundreds of carloads of the choicest oranges in the world." The Southern Pacific Railroad co-funded the campaign to promote tickets to California and posted billboards throughout Iowa with slogans such as "Oranges for Health, California for Wealth."

The Exchange directors were so amazed by the results—a stunning 50 percent increase in sales—they increased the budget to $25,000. In the fall of 1908, 6 million stickers were pasted on the Exchange's shipping boxes proudly proclaiming the Exchange's new trademark—Sunkist—the name by which it would be known around the world forevermore.[1]

Today Sunkist Growers, Inc., is a 100-year-old not-for-profit cooperative marketing organization owned and operated by over 6,000 citrus growers in California and Arizona. Membership is voluntary. Sunkist provides income to its members by marketing their fresh citrus and by licensing the Sunkist trademark for related products that use its extract.

Sunkist is also a major advertiser, though not large by national standards. And its relationship with Foote, Cone & Belding is one of the oldest and most successful in the world, spanning some 90 years. Together, Sunkist and FCB have made advertising history. •

ADVERTISING DEFINED

What is advertising?

Albert Lasker, generally regarded as the father of modern advertising, defined it as "salesmanship in print, driven by a reason why."[2] But Lasker, the owner of Lord & Thomas (the predecessor of Foote, Cone & Belding) espoused that definition around the turn of the 20th century, long before the advent of radio and television, when the nature and scope of advertising were quite limited.

Today, definitions of advertising abound. We might define it as a communication process, a marketing process, an economic and social process, a public relations process, or an information and persuasion process. In this book, we use the following definition:

> **Advertising** is the nonpersonal communication of information, usually paid for and usually persuasive in nature, about products (goods and services) or ideas by identified sponsors through various media.

Let's take this definition apart and analyze its components. Advertising is directed to groups of people rather than to individuals and is therefore *nonpersonal*. These groups might be consumers, such as people who buy fresh oranges at the store; or they might be the business people who own and manage those stores and buy oranges directly from Sunkist for resale.

Most advertising is *paid for* by sponsors. GM, Kmart, Coca-Cola, and your local fitness salon pay the newspaper or the radio or TV station to carry the ads we read, see, and hear. But some sponsors don't have to pay for their ads. The American Red Cross, United Way, and American Cancer Society are among the many national organizations whose public service messages are carried at no charge.

Most advertising is intended to be *persuasive*—to win converts to a product, service, or idea. Some ads, such as legal announcements, are intended merely to inform, not to persuade.

In addition to promoting tangible **goods** such as suits, soap, and soft drinks, advertising helps publicize the intangible **services** of bankers, beauticians, telephone companies, and auto repair shops. Increasingly, advertising is used to advocate a wide variety of **ideas,** economic, political, religious, and social. In this book the term **product** encompasses goods, services, and ideas.

An ad *identifies* its sponsor. This seems obvious: The sponsor wants to be identified—or why pay to advertise? One of the differences between advertising and *public relations* is that many PR activities, like *publicity,* aren't openly sponsored.

Advertising reaches us through a channel of communication referred to as a **medium.** In addition to the traditional **mass media** (the plural of *medium*)—radio, TV, newspapers, magazines, and billboards—advertising uses other media such as direct mail, brochures, shopping carts, blimps, and videocassettes.

• An advertisement is a marketing communication paid for by the sponsor. In this ad campaign, Utz Quality Foods' potato chips tells Baltimore customers there's no Utz in LA, Miami, Dallas, or Paris—"too bad for the rest of the world." Utz advertises on local billboards and buses and in a regional radio campaign.

What Kills Bugs Dead? *Ad Lab 1-A*

Successful marketing communications sometimes take on a life of their own. During its long history, Foote, Cone & Belding and its predecessor agency, Lord & Thomas, created dozens of slogans for clients that became a part of the popular culture. Below are 14 of the best known. See how many you can match with the advertiser. *Hint: Two of the slogans are for the same product.*

1. "Aren't you glad you use _____? Don't you wish everybody did?"
2. "Do blondes really have more fun?"
3. "_____ kills bugs dead!"
4. "600 tiny time pills."
5. "Food shot from guns."
6. "Reach for a _____ instead of a sweet."
7. "Does she . . . or doesn't she?"
8. "Button your fly."
9. "When you care enough to send the very best."
10. "You'll wonder where the yellow went . . ."
11. "Drink your vegetables."
12. "Keep that schoolgirl complexion."
13. "Which twin has the _____?"
14. "Don't put a cold in your pocket."

Answers

1. Dial 2. Clairol 3. Raid 4. Contac 5. Quaker Oats 6. Lucky Strike 7. Clairol 8. Levi's 9. Hallmark 10. Pepsodent 11. V8 juice 12. Palmolive 13. Toni 14. Kleenex

First and foremost, advertising is communication. Successful advertisers and the advertising specialists they employ work as a team to apply the elements of the communication process in the marketplace. To understand how advertising works, students must understand the basic processes involved in *marketing communications.* Ad Lab 1–A lists some successful marketing communications from Foote, Cone & Belding.

ADVERTISING IS COMMUNICATION

The Human Communication Process

From our first cry at birth, our survival depends on our ability to inform others or persuade them to take some action. As we develop, we learn to listen and respond to others' messages.

The traditional model in Exhibit 1–1 summarizes the series of events that take place when people share ideas in oral communication. The process begins when one party, called the **source,** formulates an idea, *encodes* it as a **message**, and sends it via some *channel* to another party, called the **receiver**. The receiver must *decode* the message in order to understand it. To respond, the receiver formulates a new idea, encodes it, and then sends the new message back through some channel, or medium. A message that acknowledges or responds to the original message constitutes *feedback,* which also affects the encoding of a new message.[3]

Applying this model to advertising, we could say that the source is the sponsor, the message is the ad, the channel is the medium, and the receiver is the consumer or prospect. But this model oversimplifies the process that occurs in advertising or other sponsored marketing communications. We need to consider some of the many complexities involved, especially with the advent of *interactive media,* which let consumers manipulate what they see on their computer or TV screens in real time.

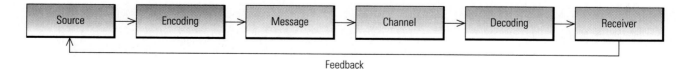

Feedback

Exhibit • 1–1
The human communication process.

The Marketing Communication Process

Barbara Stern at Rutgers University proposed a more sophisticated communication model, derived from the traditional oral one but more specific to advertising, as *composed commercial text* rather than informal speech. The Stern model acknowledges that the source, the message, and the receiver all have multiple dimensions (see Exhibit 1–2). For a more detailed presentation, see RL 1–1 in the Reference Library.

Source dimensions: *The sponsor, the author, and the persona*

In advertising, who really is the source of the communication? The sponsor named in the ad? Certainly the sponsor is legally responsible for the communication, but it usually does not actually produce the message. That is done by the sponsor's advertising agency. So the *author* of the communication is actually a copywriter, an art director, or, most often, a group at the agency—people *outside the text* of the message. However, *within the text* of the ad, some spokesperson, real or imagined, usually gives the ad or commercial a voice. To the consumer, this *persona* is the source of the within-text message.

Message dimensions: *Autobiography, narrative, drama*

Similarly, multiple types of messages are communicated in advertising. Some messages are *autobiographical:* "I" tell a story about myself to "you," the imaginary audience eavesdropping on my private personal experience. In contrast, in *narrative* messages a third-person persona tells a story about others to an imagined audience. Finally, in the *drama*, the characters act out events directly in front of an imagined empathetic audience.

In advertising, one of the most important decisions is what kind of persona and message to use. In the **encoding** process, the advertising professional usually begins by studying the emotions, attitudes, and concepts that drive particular customers. Once those are identified, symbols are developed. These symbols, in the form of images and text, are then placed in the most suitable format for the message dimension and the medium in which they are to appear.

Receiver dimensions: *Implied, sponsorial, and actual consumers*

Finally, in advertising, receivers are also multidimensional. First, within the text, every ad or commercial presumes recipients. These *implied consumers* addressed by the ad's persona are not real. They are imagined by the ad's creators to be ideal—acquiescing in whatever beliefs the text requires. When we move outside the text of the ad, the first line of consumers is the group of decision makers at the sponsor's company or organization. These *sponsorial consumers* are the gatekeepers who decide if the ad will run or not. So, before an ad ever gets a chance to persuade a real consumer, it must first

Exhibit • 1–2
Advertising communications model.

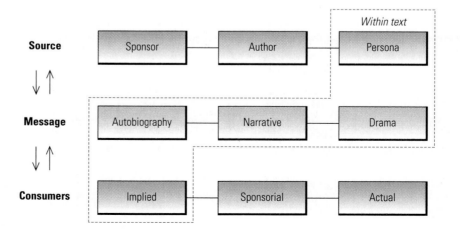

MUSIC: Theme from "A Man and A Woman"

ANNCR: Paulo has just enjoyed his fabulous meal of Capellini al Pomodoro at Prego, the restaurant. He pays the bill and makes his way toward the bar. Everyone admires him. Or so it seems to Paulo. He is on the prowl. He is a cat. A panther. He is . . . Paulo. Does he care that his fly is down? No, he doesn't care. He doesn't know! So why should he care? He waves to the Prego staff and calls them by name. Giancarlo! Guiseppe! Roberto! They do not answer. These are not their names. But Paulo is pleased. He believes he has made an impression on the leggy brunette perched at the end of the bar. She is kittenish, thinks Paulo. But I am the bigger cat. A lion, thinks Paulo. She looks up. What is it that she sees? Is it the blueness of his eyes? The strength of his chin? No, it is the spinach caught between his teeth. It has been there for hours.

Prego. Union Street, San Francisco: See. Be seen. Be seen eating.

● Good radio commercials paint vivid pictures with words. This tongue-in-cheek spot for Prego Restaurant allowed people to use their imaginations. The campaign won the Best of Show Gold Pencil award out of 12,000 entries in the 18th annual One Show—the first time in its history that radio work won top prize.

persuade the sponsor's agents. The *actual consumers* are people in the real world who comprise the ad's target audience.[4]

The advertiser has to be concerned about how the actual consumer will **decode,** or interpret, the message. The actual consumer does not usually think or behave the same as the sponsorial consumer, or even the implied consumer. And the last thing an advertiser wants is to be misunderstood. Unfortunately, message interpretation is only partially determined by the words, the symbols, and the medium used. The unique characteristics of the *receivers* themselves are also very important, and the sponsor may know little or nothing about them. As we shall see in Chapter 4, attitudes, perceptions, personality, self-concept, and culture are just some of the many influences that affect the way people receive and respond to messages and how they behave as consumers in the marketplace.

Complicating this problem is the fact that the sender's advertising message must compete with hundreds of other commercial and noncommercial messages every day. This is referred to as **noise.** So the sender doesn't know *how* the message is received, or even *if* it's received, until some acknowledgment takes place.

Feedback

That's why feedback is so important. It completes the cycle, verifying that the message was received. **Feedback** employs the same sender–message–receiver pattern except that it is directed from the receiver back to the source.

In advertising, feedback may take a variety of forms: redeemed coupons, telephone inquiries, visits to a store, requests for more information, sales, or responses to a survey. Dramatically low responses to an ad indicate a break in the communication process. Questions arise: Is the product wrong for the market? Is the message unclear? Are we using the right medium? Without feedback, these questions cannot be answered.

CLASSIFICATIONS OF ADVERTISING

Advertising can be classified by four main criteria: target audience, geographic area, medium, and purpose (see Exhibit 1–3). Each of these classifications includes several categories, some of which we'll discuss here.

Classification by Target Audience

Advertising is usually aimed at a particular segment of the population—the **target audience.** When you see an ad that doesn't appeal to you, it may be because the ad is not aimed at any of the groups you belong to. For example, a TV commercial for denture cream isn't relevant to young adults. They're not part of the target audience, so the ad isn't designed to appeal to them. There are two main types of target audiences, *consumers* and *businesses.*

Exhibit ● 1–3
The classifications of advertising.

By target audience

Consumer advertising: Aimed at people who buy the product for their own or someone else's use.

Business advertising: Aimed at people who buy or specify products and services for use in business.

- *Trade:* Aimed at middlemen (wholesalers and retailers) of products and services who buy for resale to their customers.
- *Professional:* Aimed at people licensed under a code of ethics or set of professional standards.
- *Agricultural:* Aimed at people in farming or agribusiness.

By geographic area

Local (retail) advertising: Advertising by businesses whose customers come from only one city or local trading area.

Regional advertising: Advertising for products sold in one area or region, but not the entire country.

National advertising: Advertising aimed at customers in several regions of the country.

International advertising: Advertising directed at foreign markets.

By medium

Print advertising: Newspapers, magazines.

Broadcast (electronic): Radio, TV.

Out-of-home advertising: Outdoor, transit.

Direct-mail advertising: Advertising sent through the mail.

By purpose

Product advertising: Promotes the sale of products and services.

Nonproduct (corporate or institutional) advertising: Promotes the organization's mission or philosophy rather than a specific product.

Commercial advertising: Promotes products, services, or ideas with the expectation of making a profit.

Noncommercial advertising: Sponsored by or for a charitable or nonprofit institution, civic group, or religious or political organization.

Action advertising: Attempts to stimulate immediate action by the reader.

Awareness advertising: Attempts to build the image of a product or familiarity with the product's name and package.

Consumer advertising

Much of the advertising we see daily in the mass media—TV, radio, newspapers, and magazines—is **consumer advertising**. Sponsored by the producer (or manufacturer) of the product or service, these ads are typically directed at **consumers**, people who buy the product for their own or someone else's personal use. Consumer advertising also includes the noncommercial *public service announcements* we see from the American Cancer Society or the Partnership for a Drug-Free America, a topic we discuss in Chapter 17.

Business advertising

Business advertising—directed to people who buy or specify goods and services for business use—tends to appear in specialized business publications or professional journals, in direct-mail pieces sent to businesses, or in trade shows. Since business advertising (also called *business-to-business advertising*) rarely uses the mass media, it is often invisible to consumers. However, some business-to-business commercials and print ads—by computer manufacturers and firms like Federal Express—do appear on prime-time TV and in consumer magazines.

Business advertising is aimed at the people who buy or influence the purchase of: *capital products,* expensive items used in business operations that do not become part of a finished product (plants, machinery, equipment); *production products,* which do become part of other products (raw materials, semimanufactured goods, components); and *operational products,* goods and services the firm uses to conduct business (lightbulbs, cleaning materials, insurance, maintenance, and advertising).

There are three types of business advertising: trade, professional, and agricultural. Companies aim **trade advertising** at **resellers** (wholesalers, dealers, and retailers) to obtain greater distribution of their products. For example, the objective of Sunkist's trade advertising in publications such as *California Grocer* is to develop more grocery outlets or to increase sales to existing outlets.

Advertising aimed at teachers, accountants, doctors, dentists, architects, engineers, and lawyers is called **professional advertising** and typically appears in official publications of professional societies (such as the *Archives of Ophthalmology* published by the American Medical Association). Professional advertising has three objectives: to convince professional people to buy particular brands of equipment and supplies for

use in their work; to encourage professionals to recommend or prescribe a specific product or service to their clients or patients; and to persuade professionals to use the product personally.

Companies use **agricultural** (or **farm**) **advertising** to promote products and services used in agriculture to farm families and to individuals employed in agribusiness. FMC Corp., for example, might advertise its plant nutrition products in *California Farmer* magazine to growers of Sunkist oranges in Southern California. Agricultural advertising typically shows farmers how the advertised product will increase efficiency, reduce risks, and widen profit margins.

Classification by Geographic Area

A neighborhood store or restaurant usually uses **local advertising** in its immediate trading area because that's where the majority of its customers come from. Local advertisers face special challenges that we'll discuss in Chapter 17.

On the other hand, a business such as Burger King or Nordstrom that is part of a well-known chain might use any of the four classifications of advertising based on geography: *local, regional, national,* or even *international.*

In recent years, the world has experienced dramatic political realignment, and many traditional trade barriers have disappeared. In Scandinavia you see ads for Crest toothpaste in Norwegian. Sunkist advertises lemons in Japan. Visitors to Spain see TV ads for products advertised every day in the U.S. and Canada, such as Levi's or Coca-Cola. As a result, the field of **international advertising**—advertising aimed at foreign markets—has become so important that we discuss global advertising issues wherever applicable in every chapter of this book.

● In the explosion of international advertising, the Mexican Secretariat of Tourism advertises in Japan. The headline of this print ad exclaims, *Mexico has multiple faces,* and proves it with stunning visuals. The ad offers another enticement to Japanese travelers: a 2-to-3-hour flight from Los Angeles.

Classification by Medium

Advertising can be classified on the basis of the medium used to transmit the message (radio, television, newspaper, directory). An **advertising medium** is any *paid* means used to present an ad to its target audience. Word-of-mouth, therefore, while it is a medium of communication, is not an *advertising* medium. We consider the planning, scheduling, and buying of media space and time in Chapters 8 and 12 through 14.

Classification by Purpose

Advertising can also be classified by the sponsor's objectives. Some ads promote a product or service; others promote ideas. Some advertising is meant to help generate profits for the advertiser; some is sponsored by nonprofit groups. Some ads try to spur the target audience to immediate action, others to create awareness or understanding of the advertiser's offering.

Product versus nonproduct advertising

To promote their goods and services, companies use **product advertising**. To sell ideas, though, organizations use **nonproduct advertising**. A Citgo ad for its gasoline is a product ad. So are ads for banking, insurance, or legal services. But a Citgo ad promoting the company's mission or philosophy (how the company protects the environment while drilling for oil) is considered **nonproduct, corporate,** or **institutional advertising.** Corporate advertising is the focus of Chapter 16.

Commercial versus noncommercial advertising

While commercial advertising seeks profits, **noncommercial advertising** is used around the world by governments and nonprofit organizations to seek donations, volunteer support, or a change in consumer behavior. Chapter 17 discusses noncommercial advertising.

Piétons *montrez-vous* prudents.

Au Québec, près de 5 000 piétons sont blessés ou tués chaque année sur la voie publique. Les principales causes de ces accidents sont le manque de visibilité, la négligence et l'inattention des piétons.

Rappelez-vous: vous êtes bien petit face à un véhicule. Alors pour votre sécurité, utilisez les passages piétonniers et conformez-vous aux feux de piétons.

SOCIÉTÉ DE L'ASSURANCE AUTOMOBILE DU QUÉBEC

● This ad is an example of noncommercial advertising. The Société d'Assurance Auto du Québec admonishes: *Pedestrians, watch your step!* The ad won a *Reader's Digest* Pegasus award for excellence.

Action versus awareness advertising

Some ads are intended to bring about immediate action by the reader; others have a longer-term goal. The objective of **awareness advertising**, for example, is to create interest in, and an image for, a product and to influence readers or viewers to select a specific brand the next time they shop.

A direct-mail ad, on the other hand, exemplifies **action advertising** because it seeks an immediate, direct response from the reader. Most ads on TV and radio are awareness ads, but some are a mixture of awareness and action. For example, a 60-second TV commercial may devote the first 50 seconds to image building and the last 10 to a local phone number for immediate information.

Throughout history, technological developments dramatically affected advertising and communication. The popular phrase "The medium is the message," coined by Marshall McLuhan, refers to this connection between technology and communication.[5] McLuhan's legacy is the concept that throughout history technological advances have been responsible for fundamental changes in the way people communicate. As we examine the evolution of modern advertising, we'll see ample proof for his theory.

Thousands of years ago, people used primitive hand tools to make products. They lived in small, isolated communities where artisans and farmers bartered products and services among themselves. Distribution was limited to how far vendors could walk and "advertising" to how loud they could shout.

Eventually, Greek and Roman merchants expanded contact with other societies. With the development of more sophisticated tools, people achieved a higher level of production. These factors increased the demand for products and created a need to

TECHNOLOGY AND THE EVOLUTION OF ADVERTISING

advertise their availability. Merchants hung carved signs in front of their shops so passersby could see what products were being offered. Most people couldn't read, so the signs often used symbols, such as a boot for a cobbler. This was the *ancient* or *early period* of advertising history.

The Impact of Printing

Advertising's *formative stage* began with the invention of the printing press by Johannes Gutenberg in Germany in the 1440s. The press, with its system of changeable metal letters, was not only the most important development in the history of advertising; it also revolutionized the way people lived and worked.

Prior to the printing press, most people were illiterate. Only monks and scholars could read and write; the average person had to memorize important information and communicate orally. Since oral communication could not be substantiated, people lived without documentable facts. And because dialects varied from region to region, most news never traveled more than 50 miles.

The introduction of printing meant that facts could be established, substantiated, recorded, and transported. People no longer had to rely on their memories. Movable letters provided the flexibility to print in local dialects. The slow hand transcription of the monks gave way to more rapid, volume printing by a less select group. Some entrepreneurs bought printing presses, mounted them in wagons, and traveled from town to town selling printing. This new technology made possible the first formats of advertising—posters, handbills, and signs—and the first mass medium—the newspaper. In effect, the cry of the vendor could now be multiplied many times and heard beyond the immediate neighborhood.

In 1472, the first ad in English appeared: a handbill tacked on church doors in London announcing a prayer book for sale. It was 200 years later, though, before the first newspaper ad appeared, offering a reward for the return of 12 stolen horses. Soon newspapers carried ads for coffee, chocolate, tea, real estate, and medicines, even "personals." These early ads were still directed to a limited number of people: customers of the coffeehouses where newspapers were read.

● It wasn't until 1729 that Ben Franklin, innovator of advertising art, made ads more readable by using larger headlines and adding art. This 1746 ad announces the availability of the brigantine *Elizabeth* to carry goods and passengers to Antigua.

By the early 1700s, the world's population had grown to about 600 million people, and some major cities were sufficiently populated to support large volumes of advertising. In fact, the greater volume caused a shift in advertising strategy. Samuel Johnson, the famous English literary figure, observed in 1758 that advertisements were now so numerous that they were "negligently perused" and that it had become necessary to gain attention "by magnificence of promise."

In the American colonies, the *Boston Newsletter* began carrying ads in 1704. About 25 years later, Benjamin Franklin, the father of advertising art, made ads more readable by using large headlines and considerable white space. In fact, Franklin was the first American known to use illustrations in ads.

The Impact of the Industrial Revolution

In the mid-1700s, the Industrial Revolution began in England, and by the early 1800s it had reached North America. Machinery began to replace animal power. Manufacturers could mass-produce goods with uniform quality; and for the first time, it cost people less to buy a product than to make it themselves.

To manufacture a high volume of goods, however, producers needed mass consumption. They soon realized the tremendous value of advertising, which helped them widen their reach to the frontier markets in the West and the growing industrial markets in the East. By the mid-1800s, the world's population had doubled to 1.2 billion. The need for and the use of advertising and mass marketing techniques had also grown.

For Americans, advertising as a profession began when Volney B. Palmer set up business in Philadelphia in 1841. He contracted with newspapers for large volumes of advertising space at discount rates and then resold the space to advertisers at a higher rate. The advertisers usually prepared the ads themselves.

In 1869, Francis Ayer founded an advertising agency in Philadelphia and named it after his father. N. W. Ayer & Sons was the first agency to charge a commission based on the "net cost of space" (1876) and the first to conduct a formal market survey in support of advertising.

In 1890, Ayer became the first to operate as ad agencies do today—planning, creating, and executing complete ad campaigns for media-paid commissions or fees from

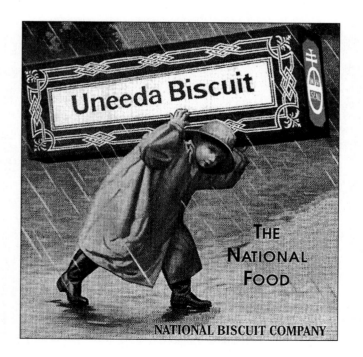

● In 1890, N. W. Ayer & Sons became the first agency to operate as agencies do today, planning, creating, and executing complete ad campaigns for advertisers. This 1899 Ayer ad for Uneeda biscuits (catch the play on words!) was one of a series of popular ads of the times.

advertisers. In 1892, Ayer set up a copy department and hired the first full-time agency copywriter. Still operating today, Ayer is considered the oldest ad agency in the U.S.

The Communications Revolution

The technological advances of the Industrial Revolution created the greatest changes in advertising since the 1400s. Photography, introduced in 1839, added credibility and a whole new world of creativity. Now ads could show products, people, and places as they really were, rather than as an artist visualized them.

In the 1840s, manufacturers began using magazine ads to reach the mass market and stimulate mass consumption. Magazines were ideal because they made national advertising possible and offered the best quality of reproduction.

The telegraph, telephone, typewriter, phonograph, and motion pictures all enabled people to communicate as never before. With the development of a nationwide railroad system, the U.S. entered a period of spectacular economic growth. And in 1896, when the federal government inaugurated rural free mail delivery, direct-mail advertising and mail-order selling flourished. Manufacturers now had an ever-increasing variety of products to sell and a new way to deliver their advertising media and their products to the public.

With the advent of public schooling, the nation reached an unparalleled 90 percent literacy rate. Manufacturers gained a large reading public that could understand print ads. The U.S. thus entered the 20th century as a great industrial nation with a national marketing system propelled by advertising. With the birth of a new century, the *modern period* in advertising emerged.

The Era of Responsibility

During the first two decades of the 1900s, the advertising profession was forced to mend its ethical ways. Consumers had suffered for years from unsubstantiated product claims, especially for patent medicines and health devices. The simmering resentment finally boiled over into a full-blown consumer movement, which in turn led to government regulation and ultimately to industry efforts at self-regulation.

In 1906, Congress responded to public outrage by passing the Pure Food and Drug Act to protect the public's health and control drug advertising. In 1914, it passed the Federal Trade Commission Act to protect the public from unfair business practices, including misleading and deceptive advertising.

● This ad for Hunt's Remedy— "the greatest kidney & liver medicine"—typifies the patent medicine claims that were prevalent at the turn of the century. Consumer protests eventually led to government regulation and industry efforts to mend its ways.

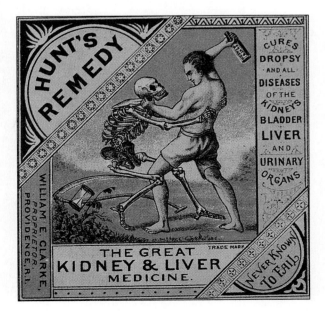

Advertising practitioners themselves formed groups to improve advertising effectiveness and promote professionalism and initiated vigilance committees to safeguard the integrity of the industry. The Association of National Advertisers (ANA), the American Advertising Federation (AAF), and the Better Business Bureau (BBB) are today's outgrowths of those early groups.

However, in the 1920s following World War I, the U.S. was rich, powerful, and in no mood for responsibility. As the war machine turned back to peacetime production, the U.S. became a consumption-driven society. The era of salesmanship had arrived and its bible was *Scientific Advertising*, written by the legendary copywriter Claude Hopkins at Lord & Thomas. Published in 1923, it became a classic and was republished in 1950 and 1980. "Advertising has reached the status of a science," Hopkins proclaimed. "It is based on fixed principles." His principles outlawed humor, style, literary flair, and anything that might detract from Hopkins' basic copy strategy of a preemptive product claim repeated loudly and often.[6]

On October 29, 1929, the stock market crashed, the Great Depression began, and advertising expenditures plummeted. But false and misleading advertising continued, perhaps out of advertisers' desperation. Several best-selling books exposed the advertising industry as an unscrupulous exploiter of consumers, giving birth to a new consumer movement and further government regulation.

In the face of consumer sales resistance and corporate budget-cutting, the advertising industry needed to improve its effectiveness and regain its credibility. It turned to research. Daniel Starch, A. C. Nielsen, and George Gallup had founded research groups to study consumer attitudes and preferences. By providing information on public opinion, the performance of ad messages, and sales of advertised products, these companies started a whole new business—the marketing research industry.

The Rise of Broadcast Advertising

As technology fostered the growth of advertising, it also opened the doors of opportunity to millions of people. Born in 1920, radio rapidly became the nation's primary means of mass communication and a powerful new advertising medium with greater immediacy. World and national news now arrived direct from the scene, and a whole new world of family entertainment—music, drama, and sports—became possible. Suddenly, national advertisers could reach huge audiences. In fact, the first radio shows were produced by their sponsors' ad agencies.

The greatest expansion of any medium, though, occurred with the introduction of television in 1941. Following World War II, television advertising grew rapidly, and today, TV is the second largest advertising medium (after newspapers) in terms of total dollars spent by advertisers.

During the postwar prosperity of the late 1940s and early 50s, consumers tried to climb the social ladder by buying more and more modern products. Advertising entered its golden era. A virtual creative revolution ensued in which ads focused on product features that implied social acceptance, style, luxury, and success. Giants in the field emerged—people like Leo Burnett, David Ogilvy, and Bill Bernbach, who built their agencies from scratch and forever changed the way advertising was planned and created.[7] (RL 1–2 in the Reference Library profiles outstanding professionals from advertising's history.)

Rosser Reeves of the Ted Bates Agency introduced the idea that every ad must point out the product's **USP (unique selling proposition)**—features that differentiate it from competitive products. The USP was a logical extension of the Lasser and Hopkins "reason why" credo, but as it was used over and over, consumers found it difficult to see what was "unique" any more.

The image era of the 1960s was thus the natural culmination of the creative revolution. Advertising's emphasis shifted from product features to product image or personality.

THE DEVELOPMENT OF CONTEMPORARY ADVERTISING

● By the 1960s, ads shifted from listing product features to promoting a product's image. The "man in the Hathaway shirt" tripled Hathaway's annual sales and became a classic campaign of the era. The use of the eye-patched actor gave David Ogilvy his first big advertising hit and lent an aura of aristocratic British class and discriminating taste to the product's image.

The Gun is a $2,000 Purdey from England

Cadillac became the worldwide image of luxury, the consummate symbol of success, surpassed only by the aristocratic Rolls-Royce.

The Positioning Era

The 1970s saw a new kind of advertising strategy, where competitors' strengths became as important as the advertiser's. Jack Trout and Al Ries trumpeted the arrival of the **positioning era**. Although they acknowledged the importance of product features and image, they insisted that what really mattered was how the brand ranked against the competition in the consumer's mind. The most famous American ads of the positioning era were Volkswagen ("Think small"), Avis ("We're No. 2"), and 7UP ("The uncola"). Other manufacturers tried the approach with great success. And product failures of the period, like Life Savers gum and RCA computers, were blamed on flawed positioning.

Meanwhile, across the Atlantic, a new generation of advertising professionals had graduated from the training grounds of Procter & Gamble and Colgate-Palmolive and were now teaching their clients the secrets of mass marketing. Lagging somewhat behind their U.S. counterparts, European marketers discovered the USP and the one-page "strategic brief" that P&G had popularized to bring focus to ad campaigns. French advertising pioneer Marcel Bleustein-Blanchet had waged a frustrating battle to introduce U.S. research techniques to his countrymen a decade or two earlier; now in-depth attitude and behavioral research was all the rage.[8] Since commercial TV was not so big as in the U.S., the European advertisers divided their media money between newspapers and outdoor media, along with a healthy dose of *cinema advertising*. Germany, Holland, and Scandinavia wouldn't get commercial TV for another decade.[9]

In the 70s, though, the European Common Market already offered untapped opportunities. Following the American example, agencies and clients began to think multinationally to gain economies of scale. But it was not easy. Physically close, the countries of Europe were separated by a chasm of cultural diversity, making the use of single Europe-wide campaigns nearly impossible.[10]

Perfume won't hide it.

SMOKELINE 0800 84 84 84 ⊛ HEALTH EDUCATION BOARD FOR SCOTLAND

● In a *demarketing campaign,* the Health Education Board for Scotland targets pre-teen and teenage girls with this startling, persuasive antismoking poster, whose model's horrifying hair is composed of lipstick-stained cigarette butts.

The "Me" Decade

In the 1970s a new American consumer movement grew out of the widespread disillusionment following the Kennedy assassination, the Vietnam war, the Watergate scandals, and the sudden shortage of vital natural resources—all communicated instantly to the world via new satellite technology. These issues fostered cynicism and distrust of the establishment and everything traditional by the first wave of baby boomers, and gave rise to a new twist in moral consciousness. On the one hand, people justified their personal irresponsibility and self-indulgence in the name of self-fulfillment. On the other, they attacked corporate America's quest for self-fulfillment (profits) in the name of social accountability.

By the mid-1980s, an avalanche of ads—especially in the toiletry and cosmetics industries—was aimed at the "me" generation ("L'Oreal. Because I'm worth it."). At the same time, the nation's largest industrial concerns spent millions of dollars on corporate advertising to extol their social consciousness and good citizenship for cleaning up after themselves and protecting the environment.

During the energy shortages of the 1970s and 80s, a new marketing tactic called **demarketing** appeared. Producers of energy and energy-consuming goods used advertising to *slow* the demand for their products. Ads asked people to refrain from operating washers and dryers during the day when electricity use peaked. In time, demarketing became a more aggressive strategic tool for advertisers to use against competitors, political opponents, and social problems. The California Department of Health Services, for example, is one of many organizations today that actively seek to demarket smoking.

The Age of Marketing Warfare

In 1986 the priests of positioning, Al Ries and Jack Trout, published *Marketing Warfare,* which portrayed marketing in the 80s as a war that businesses must be prepared to wage. Many of their ideas came from a classic book on military strategy written in 1831 by a Prussian general. Ries and Trout outlined four strategic positions in the mar-

Ethical Dilemma or Ethical Lapse?

Advertising people face ethical decisions every day. But what is ethics? Dictionaries define it vaguely as moral philosophy. Substitute conscience, principles, high standards, integrity, honesty, propriety, decency, and the Ten Commandments, and the picture becomes clearer. These are pretty heady concepts to keep in mind when all you want to do is nudge someone to buy your brand of shampoo. But in our litigious society, ethical conduct and social responsibility are more important than ever.

An *ethical dilemma* arises when there is an unresolved interpretation of an ethical issue. For example, mockups and demonstrations are frequently used in ads. But is it really okay to use mashed potatoes for ice cream in a TV commercial because they don't melt? Or soap suds to create the frothy head on a mug of beer?

Incomplete information is another issue. One ad created by the American Gas Association showed two pots of spaghetti cooking, one over a gas burner, the other over electric. When the pots threatened to boil over, both burners were quickly turned down. The pot on the gas burner stopped boiling immediately. The pot on the electric burner, which doesn't dissipate so quickly, spilled its contents and made a mess. But electricity has its good points, too, and this ad didn't tell the whole story. Advertisers sometimes highlight the good things about their brands and omit the neutral and bad. Nothing that's said is false, yet the ad does not tell the whole truth.

According to Minette E. Drumwright, ethical issues are embedded in the practice of advertising, mostly involving truthfulness. Some ethical issues involve the essence of advertising itself—its social and economical appropriateness and potentially beneficial or harmful effects on individuals and society at large. There is a distinction between "having a right" and "the right thing to do." For example, should advertisers target children? Should they attempt to persuade inner-

---

There is a distinction between "having a right" and "the right thing to do."

---

city young people to buy sneakers priced at more than $170 a pair?

An *ethical lapse* is a clear case of unethical behavior and may even lead to action by government regulators. In one case, Colgate-Palmolive created a TV commercial demonstrating the superiority of its shaving cream. The shaving cream appeared to be applied to sandpaper, after which the sand was quickly and easily shaved off. Actually, sandpaper was not used; sand was sprinkled on clear plexiglass. The FTC and the Supreme

---

ketplace: *defensive, offensive, flanking,* and *guerrilla.* Companies had to operate from one of these strategic positions, they said, based on their relative strengths and weaknesses. (For an in-depth review of Ries and Trout's comparison of war to marketing strategies, see Chapter 7, Ad Lab 7–A.)

By this time European and Asian advertising had caught up with the U.S. TV was suddenly the hot medium, and agencies focused on growth, acquisitions, and superior creative executions. For several years, Young & Rubicam in New York and Dentsu in Japan alternated as the largest advertising agency in the world. Then two brothers in London, Charles and Maurice Saatchi, started acquiring agencies around the world. In rapid succession, a number of high-profile U.S. agencies disappeared under the Saatchi & Saatchi umbrella—big companies like Ted Bates Worldwide and Dancer, Fitzgerald, Sample. Saatchi & Saatchi was suddenly the largest agency in the world. Then came additional buyouts as the big agencies from Europe, the U.S., and Japan emulated the merger mania of their huge multinational clients. Names of agency founders disappeared from the doors, replaced by initials and acronyms: WPP Group, RSCG, TBWA, FCA, DDB Needham, and FCB/Publicis, to mention just a few.[11]

The European agencies fueled their growth by establishing huge bulk media-buying conglomerates, but their now-sophisticated clients stopped looking to the agencies for research and marketing advice. Rather, they expected extraordinary creative executions to give their brands an edge, and the agencies provided it. Awards at the Cannes film festival disclosed the blossoming of creative advertising from Spain and confirmed the creative leadership of the British, who were only slightly ahead of the French.[12]

The Nervous 90s: Recession and Reevaluation

Toward the end of the 80s, the U.S. economy slowed, and too many companies chased too few consumer dollars. Clients began to trim ad budgets, and many turned to cost-effective alternatives, such as coupons, direct mail, and direct marketing. By the end of the decade, advertising had lost 25 precent of its share of the marketing budget to other forms of marketing communications.[13]

Court found the commercial deceptive and ruled that a demonstration must be real or the consumer must be informed otherwise.

University of Wisconsin professor Ivan L. Preston notes that one reason for deception is that advertisers typically sell *brands*, not just products. Since each brand must be presented as different from other brands—even though functionally it may not be—advertisers are tempted to create false differences. Some advertising claims fall on the slippery slope that runs down from what is fully true to what is false enough to be illegal.

Myriad federal, state, and local laws govern what is legal in advertising, but laws ultimately reflect ethical judgments. It's interesting that the Creative Code of the American Association of Advertising Agencies reflects legalities rather than philosophies. To Preston it appears advertising professionals find ethics largely synonymous with legality.

But is this enough? Should legislators have the final say in ethical issues? Shouldn't advertisers be careful about crossing the line between ethical and unscrupulous behavior? For example, the use of technology to totally change and distort images throws a whole new wrench into the discussion of ethical issues. The manipulation of an O. J. Simpson portait by a national news magazine generated much criticism. The possibilities for such deception are endless.

As Preston says, "You can be ethical only when you have the option of being unethical. You can't choose to be ethical when you can't choose at all, so ethics begins only where the law ends."

Questions

1. Would you mind bending your moral rules a little to sell a product with a misleading comparison or a visual distortion? What would justify such a decision? Where would you draw the line?

2. The next time you watch TV commercials, think ethics. Look for both good and bad examples of ethical presentations of the advertised products. What ethical issues might have been discussed before those ads were approved?

Sources: Ivan L. Preston, *The Tangled Web They Weave: Truth, Falsity and Advertisers* (Madison, WI: The University of Wisconsin Press, 1994); Minette E. Drumwright, "Ethical Issues in Advertising and Sales Promotion," in *Ethics in Marketing,* ed. N. Craig Smith and John A. Quelch (Burr Ridge, IL: Richard D. Irwin, 1993); and Shelby D. Hunt and Scott J. Vitell, "The General Theory of Marketing Ethics: A Retrospective and Revision," in *Ethics in Marketing.*

As the 90s unfolded, the recession deepened. The traditional advertising industry found itself threatened on all sides and suffering from overpopulation.[14] Clients demanded better results from their promotional dollars; small, imaginative, upstart agencies competed for (and won) some big accounts that had never been available to them; TV viewers appeared immune to conventional commercials; and new technology promised to reinvent the very process of advertising. In three short years, the advertising business lost over 13,500 jobs. Major clients like Coca-Cola defected from Madison Avenue, giving various portions of their business to specialists in small, regional creative shops and media-buying services. But the setback went far beyond the agency business. Throughout the media world, newspapers, magazines, and TV networks all lost advertising dollars. About 40 magazines went out of business during the two-year slump.[15]

At the same time, a five-year study by the Ayer ad agency found consumers and marketers moving in opposite directions. Corporate management felt pressure to simplify and consolidate operations, but consumer markets were becoming increasingly diverse and fragmented. Armed with remote controls, VCRs, 50 channels, and pockets full of competitors' coupons, consumers had become too sophisticated, too quick, and too fickle for slow-moving, traditional marketers who were disarmed by shrinking budgets. To counter this, Fred Posner, Ayer's director of research, urged marketers to redefine and reembrace the concept of *branding* (a subject we discuss in Chapters 5 and 15).[16]

Other industry leaders echoed the need to get back to basics. Hank Seiden, former chair of Ketchum Advertising, denounced the glut of irrelevant and costly product commercials that were "99 percent show biz and 1 percent advertising." In an era when most sales are *conquest sales* (won at the expense of a competitor), he maintained that a "mean, lean sales point the advertiser believes in should come wrapped in a commercial without a trace of fat on it."[17]

But more and more, industry spokespeople viewed the problems as systemic. Keith Reinhard, CEO of DDB Needham Worldwide, acknowledged, "This isn't [just] a recession we're in, and we're not going to go back to the good old days."

● This *Robert Post, One Man Theatre* poster is an example of how technology is changing the way advertising is created. Transferring 80 to 120 shots from a VHS tape into a computer, the design firm manipulated the images to capture the essence of Robert Post and his many different performance acts.

In 1992 and 1993, U.S. marketers began shifting dollars back from sales promotion to advertising to build their brands. In 1994, ad budgets surged ahead by 8.1 percent to $150 billion nationally. But hardly anybody thought the problems were over.[18] Technology, evolving lifestyles, and the rising cost of reaching consumers had already changed the advertising business forever. We were on the threshold of a new electronic frontier, entering what Tom Cuniff, VP/creative director at Lord, Dentsu & Partners, calls "the second creative revolution."[19] The future would not be business as usual.

Looking toward the 21st Century: The Global Interactive Age

In the last 15 years, expenditures by foreign advertisers increased more rapidly than either U.S. or Canadian expenditures, thanks to improved economic conditions and a desire for expansion. Recent estimates of worldwide advertising expenditures outside the U.S. exceed $193 billion per year.[20] The importance of advertising in individual countries depends on the country's level of development and national attitude toward promotion. Typically, advertising expenditures are higher in countries with higher personal incomes. As Exhibit 1–4 shows, the top 10 worldwide advertisers are based in many different countries.

British historian Raymond Williams called advertising "nothing other than the official art of capitalism."[21] While the communist countries once condemned it as an evil of capitalism, now, with the Cold War ended, Eastern European countries are encouraging private enterprise and realizing the benefits of advertising. Even China appears to have inherited the capitalist sensibility of Hong Kong.[22]

The explosion of new technologies in the last decade has affected advertising considerably. With cable TV and satellite receivers, viewers can watch channels devoted to single types of programming, such as straight news, home shopping, sports, or comedy. This has transformed television from the most widespread of mass media to a more specialized, "narrowcasting" medium.[23] Now small companies and product marketers who appeal to a limited clientele can use TV to reach audiences with select interests.

Exhibit • 1–4
Top 10 international advertisers.

Rank	Advertiser	Headquarters	Primary business	Countries in which spending was reported
1	Unilever NV	Rotterdam/London	Soaps	Argentina, Australia, Brazil, Britain, Canada, Denmark, France, Germany, Greece, India, Italy, Japan, Malaysia, Mexico, Netherlands, Pan Arabia, Portugal, Puerto Rico, South Africa, Spain, Switzerland, Taiwan, Thailand, Turkey, U.S.
2	Procter & Gamble	Cincinnati	Soaps	Australia, Austria, Britain, Canada, France, Germany, Greece, India, Italy, Japan, Malaysia, Mexico, Netherlands, Pan Arabia, Puerto Rico, Taiwan, Thailand, Turkey, U.S.
3	Nestlé SA	Vevey, Switzerland	Food	Argentina, Australia, Austria, Brazil, Britain, France, Germany, India, Japan, Malaysia, Mexico, Netherlands, Pan Arabia, Portugal, Puerto Rico, Spain, Switzerland, Taiwan, Thailand, Turkey, U.S.
4	Renault SA	Paris, France	Automotive	Argentina, Austria, Britain, France, Germany, Italy, Netherlands, Pan Arabia, Portugal, Spain, Switzerland, Thailand, U.S.
5	Philip Morris	New York	Food	Argentina, Australia, Austria, Brazil, Britain, Canada, Denmark, France, Germany, Hong Kong, Japan, Malaysia, Mexico, Netherlands, Pan Arabia, Spain, Taiwan, Thailand, U.S.
6	Fiat SpA	Turin, Italy	Automotive	Brazil, Britain, Denmark, France, Germany, Italy, Netherlands, Portugal, Spain, Switzerland, U.S.
7	Matsushita Electric Industrial	Osaka, Japan	Electronics	Brazil, Britain, Hong Kong, Japan, Malaysia, Pan Arabia, Taiwan, Thailand, U.S.
8	PSA Peugeot-Citroen SA	Paris, France	Automotive	Argentina, Austria, Britain, Denmark, France, Germany, Netherlands, Pan Arabia, Portugal, Spain, Switzerland, Thailand, U.S.
9	Nissan Motor	Tokyo, Japan	Automotive	Australia, Britain, Germany, Japan, Mexico, Pan Arabia, Switzerland, Thailand, U.S.
10	Volkswagen AG	Wolfsburg, Germany	Automotive	Brazil, Britain, France, Germany, Mexico, South Africa, Spain, Sweden, Switzerland, Thailand, U.S.

A concurrent change has been the growing presence of videocassette recorders (VCRs) and remote controls, which allow viewers to avoid commercials altogether by channel surfing during breaks or simply zipping through them when watching a previously recorded show. Advertisers have tried placing some commercials on rented videos, but this trend has yet to take hold, perhaps because viewers can still zap them.

Computer technology has had an impact, too. Personal computers, modems, electronic mail and bulletin boards, even facsimile machines give advertisers new media for reaching potential customers. Now even the smallest companies can maintain computer databases of customers' names to integrate their marketing campaigns.

But what is coming is even more dynamic—the global information highway, and with it an interactive revolution. Advertising is evolving into a two-way medium in which consumers with PCs, modems, CD-ROMS, and cable TV can choose what information to access and then spend 20 minutes or more drilling down to the in-depth product information they desire.[24] With interactivity, rather than zipping or zapping commercials, consumers will seek them out. As we discuss in Chapter 13, this will be a revolutionary way for advertisers to reach consumers. Agencies will have the opportunity to prove once again that advertising creativity is not about winning awards, but about *selling* things.[25]

Advertising has come a long way from the simple sign on the bootmaker's shop. Today it is a powerful device that announces the availability and location of products, describes their quality and value, imbues brands with personality, and simultaneously defines the personality of the people who buy them. More than a reflection of society and its desires, advertising can start and finish fads, trends, and credos—occasionally alone.[26]

In turn, advertising is shaped by the very technology used to convey its message. In the past it was always a monolog. But today it's evolving into a dialog. The medium and the message have become virtually inseparable.

FUNCTIONS AND EFFECTS OF ADVERTISING

• The new Sunkist logo introduced in 1995.

For any business, advertising performs several functions, and its effects may be dramatic. Consider the beginnings of Sunkist. The citrus growers decided to write their product's name in a unique way. Later, the name and style of lettering were trademarked with the U.S. Patent Office to reserve use of the Sunkist name and logo solely for the advertising and packaging of the California Fruit Growers Exchange. This demonstrates one of the most basic marketing functions of advertising: *to identify products and differentiate them from others*. (Some of advertising's functions and effects are listed in Exhibit 1–5.)

Once the growers named the product, they ran ads to promote the oranges and where people could get them. Here is another basic function of advertising: *to communicate information about the product, its features, and its location of sale*.

Prior to World War I, there was an enormous overproduction of oranges and no place to sell them. So the marketing department of Sunkist working with Lord & Thomas came up with a remarkable notion: to educate consumers about the idea of orange juice. They manufactured millions of glass reamers and ran ads telling people how they could make fresh juice in their homes. The campaign changed the whole demand pattern for oranges and demonstrated another reason for advertising: *to induce consumers to try new products and to suggest reuse*.[27]

As more people tried the oranges, liked them, and requested them, more grocery stores stocked the brand. *Stimulating the distribution of a product* is yet another function of advertising.

In the 1920s and 30s, the benefits of vitamin C became evident, but not everybody knew how to get it. One of the many purposes of advertising, though, is *to increase product use* . Sunkist and L&T introduced the word *vitamin* to the public in a campaign that told the world oranges contain vitamin C.[28]

As with any popular product, imitators with confusingly similar names appeared. The battle against competitors has been continuous ever since. Another function of advertising is *to build value, brand preference, and loyalty*. Sunkist's ongoing, consistent promotional campaign has helped accomplish this.

For more than 100 years, Sunkist has used the media to communicate advertising messages to mass audiences. This satisfies the most important function of advertising: *to lower the cost of sales*. The cost of reaching a thousand people through advertising is usually far less than the cost of reaching just one prospect through personal selling. According to a Cahners Advertising Research Report, the average cost to make a face-to-face, field sales call in 1994 was $292—and growing.[29] Multiply $292 by the more than 10 million people who watch a top-rated prime-time show, and the cost comes to a mind-boggling $2.9 billion. However, for only $175,000, Sunkist can buy 30-second TV commercials during "Beverly Hills 90210" and reach the same 10 million people. In fact, through television, advertisers can talk to a *thousand* prospects for only $7.50 total—about 3 percent of what it costs to talk to *one* prospect through personal selling.

(continued on page 30)

Exhibit • 1–5
Functions and effects of advertising as a marketing tool.

• To identify products and differentiate them from others.
• To communicate information about the product, its features, and its location of sale.
• To induce consumers to try new products and to suggest reuse.
• To stimulate the distribution of a product.
• To increase product use.
• To build value, brand preference, and loyalty.
• To lower the overall cost of sales.

In 1893, 60 orange growers met to organize a farmers' cooperative that became the California Fruit Growers Exchange. Their objective was to gain a stronger voice in the marketplace and to help coordinate distribution. In 1907, they hired the Lord & Thomas advertising agency (now Foote, Cone & Belding), which helped them create the Sunkist brand name.

The client–agency relationship remains to this day one of the longest associations in advertising history. Sunkist Growers, Inc., is the largest citrus cooperative in the world, with total yearly sales of over $800 million. By national standards, though, it only spends a small amount on media advertising annually.

The first Exchange advertisement ran in the *Des Moines Register* on March 2, 1908. Surprisingly, the ad ran in three colors (orange, green, and black), an unheard-of accomplishment. The campaign celebrated "Orange Week" with fruit shipped via rail from California to Iowa—another unheard-of feat in those days.

Early Sunkist ads offered recipes and suggestions for additional citrus uses. By the time this 1915 ad was produced, the Exchange's advertising budget totaled $250,000 per year, up from $25,000 in 1908.

Creation of the Sunkist brand was the first branding of a commodity. Early on, the decision was made to select only the finest oranges and lemons and to wrap them in tissue printed with the Sunkist label. Thus the Sunkist name rapidly became more than just a trademark; it also became a grade mark that stood for superior quality.

Up until 1916, oranges had only been eaten as a fruit. But sales quadrupled after Sunkist introduced its "Drink an Orange" ads. Sunkist introduced juice extractors to restaurants and soda fountains in 1917 and later to consumers for home use.

The new 1995 fruit labels show the brand name (Sunkist) and the variety (Valencia).

Because of its track record, the fine quality of Sunkist fruit remains undisputed. Sunkist's advertising strategy, then, was to advise customers to read the brand name on the fruit to ensure selection of the best orange—Sunkist.

Outdoor advertising further demonstrated brand differentiation with a catchy one-line statement set below vivid photography that enhanced the naturally evocative visual qualities of the product.

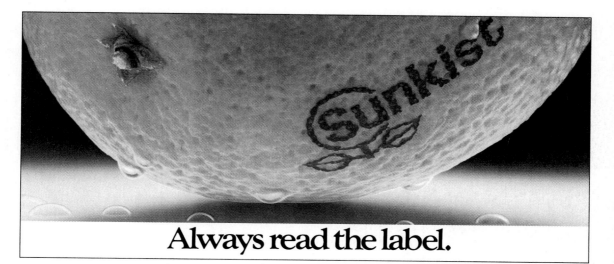

In television, the task was to show brand differentiation in a memorable, engaging, entertaining, and informative manner. To find the best orange, the commercials said, some customers squeeze, shake, or study every orange. But all they really need to do is "twist the wrist" and "always read the label."

Have you ever watched people at the market?

They all think they know how to pick the best orange.

They squeeze . . . They tap . . . They shake . . .

I have no idea what she's doing.

But all they have to do is twist the wrist. If it says Sunkist . . . you pick it.

Hey, always read the label.

Advertising to the trade: Sunkist aims messages at customers in the supermarket trade—produce buyers and merchandisers. These customers have a profit motive. If they believe customers prefer Sunkist, that is the brand they will buy.

IT'S NOT JUST a PEEL.
IT'S WHERE PROMISES are KEPT.

In fact, it's not an ordinary peel at all.

Because Sunkist® lemons are the finest, freshest lemons found anywhere in the world. What's more, we offer a year-round supply. In all the quantities and sizes you need.

Add to that our innovative, yet well established marketing support programs.

Plus a sales force which is not only professional, but highly accessible, with thirty one offices located throughout North America.

And perhaps, most importantly, a name your customers look for. A name they've known for nearly 100 years. And one they've come to respect.

Indeed, what you'll find inside that fresh yellow peel, is a promise fulfilled.

A promise that from Sunkist, when it comes to lemons, or any fresh citrus, you can expect nothing less than the best.

You have our word on it.

Consumers of oranges want the juiciest and best-tasting oranges available. The photography in this outdoor ad vividly shows the product to its best and juiciest advantage. The clever alliteration of the headline copy emphasizes the tangy qualities of the fruit. Everything else that needs to be said is implicit in the Sunkist name at the base of the ad.

OPEN on a lightly treed suburban street. We see two strong men in their early 20s earning some pin money by unloading a lorry stacked with crates of Sunkist oranges. They are working near the local greengrocer's shop.

CUT to see two girls working in the green-grocer's. CUT to the stackers as they pass crates to each other. CUT to see the girls have moved into the sunlight to open a can of Diet Sunkist to enjoy during their break.

CUT to one of the stackers noticing a spot of sunlight moving up his body. He wriggles as the beam of sunlight moves around.

CUT to see the source of light is a reflection from the underside of a Diet Sunkist can. The can is being maneuvered by a girl from the greengrocer's, egged on by her friend. She has nearly finished the can and is using the sunlight to tease the man.

CUT to the men realizing where the ray of sunlight is emanating from. But just as they look toward the can the girl puts it to her mouth and drinks the remaining amount of Diet Sunkist. The girls smile at the men and the taunting one purses her lips in a flirtatious manner.

CUT to one of the stackers wryly smiling at being caught by one of the girls.
CUT to a can of Diet Sunkist.

Under its licensing program, Sunkist authorizes use of its trademark on related products. In the mid-1950s, Hong Kong Bottlers received a license to market Sunkist Orange Drink. In 1977, the trademark for Sunkist Orange Soda was licensed to Sunkist Soft Drinks, Inc. (now a division of Cadbury-Schweppes); and in 1981 the Sunkist trademark was licensed to the Thomas J. Lipton Company for Sunkist fruit juices and fruit snack products. Sunkist Fruit Gem pectin jelly candies are marketed by The Ben Myerson Candy Company. Sunkist Growers members receive royalties from the companies that produce the licensed products.

THE ECONOMIC IMPACT OF ADVERTISING

Advertising accounts for approximately 2.3 percent of the U.S. gross domestic product. In relation to the total U.S. economy, this percentage is small. But as the father of modern French advertising, Marcel Bleustein-Blanchet, noted in the early 70s, it's no coincidence that the level of advertising investment in a country is directly proportional to its standard of living.[30]

The economic effect of advertising is like the break shot in billiards, as shown in Exhibit 1–6. The moment a company begins to advertise, a chain reaction of economic events takes place. The extent of the chain reaction, although hard to measure, is related to the force of the shot. But because it occurs at the same time as many other economic events, the direction is often disputed.

For example, does advertising affect the value of products? Does advertising raise or lower prices? Does advertising promote competition or discourage it? How does advertising affect the total demand for a product category? Does advertising make more consumer choices available or fewer? How does advertising influence the business cycle? These are just some of the frequently asked (and difficult to answer) questions related to the chain reaction of economic events.

Effect on the Value of Products

Why do most people prefer Coca-Cola to some other cola? Why do more women prefer Estee Lauder to some unadvertised, inexpensive perfume? Are the advertised products functionally better? Not necessarily. But advertising can add value to a product in the consumer's mind.

In the mid-1960s, Ernest Dichter, a psychologist known as the father of motivational research, said that a product's image, produced partially by advertising and promotion, is an inherent feature of the product itself.[31] Subsequent studies showed that while an ad may not speak directly about a product's quality, the positive image conveyed by advertising may imply quality, make the product more desirable to the consumer, and

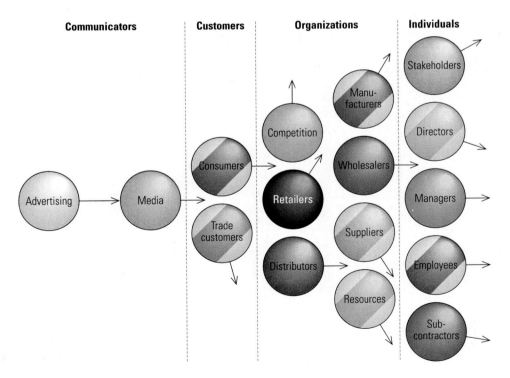

Exhibit • 1–6
The economic effect of advertising is like the opening break shot in billiards.

• Ads that encourage new uses for established products or educate customers on how to use them create the perception of added value. In this ad, Minute Maid Foodservice advises restauranteurs to feature its juices in a variety of menu styles, at different times of the day, and with different types of customers to increase sales.

thereby add value to the product.[32] That's why people pay more for Bufferin than an unadvertised brand displayed right next to it—even though all buffered aspirin, by law, is functionally the same.[33]

Advertising also creates added value by educating customers about new uses for a product. Kleenex was originally advertised as a makeup remover, later as a disposable handkerchief. Sunkist promoted oranges as a food and later as a drink.

One advantage of the free market system is that consumers can choose the values they want in the products they buy. If low price is important, for example, they can buy an inexpensive economy car. If status and luxury are important, they can buy a fancy sedan or racy sports car. Many of our wants are emotional, social, or psychological rather than functional. One way we communicate who we are (or want to be) is through the products we purchase and display. Advertising allows people the opportunity to satisfy those wants or needs.

Effect on Prices

If advertising adds value to products, it follows that advertising also adds cost. Right? And if companies stopped all that expensive advertising, products would cost less. Right?

Wrong.

Some advertised products do cost more than unadvertised products; but the opposite is also true. The FTC and the Supreme Court have ruled that advertising has the competitive effect of keeping prices down, so professionals such as attorneys and physicians must be allowed to advertise.

Sweeping statements about advertising's positive or negative effect on prices are likely to be too simplistic. But we can make some important points.

- As one of the many costs of doing business, advertising is indeed paid for by the consumer who buys the product. In most product categories, though, the amount spent on advertising is usually very small compared to the total cost of the product.

- Advertising is one element of the mass-distribution system that enables many manufacturers to engage in mass production, which in turn lowers the unit cost of products. These savings can then be passed on to consumers in the form of lower prices. In this indirect way, advertising helps lower prices.

- In industries subject to government price regulation (agriculture, utilities), advertising has historically had no effect on prices. In the 1980s, though, the government deregulated many of these industries in an effort to restore free market pressures on prices. In these cases, advertising does affect price—often downward, sometimes upward.

- In retailing, price is a prominent element in many ads, so advertising tends to hold prices down. Manufacturing firms advertise to stress features that make their products better, so advertising tends to support higher prices.

Effect on Competition

Some observers complain that small companies or industry newcomers can't compete with the immense advertising budgets of large firms and eventually go out of business. They think advertising restricts competition.

Intense competition does tend to reduce the number of businesses in an industry. However, the firms eliminated by competition may be those that served customers least effectively.

In many cases, advertising by big companies has only a limited effect on small businesses because no advertiser is large enough to dominate the whole country. Regional oil companies, for example, compete very successfully with national oil companies on the local level. And nonadvertised store brands of food compete effectively with nationally advertised brands on the same shelves.

In industries characterized by heavy advertising expenditures, advertising does inhibit the entry of new competitors. In some markets, the original brands probably benefit greatly from this barrier. But heavy spending on plants and machinery is usually a far more significant barrier.

Effect on Consumer Demand

The question of advertising's effect on total consumer demand is extremely complex. Numerous studies show that promotional activity does affect aggregate consumption, but they don't agree on the extent. Many social and economic forces, including technological advances, the population's educational level, increases in population and per capita income, and revolutionary changes in lifestyle, are more significant.

For example, the demand for CD players, cellular phones, and personal computers expanded at a tremendous rate, thanks in part to advertising but more to favorable market conditions. At the same time, advertising has not reversed sales declines for such items as hats, fur coats, and manual typewriters.

Advertising can help get new products off the ground by stimulating demand for a product class. But in declining markets, advertising can only slow the rate of decline. In growing markets, advertisers generally compete for shares of that growth. In mature, static, or declining markets, they compete for each other's shares—conquest sales.

● Advertisers must find a way to differentiate their products in an overcrowded market. To show how small its subcompact Mazda 121 is, the Japanese firm placed ads displaying a car and a half on 150 outdoor boards in Israel in a campaign to attract new customers. Only the brand name—Mazda 121—is shown on the board.

Effect on Consumer Choice

For manufacturers, the best way to beat the competition is to make their product different. For example, look at the long list of car models, sizes, colors, and features used to attract different buyers. And grocery shelves may carry 15 to 20 different brands of breakfast cereals—something for everybody.

The freedom to advertise encourages businesses to create new brands and improve old ones. When one brand reaches market dominance, smaller brands may disappear for a time. But the moment a better product comes along and is advertised skillfully, the dominant brand loses to the new, better product.

Effect on the Business Cycle

The relationship between advertising and gross domestic product (GDP) has long been debated. John Kenneth Galbraith, a perennial critic of advertising, concedes that, by helping to maintain the flow of consumer demand, advertising helps sustain employment and income. But he maintains that, despite decline in the value of the dollar, the U.S. trade deficit persists because advertising and marketing activities create consumer preference for certain foreign products.[34]

Historically, when business cycles dip, companies cut advertising expenditures. That may help immediate short-term profits, but studies prove that businesses that continue to invest in advertising during a recession are better able to protect, and sometimes build, market shares.[35] However, no study has shown that if everybody keeps advertising, the recessionary cycle will turn around. We conclude that when business cycles are up, advertising contributes to the increase. When business cycles are down, advertising may act as a stabilizing force.

THE ECONOMIC IMPACT OF ADVERTISING: THE ABUNDANCE PRINCIPLE

To individual businesses like Sunkist, the local car dealer, and the convenience store on the corner, advertising pays back more than it costs. If advertising didn't pay, no one would use it; and the various news and entertainment media that depend on advertising for financial support would go out of business.

For the consumer, advertising costs less than most people think. The cost of a bottle of Coke includes about a penny for advertising. And the $15,000 price tag on a new car usually includes a manufacturer's advertising cost of less than $300.

To the economy as a whole, the importance of advertising may best be demonstrated by the **abundance principle.** This states that in an economy that produces more goods and services than can be consumed, advertising serves two important purposes: It keeps consumers informed of their alternatives, and it allows companies to compete more effectively for consumer dollars.

In North America alone, the U.S. and Canadian economies produce an enormous selection of products. Most supermarkets carry more than 10,000 different items. Each carmaker markets dozens of models. And many suppliers compete for the consumer dollar. This competition generally results in more and better products at similar or lower prices.

● Advertising stimulates competition. It also stimulates innovation and added value, as shown
in this ad for Jergens lotions. The
new refill pouches are more economical and are also environmentally responsible, which
signifies added value to many
people today.

Advertising stimulates competition. In countries where consumers have more income to spend after their physical needs are satisfied, advertising also stimulates innovation and new products. However, no amount of advertising can achieve long-term
acceptance for products that do not meet consumer approval. Despite massive advertising expenditures, fewer than a dozen of the 50 best-known cars developed this century are still sold today.

Advertising stimulates a healthy economy. It also helps create financially healthy
consumers who are more informed, better educated, and more demanding. Consumers
now demand that manufacturers be held accountable for their advertising. This has led
to an unprecedented level of social and legal regulation, the subject of the next chapter.

Summary

Advertising is the nonpersonal communication of information, usually
paid for and usually persuasive, about products, services, or ideas, by
identified sponsors through various media.

Since advertising is first and foremost communication, advertisers
cannot afford to take the communication process for granted. The basic
process begins when one party (the source) formulates an idea, encodes it as a message, and sends it via some channel or medium to another party (the receiver). The receiver must decode the message in
order to understand it. To respond, the receiver formulates a new idea,
encodes that concept, and then sends a new message back through
some channel. A message that acknowledges or responds to the original message constitutes feedback, which also affects the encoding of a
new message. In advertising the communication process is made more
complex by the multidimensional nature of the source, the message,
and the recipient.

There are many types of advertising. It can be classified by target
audience (consumer, business), by geographic area (local, international), by medium (radio, newspaper, television), or by function or
purpose (product, noncommercial, or action advertising).

In ancient times when most people could not read or write, marketers used symbols on signs to advertise their products. As manufacturing and communication technologies developed, so did advertising.
Printing was the first major technology to affect advertising; cable TV
and computers are the most recent. Since World War II, advertisers
have attempted to differentiate products through positioning strategies
and other techniques. Recently the advertising industry underwent a
period of retrenchment and reevaluation; but the future offers new opportunities for advertisers and agencies that can harness the interactive
revolution.

As a marketing tool, advertising serves several functions. It identifies
and differentiates products; communicates information about them; in-
duces nonusers to try products and users to repurchase them; stimulates products' distribution; increases product use; builds value, brand
preference, and loyalty; and lowers the overall cost of sales.

Aside from marketing, advertising serves several other functions in the economy and in society.

Its economic impact can be likened to the opening shot in billiards—a chain reaction that affects the company as well as its competitors, customers, and the business community.

On a broader scale, advertising is often considered the trigger on a country's mass-distribution system, enabling manufacturers to produce the products people want in high volume, at low prices, with standardized quality. People disagree, however, about whether advertising adds value to products, makes them more or less expensive, encourages or discourages competition, affects total consumer demand, narrows or widens consumer choice, and affects national business cycles.

Although controversy surrounds most of these economic issues, few dispute the abundance principle, which states that in an economy that produces more goods and services than can be consumed, advertising keeps consumers informed of their choices and helps companies compete more effectively.

Questions for Review and Discussion

1. How does advertising for the American Cancer Society compare with the standard definition of advertising?

2. How does advertising differ from public relations activities?

3. In the marketing communication process, what are the various dimensions of the source, the message, and the receiver?

4. What is the difference between the media used for local advertising and for national advertising?

5. How did the railroad affect the growth of advertising?

6. What examples can you think of in which companies or organizations use a demarketing strategy?

7. What companies can you think of that are engaged in marketing warfare?

8. As a consumer, will you save money buying at a store that doesn't advertise? Explain.

9. In what ways can advertising increase a product's value?

10. How would you explain the overall effect of advertising on consumer choice?

Chapter

2

The Social, Legal, and Ethical Aspects of Advertising

Objective: To identify and explain the social, ethical, and legal issues advertisers must consider. Society determines what is offensive, excessive, and irresponsible; government bodies determine what is deceptive and unfair. To be law abiding, ethical, and socially responsible, as well as effective, an advertiser must understand these issues.

After studying this chapter, you will be able to:

- Recognize some of the many legal issues advertisers face here and abroad.

- Debate common social criticisms of advertising.

- Discuss advertising's effect on society.

- Discuss the difference between social responsibility and ethics in advertising.

- Explain how federal agencies regulate advertising to protect consumers and competitors.

- Describe the roles regional and local governments play in advertising regulation.

- Discuss recent court rulings that affect advertisers' freedom of speech.

- Evaluate the effectiveness of nongovernment organizations in regulating advertising.

or a movie, it was the largest marketing extravaganza ever, with a total integrated communications budget of over $60 million! Steven Spielberg himself worked closely with the studio, MCA/Universal, to marshal the plans—not just to promote the movie but to merchandise it through extensive cooperative marketing agreements. Unquestionably, *Jurassic Park* was an enormous project.

In early 1992, MCA secured Kenner Products as the first partner to manufacture and distribute *Jurassic Park* toys worldwide. Several months later, McDonald's jumped on board for a cross-promotion to be used in the U.S. and a handful of foreign countries. Within a year, over 500 licensees were marketing more than 5,000 products worldwide, all bearing the *Jurassic Park* logo.[1] Among them were Kmart, Kellogg (Canada), Weetabix (France, Portugal, and the U.K.), Coca-Cola (Latin America), PepsiCo (Scandinavia), and Panasonic, to name just a few.

However, MCA/Universal Merchandising, the company overseeing the marketing of *JP* products, confronted immense legal challenges—namely, how to protect the name and the movie's trademarks from infringement by the many counterfeiters, bootleggers, and trademark pirates around the world.

The legal staff for MCA/Universal Merchandising developed a five-step approach to the problem. First, secure a distinguishing mark for the movie and all the merchandise. Second, ensure confidentiality and secrecy during the prerelease development stages. Next, establish a claim on the name and trademark. Then, secure registration of the copyrights and trademarks. Finally, enforce ownership claims.

The distinguishing mark was relatively simple to determine. Early on, Kenner Products wanted to use the same red, black, and yellow logo that appeared on the cover of Michael Crichton's *Jurassic Park* novel. Others felt the same. The publisher, Ballantine Books, granted the rights, and MCA published a style guide on how to treat the specific design elements of the logo and where and how it should be used.

The second issue, confidentiality, was also fairly straightforward. "We made sure that every licensee we solicited to create merchandise first signed confidentiality agreements and enhanced nondisclosure agreements before we shipped them any slides from the movie or the style guides and sales kits," said Michelle Katz, general counsel for Merchandising. "And we prohibited the actual release of any licensed products that bore certain elements from the film until a few weeks before the movie was released."

However, the third element, establishing the claim, posed a serious problem. Confidentiality was essential for two reasons. It kept knockoff and illegal products from jumping in early. The shroud of secrecy was critical to promoting the film—building the market's expectations and craving for it. But to protect the images and the *JP* concept in some countries, they would have to publish them prior to the film's release. The question was how to release the minimum information required for trademark protection without revealing the nature of the images and products, particularly since so much would not be available until the following year.

Advertising was the answer. MCA/Universal Merchandising created a series of ads based on the logo. Fortunately, the logo did not reveal any actual images from the film. The rights for its use had already been attained. And it enjoyed some awareness in the marketplace with those who had read the book.

One full-page magazine ad featured a huge headline: "If you think this dinosaur has a ferocious appetite, wait until you meet our attorneys." The logo appeared in a moderate size below the headline. In small type at the bottom of the page was the line, "To report unauthorized sightings: call 1-800-DINO-COP." Months before the film's release, the company ran the print ads in the U.S. as well as overseas in different languages.[2]

Advertising mitigated a number of challenges. Some countries, like the U.S., require that marks be published before being registered. By placing ads in the trade journals read by people who market licensed products, MCA limited exposure of the concept to a select audience and avoided alerting the general moviegoing public. By using paid advertising, rather than relying on news releases or media interviews, the company maintained complete control over how the logo was displayed and the message it conveyed.

In addition, most media afford some protection to the ads they carry. For example, magazines and newspapers feature a publication date, and they copyright the material within their pages. Broadcast media run ads according to a schedule listed on a notarized statement. All of these verify the mark's first use, a critical factor in determining who has the legitimate right to use a trademark.

As the ads were being produced, the trademark was registered in certain areas (phase four). "Many countries don't require you to use a mark in commerce before registering it, so if you don't register your mark early in those countries, others will," Katz stated. Eventually, trademarks were filed on the film's title, its designs, and its logo in all major markets worldwide and for all categories where licensing might occur.

The ads also helped support the last phase of the strategy, enforcement of the claim. By announcing the memorable "1-800-DINO-COP" telephone number, the company signaled its intent to protect the *Jurassic Park* logo and other intellectual property associated with the mark.[3] The ads also served as a grassroots awareness program aimed at customs agents in the U.S., Japan, and the U.K. "We let them know," said Katz, "what our products, logos, and trademarks looked like."

The program was immensely successful. Copycats—even at flea markets and on street corners—were quickly dealt with by the firm's lawyers. Eventually, MCA generated more than *$1 billion* retail in revenue from sales of licensed products—more than the movie itself produced, and substantially more than the company would have realized had it not protected itself from illegal operators.[4] The Film Information Council voted *Jurassic Park* the best-marketed picture of 1993 and cited the use of the *JP* logo in advertising, publicity, and merchandising as the key element that made the film the "super movie event experience of the year."[5] •

Protection of a company's brands and trademarks is just one of the many legal issues confronting advertisers. Moreover, marketers also face many social and ethical challenges in their efforts to communicate with people about their products.

This chapter addresses the major social criticisms of advertising and contrasts them with the benefits advertising offers. It examines the ethics of advertising and the social responsibility of advertisers. Finally, it discusses the regulatory methods used to remedy abuses.

SOCIAL CRITICISM OF ADVERTISING

John O'Toole, the late chair of Foote, Cone & Belding and president of the American Association of Advertising Agencies, pointed out that many critics attack advertising because it *isn't something else*. Advertising isn't journalism, education, or entertainment—although it often performs the tasks of all three. To go back to Albert Lasker's original definition, advertising is *salesmanship in print* (or, in today's parlance, *in the paid space and time of mass media*). As a means of communication, advertising shares certain traits of journalism, education, and entertainment, but it shouldn't be judged by those standards. Sponsors advertise because they hope it will help them sell some product, service, or idea.[6]

Advertising is the most visible activity of business. By inviting people to try their products, companies also risk public criticism and attack if their products don't measure up or if their advertising displeases the audience. Proponents of advertising say it's safer to buy advertised products because, when manufacturers put their company name and reputation on the line, they try harder to fulfill their promises (especially when they list product benefits).

Advertising is both applauded and criticized for its role in selling products and its influence on society. For years, critics have denigrated advertising for a wide range of sins—some real, some imagined. The result has been a steady growth in the number of consumer groups, business organizations, and government bodies that now regulate virtually everything advertisers say and do. Let's look at some common criticisms of advertising, debunk some of the misconceptions about it, and acknowledge the problems that do exist.

The Proliferation of Advertising

One of the most common complaints about advertising is that there's just too much of it. In the U.S. alone, the average person may be exposed to 500 to 1,000 commercial messages a day. With so many products competing for attention (over 15,000 in the average supermarket), advertising professionals themselves worry about the negative impact of excessive advertising. A recent study by the Association of National Advertisers and the American Association of Advertising Agencies showed that TV networks added to the problem of ad clutter by jamming every possible moment with promotions for their shows. The more commercials hit the consumer's brain, the less effective paid advertising is. The cable channels used to be a haven for the weary, but now they are even worse. Some run as much as 17 minutes per hour of nonprogramming material, not to mention those that run continuous infomercials.[7]

● French government-owned TV stations severely limit commercial air time, which encourages advertisers to make every minute count, as in this humorous spot for Miss Dior perfume.

VIDEO: A woman in a purple bridal dress storms through a door.
AUDIO: Operatic music throughout the entire film.
VIDEO: She starts to descend a spiral staircase.

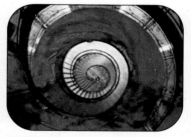

PRIEST: "You are now ready to marry this man . . ."
VIDEO: Cut to a man (the groom?) waiting at the foot of the spiral staircase. Cut to a view of the staircase from above. The train

of the bridal dress covers every step along the way.
PRIEST: ". . . to take him as your husband, for better or worse . . ."
VIDEO: Two little pages are "riding" on the train of the dress.

PRIEST: " . . . if he's rich or if he's poor . . . to obey his requests, to serve his demands . . . to respect him."
PRIEST: (Hysterical voice) "Are you ready to love this man . . ."

VIDEO: The bride has almost reached the bottom of the stairs.
PRIEST: ". . . are you ready to stay with this man . . ." The music drowns out the rest of the litany.

VIDEO: Cut to the waiting man, who is obviously nervous. Cut to the bride as she steps off the staircase, leaves behind her wedding dress, train and all, and, in her underwear, jumps into the arms of the man. Cut to a bottle of "Miss Dior."
VO: Miss Dior. Trés Miss. Trés Dior.

Clutter is not so evident in other countries. In France, for example, government-owned stations can carry no more than 12 minutes of commercials per hour. During movies there is only one four-minute commercial break, although the government is considering changing that rule to allow two breaks.[8]

In North America we should be so lucky. During election periods, the clutter problem is exacerbated, which seriously devalues the advertiser's commercial. The Association of Canadian Advertisers, in fact, called on its members to renegotiate the prices they had been charged for air time after an overwhelming number of political ads ran during the fall of 1993.[9]

While this problem is irksome to viewers and advertisers alike, most people tolerate it as the price for free TV, freedom of the press, and a high standard of living. And with the proliferation of new media choices, it's likely to get worse. But recently the FCC began considering reinstating commercial time limits on television.[10]

The Effect of Advertising on Our Value System

Some professional critics—academics, journalists, consumer advocates, and government regulators—believe advertising adversely affects people's value systems by promoting a hedonistic, materialistic way of life. Advertising, they say, encourages us to buy more cars, more CDs, more clothing, and more junk we don't need. It is destroying the essence of our "citizen democracy," replacing it with a self-oriented consumer democracy.[11]

A variation on this theme is that advertising manipulates us to buy things by playing on our emotions and promising greater status, social acceptance, and sex appeal. Critics claim advertising causes people to take up harmful habits, makes poor kids buy $175 sneakers, and tempts ordinary people to buy useless products in the vain attempt

• Beverly Center's previous campaign focused on the center itself, but the new campaign featured the Beverly shopper. The 80s power shopper was passé; instead, the ads used stream-of-consciousness copy to focus on the anxiety of people who *have* to shop.

to emulate celebrity endorsers.[12] Advertising, they think, is so powerful consumers are helpless to defend themselves against it.

Advertisers do indeed spend millions trying to convince people their products will make them sexier, healthier, and more successful. But some observers point out that advertising's powers have been greatly exaggerated. In fact, Americans in particular are highly skeptical of it. Studies show that only 17 percent of U.S. consumers see advertising as a source of information to help them decide what to buy.[13] Perhaps that's why more advertised products fail than succeed in the marketplace.

The Use of Stereotypes in Advertising

Advertising has long been criticized for insensitivity to minorities, women, immigrants, the disabled, and myriad other groups—that is, for not being "politically correct."[14] This is ironic, since marketing and advertising practitioners are supposed to be professional students of consumer behavior (a subject we cover in Chapter 4) and the communication process. But, in fact, they sometimes lose touch with the very people they're trying to reach. This is one reason the discipline of account planning (discussed in Chapter 3) is growing so rapidly at agencies in the U.S and abroad.

Since the 80s, national advertisers have actually become more sensitive to the concerns of minorities and women. Latinos, African-Americans, Asians, Native Americans, and others are now usually portrayed more favorably in ads, not only because of pres-

• Marketers today are more sensitive to the concerns of minorities and are aware of their purchasing power. Advertising reflects this focus, avoiding the old stereotypes and portraying these consumers as good role models. This Southwestern Bell commercial, broadcast in Spanish for the Hispanic market, informs potential customers of the low cost and high value of its telephone services.

DAUGHTER: Me daban nervios por no saber como seguía mamá. *(I was always nervous because I couldn't check on how mom was doing.)*

DAUGHTER: Ella vive en otro barrio, *(She lives in another neighborhood,)*
DAUGHTER: y no teníamos teléfono. *(and we just didn't have a phone.)*

DAUGHTER: Ella si, pero nosotros . . . *(She did, but we . . .)*
DAUGHTER: Pensábamos que era muy caro. *(We thought it was too expensive.)*
DAUGHTER: ¡Ay que equivocados! *(Boy, were we wrong!)*

ANNCR: Usted puede tener servicio telefónico básico por sólo $17 al mes. *(You can have basic phone service for only $17 a month.)*
ANNCR: La instalación es menos de $53. *(Installation? It's less than $53.)*

ANNCR: Llame a Southwestern Bell Telephone *(Call Southwestern Bell Telephone)*
ANNCR: al 1-800-559-0050 y ordene su servicio hoy. *(at 1-800-559-0050 and order your service today.)*

ANNCR: Hablamos español. *(We speak Spanish.)*
DAUGHTER: ¿Mama? *(Mom?)*
MOM: ¡Mija! *(Daughter!)*

sure from watchdog groups, but also because it's just good business; these consumers represent sizable target markets. Marilyn Kern-Foxworth, a Texas A&M professor and an expert on minorities in advertising, points out, for example, that positive role portrayal in some mainstream ads has had a positive effect on the self-esteem of black youth.[15] As we'll see in Chapter 3, this positive trend has accelerated with the emergence of many ad agencies owned and staffed by minorities that specialize in reaching minority markets.

In national advertising, the image of women is also changing from their historic depiction as either subservient housewives or sex objects (see the Ethical Issue: "Does Sex Appeal?" in Chapter 9). Recent research indicates that since the early 80s, these traditional depictions of women have decreased and "equality" portrayals are on the rise.[16] More than 57 percent of all women now work outside the home, and more than 38 million of them are in professional, managerial, technical, sales, or administrative careers.[17] Advertisers want to reach, not offend, this sizable market of upwardly mobile consumers. Some agencies now retain feminist consultants to review ads that may risk offending women.[18]

However, problems still exist, especially in local and regional advertising and in certain product categories like beer and sports promotions. Some advertisers are not aware of the subtle meanings ads communicate, and they may inadvertently perpetuate male and female stereotypes.[19] Other advertisers resort to stereotypes for convenience. All too often, women are still not represented accurately. And the minimal use of minorities in mainstream ads, both local and national, smacks of tokenism. Observers hope that with increasing numbers of women and minorities joining the ranks of marketing and advertising professionals, and with continuing academic studies of minority and sex-role stereotyping, greater attention will be focused on these issues.

Offensiveness in Advertising

Taste is highly subjective: What is bad taste to some is perfectly acceptable to others. And tastes change. What is considered offensive today may not be so tomorrow. People were outraged when the first ad for underarm deodorant appeared in a 1927 *Ladies Home Journal*; today no one questions such ads. Yet, even with the AIDS scare, all the broadcast networks except Fox still restrict condom ads to local stations, and all four forbid any talk of contraception.[20]

Taste is also geographic. A shockingly bloody ad for a small surfwear company in Sydney, Australia, showed a gutted shark lying on a dock. Protruding from its cut-open belly were a human skeleton and an intact pair of surfer shorts. The tagline: "Tough clothes by Kadu—Triple stitched. Strongest materials available. Homegrown and sewn."

While we might consider that ad quite offensive in North America, it won the Grand Prix at the International Advertising Festival in Cannes, France. In Australia it received wide media coverage, since two surfers were killed by sharks while it was running. Rather than pulling the ad out of respect, the company reveled in its timeliness, and the local surfer set responded very favorably.[21]

Today, grooming, fashion, and personal hygiene products often use nudity in their ads. Where nudity is relevant to the product, people are less likely to regard it as obscene or offensive. And in international markets, nudity in commercials may be commonplace. Some industry observers predict that nudity in U.S. advertising will increase in the 21st century, but there will be fewer overt sexual scenes of the Calvin Klein style.[22]

Some consumers get so offended by both advertising and TV programming that they boycott sponsors' products.[23] Of course, they also have the option of just changing the channel. Ultimately, the market has veto power. If ads don't attract the target audience, the campaign will falter and die.

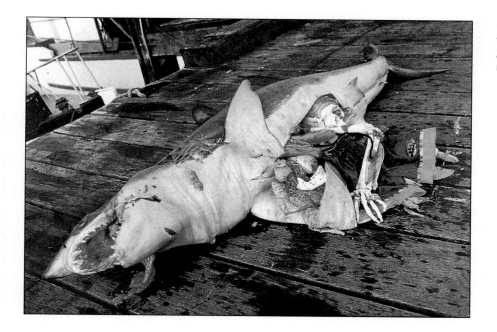

● Tastes of consumers—and advertisers—may differ geographically, as shown in this award-winning Australian surfwear ad. Local Sydney surfers responded quite favorably to the ad.

Deception in Advertising

Professor Ivan Preston notes that the essence of a marketplace lies in the willingness of buyers and sellers to enter commercial transactions. Anything that detracts from the satisfaction of the transaction produces a loss of activity that is unfortunate for both parties.[24] If a product does not live up to its ads, dissatisfaction occurs—and it is ultimately as harmful to the advertiser as to the buyer.

For advertising to be effective, consumers must have confidence in it. So any kind of deception risks being self-defeating. Even meaningless (but legal) *puffery* might be taken literally and therefore become deceptive. **Puffery** is exaggerated, subjective claims that can't be proven true or false such as "the best," "premier," or "the only way to fly."

Under current advertising law, the only product claims—explicit or implied—that are considered deceptive are those that are *factually false* and have the potential to deceive or mislead reasonable people.[25] Critics would broaden that definition to include false impressions conveyed, whether intentional or not. Preston points out that advertisers regularly use puffery and nonproduct facts to enhance the image of their products. **Nonproduct facts** are not about the brand but about the consumer or the social context in which the consumer uses the brand. An example is "Pepsi. The choice of a new generation."

Preston would require advertisers to have a reasonable basis for *any* claims they make, whether those claims are facts about the product, *nonfacts* such as "Coke is it," or nonproduct facts.[26] Ad Lab 2–A lists common deceptive practices.

The Subliminal Advertising Myth

Wilson Bryan Key (who has sold thousands of books on subliminal advertising) promotes the notion that, to seduce consumers, advertisers intentionally embed sexual messages in ads just below the threshold of perception. But academic studies completely debunk this theory.[27] There is absolutely no proof that such embedding either exists or that if it did it would have any effect. Unfortunately, by promulgating this fiction, Key has helped to create a generation of consumers who believe in the poppycock of subliminal advertising.[28]

Ethical Issue   Truth in Advertising: Fluffing and Puffing

The best. Tops. The most. The country's #1 _____ (fill in the blank). These may be useful superlatives in the right context, but in advertising they often don't signify much and are referred to as puffery.

Puff comes from the Old English word *pyffan*, meaning "to blow in short gusts" or "to inflate; make proud or conceited." And from the powder puff, a soft and fluffy pad for dispensing talc, came the puff piece, or "adoring article." In advertising, puffery is exaggerated commendation, or hype.

Because advertisers "adore" their products, fluff and puff hover about most advertising communications. Regulators find puffery generally tolerable and contend reasonable consumers aren't taken in by it. People are expected to find an exaggerated claim obvious and not to believe when

Prudential says "Own a piece of the rock" that they will be receiving a chunk of granite.

Legally, puffery is a dichotomy. The law says that puffed-up claims can be false yet acceptable. In other words, a product's quality can be exaggerated with opinions or superlatives if they state no specifics. Bayer's claim to be "the world's best aspirin" is acceptable since the FTC decided such phrases "are merely puffing because the ad does not discuss any comparison of Bayer's quality."

Puffery's key legal distinction is between deception and falsity. Deception is *subjectively* interpreted as injurious to consumers and therefore illegal, while falsity is an *objective* characteristic that may or may not be deceptive and illegal. The characteristics puffed must actually exist. A few examples of permissible (legal) puffery follow:

- "The legendary marque of high performance." (Alfa Romeo)
- "The lightest, most compact cellular phone on earth." (Motorola)
- "A perfect partner for American business." (Sunkyong)
- "We do more to keep you at the top." (Credit Suisse)
- "The right fund at the right time." (Dreyfus)

Puffery can be found in another area, *nonproduct facts*, which are not about the product and therefore cannot say anything true or false about it. Nonproduct facts are typically about consumers: their personalities, lifestyles, fears, anxieties. An example is Vic Tanny's claim, "You don't just shape your body, you shape your life." The claim is really about the newspaper ad's readers,

Ad Lab 2-A   Unfair and Deceptive Practices in Advertising

The courts have held that these acts constitute unfair or deceptive trade practices and are therefore illegal.

False Promises

Making an advertising promise that cannot be kept, such as "restores youth" or "prevents cancer." When Listerine claimed to prevent or reduce the impact of colds and sore throats, the FTC banned the campaign and required the company to run millions of dollars' worth of corrective ads.

Incomplete Description

Stating some, but not all, of a product's contents, such as advertising a "solid oak" desk without mentioning that only the top is solid oak and the rest is pine.

False and Misleading Comparisons

Making false comparisons, either explicitly or by implication, such as "Like Tylenol, Advil doesn't upset my stomach." That implies that Advil is equal in avoiding stomach upset, though in truth Tylenol is better. To some people, Advil's claim might even suggest that Tylenol upsets the stomach, which is also false.

Bait-and-Switch Offers

Advertising an item at an unusually low price to bring people into the store and then "switching" them to a higher-priced model by claiming that the advertised product is out of stock or poorly made.

Visual Distortions and False Demonstrations

Using trick photography or computer manipulation to enhance a product's appearance—for example, a TV commercial for a "giant steak" dinner special showing the steak on a miniature plate that makes it look extra large. In one classic case, General Motors and its window supplier Libby Owens-Ford rigged a demonstration to show how clear their windows were versus the competition. The GM cars were photographed with the windows down, the competitor's car with the windows up—and Vaseline smeared on them.

False Testimonials

Implying that a product has the endorsement of a celebrity or an authority who is not a bona fide user, or implying that endorsers have a certain expertise that in fact they don't.

Partial Disclosures

Stating certain facts about the advertised product but omitting other material information. An example is claiming, "Kraft's Singles processed cheese slices are made from five ounces of milk which give Singles more calcium than the imitators" without mentioning that processing loses about two ounces of the milk.

Small-Print Qualifications

Making a statement in large print, such as Beneficial's "Instant Tax Refund," only to qualify or retract it in obscure, small, or unreadable type elsewhere in the ad: "If you qualify for one of our loans." To the FTC, if the readers don't see the qualification, it's not there.

Laboratory Applications

1. Describe some examples of deception you have seen in advertising.

2. Do you think the rules that apply to commercial speech should also apply to political advertising?

who are Tanny's prospective customers. While it may be true or false about such people, the claim is neither true nor false about Vic Tanny.

Consumers must make up their own minds about advertising and separate fact from fiction.

Consumers must make up their own minds about advertising and separate fact from fiction. But can they do this only on the seller's say-so? Suppose a soft drink or coffee claims it's the best tasting. We won't really know until we take a sip for ourselves. (Of course, we have to buy the product to get that sip.) Brands that turn out not to taste good can't be saved by any advertising.

Puffery is as old as the first ads ever written to distinguish one product from another—and it's here to stay. How else can the advertiser focus attention on its product? But how much puffery is allowable? Traditionally, puffery has enjoyed immunity from legal constraints because it is considered opinion rather than fact. In the end, an ad's effectiveness depends on the actions people actually take rather than what they merely think about an advertised product. Whether an advertiser puffs or not, the consumer's best bet is to heed the ancient admonition *caveat emptor:* let the buyer beware.

Questions

1. How do you react to an ad that proclaims a product "is the greatest ever," "will change your life," or "can't be beat"? Does it pique your interest to give it a try—or do just the opposite?

2. If puffery were outlawed, how would similar products (toothpaste, detergents, cereals, for example) differentiate themselves? If advertisers were restricted to telling only the literal truth, how would that affect creativity in advertising?

Sources: William Safire, "On Language—Huff and Puff Stuff of Old England and the Wolf," *San Diego Union-Tribune,* October 9, 1994, p. E-8; Ivan L. Preston, *The Tangled Web They Weave: Truth, Falsity and Advertisers* (Madison, WI: The University of Wisconsin Press, 1994), pp. 103, 107, 110; Minette E. Drumwright, "Ethical Issues in Advertising and Sales Promotion," in N. Craig Smith and John A. Quelch, eds., *Ethics in Marketing* (Burr Ridge, IL: Richard D. Irwin, 1993), p. 611; Ivan L. Preston, "A New Conception of Deceptiveness," paper presented to Advertising Division, AEJMC, August 12, 1993.

THE SOCIAL BENEFITS OF ADVERTISING

Critics often forget that advertising benefits society. Advertising encourages the development and speeds the acceptance of new products and technologies. It fosters employment. It gives consumers and business customers a wider variety of choices. It helps keep prices down by encouraging mass production. And it stimulates healthy competition between producers, which benefits all buyers.[29] Advertising also promotes a higher standard of living, subsidizes the media and the arts, supports freedom of the press, and provides a means to disseminate public information about health and social issues.

SOCIAL RESPONSIBILITY AND ADVERTISING ETHICS

Numerous laws determine what advertisers can and cannot do, but they also allow a significant amount of leeway. That's where ethics and social responsibility come into play. An advertiser can act unethically or irresponsibly without breaking any laws. Beer and tobacco companies can sponsor rock concerts for college students, and a shoe company can market a basketball sneaker to urban youth as the "Run 'N Gun" brand. As Ivan Preston says, ethics begin where the law ends.[30] Ethical advertising means doing what the *advertiser* and the advertiser's peers believe is morally right in a given situation. Social responsibility means doing what *society* views as best for the welfare of people in general or for a specific community of people.

Advertisers' Social Responsibility

The foundation of any human society is the amicable relationship among its members. Without harmony, a society will collapse. So all the institutions within a society have some responsibility for helping to maintain social harmony through proper stewardship of families and companies, exercise of integrity in all relationships, adherence to accepted ethical standards, willingness to assist various segments of the society, and the courtesy to respect the privacy of others.

Advertising plays an important role in developed countries. It influences the society's stability and growth. It helps secure large armies, creates entertainment events at-

● One of the many ways advertising benefits society is by alerting qualified individuals to employment opportunities. This MCI recruiting ad ran in magazines such as *Hispanic Business* as part of the company's efforts to achieve diversity in the workplace.

tracting hundreds of thousands of fans, and often influences the outcome of political elections. Such power places a burden of responsibility on those who buy, create, produce, and sell advertising to maintain ethical standards that support society.

In the U.S., for example, the advertising industry is part of a large business community. Like any good neighbor, it has responsibilities: to keep its property clean, participate in civic events, support local enterprises, and improve the community. U.S. advertising professionals have met these challenges by forming local advertising clubs, the American Advertising Federation (AAF), the American Association of Advertising Agencies (AAAA), and the Ad Council. These organizations provide thousands of hours and millions of dollars worth of pro bono work to charitable organizations and public agencies. They also provide scholarships and internships, contributions that serve the whole society. As we discuss later, they even regulate themselves effectively.

Many advertisers, including Chevron, Mobil, General Electric, and even local quick-lube shops, have demonstrated their social responsibility by reformulating their products and packaging to be more environmentally responsible and by launching major "green" advertising campaigns. Similarly, many retailers have jumped on the green bandwagon, advertising environmentally friendly merchandise in their local communities.[31] Advertisers like AT&T, IBM, and Honda commit significant dollars to supporting the arts, education, and various charitable causes as well as their local Better Business Bureaus and Chambers of Commerce.

Still, advertisers are regularly chided when they fail the social responsibility litmus test. Concerned citizens, consumer advocates, and special-interest groups pressure advertisers when they perceive the public's welfare is at risk. RJR Nabisco canceled plans for two new cigarette brands—Uptown, aimed at African-Americans, and Dakota, aimed at uneducated young women—in the heat of opposition from consumer advocacy groups.

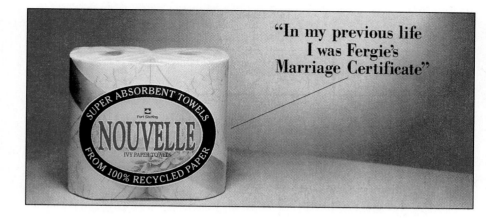

"In my previous life I was Fergie's Marriage Certificate"

SUPER ABSORBENT TOWELS
NOUVELLE
IVY PAPER TOWELS
FROM 100% RECYCLED PAPER

• Advertisers today are increasingly aware of the imperative to exhibit social responsibility. In this series of U.K. ads, Nouvelle takes a humorous approach to announce the use of recycled paper in its toweling—and no other copy except the package label to promote the product itself.

Advertising Ethics

Philosophies of ethics span the centuries since Aristotle. We can hardly do them justice here. But for practical purposes, let's consider three levels of ethical responsibility and apply them to advertising.

On one level, ethics comprises two interrelated components: the traditional actions taken by people in a society or community; and the philosophical rules it establishes to justify such past actions and decree future actions. These components create the **primary rules** of ethical behavior in the society and enable us to measure how far an individual or company (or advertiser) strays from the norm. Here, the individual's rights are subject to the standards of what is customary (and therefore proper) for the group.

Every individual also faces a second set of ethical issues: the attitudes, feelings, and beliefs that add up to a **personal value system**. When these two systems conflict, should the individual act on personal beliefs or on the obligation to serve the group and its policies?

For example, nonsmoking ad agency people may create ads for a tobacco client. At the first, societal level of ethics there is some conflict: smoking has been a custom in the U.S. for centuries and is not illegal today. However, the U.S. Surgeon General has declared that smoking is a national health problem (harmful to the group). This conflict at the first ethical level passes the responsibility for decision making to the second, individual level. Since the penalty may be the loss of income, nonsmokers may decide to produce the ads while keeping their own work area smoke-free. The ethical issue is at least temporarily and partially resolved—or at least rationalized—at the second ethical level.

A third level of ethics concerns **singular ethical concepts** such as duty, integrity, truth, empathy, good, bad, right, wrong. Are these concepts absolute, universal, and binding? Or are they relative, dependent on situations and consequences? A person's ethical philosophy, influenced by society and individual values, determines the answer (see Exhibit 2–1).

At the third level, the nonsmoker writing a cigarette ad may purposely select wording that does not defend smoking. That may alleviate the nonsmoker's anxiety over integrity. But someone else might think the ad should have described the dangers of smoking and believe the copywriter acted unethically.

Because ethics are so important, we address issues that pertain to advertising in Ethical Issue sidebars in each chapter. They discuss the legal, moral, or practical considerations surrounding the issue, along with cases and examples. Exhibit 2–2 lists the Ethical Issue in each chapter.

Most advertisers strive to maintain fair ethical standards and practice socially responsible advertising. Once a free-swinging, unchecked business, advertising is today

Exhibit ● 2–1
Levels of ethical responsibility.

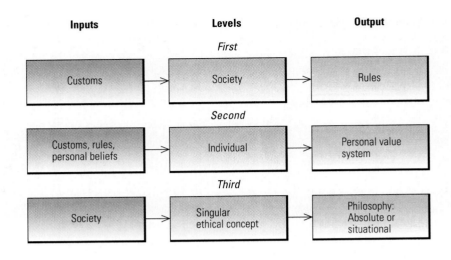

	Inputs	Levels	Output

First

Customs → Society → Rules

Second

Customs, rules, personal beliefs → Individual → Personal value system

Third

Society → Singular ethical concept → Philosophy: Absolute or situational

a closely scrutinized and heavily regulated profession. Advertising's past shortcomings have created layer upon layer of laws, regulations, and regulatory bodies. Consumer groups, governments, special-interest groups, and even other advertisers now review, control, and change advertising.

FEDERAL REGULATION OF ADVERTISING

The U.S government imposes strict controls on advertisers through laws, regulations, and judicial interpretations. Among the many federal agencies and departments that regulate advertising are the Federal Trade Commission, the Food and Drug Administration, the Federal Communications Commission, the Patent and Trademark Office, and the Library of Congress. Because their jurisdictions often overlap, advertisers may have difficulty complying with their regulations. (See RL 2–2 in the Reference Library).

Exhibit ● 2–2
Ethical issues discussed in this text.

Chapter/ethical issue	Issue discussed
1. Ethical Dilemma or Ethical Lapse?	Ignoring ethical issues and being confused about them
2. Truth in Advertising: Fluffing and Puffing	How exaggeration spans acceptable limits to illegality
3. Accounting for Account Reviews	Etiquette between agencies and prospective clients
4. Is It Marketing or Is It Exploitation?	Taking advantage of markets in a crisis
5. Niching May Cause Twitching	Targeting markets can lead to ethical problems
6. Research Statistics Can Be Friends or Foes	How statistics can be misunderstood and/or misrepresented
7. The Winds of Ad Wars	Comparative advertising must be done with care
8. The Ethical Cost of Gifts and Commissions	Influence and the appearance of it can be illegal
9. Does Sex Appeal?	Sexual inferences can lead to real consequences
10. Manipulating Morphing's Magic	Artistic changes may create new meaning and violate rights
11. Ethics, Ergonomics, and Economics	Ethical decisions or indecision may create medical problems
12. Imitation, Plagiarism, or Flattery?	It's a close call between borrowing and stealing
13. Children's Advertising: Child's Play?	Protecting the innocent from calculated sales pitches
14. Does Spillover Need Mopping Up?	Messages designed for one audience may hurt others
15. Is Privacy Going Public?	The individual's rights versus the public's rights
16. When Is Advertising Not Really Advertising?	Editorials promoting products can be misleading
17. Political Advertising: Positively Negative?	Pointing out individual failures is legal but not necessarily ethical

In Canada, there is a similar maze of federal regulators. But the Canadian legal situation is considerably more complex than in the States due to the separate (but often concurrent) jurisdictions of paternalistic federal and provincial governments, the broad powers of government regulators, the vast array of self-regulatory codes, and the very nature of a bilingual and bicultural society. One simple example of this is the fact that all packages and labels must be printed in both English and French throughout Canada.[32]

The U.S. Federal Trade Commission (FTC)

The **Federal Trade Commission (FTC)** is the major regulator of U.S. advertising for products sold in interstate commerce. Initially, the FTC just protected competitors from false advertising. But in 1938, Congress passed the Wheeler-Lee Amendment, which gave the FTC power to protect both consumers and competitors from unfair or deceptive acts or practices and unfair competition (including advertising). Unfortunately, the definitions of *deceptive* and *unfair* are controversial.

Defining deception

The FTC defines **deceptive advertising** as any ad in which there is a misrepresentation, omission, or other practice that can mislead a significant number of reasonable consumers to their detriment. Proof that consumers were deceived is not required, and the representation may be expressed or implied. The issue is whether the ad conveys a false impression—even if it is literally true.[33]

Take the case of the FTC against the weight-loss industry. Weight Watchers, Jenny Craig, Nutri System, and others used print and broadcast ads featuring customer testimonials. Jenny Craig even offered consumers the chance to "lose all the weight you want" for a fixed price. The FTC filed a complaint against the firms alleging false and deceptive advertising. Why? Because the ads *implied*—but gave no substantiation—that customers are successful at losing weight and maintaining weight loss. The FTC additionally accused Jenny Craig of falsely representing that the advertised prices were the only costs associated with the programs and of failing to adequately disclose additional mandatory expenses.[34]

Ultimately the FTC signed consent orders with several of the firms requiring them to disclose in their ads how many customers lose weight, report how much they lose over how long a time, and provide a warning that most dieters eventually regain lost weight. But Jenny Craig and Weight Watchers decided to fight the charges as a matter of principle, claiming that they had never misled the public and the FTC requirements would create an unfair burden on them.[35]

Critics of the FTC agreed. To comply, firms making a weight-loss claim would have to provide a table listing the average weight loss by past participants and its duration. The companies would have to collect large amounts of data, often covering two years or more, involving all customers who had stayed in the program for more than two weeks. If a seller makes a comparative claim, the data acquisition problem increases

• Understandably, advertisers today are careful about claims they make about their products, as this tongue-in-cheek cartoon illustrates.

geometrically. As one former FTC staffer points out, requirements such as these are little more than disguised prohibitions. Suddenly comparative ads are out, as are simple effectiveness claims.[36]

Regardless of the criticisms, the FTC remains a powerful regulator. The commission cracked down on program-length TV ads (*infomercials*) that might deceive viewers into mistaking them for regular programming. Now infomercials must be clearly identified as ads.[37] The FTC also looks at environmental claims (such as biodegradable, degradable, photodegradable, and recyclable). To avoid confusing terminology, the National Association of Attorneys General requested the FTC and EPA to work jointly with the states to develop uniform national guidelines for environmental marketing claims.[38]

Defining unfairness

According to FTC policy, some ads that are not deceptive may be considered unfair to the consumer. **Unfair advertising** occurs when a consumer is "unjustifiably injured" or there is a "violation of public policy" (such as other government statutes). Practices considered unfair are claims made without prior substantiation, claims that exploit vulnerable groups such as children and the elderly, and cases where the consumer cannot make a valid choice because the advertiser omits important information about the product or about competing products mentioned in the ad.[39]

For example, the FTC found that an automaker's failure to warn of a safety problem is not deceptive but is unfair. Advertising organizations have argued that the word *unfair* is so vague it can mean whatever any given individual wants it to. They have lobbied Congress to eliminate the FTC's power to prosecute on unfairness grounds, and Congress did pass a compromise bill requiring the FTC to show that an alleged unfair practice involves substantial, unavoidable injury to consumers, the injury is not reasonably avoidable by consumers themselves, and the injury is not outweighed by benefits to consumers or competition.[40] This legislation suggests that in the future the FTC will have to balance on a far narrower beam in its effort to regulate unfairness.[41]

Investigating suspected violations

If it receives complaints from consumers, competitors, or its own staff members who monitor ads in various media, the FTC may decide to investigate an advertiser. The agency has broad powers to pursue suspected violators and demand information from them. Typically, the FTC looks for three kinds of information: *substantiation, endorsements,* and *affirmative disclosures.*

If a suspected violator cites survey findings or scientific studies, the FTC may ask for **substantiation.** Advertisers are expected to have supporting data before running an ad, although the FTC sometimes allows postclaim evidence. The FTC does not solicit substantiation for ads it is not investigating.

The FTC also scrutinizes ads that contain questionable **endorsements** or **testimonials**. If a noncelebrity endorser is paid, the ad must disclose this on-screen.[42] The endorsers may not make claims the advertiser can't substantiate. Further, celebrity endorsers must actually use the product or service (if portrayed), and they can be held personally liable if they misrepresent it.[43]

Advertisers must make **affirmative disclosure** of their product's limitations or deficiencies: for example, EPA mileage ratings for cars, pesticide warnings, and statements that saccharin may be hazardous to one's health.

Remedies for unfair or deceptive advertising

When the FTC determines that an ad is deceptive or unfair, it may take three courses of action: negotiate with the advertiser for a consent decree, issue a cease-and-desist order, and/or require corrective advertising.

A **consent decree** is a document the advertiser signs agreeing to stop the objectionable advertising without admitting any wrongdoing. Before signing, the advertiser

KENT STEFFES, WORLD BEACH VOLLEYBALL CHAMPION, RELAXING OFF THE COURT IN HIS POLAR FLEECE AND DELPHI LEATHER RUNNING SHOES — FROM FILA.

CHANGE THE GAME.™ FILA

• FTC regulations mandate that celebrity endorsers portrayed as users of a product must in fact use it and can be held personally responsible if they misrepresent the product or service.

can negotiate specific directives with the FTC that will govern subsequent advertising claims.

If an advertiser won't sign a consent decree, the FTC may issue a **cease-and-desist** order prohibiting further use of the ad. Before the order is final, it is heard by an administrative law judge. (RL 2–1 in the Reference Library shows a flowchart of the FTC complaint procedure.) Most advertisers sign the consent decree after the hearing and agree, without admitting guilt, to halt the advertising. Advertisers who violate either a consent decree or a cease-and-desist order can be fined up to $10,000 per showing of the offending ad.

The FTC may also require **corrective advertising** for some period of time to explain and correct offending ads. A classic case of corrective advertising was Listerine's $10.2 million worth of ads stating, "Listerine will *not* help prevent colds or sore throats or lessen their severity." To help advertisers avoid such expense, the FTC will review advertising before it runs and give "advance clearance" in an advisory opinion. It also publishes *Industry Guides and Trade Regulation Rules,* which gives advertisers, agencies, and the media ongoing information about FTC regulations.

In Canada, the laws are even tougher and the consequences stiffer. It's an offense for any public promotion to be "false or misleading in a material respect." For an offense to occur, it is not necessary that anyone be misled by the representation, only that it be false. An *offense* is a crime. If convicted, an advertiser or agency could go to jail for up to five years, pay a fine, or both.[44]

The Food and Drug Administration (FDA)

The **Food and Drug Administration (FDA)** has authority over the labeling, packaging, and branding of packaged foods and therapeutic devices. The FDA requires manufacturers to disclose all ingredients on product labels, in in-store product advertising, and in product literature. The label must accurately state the weight or volume of the

● Under the FDA labeling laws, food packages must list nutrition facts per serving (and the serving size) in a format easy for consumers to understand and compare with competing products.

Nutrition Facts		
Serving Size ¾ cup (30g)		
Servings Per Container About 11		

Amount Per Serving	Whole Grain Total	with ½ cup Skim milk
Calories	100	140
Calories from Fat	5	10
	% Daily Value**	
Total Fat 0.5g*	1%	1%
Saturated Fat 0g	0%	0%
Cholesterol 0mg	0%	1%
Sodium 200mg	8%	11%
Potassium 100mg	3%	9%
Total Carbohydrate 24g	8%	10%
Dietary Fiber 3g	10%	10%
Sugars 5g		
Other Carbohydrate 16g		
Protein 3g		
Vitamin A (10% as Beta Carotene)	100%	110%
Vitamin C	100%	100%
Calcium	25%	40%
Iron	100%	100%

Vitamin D	10%	25%
Vitamin E	100%	100%
Thiamin	100%	100%
Riboflavin	100%	110%
Niacin	100%	100%
Vitamin B$_6$	100%	110%
Folic Acid	100%	100%
Vitamin B$_{12}$	100%	110%
Pantothenic Acid	100%	100%
Phosphorus	20%	30%
Zinc	100%	100%

*Amount in Cereal. A serving of cereal plus skim milk provides 1g fat, <5mg cholesterol, 260mg sodium, 300mg potassium, 30g carbohydrate (11g sugar) and 7g protein.
**Percent Daily Values are based on a 2,000 calorie diet. Your daily values may be higher or lower depending on your calorie needs:

		Calories: 2,000	2,500
Total Fat	Less than	65g	80g
Sat Fat	Less than	20g	25g
Cholesterol	Less than	300mg	300mg
Sodium	Less than	2,400mg	2,400mg
Potassium		3,500mg	3,500mg
Total Carbohydrate		300g	375g
Dietary Fiber		25g	30g

Calories per gram:
Fat 9 ● Carbohydrate 4 ● Protein 4

contents. Labels on therapeutic devices must give clear instructions for use. The FDA can require warning statements on packages of hazardous products. It regulates "cents off" and other promotions on package labels, and also has jurisdiction over the use of words such as *giant* or *family* used to describe package sizes.

When consumer-oriented drug ads became common in the mid-80s, the FDA ruled that any ad for a brand-name drug must include all information in the package insert.[45] That meant advertisers would have to run lengthy commercials or use minuscule type in print ads. However, pharmaceutical companies found a way around the FDA ruling by omitting the brand name. Upjohn's successful ads for its antibaldness drug Rogaine used only the Upjohn name, talked about baldness in general, and suggested that consumers see their doctors for further information.[46]

In 1990, Congress passed the **Nutritional Labeling and Education Act (NLEA)**, which went into effect in 1994. The new law gives the FDA additional muscle by setting stringent legal definitions for terms such as *fresh, light, low fat,* and *reduced calories*. It also sets standard serving sizes and requires labels to show food value for one serving alongside the total recommended daily value as established by the National Research Council.[47]

Procter & Gamble was affected by the FDA's tougher stand. The FDA seized 2,400 cases of the company's Citrus Hill Fresh Choice orange juice—the first time the agency ever took such severe action against a prominent marketer over a labeling dispute. Fresh Choice was made from concentrate, not fresh-squeezed juice as P&G claimed.[48] Due to increased FDA scrutiny, many advertisers are now more cautious about their health and nutritional claims.

The Federal Communications Commission (FCC)

The seven-member **Federal Communications Commission (FCC)**, established by the Communications Act of 1934, has jurisdiction over the radio, television, telephone, and telegraph industries. The FCC's control over broadcast advertising is actually indirect, stemming from its authority to license broadcasters (or take away their licenses). The FCC stringently controls the airing of obscenity and profanity, and it can restrict both the products advertised and content of ads. For example, the FCC required stations to run commercials about the harmful effects of smoking even before Congress banned cigarette advertising on TV and radio.

In the 1980s, the FCC decided that marketplace forces can adequately control broadcast media, so it deregulated both radio and TV stations. The FCC no longer limits commercial time or requires stations to maintain detailed program and commercial logs. However, stations still keep records of commercial broadcasts to assure advertisers they ran.

The 1992 Cable Television Consumer Protection and Competition Act gave the FCC additional teeth. It placed new controls on the cable TV industry to encourage a more service-oriented attitude and to improve the balance between rates and escalating ad revenues.[49] The FCC can set subscriber rates for cable TV, so subscription revenues should slow while advertising rates rise.

Studies show violence on TV is linked to violent behavior (a public health issue). Congress responded by enacting the 1992 Television Violence Act exempting network and cable companies from antitrust laws if they agree to self-regulate violence. Because network and cable companies deny that violence on TV is related to violence in life, government intervention is a possibility.[50]

The Patent and Trademark Office

As we saw at the beginning of this chapter, a trademark like *Jurassic Park* is a valuable asset. According to the Lanham Trade-Mark Act (1947), a **trademark** is "any word, name, symbol, or device or any combination thereof adopted and used by a manufacturer or merchant to identify his goods and distinguish them from those manufactured or sold by others."

Ownership of a trademark may be designated in advertising or on a label, package, or letterhead by the word *Registered,* the symbol ®, or the symbol ™. If someone persists in using a trademark owned by another, the trademark owner can ask for a court order and sue for trademark infringement.

Ironically, advertising success can sometimes cause the loss of a trademark. That's what happened to *thermos, escalator,* and *cellophane.* The owners lost their trademark rights when the courts declared the trademarks "generic," meaning the names had come into common use and are now the dictionary names for the products.

a. Trademark, brand
Initials, words, or symbols that identify one particular product or line of products from a single source

b. Trade name
Name under which a company does business; in some instances trade name and trademark may be identical (such as General Motors' GM)

c. House mark
A trademark used on all or most of the products of a particular company

d. Service mark
The name or symbol for a service as opposed to a product

e. Trade character
A person, animal, or other character used to identify a business

f. Certification mark
A mark guaranteeing the origin, trade, or quality of a product

g. Collective
A mark used to indicate membership in an organization

• As we saw in the opening story of this chapter, the owners of the *Jurassic Park* trademark went to extraordinary lengths up front to protect their exclusive right to use, promote, and license every aspect of this very successful product.

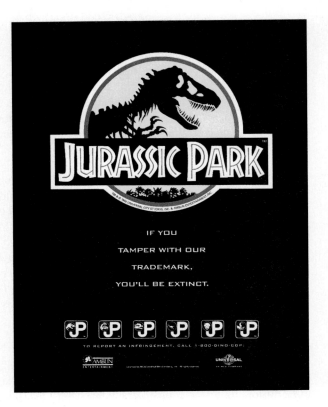

Most trademark owners take precautions to prevent their trademarks from becoming generic. They capitalize the trademark and follow it with the generic name of the product (Band-Aid brand adhesive bandages, Scotch brand tape, Kleenex tissues, Jell-O brand gelatin). They never refer to the trademark in the plural or use it as a verb. Many companies even advertise the fact that their name is a registered trademark: "You can't Xerox a Xerox on a Xerox."

The Library of Congress

The **Library of Congress** registers and protects all copyrighted material, including advertising, in the United States. A **copyright** issued to an advertiser grants the exclusive right to print, publish, or reproduce the protected ad for the life of the copyright owner plus 50 years. An ad can be copyrighted only if it contains original copy or illustrations. Slogans, short phrases, and familiar symbols and designs cannot be copyrighted (although they may be trademarkable). Nor can an idea. Although a copyright prevents a whole ad from being legally used by another, it does not prevent others from using the general concept or idea of the ad or paraphrasing the copy. An advertiser that uses original written, musical, illustrative, or other material from an outside source without its creator's express written consent is infringing on the copyright and may be subject to legal action. Advertisers and agencies must obtain permission before they use creative material, like music, from any outside source.

Copyright is indicated by the word *Copyright,* the abbreviation *Copr.,* or the symbol © near the name of the advertiser. Ads with foreign or international copyright protection usually contain the year of copyright as well.

STATE AND LOCAL REGULATION

Advertisers are also subject to state or local laws. Since the U.S. federal deregulation trend of the 1980s, state and local governments have taken a far more active role.

Regulation by State Governments

State legislation governing advertising is often based on the truth-in-advertising model statute developed in 1911 by *Printer's Ink,* for many years the major trade paper of the industry. The statute holds that any maker of an ad found to contain "untrue, deceptive, or misleading" material is guilty of a misdemeanor. Today 46 states (all except Arkansas, Delaware, Mississippi, and New Mexico) enforce laws patterned after this statute.

All states also have "little FTC acts," consumer protection laws that govern unfair and deceptive business practices. States themselves can investigate and prosecute cases, and individual consumers can bring civil suits against businesses. To increase their clout, some states team up on legal actions—for example, to challenge deceptive ad promotions in the airline, rental-car, and food-making industries. As one observer pointed out, "Many of the food manufacturers could litigate some of the smaller states into the ground, but they might not be willing to fight it out against 10 states simultaneously."[51]

Different states have different regulations governing what can be advertised. Some states prohibit advertising for certain types of wine and liquor, and most states restrict the use of federal and state flags in advertising.

This presents a major problem to national marketers. In some cases, it actually hurts consumers. For example, many companies trying to conduct environmentally responsible marketing programs feel stymied by the plethora of state laws governing packaging materials and recycling.[52]

Regulation by Local Governments

Many cities and counties have consumer protection agencies to enforce laws regulating local advertising practices. The chief function of these agencies is to protect local consumers against unfair and misleading practices by area merchants.

In 1993 alone, the Orange County, California, district attorney's office received over 1,200 complaint letters from consumers about everything from dishonest mechanics and phony sale ads to a taco stand that skimped on the beef in its "macho" burrito.[53] In one case the DA collected $310,000 in civil penalties from Montgomery Ward to settle a false advertising suit. The company was charged with a variety of deceptions, including increasing retail prices before applying sale discounts and advertising that sales were of limited duration when in fact they were ongoing. It was the third time in a decade that the company was ordered to halt misleading advertising.[54]

RECENT COURT RULINGS AFFECTING ADVERTISERS

Recently, both federal and state courts made a number of significant rulings pertaining to advertising issues, including First Amendment rights, privacy rights, and comparative advertising.

First Amendment Rights

The Supreme Court historically distinguishes between "speech" and "commercial speech" (speech that promotes a commercial transaction). But decisions over the last two decades suggest that truthful commercial speech is also entitled to significant, if not full, protection under the First Amendment.

The trend started in 1976 when the Supreme Court held in *Virginia State Board of Pharmacy v. Virginia Citizens Consumer Council* that ads enjoy protection under the First Amendment as commercial speech.[55] The next year the Court declared that the ban by state bar associations on attorney advertising also violated the First Amendment. Now, a third of all lawyers advertise; and a few states even permit client testimonials. One Wisconsin lawyer said his firm gained 200 new clients after a

• In 1982, the U.S. Supreme Court decreed that physicians and dentists could advertise. In Canada, too, dentists may advertise, as shown in this outdoor campaign that runs in both English and French for the Quebec Order of Dentists. This ad uses a shark displaying fierce-looking teeth to remind people to have regular checkups.

$25,000 local TV ad campaign featuring client testimonials.[56] To help guard against deceptive and misleading legal ads, the American Bar Association issues guidelines for attorneys.

In 1980 the Court used *Central Hudson Gas v. Public Service Commission* to test whether specific examples of commercial speech can be regulated.[57] The four-pronged *Central Hudson* test includes the following parts:

1. **Does the commercial speech at issue concern a lawful activity?** The ad in question must be for a legal product and must be free of misleading claims.
2. **Will the restriction of commercial speech serve the asserted government interest substantially?** The government would have to prove that the absence of regulation would have a substantial negative effect.
3. **Does the regulation directly advance the government interest asserted?** The government must be able to establish conclusively that cessation of the advertising would be effective in furthering the government's interest.
4. **Is the restriction no more than necessary to further the interest asserted?** The government would have to establish that there are no other means to accomplish the same end without restricting free speech.[58]

In 1982, the Supreme Court upheld an FTC order allowing physicians and dentists to advertise. Since then, their advertising has exploded.

In 1993, the Supreme Court gave the advertising industry the biggest win in years. It said the Cincinnati City Council violated the First Amendment when it banned racks of advertising brochures from city streets for "aesthetic and safety reasons" while permitting newspaper vending machines.[59]

The issue of freedom of commercial speech is far from settled. The heated controversies surrounding issues like tobacco advertising and advertising to children are sure to keep the debate lively for years to come.

Privacy Rights

Most advertisers know it's illegal to use a person's likeness in an ad without the individual's permission, but since a 1987 court ruling, even using a celebrity lookalike (or soundalike) can violate that person's rights. Other courts have ruled that privacy rights continue even after a person's death.

The privacy issue is coming up again now with the increased use of computers and fax machines for advertising directly to prospects. As we shall see in Chapter 13, privacy is an ethical as well as a legal issue.

Comparative Advertising

Advertisers use **comparative advertising** to claim superiority to competitors in some aspect. In the U.S., such ads are legal so long as the comparison is truthful.

The 1988 Trademark Law Revision Act closed a loophole in the Lanham Act, which governed comparison ads but did not mention misrepresenting another company's product. Under the new law, any advertiser that misrepresents its own or another firm's goods, services, or activities is vulnerable to a civil action.

In addition to being truthful, comparative ads must compare some objectively measurable characteristic. Wilkinson Sword encountered a million-dollar problem when it claimed its Ultra-Glide razor blade's lubricant strip was six times smoother than Gillette's and preferred by more men. Gillette sued and won.[60]

GOVERNMENT RESTRAINTS ON INTERNATIONAL ADVERTISERS

Advertising is becoming more global. More and more campaigns use similar themes and even the same ads across frontiers. But foreign governments often regulate advertising considerably more than either the U.S. or Canada. And while Europe has moved toward uniformity in marketing activities, the laws governing advertising remain largely national.[61] So advertisers need to keep up with the changing legal environment of national markets.

Foreign governments not only regulate what ads say, show, or do; they often prohibit advertising altogether. Throughout Europe, broadcast advertising for tobacco products is prohibited, and liquor ads are sharply restricted. In fact, in 1994 a British parliamentary committee demanded a ban on tobacco-sponsored sporting events—even though these events earned $14 million a year in ad revenues. The British commercial networks, ITV and Channel 4, stopped broadcasting them, and the BBC pledged not to renew existing contracts.[62]

Many countries prohibit superlatives in puffery. In Germany, for example, advertisers may use only scientifically provable superlatives. McCann-Erickson once had to re-translate the old Coca-Cola slogan, "Refreshes you best," because it implied a leadership position that was unprovable. The agency substituted "Refreshes you right" in Germany. In Austria, however, which typically follows Germany's lead in advertising law, the original line would be permissible.[63]

Many European countries also ban coupons, premiums, free tie-in offers, and the like. Companies may advertise price cuts only during "official sales periods," and advertisers often need government approval before publishing a sale ad. Across Europe, TV ads must be clearly recognizable and kept separate from other programming. Paid *product placements* in programs, therefore, are typically prohibited.[64] RL 2–3 in the Reference Library lists the regulations some Western European countries now impose on advertising.

• Many countries strongly regulate advertising claims. This ad for Obira antacid gel from the German drug marketer Boehringer Ingelheim uses humor to advertise the benefit of its fast-acting formula in Taiwan. The headline says: *"With a long neck like mine, thank God Obira gel works quickly."* It gets the point across without using superlatives or puffery.

Ad Lab 2-B   How Strictly Should Government Regulate Advertising?

Singapore is one of the strictest societies in the world. Chewing gum is not allowed. Vandalism is punished by painful caning. And now the Advertising Standards Authority of Singapore (ASAS) is tightening its guidelines to fend off "immoral and offensive ads." The ASAS, an industry watchdog group, is composed of industry representatives and the Ministry of Information and the Arts (MITA).

The rewrite follows Prime Minister Goh Chok Tong's National Day Rally speech in August 1994, in which he criticized the Western media for Western-style democracy and freedom of the press for every country, regardless of cultural and historical differences. The ensuing ripple effect led to a number of ads being pulled or modified. It also created a clamor of discussion among industry associations representing media, agencies, and advertisers. Historically, the ASAS Code of Advertising Practice said ads should be "legal, decent, and honest," but made no reference to the social responsibility of advertising. "Now [we have] to look at the traditional core values that are being promoted by our government on top of taking to task errant advertisers who mislead,

misrepresent or overclaim in ads," stated Ivan Chong, ASAS chairman.

One ad singled out by the prime minister was for Bristol Myers Squibb's Sustagen, a line of milk-based nutritional products, including flavored drinks and puddings. The print ad features a little baseball-capped Asian boy shaking his fist. He appears to be shouting at his father, and the tagline reads: "Come on, Dad. If you can play golf five times a week, I can have Sustagen once a day." In his speech, Goh said, "I found the language and the way the boy speaks most objectionable. Do your children really speak to you like that these days?" The ad had been running since 1993 in Malaysia and Singapore without consumer complaint and, according to a spokesperson from Leo Burnett/Kuala Lumpur, was conceived and produced by Asians.

Phyllis Chan, group account director for the agency, said the ad for Sustagen was meant to be light-hearted and entertaining. "But we take the prime minister's comments seriously," she said.

Since the government controls the Singapore Broadcast Co. and can withdraw newspaper licenses at will, MITA can flex considerable govern-

ment clout to prevent Western-influenced advertising from corrupting Asian family values. Thus, when a ministry spokesman said, "We should discourage advertisements which show Singapore men, women, and children behaving as if they are Westerners," the media responded immediately.

Bernard Chan, president of the Association of Accredited Advertising Agents, the local agency association, welcomed the new, more specific guidelines. He said, "It is difficult to police the industry on an ad-hoc basis."

Following the prime minister's speech, ads for Spin laundry detergent, Citibank, and Qantas Airlines were pulled or modified demonstrating the fear a threat of government intervention can create.

Laboratory Applications

1. Since many people in North America criticize advertising for being offensive, should the U.S. adopt a code of standards requiring ads to promote traditional family values?

2. Should the U.S. government use the threat of intervention to curb false and misleading political advertising?

In Singapore, the state-owned broadcasting company yanked a Qantas Airline spot after the Ministry of Information and the Arts criticized its "harmful values." The ad had used the line "last of the big spenders," which the ministry felt encouraged reckless spending by consumers (see Ad Lab 2–B).[65]

Costa Rica has more than 250 laws regulating advertising. Recently, government officials agreed to consider an industry proposal that would overturn the particularly onerous law mandating preclearance of all advertising.[66]

Regulators are cracking down in China as well. A new comprehensive advertising law targets false, "unscientific, and superstitious" claims and requires preclearance of all advertising in all media. However, China now allows Taiwanese advertising on mainland billboards—after preclearance, of course.[67]

In international advertising, the only solution to this morass of potential legal problems is to retain a local lawyer who specializes in advertising law.

NONGOVERNMENT REGULATION

Nongovernment organizations also issue advertising guidelines (see Exhibit 2–3). In fact, advertisers face considerable regulation by business-monitoring organizations, related trade associations, the media, consumer groups, and advertising agencies themselves.

The Better Business Bureau (BBB)

The largest of the U.S. business-monitoring organizations is the **Better Business Bureau (BBB)**, established in 1916. Funded by dues from over 100,000 member companies, it operates primarily at the local level to protect consumers against fraudulent and

The Board of Directors of the American Association of Advertising Agencies recognizes that when used truthfully and fairly, comparative advertising provides the consumer with needed and useful information.

However, extreme caution should be exercised. The use of comparative advertising, by its very nature, can distort facts and, by implication, convey to the consumer information that misrepresents the truth.

Therefore, the Board believes that comparative advertising should follow certain guidelines:

1. The intent and connotation of the ad should be to inform and never to discredit or unfairly attack competitors, competing products, or services.

2. When a competitive product is named, it should be one that exists in the marketplace as significant competition.

3. The competition should be fairly and properly identified but never in a manner or tone of voice that degrades the competitive product or service.

4. The advertising should compare related or similar properties or ingredients of the product, dimension to dimension, feature to feature.

5. The identification should be for honest comparison purposes and not simply to upgrade by association.

6. If a competitive test is conducted, it should be done by an objective testing source, preferably an independent one, so that there will be no doubt as to the veracity of the test.

7. In all cases the test should be supportive of all claims made in the advertising that are based on the test.

8. The advertising should never use partial results or stress insignificant differences to cause the consumer to draw an improper conclusion.

9. The property being compared should be significant in terms of value or usefulness of the product to the consumer.

10. Comparatives delivered through the use of testimonials should not imply that the testimonial is more than one individual's thought unless that individual represents a sample of the majority viewpoint.

Exhibit • 2–3

American Association of Advertising Agencies policy statement and guidelines for comparative advertising.

deceptive advertising and sales practices. When local bureaus contact violators and ask them to revise their advertising, most comply.

The BBB's files on violators are open to the public. Records of violators who do not comply are sent to appropriate government agencies for further action. The BBB often works with local law enforcement agencies to prosecute advertisers guilty of fraud and misrepresentation. Each year, the BBB investigates thousands of ads for possible violations of truth and accuracy.

The Council of Better Business Bureaus is the parent organization of the Better Business Bureau and a sponsoring member of the National Advertising Review Council. One of its functions is to help new industries develop standards for ethical and responsible advertising. The Code of Advertising of the Council of Better Business Bureaus (the BBB Code) has been called the most important self-regulation of advertising.[68] The BBB Code is only a few pages long, but it is supplemented by a monthly publication called *Do's and Don'ts in Advertising Copy,* which provides ongoing information about advertising regulations and recent court and administrative rulings that affect advertising.[69] Since 1983, the National Advertising Division (NAD) of the Council of Better Business Bureaus has published guidelines for advertising to children, a particularly sensitive area.

The National Advertising Review Council (NARC)

The **National Advertising Review Council (NARC)** was established in 1971 by the Council of Better Business Bureaus, the American Association of Advertising Agencies, the American Advertising Federation, and the Association of National Advertisers. Its

● Advertising to children and adolescents is a particularly sensitive area, and advertisers are careful about what they say and how they say it. In the U.K., National Westminster Bank promotes a bank account that lets teenagers get cash from 6,000 ATMs instead of two parents.

primary purpose is to promote and enforce standards of truth, accuracy, taste, morality, and social responsibility in advertising.

NARC is one of the most comprehensive and effective mechanisms for regulating American advertising. A U.S. district court judge noted in a 1985 case that its "speed, informality, and modest cost," as well as its expertise, give NARC special advantages over the court system in resolving advertising disputes.[70]

NARC operating arms

The NARC has two operating arms: the **National Advertising Division (NAD)** of the Council of Better Business Bureaus and the **National Advertising Review Board (NARB).** The NAD monitors advertising practices and reviews complaints about advertising from consumers and consumer groups, brand competitors, local Better Business Bureaus, trade associations, and others. The appeals board for NAD decisions is the NARB, which consists of a chairperson and 70 volunteer members (39 national advertisers, 21 agency representatives, and 10 laypeople).

The NAD/NARB review process

To encourage consumers to register complaints, the NAD itself runs ads that include a complaint form. Most concern untruthfulness or inaccuracy.

When the NAD finds a valid complaint, it contacts the advertiser, specifying any claims to be substantiated. If substantiation is inadequate, the NAD requests modification or discontinuance of the claims.

The Texaco–Chevron dispute shows how well the NAD process works. In 1994, Texaco introduced a new gasoline, CleanSystem3, amid much hoopla. It claimed the product represented a new generation of fuel and would provide the "highest performance" and the "best mileage." Chevron tested the stuff and protested to the NAD that its gas was just as good as Texaco's. The NAD pored over 1,500 pages of test data and eventually sided with Chevron. Texaco agreed to alter its ads to say "a breakthrough in Texaco technology" and "higher performance" instead of "highest performance."[71]

If the NAD and an advertiser reach an impasse, either party has the right to a review by a five-member NARB panel (consisting of three advertisers, one agency representative, and one layperson). The panel's decision is binding. If an advertiser refuses to comply with the panel's decision (which has never yet occurred), the NARB refers the matter to an appropriate government body and so indicates in its public record. (For a flowchart of the NAD/NARB review process, see Reference Library 2–4.) Of 3,000 NAD investigations conducted between 1971 and 1990, only 70 were disputed and referred to the NARB for resolution.[72]

Regulation by the Media

Almost all media review ads and reject material they regard as objectionable, even if it isn't deceptive. Many people think the media are more effective regulators than the government.

Television

Of all media, the TV networks conduct the strictest review. Advertisers must submit all commercials intended for a network or affiliated station to its broadcast standards department. Many commercials (in script or storyboard form) are returned with suggestions for changes or greater substantiation. Some ads are rejected outright if they violate network policies. (See Ad Lab 2–C.)

The three major U.S. broadcast networks base their policies on the original National Association of Broadcasters Television Code. But network policies vary enough that it's difficult to prepare universally acceptable commercials. Cable networks and local stations tend to be much less stringent, as demonstrated by their acceptance of condom ads.

Radio

The 19 U.S. radio networks, unlike TV networks, supply only a small percentage of their affiliates' programming, so they have little or no say in what their affiliates advertise. A radio station is also less likely to return a script or tape for changes. Some stations, like KLBJ in Austin, Texas, look mainly at whether the advertising is illegal, unethical, or immoral.[73] Radio stations are concerned that spots might offend listeners or detract from the rest of the programming.

Every radio station typically has its own unwritten guidelines. KDWB, a Minneapolis/St. Paul station with a large teenage audience, turned down a psychic who wanted to buy advertising time but did allow condom and other contraceptive ads.[74] KSDO in San Diego, a station with a business and information format, won't air commercials for X-rated movies or topless bars.[75]

Magazines

National magazines monitor all advertising, especially by new advertisers and for new products. Newer publications eager to sell space may not be so vigilant, but established magazines, like *Time* and *Newsweek,* are highly scrupulous. Many magazines will not accept advertising for certain types of products. *The New Yorker* won't run discount retail store advertising or ads for feminine hygiene or self-medication products. *Reader's Digest* won't accept tobacco ads.

Some magazines test every product before accepting the advertising. *Good Housekeeping* rejects ads if its tests don't substantiate the advertiser's claims. Products that pass may feature the Good Housekeeping seal of approval.

Ad Lab 2-C   The Issue of Issue Ads

The commercials pictured an educated, two-career, middle-aged yuppie couple, "Harry and Louise." The cappuccino-sipping duo paid their bills, flossed every day, and had time to discuss current events. Dressed casually in the comfort of their warmly lit home, they chatted while scanning books and papers. Their conversation described how the newly proposed Clinton health care plan would be an elaborate government intervention, a threat to existing insurance plans, and a precursor of price controls and rationing.

The first run of the $10 million campaign by the Health Insurance Association of America stimulated 286,000 calls to a toll-free phone number between September and March 1994. As the public waited for a rebuttal from the president, the news media and others joined in to reinforce the commercial's points. Soon, opinion shifted away from the Clinton plan. Clinton finally counterattacked, but this only led to more exposure for the ads on the evening news, current affairs programs, and talk shows. The president's tardiness also added credibility to Harry and Louise—leverage that eventually led to removal of the plan.

The ads struck a nerve with the Democratic National Committee, which ran an ad satirizing Harry and Louise. Of course, politicians could find it frustrating to debate an issue with personae that "talked the talk and walked the walk" of their electorate. And Harry and Louise represented Everyman, according to Ben Goddard, president of the ad agency Goddard/First Tuesday and the man who cast the two actors.

Advocates of issue ads believe there are a number of lessons to be learned from this example. First, commercial speech can have a corrective effect on political speech. Also, corporations under political attack often find press releases and campaign donations weak defenses, especially if a president is popular and skilled at using the power of his bully pulpit. Paid advertising can

be an effective recourse and is more open and honorable than backdoor lobbying or political fundraising.

Second, issue advertising depends more on the credibility of your message than on how much you spend. Credibility is measured by how favorably the message survives the rebuttal. Issue ads give the advertiser the chance for an open exchange.

Finally, issue ads can stimulate skepticism and bring to bear the self-correcting forces that govern all open markets. An article in *Advertising Age* said, "The Harry and Louise ads gained their power not by stifling debate but by inspiring it."

Critics dismiss issue advertising as a tool of wealthy corporations and lobbying groups. They believe these ads (also called *advertorials*) oversimplify the complexities of important political issues and misuse the public airwaves.

Margaret Carlson wrote in *Time* magazine, "Harry and Louise shed no more light on health care than their counterparts selling Taster's

Choice shed on instant sex or coffee. For now, viewer discretion advised." Many broadcasters agree and refuse to air issue ads, making it more difficult for the sponsors to reach the audience they're targeting.

Right or wrong, Harry and Louise represent a successful use of issue advertising—particularly to stimulate debate and counter the effects of the prevailing social mindsets.

Laboratory Applications

1. To what degree, if any, should government be able to control advertising that deals with issues important to the entire nation such as pollution, election reform, the national debt, and health issues?

2. What effect, if any, could advertorials have on national problems such as age discrimination, racism, sexism, and teenage pregnancy? Be specific.

Newspapers

Newspapers also monitor and review advertising. Larger newspapers have clearance staffs that read every ad submitted; most smaller newspapers rely on the advertising manager, sales personnel, or proofreaders.

The advertising policies set forth in *Newspaper Rates & Data* specify "No objectionable medical, personal, matrimonial, clairvoyant, or palmistry advertising accepted; no stock promotion or financial advertising, other than those securities of known value." Another rule prohibits ads that might easily be mistaken for regular reading material unless they feature the word *advertisement* or *advt.*

In addition, most papers have their own acceptability guidelines, ranging from one page for small local papers to more than 50 pages for large dailies such as the *Los Angeles Times*. Some codes are quite specific. The *Detroit Free Press* won't accept classified ads containing such words as "affair" or "swinger." Some newspapers require advertisers who claim "the lowest price in town" to include a promise to meet or beat any price readers find elsewhere within 30 days.

One problem advertisers face is that newspapers' codes are far from uniform. Handgun ads may be prohibited by one newspaper, accepted by another if the guns are antique, and permitted by a third so long as the guns aren't automatic. And newspapers do revise their policies from time to time.

Regulation by Consumer Groups

Of all the regulatory forces governing advertising, consumer protection organizations have shown the greatest growth. Starting in the 1960s, the consumer movement became increasingly active in fighting fraudulent and deceptive advertising. Consumers demanded that products perform as advertised and that more product information be provided for people to compare and make better buying decisions. The consumer movement gave rise to **consumerism**, social action to dramatize the rights of the buying public. It is clear now that the U.S. consumer has the power to influence advertising practices dramatically.

Today, advertisers and agencies pay more attention to product claims, especially those related to energy use (such as the estimated miles per gallon of a new car) and the nutritional value of processed foods. Consumerism fostered the growth of consumer advocacy groups and regulatory agencies, and promoted more consumer research by advertisers, agencies, and the media in an effort to learn what consumers want—and how to provide it. Investment in public goodwill pays off in improved consumer relations and sales.

Consumer information networks

Organizations like the Consumer Federation of America (CFA), the National Council of Senior Citizens, the National Consumer League, and the National Stigma Clearinghouse exchange and disseminate information among members. They help develop state, regional, and local consumer organizations, and they work with national, regional, county, and municipal consumer groups.

Consumer interests also are served by private, nonprofit testing organizations such as Consumers Union, Consumers' Research, and Underwriters Laboratories.

Consumer advocates

Consumer advocate groups act on advertising complaints received from the public and those that grow out of their own research by investigating the complaint. If it is warranted, they ask the advertiser to halt the objectionable ad or practice. If the advertiser does not comply, they release publicity or criticism about the offense to the media and submit complaints with substantiating evidence to appropriate government agencies for further action. In some instances, they file a lawsuit to obtain a cease-and-desist order, a fine, or other penalty against the violator.

Today, there are so many special-interest consumer advocacy groups that even the most sensitive advertisers feel challenged. To attract attention, advertising must be creative. It has to stand out from competing noise. Yet today, advertisers fear drawing attention from politically correct activists—the "PC police." Calvin Klein ads were attacked by the Boycott Anorexic Marketing group. A Nike ad starring Porky Pig was protested by the National Stuttering Project in San Francisco. An animated public service spot from Aetna Insurance recently drew curses from a witches' rights group.[76]

Don't call it advertising.

A distraught woman is persuaded to appear in a commercial where she accuses the Governor of New York of being responsible for the murder of her son.

A gubernatorial candidate is forced to do a commercial denying the charges that his recent divorce was a result of his beating his wife.

In a local race for Comptroller, a commercial was created that opened with white letters against a black screen asking "KILL THE JEWS?"

This is filth.

Political filth that is not advertising and shouldn't be dignified by being called advertising.

Whether you are a Democrat, Republican, Conservative or Liberal, if you are a decent, thinking human being you must be appalled at the political communication that came into your home during this dirty election.

Once again let us reiterate: This is not advertising.

The practitioners of the bulk of this trash are those so-called "political consultants" who might have been part of a "dirty tricks" team in the 1970s. Now, in 1994, they publish and broadcast their "dirty tricks" and they claim that it's advertising.

If a reputable corporation produced advertising with the same exaggerated claims and promises for their products and then failed to deliver on these claims, their executives would be fined or led off to jail in handcuffs. And, standing on the sidelines, shouting, "How dare they not deliver on what they promised!" would be those politicians who have condoned this year's group of political lies and exaggerations.

We say it must stop.

And it must stop now.

Let it start with this advertisement.

Let it start today, November 9, 1994, the day after one of the dirtiest elections in the history of this country.

Let those of us in advertising, broadcasting, publishing and business stand up together and say, "Stop."

Stop the character assassination.

Stop the lies.

Stop the ugliness.

And, above all, stop calling what you're doing advertising.

Advertising enhances a product. What you do tears it down.

Advertising that is effective is built on truth. What you are doing is built on lies.

We at Ketchum Advertising are calling on the broadcasting and publishing community to hold political advertising to the same standards you hold consumer advertising.

We're calling on you to set up a bi-partisan group, to screen all future political advertising.

A group made up of broadcasting executives, publishing executives, and bona fide advertising executives.

We are calling on you to hold political advertisers to the same rules of disparagement you hold other advertisers.

But most of all, we're calling on you and every concerned citizen to get involved.

Now at this point you might be asking how you and your company can make a contribution towards bringing about this change.

Our answer is we don't want your money, we want your name.

If you want to register your vote for a change in the nature and tone of political advertising in the United States, write to:

Ketchum Advertising
527 Madison Avenue
New York, NY 10022
Or fax: (212) 907-9332

We promise your voice will be heard.

This advertisement was developed from an idea by Dianne Snedaker who heads up the San Francisco office of Ketchum Advertising. Art direction by Bruce Campbell, Creative Director, Ketchum/S.F. The body copy was written by Jerry Della Femina in New York. The sentiments are those of the 1,200 employees of Ketchum Communications.

● In the aftermath of the vicious political advertising for the November 1994 elections, Ketchum Advertising published this ad in *The Wall Street Journal* calling on the broadcasting and publishing community to hold political advertising to the same standards as consumer advertising.

When the protests start flying, the ads usually get pulled. Steve Hayden, chair of BBDO Los Angeles, believes it would be possible to get any spot pulled with "about five letters that appear on the right stationery."[77] As Shelly Garcia noted in *Adweek,* "The way things are these days, nothing motivates middle managers like the need to avoid attention." She laments the fact that "there are fewer and fewer opportunities to have any fun in advertising."[78]

Self-Regulation by Advertisers

Advertisers also regulate themselves. They have to. In today's competitive marketplace, consumer confidence is essential. Most large advertisers gather strong data to substantiate their claims. They maintain careful systems of advertising review to ensure that ads meet both their own standards and industry, media, and legal requirements. Most advertisers also aim for a sense of social responsibility in their advertising. Pizza Hut, for example, became a promotional partner with the 20th Century Fox movie *Pagemaster,* about libraries and literature, because the film enabled it to tie social responsibility to its brand.[79]

Many industries maintain advertising codes that companies agree to follow. These codes also establish a basis for complaints. However, industry advertising codes are only as effective as the enforcement powers of the individual trade associations. And since enforcement may conflict with antitrust laws, trade associations usually use peer pressure rather than hearings or penalties.

Self-Regulation by Ad Agencies and Associations

Most ad agencies monitor their own practices. In addition, professional advertising associations oversee members' activities to prevent problems that might trigger government intervention. Advertising publications report issues and court actions to educate agencies and advertisers about possible legal infractions.

Advertising agencies

Although advertisers supply information about their product or service to their agencies, the agencies must research and verify product claims and comparative product data before using them in advertising. The media may require such documentation before accepting the advertising, and substantiation may be needed if government or consumer agencies challenge the claims.

Agencies can be held legally liable for fraudulent or misleading advertising claims. (See the Ethical Issue in Chapter 7: "When Advertisers Dare to Compare.") For this reason, most major advertising agencies have in-house legal counsel and regularly submit their ads for review. If any aspect of the advertising is challenged, the agency asks its client to review the advertising and either confirm claims as truthful or replace unverified material.

Advertising associations

Several associations monitor industrywide advertising practices. The **American Association of Advertising Agencies (AAAA),** an association of the largest advertising agencies throughout the United States, controls agency practices by denying membership to any agency judged unethical. The AAAA *Standards of Practice and Creative Code* set advertising principles for member agencies.

The **American Advertising Federation (AAF)** helped to establish the FTC, and its early vigilance committees were the forerunners of the Better Business Bureau. The AAF Advertising Principles of American Business, adopted in 1984, define standards for truthful and responsible advertising (see Exhibit 2–4). Since most local advertising clubs belong to the AAF, it is instrumental in influencing agencies and advertisers to abide by these principles.

The **Association of National Advertisers (ANA)** comprises 400 major manufacturing and service companies that are clients of member agencies of the AAAA. These companies, pledged to uphold the ANA code of advertising ethics, work with the ANA through a joint Committee for Improvement of Advertising Content.

Exhibit • 2–4
Advertising Principles of American Business of the American Advertising Federation (AAF).

1. **Truth.** Advertising shall reveal the truth, and shall reveal significant facts, the omission of which would mislead the public.

2. **Substantiation.** Advertising claims shall be substantiated by evidence in possession of the advertiser and the advertising agency prior to making such claims.

3. **Comparisons.** Advertising shall refrain from making false, misleading, or unsubstantiated statements or claims about a competitor or his products or service.

4. **Bait advertising.** Advertising shall not offer products or services for sale unless such offer constitutes a bona fide effort to sell the advertised products or services and is not a device to switch consumers to other goods or services, usually higher priced.

5. **Guarantees and warranties.** Advertising of guarantees and warranties shall be explicit, with sufficient information to apprise consumers of their principal terms and limitations or, when space or time restrictions preclude such disclosures, the advertisement shall clearly reveal where the full text of the guarantee or warranty can be examined before purchase.

6. **Price claims.** Advertising shall avoid price claims that are false or misleading, or savings claims that do not offer provable savings.

7. **Testimonials.** Advertising containing testimonials shall be limited to those of competent witnesses who are reflecting a real and honest opinion or experience.

8. **Taste and decency.** Advertising shall be free of statements, illustrations, or implications that are offensive to good taste or public decency.

THE ETHICAL AND LEGAL ASPECTS OF ADVERTISING IN PERSPECTIVE

Unquestionably, advertising offers considerable benefits to marketers and consumers alike. However, there's also no disputing that advertising has been and still is too often misused. As *Adweek* editor Andrew Jaffe says, the industry should do all it can to "raise its standards and try to drive out that which is misleading, untruthful, or downright tasteless and irresponsible." Otherwise, he warns, the pressure to regulate even more will become overwhelming.[80]

Advertising apologists, of course, believe the abuse heaped on advertising is no longer warranted. They point out that of all the advertising reviewed by the Federal Trade Commission in a typical year, 97 percent is found to be satisfactory.[81] In the end, advertisers and consumers need to work together to ensure that advertising is used intelligently, ethically, and responsibly for the benefit of all.

Summary

As advertising proliferated, criticism of it intensified. Advertising is both lauded and criticized for the role it plays in selling products and influencing society. Critics say there's too much of it; it makes people too materialistic and manipulates them into buying unneeded products. Further, they say, advertising perpetuates stereotypes, is offensive, often in bad taste, and even deceptive.

Proponents admit that advertising is sometimes misused. However, they point out that despite its problems, advertising offers many social benefits. It encourages the development of new products and speeds their acceptance. It fosters employment, gives consumers and businesses a wider variety of product choices, and helps keep prices down by encouraging mass production. It stimulates healthy competition between companies, and it raises the overall standard of living. Moreover, sophisticated marketers know the best way to sell their products is to appeal to genuine consumer needs and be honest in their advertising claims.

Under growing pressure from consumers, special-interest groups, and government regulation, advertisers developed higher standards of ethical conduct and social responsibility. Advertisers confront three levels of ethical consideration: the primary rules of ethical behavior in society, their personal value system, and their personal philosophy of singular ethical concepts.

Advertising is regulated by federal, state, and local government agencies, business-monitoring organizations, the media, consumer groups, and the advertising industry itself.

The Federal Trade Commission (FTC), the major federal regulator of advertising in the U.S., is responsible for protecting consumers and competitors from deceptive and unfair business practices. If the FTC finds an ad deceptive or unfair, it may issue a cease-and-desist order or require corrective advertising.

The Food & Drug Administration (FDA) monitors advertising for food and drugs and regulates product labels and packaging. The Federal Communications Commission (FCC) has jurisdiction over the radio and television industries, but deregulation severely limited its control over advertising in these media. The Patent and Trademark Office governs ownership of U.S. trademarks, trade names, house marks, and similar distinctive features of companies and brands. The Library of Congress registers and protects copyrighted materials.

State and local governments also enact consumer protection laws that regulate advertising.

The federal and state courts are involved in several advertising issues, including First Amendment protection of commercial speech, professionals' right to advertise, infringements of the right to privacy, and lawsuits over comparative advertising.

Nongovernment regulators include the Council of Better Business Bureaus and its National Advertising Division. The NAD, the most effective U.S. nongovernment regulatory body, investigates complaints from consumers, brand competitors, or local Better Business Bureaus and suggests corrective measures. Advertisers that refuse to comply are referred to the National Advertising Review Board (NARB), which may uphold, modify, or reverse the NAD's findings.

Other sources of regulation include the codes and policies of the print media and broadcasting. Consumer organizations and advocates also control advertising by investigating and filing complaints against advertisers and by providing information to consumers. Finally, advertisers and agencies also regulate themselves.

Questions for Review and Discussion

1. What legal issues do advertisers face here and abroad?

2. Does advertising affect our value system? In what ways?

3. What is puffery? Give some examples. Do you ever feel deceived by puffery in advertising?

4. What is the difference between an advertiser's ethics and an advertiser's social responsibility?

5. What is the role of the FTC in advertising? Do you think this role should be expanded or restricted?

6. How does commercial speech differ from political speech? Do you think advertisers should have the same First Amendment rights as everyone else? Explain.

7. How do regional and local governments affect advertisers?

8. How well do advertisers regulate themselves? In what areas do you think advertisers have done well, and where should they "clean up their act"?

9. Do advertisers face greater regulation in North America or Europe? How do they differ?

10. How does the NAD/NARB system contribute to truth in advertising? Do you think it is an effective mechanism?

3

The Advertising Business
Agencies, Clients, Media, and Suppliers

Objective: To introduce the people and groups who create, produce, and run advertising. Advertising people may serve in a variety of roles. This chapter discusses the basic tasks of both the agency and the client, the roles of the media and suppliers, the way agencies acquire clients and are compensated, and the overall relationship between the agency and the client.

After studying this chapter, you will be able to:

- Describe the various groups in the advertising business and explain their relationship to one another.

- Define the main types of advertising agencies.

- Explain the range of work people do in an ad agency and an advertising department.

- Discuss how agencies get new clients and how they make money.

- Debate the pros and cons of an in-house advertising agency.

- Discuss factors that affect the client-agency relationship.

- Explain how the media and suppliers help advertisers and agencies.

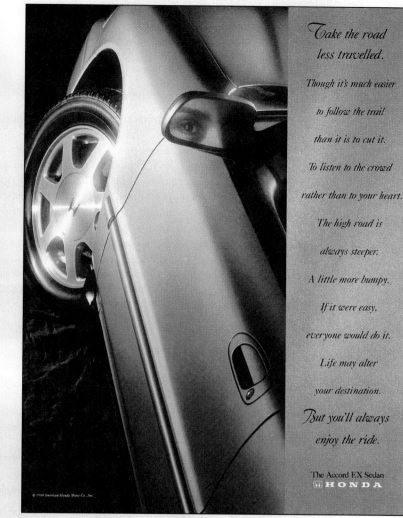

When Mike Whitlow first got the project assignment, it was anything but exciting. As a creative director at Muse Cordero Chen, he was accustomed to getting the juicy jobs for the agency's plum accounts: Nike, Honda, Snapple. Those were the projects you could win awards for, the kind of jobs that made other creatives envious.

But with this one—well, he could already imagine the grumblings from his art directors and copywriters. Lisa Wright, the account executive on Honda, had just handed him the creative brief for the project. They needed some ideas for a dealer kit: a package, usually in the form of a binder, containing information and sample ads that the car dealers could use to plan and create their local advertising. Typically not Emmy award-winning stuff.

Lisa sensed his ambivalence. "Look, Mike," she said. "I really want something spectacular, something that will get these dealers to sit up and take notice of our market."

"Oh, and Mike, there's no budget on this."

Whitlow smiled. Lisa was good. She not only worked with clients well, she knew how to challenge the creatives, dangling just the right amount of bait to pique their interest and get their creative juices flowing.

The market Wright referred to was the 31 million-strong African-American market. This group spends $15 billion on vehicle purchases every year, so it's an important market to Honda. Muse Cordero Chen is a full-service advertising agency that specializes in multicultural communications. Founded in 1986, the Los Angeles-based shop is one of the fastest-growing ethnic agencies in the country. Its 29 employees speak a total of 19 languages. Over the years, the agency has worked very closely with Rubin/ Postaer, Honda's general-market agency of record, to ensure that the work it produced for the African-American market reflected the overall Honda strategy. In the process, MCC has won numerous awards for outstanding national ads. Lisa wanted the dealer kits to be conceived with the same pride.

Mike assembled his creative team of art directors and copywriters and gave them the same challenge. "Remember, you guys, there are no bad assignments," he said, "just bad work. Let's do something out of the ordinary and have some fun with this, OK?"

They did, as we shall see. ●

THE ADVERTISING INDUSTRY

People and organizations in many industries other than advertising—car dealers, for example—are also involved in the advertising business. That's because every successful company needs to advertise. And the range of work performed by advertising people goes far beyond what we see on nightly TV. In fact, that's barely the tip of the iceberg.

The Organizations in Advertising

The advertising business is composed of four different groups. The two main ones are the advertisers and the agencies. The **advertisers** (or clients) are the companies—like Honda or the local Honda dealer—that advertise themselves and their products. Advertisers range in size from huge multinational firms to small independent stores and in type from service organizations to industrial concerns to political action committees. Assisting them is the second group—the **advertising agencies** that plan, create, and prepare their clients' ad campaigns and promotional materials.

The third group, the **media,** sells time (in electronic media) and space (in print media) to carry the advertiser's message to the target audience. The last group, the **suppliers,** includes the photographers, illustrators, printers, digital service bureaus, color film separators, video production houses, and others who assist both advertisers and agencies in preparing advertising materials. Suppliers also include consultants, research firms, and other professional services that work with both advertisers and agencies.

The People in Advertising

When most people think of advertising, they imagine the copywriters and art directors who work for ad agencies. But the majority of people in advertising are actually employed by the *advertisers*. Most companies have an advertising department, even if it's just one person.

● Advertisers come in all sizes and types, and so does their advertising. These whimsical ads for Lee & Perrins tomato ketchup are part of a poster campaign devised in Italy for the Belgian market. Note the sly play on words in the "Catch up" headline. Advertising runs the gamut from hilarious to heart-tugging in attempts to bring advertisers and their products and services to the attention of prospective customers.

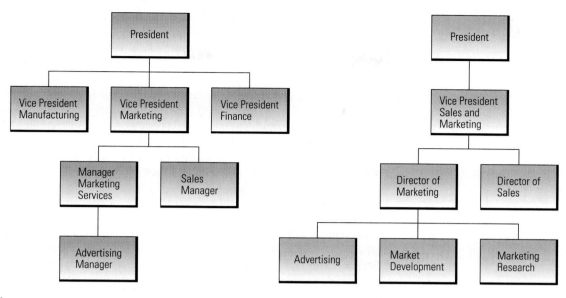

Exhibit • 3–1
Many large companies have a separate advertising department able to perform a wide variety of functions. Small departments generally subcontract for creative and camera services; larger departments handle the majority of work on site.

The importance of a company's advertising department depends on the size of the company, the type of industry it operates in, the size of its advertising program, the role advertising plays in the company's marketing mix, and most of all, the involvement of top management.

Many people are involved in a company's advertising function:

1. Company owners and top corporate executives make key advertising decisions.
2. Sales and marketing personnel often assist in the creative process, help choose the ad agency, and evaluate proposed ad programs.
3. Artists and writers produce ads, brochures, and other materials.
4. Product engineers and designers give input to the creative process and provide information about competitive products.
5. Administrators evaluate the cost of ad campaigns and help plan budgets.
6. Clerical staff coordinate various advertising activities.

A large company's advertising department may employ many people and be headed by an advertising manager who reports to a marketing director or marketing services manager (see Exhibit 3–1). These departments often resemble ad agencies in structure and function.

[handwritten margin note: importance of advertising departments & people involved in the company's advertising function]

Why would a company like Honda hire an advertising agency? Couldn't it save money by hiring its own staff and creating its own ads? How does Muse Cordero Chen win such a large account? Must an agency's accounts be that big for it to make money? This section sheds some light on these issues and gives a clearer understanding of why so many advertisers use agencies.

THE ADVERTISING AGENCY

The Role of the Advertising Agency

The American Association of Advertising Agencies (AAAA) defines an **advertising agency** as an independent organization of creative people and businesspeople who specialize in developing and preparing marketing and advertising plans, advertisements, and other promotional tools. The agency purchases advertising space and time in various media on behalf of different advertisers, or sellers—its **clients**—to find customers for their goods and services.[1]

This definition offers clues to why so many advertisers hire ad agencies. First, an agency like Muse Cordero Chen is *independent.* The agency isn't owned by the advertiser, the media, or the suppliers, so it can bring an outside, objective viewpoint to the advertiser's business—a state the advertiser can never attain.

Second, like all agencies, MCC employs a combination of *businesspeople* and *creative people,* including administrators, accountants, marketing executives, researchers, market and media analysts, writers, and artists. They have day-to-day contact with outside professional suppliers who create illustrations, take photos, retouch art, shoot commercials, record sound, and print brochures.

The agency provides yet another service by researching, negotiating, arranging, and contracting for commercial space and time with the various print and electronic *media.* Because of its *media expertise,* Muse Cordero Chen saves its clients time and money.

Agencies don't work for the media or the suppliers. Their moral, ethical, financial, and legal obligation is to their clients. Just as a well-run business seeks professional help from attorneys, accountants, bankers, or management specialists, advertisers use agencies because they can create more effective advertising and select more effective media than the advertisers can themselves. Today, almost all sizable advertisers rely on an ad agency for expert, objective counsel and unique creative skills—to be the "guardian of their brands."[2]

Finally, good agencies serve the needs of a variety of clients because of their daily exposure to a broad spectrum of marketing situations and problems both at home and abroad. As modern technology has enabled companies to work across borders with relative ease, the advertising business has boomed worldwide. Most of the large U.S. agencies, for example, maintain offices in many foreign countries. Ad Lab 3–A describes the global ad industry.

Types of Agencies

Advertising agencies are normally classified by the range of services they offer and the type of business they handle.

Full-service agencies

The modern **full-service advertising agency** supplies both advertising and nonadvertising services in all areas of communications and promotion. *Advertising services* include planning, creating, and producing ads, performing research, and selecting media. *Nonadvertising functions* run the gamut from packaging to public relations to producing sales promotion materials, annual reports, trade-show exhibits, and sales training materials. With the increasing trend toward integrated marketing communications (IMC), many of the largest agencies today are in the forefront of the emerging *interactive media.*[3]

Full-service agencies may specialize in certain kinds of clients. Most can be classified as either *general consumer agencies* or *business-to-business agencies.*

General consumer agencies A **general consumer agency** represents the widest variety of accounts, but it concentrates on consumer accounts—companies that make goods purchased chiefly by consumers (soaps, cereals, cars, pet foods, toiletries). Most of the ads are placed in consumer media (TV, radio, billboards, newspapers, and magazines) that pay a *commission* to the agency. General agencies derive much of their income from these commissions.

General agencies include the international superagency groups headquartered in world capitals like New York, London, Paris, and Tokyo, as well as many other large firms in New York, Chicago, Los Angeles, Minneapolis, Montreal, and Toronto. A few of the better-known names in North America are the Interpublic Group; Saatchi & Saatchi; Ogilvy & Mather; Foote, Cone & Belding; BBDO; Ayer; Cossette Communications-Marketing (Canada); and Young & Rubicam. But general agencies also include

How Big Is the Agency Business?   *Ad Lab 3-A*

Advertising today is a worldwide business. In 1994, New York (with $26.5 billion in billings) regained the lead from Tokyo (with $25.4 billion) as the world's advertising capital. London and Paris were third and fourth, respectively. Leading advertising centers in North America are New York, Los Angeles, Chicago, Toronto, and Montreal.

All U.S. and Canadian cities with at least 100,000 people have ad agencies. So do many smaller cities and towns. Of over 10,000 U.S. agencies, the top 500 represent about $65.1 billion in domestic billing (the amount of client money the agency spends on media and equiva-

lent activities)—almost half of all U.S. advertising expenditures.

Interestingly, the top 10 U.S. agencies handle over half the total volume of business done by the top 500 agencies, and that's just their U.S. billing. Their overseas operations often equal or exceed their U.S. billings.

The top 500 domestic ad agencies employ about 70,000 people. Agencies need fewer people than businesses in many other industries: five or six people can easily handle $1 million in annual billings. In agencies that bill $20 million or more a year, the ratio is even lower.

Basic information about advertisers and agencies can be found in the *Standard Directory of Advertising Agencies* (the "Red Book"), which lists agencies; a related volume, the *Standard Directory of Advertisers*, which lists U.S. companies that advertise; and magazines such as *Advertising Age, Adweek,* and *Marketing* (Canada).

Laboratory Application

From your library, obtain a copy of the agency Red Book. How many agencies in your town are listed? If none, what town nearest you has agency listings? How many?

Top 10 advertising organizations

Rank	Agency	Income*
1.	WPP Group	$2,768.2
2.	Interpublic Group of Cos.	2,211.0
3.	Omnicom Group	2,052.6
4.	Dentsu, Inc.	1,641.7
5.	Cordiant	1,431.5
6.	Young & Rubicam	1,059.7
7.	Euro RSCG Worldwide	813.3
8.	Grey Advertising	808.7
9.	Hakuhodo Inc.	774.2
10.	Leo Burnett Co.	677.5

*1994 worldwide gross income ($ millions).

Top 10 U.S.-based consolidated agencies

Rank	Agency	Income*
1.	McCann-Erickson Worldwide	$1,076.1
2.	Young & Rubicam	985.5
3.	BBDO Worldwide	917.7
4.	J. Walter Thompson	915.7
5.	DDB Needham Worldwide	875.7
6.	Ogilvy & Mather Worldwide	768.7
7.	Lintas Worldwide	760.5
8.	Grey Advertising	749.8
9.	Saatchi & Saatchi	690.5
10.	Leo Burnett Co.	677.5

*1994 worldwide gross income ($ millions).

Top 10 U.S.-based agency brands

Rank	Agency	Income*
1.	Leo Burnett	$322.1
2.	J. Walter Thompson	317.4
3.	Grey Advertising	302.2
4.	McCann-Erickson Worldwide	261.4
5.	BBDO Worldwide	245.9
6.	Saatchi & Saatchi	241.5
7.	True North Communications (FCB)	236.8
8.	DDB Needham Worldwide	228.2
9.	D'Arcy Masius Benton & Bowles	219.3
10.	Young & Rubicam	184.7

*1994 worldwide gross income ($ millions).

the thousands of smaller entrepreneurial agencies located in every major market across the country (Rubin/Postaer, Los Angeles; Ruhr/Paragon, Minneapolis; Wieden & Kennedy, Portland, Oregon).

Profit margins in entrepreneurial agencies are often slimmer, but these shops are typically more responsive to the smaller clients they serve. They offer the hands-on involvement of the firm's principals, and their work is frequently startling in its creativity. For these very reasons, many large agencies are spinning off smaller subsidiaries.[4] Some entrepreneurial agencies, like Muse Cordero Chen, carve a niche for themselves by serving particular market segments.

Business-to-business agencies A **business-to-business** (or *high-tech*) **agency** represents clients that market products to other businesses. Examples are electronic components for computer manufacturers, equipment used in oil and gas refineries, and MRI equipment for radiology. Business and industrial advertising requires some technical knowledge and the ability to translate that knowledge into precise, persuasive communications.

Most business-to-business advertising is placed in trade magazines or other business publications. These media are commissionable, but because their circulation is smaller, their rates are far lower than those of consumer media. Since commissions often don't cover the cost of the agency's services, business agencies typically charge their clients service fees. They can be expensive, especially for small advertisers, but

• Most business-to-business advertising is placed in trade magazines or other business publications. This 3M trade magazine ad presents a solution to a messy situation: Packaging with 3M Scotchban Protector resists ruin from leaking fluids. The photo identifies the product's value quickly and succinctly without getting into many dry details, and the ad copy invites customer response by providing a toll-free phone number.

failure to obtain a business agency's expertise may carry an even higher price in lost marketing opportunities.

Business and industrial agencies may be large international firms like MacLaren/Lintas in Toronto or HCM/New York. Or they may be smaller firms experienced in such special areas as recruitment (help wanted) advertising, health and medicine, or electronics.

Specialized service agencies

Many small agencies assist their clients with a variety of limited services. In the early 90s the trend toward specialization blossomed (see Ad Lab 3–B), giving impetus to many of the small agency-type groups called *creative boutiques* and other specialty businesses such as *media-buying services*.

Creative boutiques Some talented artists—like graphic designers and copywriters—set up their own creative services, or **creative boutiques.** They work for advertisers and occasionally subcontract to advertising agencies. Their mission is to develop exciting creative concepts and produce fresh, distinctive advertising messages. Creative Artists Agency, a Hollywood talent agency, caused a stir on Madison Avenue by taking on the role of a creative boutique, using its pool of actors, directors, and cinematographers to create a series of commercials for Coca-Cola. McCann-Erickson Worldwide remains Coke's agency of record, but the majority of creative work comes from CAA and other small agencies.[5]

Advertising effectiveness depends on originality in concept, design, and writing. However, while boutiques may be economical, they usually don't provide the research, marketing, and sales expertise full-service agencies offer. So boutiques tend to be limited to the role of creative suppliers.

Media-buying services Some experienced media specialists set up organizations to purchase and package radio and TV time. In the U.S., the largest of these **media-buying services** is Western International Media in Los Angeles, which places over $1.6 billion

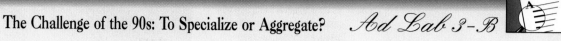

The Challenge of the 90s: To Specialize or Aggregate?   *Ad Lab 3-B*

Many ad agencies were infected by the 80s' merger mania. The biggest empire builder, London-based Saatchi & Saatchi PLC, rapidly became (for a while) the world's largest agency by acquiring Compton Advertising, Dancer Fitzgerald Sample, and the giant Ted Bates Worldwide in addition to a host of firms in related communications fields.

But the aggregation strategies used so extensively by so many companies, both advertisers and agencies, didn't always produce the desired results. With current economic realities and the recent wave of technological innovation, specialization has become the strategy of choice for the 90s. Now some of the biggest companies are spinning off divisions and focusing on their strengths.

Many agencies are debating which way to turn: specialize or aggregate. Some companies are specializing in the type of products or services they offer. Others specialize in particular markets or clients (like an agency that concentrates on business-to-business clients). Companies can now identify more market segments, and they have the tools to reach those segments. For example, an ad agency can specialize in database marketing services.

As Larry Jones of Foote, Cone & Belding says, "Compressed margins mean that agencies must run very lean, so services are viewed very pragmatically. Depending on what a client's requirements are, agencies are staffing very much to fill those needs, rather than being full service." Also, many agencies are starting to unbundle certain services, like media buying.

On the other hand, Rance Crain, president of Crain Communications and editor in chief of *Advertising Age* magazine, forecasts that (media) advertising will soon become more integrated with other forms of marketing communications. In fact, some agencies are becoming less specialized; they're changing their traditional focus from selling commissionable media advertising to providing clients with more integrated communications. Leo Burnett, for example, aggregated its diversified services in order to offer clients an integrated communications strategy.

To decide a path, an agency should picture the continuum from specialization to aggregation

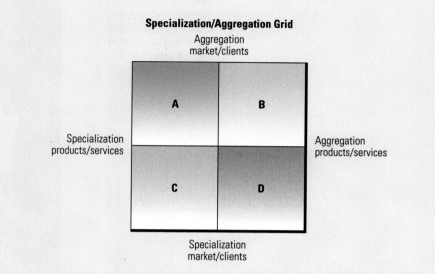

Specialization/Aggregation Grid

using the specialization/aggregation grid. The vertical axis expresses the range of clients served and the horizontal axis shows the range of products or services the agency offers. The four quadrants represent four possible strategies that can be used by any agency or company. For example, a full-service agency offers a relatively broad spectrum of services (market research, creative services, media planning and buying, etc.) useful to a range of client companies. Thus, it belongs in section B of the grid. In contrast, a creative boutique or advertising consultant offers only a specialized service to solve a client's specific need, so it fits into section C. Sections A and D are blends of specialization and aggregation. A recruitment agency exemplifies section A and a business-to-business ad agency exemplifies section D.

For the big superagencies, most of the mega-mergers seem to be over and their strategic choices are limited. The mid-size companies ($100 million to $500 million) are in the most enviable position. They're small enough to aggregate with a larger company but large enough to acquire smaller agencies.

The vast majority of U.S. and Canadian agencies, though, are small, entrepreneurial shops with billings below $100 million. In general, this group is doing well. According to *Advertising*

Age, the U.S. billings of the bottom 450 agencies rose 6.8 percent in 1991, nearly six times faster than the 1.2 percent increase of the top 50 agencies. Many small agencies may aggregate through merger. The structure and financing of large agencies supports them, and the large agency can enter niche markets with low overhead and excellent creative teams.

Laboratory Applications

1. Andy Berlin decided to leave Goodby, Berlin & Silverstein, the agency he helped to build. He wanted to expand by opening offices in New York while his partners wanted to remain in San Francisco and focus on the agency's clients there. What points can you make in favor of each position?

2. For better efficiency, some of the world's largest advertisers—IBM, PepsiCo, Campbell Soup—now consolidate all their work with one or a few agencies and dismiss the many agencies they used to employ for their global advertising efforts. Using the specialization/aggregation grid, what quadrant would the agencies receiving the consolidated work most likely fall into? What effect do you think this will have on agency mergers in the future?

worth of advertising annually for clients such as Walt Disney, Atlantic Richfield (Arco), USAir, and Times-Mirror.[6]

Radio and TV time is perishable. A 60-second radio spot at 8 P.M. can't be sold later. So radio and TV stations presell as much time as possible and discount their rates for

● Some firms supply creative services to advertising agencies. Others set up their own creative services, or creative boutiques. This ad for Printbox Electronic Imaging Services is a humorous example of the type of creative work it can offer customers.

large buys. The media-buying service negotiates a special discount with the stations and then sells the time to agencies or advertisers.

Media-buying firms provide their customers (both clients and agencies) with a detailed analysis of the media buy. Once the media package is sold, the buying service orders the spots, verifies performance, sees that stations "make good" for any missed spots, and even pays the media bills. Compensation methods vary. Some services charge a set fee; others get a percentage of the discount.

What Agency People Do

The American Association of Advertising Agencies (AAAA) is the national organization of the advertising agency business. Its 650 agency members, representing a wide spectrum of small, medium, and large agencies, place almost 75 percent of all national advertising handled by agencies in the United States.[7]

The AAAA Service Standards explain that an agency's purpose is to interpret to the public, or to desired segments of the public, information about a legally marketed product or service. How does an agency do this? First, it studies the client's product to determine its strengths and weaknesses. Next, it analyzes the product's present and potential market. Then, using its knowledge of the channels of distribution and available media, the agency formulates a plan to carry the advertiser's message to consumers, wholesalers, dealers, or contractors. Finally the agency writes, designs, and produces ads, contracts for media space and time, verifies media insertions, and bills for services and media used.

The agency also works with the client's marketing staff to enhance the advertising's effect through package design, sales research and training, and production of sales literature and displays.[8]

To understand these functions, consider the people who were involved—directly or indirectly—in the creation, production, and supervision of the Honda dealer kits created by Muse Cordero Chen.

Account management

Muse Cordero Chen's **account executives (AEs)** are the liaison between the agency and the client. Large agencies typically have many account executives, who report to **management (or account) supervisors.** They in turn report to the agency's director of account (or client) services.

Responsible for formulating and executing advertising plans (discussed in Chapter 7), mustering the agency's services, and representing the client's point of view to the agency, the account manager is often caught in the middle. As one observer commented, to succeed today, an AE like Lisa Wright needs to be more of a strategist than an advocate. She must be well versed in a far wider range of media than ever before and be able to demonstrate how her agency's creative work satisfies both her client's marketing needs and the market's product needs. That means she must be enterprising and courageous, demanding yet tactful, artistic and articulate, meticulous, forgiving, perceptive, persuasive, ethical, and discreet—all at once. And she must deliver the work on time and within budget.[9]

To grow, agencies require a steady flow of new projects. The best account and creative people always want to work for the "hot shops." Sometimes agencies get new assignments when their existing clients develop new products or enter new markets. Sometimes clients seek out agencies whose work they are familiar with. Thanks to its reputation, Muse Cordero Chen receives 10 to 15 new-business calls a week.

Research

Clients and agencies must give their creatives (artists and copywriters) a wealth of product, market, and competitive information because, at its core, advertising is based on information. Before creating any advertising, agencies research the uses and advantages of the product, analyze current and potential customers, and try to determine what will influence them to buy. After the ads are placed, agencies use more research to investigate how the campaign fared. Chapter 6 discusses some of the many types of research ad agencies conduct.

Account planning

When Goodby, Berlin & Silverstein won the Porsche Cars North America account, *Adweek* commented: "In the end, what distinguished GBS was the sophistication of its *account planning*."[10]

Account planning is a hybrid discipline that bridges the gap between research, account management, and creative. The account planner defends the consumer's point of view and the creative strategy in the debate between the agency's creative team and the client.

Account planners study consumers through phone surveys and focus groups, but primarily through personal interviews. Then they help the creative team translate their findings into imaginative, successful campaigns. Not attached to either account management or creative, the account planner is an equal, working side by side with them to make sure the research is reflected in the ads.[11]

Working on Nike, Berni Neal, an account planner at Muse Cordero Chen, spent many afternoons in L.A. just talking to young people to understand their attitudes, feelings, language, and habits. Then she represented their views in agency meetings with Nike. The result was the discovery of a new market segment for Nike: urban youth—defined not by race or ethnicity but by a cultural attitude, shaped by inner city life, that crossed demographic lines to foster the market's core values: irreverence, fitness, athleticism, and discipline.

By putting the consumer, instead of the advertiser, at the center of the process, account planning changes the task from the creation of advertising to the nurturing of a future relationship between the consumer and the brand. That requires tremendous understanding, intuition, and insight. When performed properly, though, planning provides that mystical leap into the future—that brilliant, simplifying insight that lights the

● Before creating any advertising, advertisers and their agencies must research not only the uses and advantages of the product itself and who and where its current and potential customers are, but also the type and level of the competition. Marketing research firms like CMR specialize in media intelligence. As the ad states, they find out what competitors are doing—as soon as they start to do it.

client's and the creative's way. Interestingly, the U.S. agencies that have adopted account planning in the last decade are the very ones now considered to be the hottest shops. They're performing the best work, getting the biggest accounts, and winning all the awards.[12]

Creative concepts

Most ads rely heavily on **copy**—the words that make up the headline and message. The people who create these words, called **copywriters,** must condense all that can be said about a product into a few pertinent points.

Ads also use *nonverbal communication*. That is the purview of the **art directors,** graphic designers, and production artists who determine how the ad's verbal and visual symbols will fit together. (The creative process is discussed in Chapters 9–11.) The agency's copywriters and artists work as a creative team under a **creative director.** Each team is usually assigned a particular client's business.

In the case of the Honda dealer kits, Mike Whitlow brought two copywriters, Ed Mun and Chase Connerly, together with two art directors, Alfonso ("Fons") Covarrubias and Wilky Lau. The team immediately discarded the traditional binder format as too pedestrian. They wanted to develop an overall *concept* for the kit, not just a nice package of materials. They thought of several ideas: a magic kit ("pulling sales out of a hat"); a cookbook ("the recipe for greater sales"); a tourbook ("your guide to the African-American market").

Eventually they hit on the big idea: A model car—in a kit—complete with instructions on "how to put together a model sales year." That was the concept, but developing it was not easy. They wanted the box to look like a real model kit you might buy at

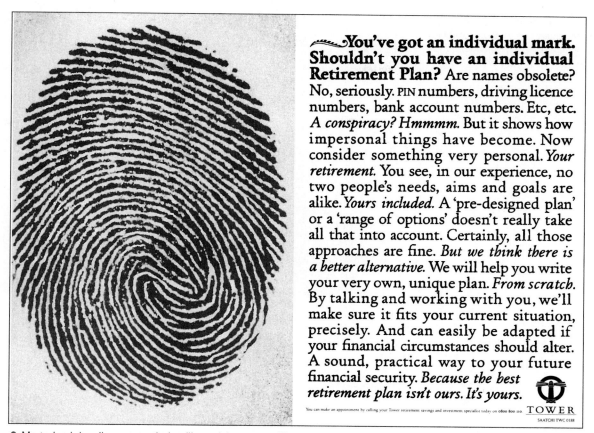

> • Most ads rely heavily on copy—the headline and the message. The strong fingerprint visual in this award-winning Tower Corp. ad captures readers' attention and curiosity, drawing them into the body copy, which compares the unique quality of an individual fingerprint to the uniquely personal Tower retirement plans. The varying type styles and the conversational tone of the copy keep readers interested to the end—at which point they might be overheard to mutter, "I can't believe I read the whole thing!"

the store. Then they had to find an actual model of a current Honda to put in the kit. Next they had to design a book of advertising plans that would fit into the box. They had to create the ads and commercials the local dealers would use for a variety of local media, and that meant the box would have to be designed to carry an audiotape and a videotape. Finally, it would all have to be executed quickly to meet the client's deadline for the new model year. So the kit had to get into production fast.

Advertising production: Print and broadcast

Once an ad (or a kit) is designed, written, and approved by the client, it is turned over to the agency's print production manager or broadcast producers.

For print ads, the production department buys type, photos, illustrations, and other components and works with printers, reproduction service bureaus, and other suppliers. For a broadcast commercial, production people work from an approved script or storyboard. They use actors, camera operators, and production specialists (studios, directors, editors) to produce a commercial on tape (for radio) or on film or videotape (for TV).

But as the Honda case shows, production work is not limited to just ads and commercials. MCC's print production manager had to find suppliers to create and print the box. Inside the box was a spiral-bound book, designed with heavy pages similar to the cardboard of the box. Covarrubias even designed a system of interlocking trays in the box to hold the tapes and the book at the bottom and keep the model at the top, safe from damage. Meanwhile Christine Sloan, the broadcast production manager, supervised production of all the commercials and had the audiocassettes and videotapes duplicated and packaged.

• Honda's advertising team at Muse Cordero Chen came up with the big idea—a dealer kit with a concept: "How to put together a model sales year." The kit included a model of the 1995 Honda Prelude for the dealer to assemble and complete promotional materials and instructions for reaching the lucrative African-American market.

Media planning and buying

Ad agencies perform a variety of media services for their clients: research, negotiating, scheduling, buying, and verifying. Media planning is critical, because the only way advertisers can communicate is through some medium. Tight budgets demand ingenious thinking, tough negotiating, and careful attention to details. Many advertisers owe their success to creative media buying more than clever ads. (We discuss the media in Chapters 8 and 12–14.)

Traffic management

One of the greatest sins in an ad agency is a missed deadline. If Muse Cordero Chen missed the deadline for a monthly magazine read by Nike's youthful customers, the agency would have to wait another month to run the ad—much to Nike's displeasure. And if the Honda dealer kits didn't arrive on time for the new model year, that could mean lost sales around the country.

• Items in the Honda dealer promotion kit included an 8½ x 11-inch spiral-bound notebook with three color magazine ad slicks, five black-and-white newspaper ad slicks, and marketing and media information; a 25-second "I Am Me" video commercial; an audiocassette with three 55-second radio commercials; and a model kit of the Honda Prelude for the dealer to assemble.

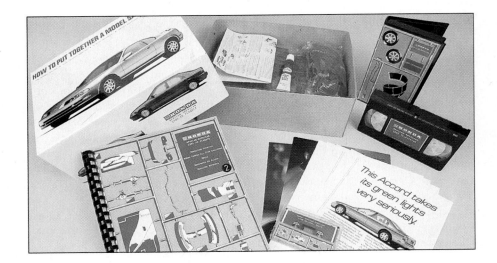

The agency traffic department coordinates all phases of production and makes sure everything is completed before media deadlines. Traffic is often the first stop for entry-level college graduates and an excellent place to learn agency operations. (See Appendix C for information on careers in advertising.)

Additional services

With the trend toward integrating marketing communications, some agencies employ specialists who provide services besides advertising. While Muse Cordero Chen uses its regular creative department for both advertising and nonadvertising services, larger agencies may have a fully staffed **sales promotion department** to produce dealer ads, window posters, point-of-purchase displays, and dealer sales material. Or, depending on the nature and needs of their clients, they may have staff public relations and direct-marketing specialists, home economics experts, package designers, or economists.

Agency administration

In small agencies, administrative functions may be handled by the firm's principals. Large agencies often have accounting, human resources, data processing, purchasing, financial analysis, and insurance departments.

How Agencies Are Structured

An ad agency organizes its functions, operations, and personnel according to the types of accounts it serves, its size, and its geographic scope.

In small agencies (annual billings of less than $15 million), each employee may wear many hats. The owner usually supervises daily business operations, client services, and new business development. Account executives generally handle day-to-day client contact. AEs may also do creative work and write copy. Artwork may be produced by an art director or purchased from an independent studio or freelance designer. Most small agencies have production and traffic departments or an employee who fulfills these functions. They may have a media buyer, but in very small agencies account executives also purchase media time and space. Exhibit 3–2 shows how Muse Cordero Chen is structured.

Medium and large agencies are usually structured in a *departmental* or *group system*. In the **departmental system,** the agency's functions—account services, creative services, marketing services, and administration—are handled by separate departments (see RL 3–1 in the Reference Library).

In the **group system,** the agency is divided into a number of "little" agencies or groups (see RL 3–2 in the Reference Library). Each group may serve one large account or, in some cases, three or four smaller ones. An account supervisor heads each group's staff of account executives, copywriters, art directors, a media director, and any other necessary specialists. A very large agency may have dozens of groups with separate production and traffic units for each.

To deal with the economic pressures of the 90s, many agencies have looked for ways to reorganize. Chiat/Day in Venice, California, invented a high-tech "virtual office" that frees employees from a regular desk, allowing them to roam around with their personal notebook computers and sit wherever the needs of the moment dictate.[13] In New York, Lintas restructured itself into six client business units (CBUs), each meant to function as an agency within an agency. And in France, Young & Rubicam encourages employees to spend more time out of the office with clients and to work from home while linked to the agency via laptop.[14]

How Agencies Are Compensated

To survive, an agency must make a profit. But recent trends in the business—mergers of superagencies, lower media advertising budgets, shifts in emphasis from advertising to sales promotion and direct marketing, increased production costs, and the fragmen-

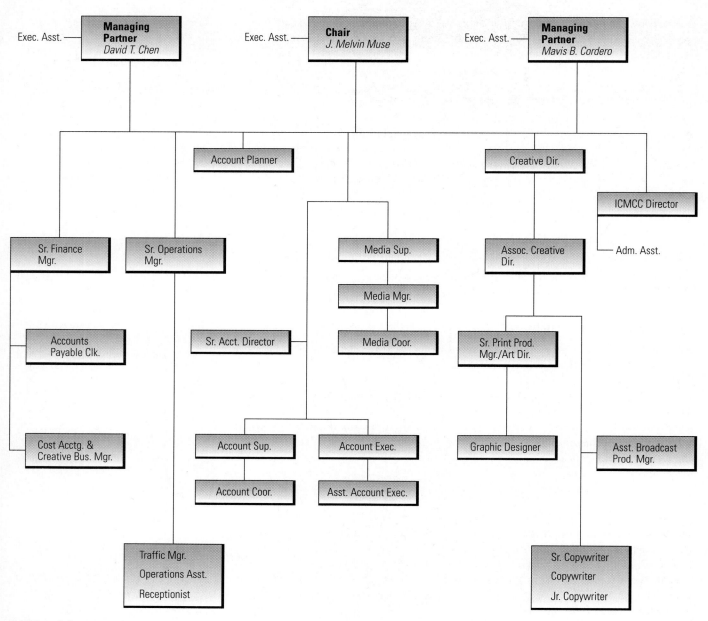

Exhibit • 3–2
Muse Cordero Chen organization.

tation of media vehicles—have all cut into agency profits.[15] Moreover, different clients demand different services, forcing agencies to develop various compensation methods. Basically, agencies make money from three sources: *media commissions, markups,* and *fees* or *retainers.*

Media commissions

Agencies save the media much of the expense of sales and collections, so the media let agencies retain a 15 percent **media commission** on the space or time they purchase for their clients. Say a magazine bills an agency $1,000 for an ad. The agency then bills the client $1,000. The client pays that total amount to the agency, and the agency sends $850 to the magazine, keeping its 15 percent commission ($150). For large accounts, the agency typically provides creative, media, accounting, and account management

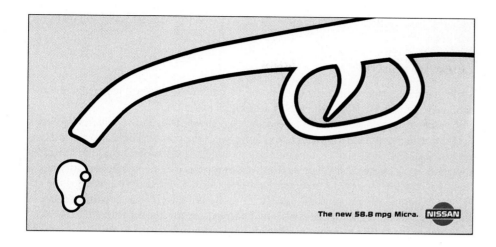

The new 58.8 mpg Micra.   NISSAN

• Agencies receive a media commission for purchasing time or space (in this case, billboards and TV commercials) for their clients. "Herbie rides again" seems to be the theme for Nissan Motors GB's Micra, the heir-apparent to the Volkswagen Beetle. The British-built Micra was voted European Car of the Year, and its bubble shape appears in premiums such as balloons, sponges, and eyeglasses.

services for this commission. However, many agencies now charge for what used to be free services.[16]

Markups

To create an ad, the agency normally buys a variety of services or materials from outside suppliers—for example, photos and illustrations. The agency pays the supplier's charge and then adds a **markup** to the client's bill, typically 17.65 percent (which becomes 15 percent of the new total).

For example, a markup of 17.65 percent on an $850 photography bill yields $150. When billing the client, the agency adds the $150 to the $850 for a new total of $1,000. When the client pays the bill, the agency keeps the $150 (15 percent of the total)—the standard agency commission.

$$\$850 \times 17.65\% = \$150$$
$$\$850 + \$150 = \$1,000$$
$$\$1,000 \times 15\% = \$150$$

Some media—local newspapers, for example—allow a commission on the higher rates they charge national advertisers but not the lower rates they charge local advertisers. So agencies use the markup formula to get their commission.

Today many agencies find that the markup doesn't cover their costs, so they're increasing their markups to 20 or 25 percent. While this helps, agency profits are still under pressure, forcing many agencies to a fee system in place of, or in addition to, commissions and markups.

Fees

Clients today expect agencies to solve problems rather than just place ads, so fees are becoming more common. In fact, one study shows that only about 33 percent of national advertisers still rely on the 15 percent commission system. An equal number now use some fee-based system.[17]

There are two pricing methods in the fee system. With the **fee–commission** combination, the agency charges a basic monthly fee for all its services to the client and retains any media commissions earned. In the **straight fee** or **retainer** method, agencies charge for all their services, either by the hour or by the month, and credit any media commissions earned to the client.

Accountability is a major issue in client–agency relationships. With a new type of agency compensation, the **incentive system,** the agency earns more if the campaign attains specific, agreed-on goals. DDB Needham, for example, offers its clients a "guaranteed results" program. If a campaign wins, the agency earns more; if it loses, the agency earns less. Kraft General Foods rewards its agencies based on their performance: A grades get an extra 3 percent commission; C grades are put on review.[18]

THE ADVERTISERS (THE CLIENTS)

The size, organization, and management of a company's advertising department depend on a variety of factors.

Large Advertisers

Some companies operate in only one part of the country. Others sell nationally or internationally. Exhibit 3–3 shows the top 15 advertisers in the U.S.

Companies advertising abroad face many challenges. They face an audience with a different value system, environment, and language. Foreign customers also have different purchasing abilities, habits, and motivations. Media customary for U.S. and Canadian advertisers may be unavailable or ineffective. Companies may need different advertising strategies too. But they face a more basic problem: How to manage and produce the advertising? Should their domestic agency or in-house advertising department do it? Should they use a foreign agency or set up a foreign advertising department?

Whether marketing at home or abroad, large companies tend to use some mix of two basic management structures: *centralized* and *decentralized.*

Centralized organization

Companies are concerned with cost efficiency and continuity in their communications programs. So many embrace the **centralized advertising department** because it gives the greatest control and offers both efficiency and continuity across divisional boundaries. In centralized departments, an advertising manager typically reports to a marketing vice president. But beyond this one feature, companies may organize the department in any of five ways:

- By product or brand.
- By subfunction of advertising (copy, art, print production, media buying).
- By end user (consumer advertising, trade advertising).
- By media (radio, TV, newspapers, outdoor).
- By geography (western advertising, eastern advertising, European advertising).

The cereal giant General Mills, for example, is one of the 25 largest national advertisers. It operates a vast advertising and marketing services department with some 350 employees. It spends $570 million annually in advertising and another $600 million in other promotional activities.[19]

General Mills' Marketing Services is really many departments within a department. Its centralized structure enables it to administer, plan, and coordinate the promotion of more than 60 brands. It also supervises nine outside ad agencies and operates its own in-house agency for new or smaller brands.[20]

Organized around functional specialties (market research, media, graphics), Marketing Services consults with General Mills' brand managers and consolidates many of their expenditures for maximum efficiency. The media department, for example, is involved in all media plans for the marketing divisions. The production and art services department handles package design for all brands and graphics for the company's in-house agency. From one spot, Marketing Services creates effective ad programs for a wide variety of brands (see Exhibit 3–4).

Exhibit • 3–3

Top advertisers in the U.S. in 1993 by total U.S. ad spending ($ millions rounded).

1.	Procter & Gamble (Cincinnati)	$2397.5	9.	Johnson & Johnson (New Brunswick, NJ)	762.5
2.	Philip Morris (New York)	1844.3	10.	Chrysler (Highland Park, MI)	761.6
3.	General Motors (Detroit)	1539.2	11.	Warner-Lambert (Morris Plains, NJ)	751.0
4.	Sears, Roebuck (Chicago)	1310.7	12.	Unilever NV (London/Rotterdam)	738.2
5.	PepsiCo (Purchase, NY)	1038.9	13.	McDonald's (Oak Brook, IL)	736.6
6.	Ford Motor (Dearborn, MI)	958.3	14.	Time Warner (New York)	695.1
7.	AT&T (New York)	812.1	15.	Toyota (Toyota City, Japan)	690.4
8.	Nestlé SA (Vevey, SW)	793.7			

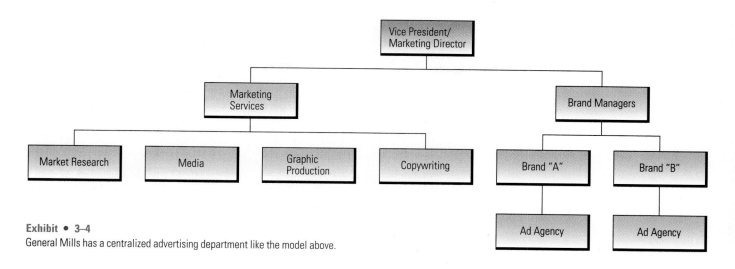

Exhibit • 3–4
General Mills has a centralized advertising department like the model above.

As advertisers break into international markets, they may start by simply exporting their existing products. At first, the home office controls all foreign marketing and advertising. Everything is centralized.

Later, as companies grow and prosper around the world, they may invest directly in many countries. True **multinational corporations** strive for full, integrated participation in world markets.[21] Foreign sales often grow faster than domestic sales. Multinationals like Exxon and IBM earn about 50 percent of their sales abroad; Kodak and Xerox, about 25 percent. Typically, the top 25 U.S. multinational corporations earn more than 40 percent of their revenues and two-thirds of their profits overseas.[22]

A multinational typically exerts strong centralized control over all its marketing activities. Multinational firms like Kodak get strong direction and coordination from headquarters and have a standardized product line and marketing structure. Exhibit 3–5 shows the largest advertisers in various countries.

Multinationals that use a *standardized approach* to marketing and advertising in all countries are **global corporations,** and they create global brands. Their assumption is that the way the product is used and the needs it satisfies are universal.[23] Max Factor, for example, markets and advertises its cosmetics globally with a campaign that makes the brand relevant through the use of strong, contemporary, self-confident women. The campaign has drawn favorable reactions from women worldwide.[24] Other global advertisers include Coca-Cola, British Airways, British Petroleum, TGI Friday's, Federal Express, and Chiclets.[25]

Companies must do a lot of research before attempting a global advertising strategy. So much depends on the product and where they try to sell it. A no answer to any of the following questions means the attempt will probably fail.

1. **Has each country's market for the product developed in the same way?** A Ford is a Ford in most markets. On the other hand, many Europeans use clotheslines, so they don't need fabric softeners for dryers.

1. Procter & Gamble (Cincinnati)	$1,901	8. Ford Motor (Dearborn, MI)	534
2. Unilever NV (Rotterdam/London)	1,888	9. L'Oreal (Paris)	527
3. Nestlé SA (Vevey, SW)	1,128	10. Mars (McLean, VA)	518
4. Philip Morris (New York)	713	11. Fiat SpA (Turin, Italy)	504
5. Volkswagen AG (Wolfsburg, Germany)	707	12. Renault SA (Paris)	462
		13. Coca-Cola (Atlanta)	448
6. PSA Peugeot-Citroen SA (Paris)	701	14. Kao Corp. (Tokyo)	436
7. General Motors (Detroit)	601	15. Toyota (Toyota City, Japan)	422

Exhibit • 3–5
Top advertisers outside the U.S. in 1993 ($ millions rounded).

• Global advertisers such as Patek Philippe use a standardized approach to marketing and advertising when their products satisfy universal needs. Patek Philippe's multinational campaign results from research conducted in major markets throughout the world. The ads appear in women's magazines in Switzerland, Japan, France, Spain, Singapore, Italy, Austria, Hong Kong, Germany, the U.K., and the U.S.

2. **Are the targets similar in different nations?** Japanese consumers like jeans, running shoes, and rock and roll. The same is true in Europe and the U.S. But it might not be true for certain foods or fashions.

3. **Do consumers share the same wants and needs?** Breakfast in Brazil is usually a cup of coffee. Kellogg's Corn Flakes won't be served the same way there as in the U.S., where people commonly eat cereal for breakfast.[26]

According to the worldwide creative director of J. Walter Thompson, the secret to success in global advertising is knowing how to tap into basic human emotions and uncover universal appeals that don't depend solely on language.[27]

Decentralized organization

As some companies become larger, diversify their product line, acquire subsidiaries, and establish divisions in different regions or different countries, a centralized advertising department often becomes impractical.

In a **decentralized system,** the company sets up separate advertising departments for different divisions, subsidiaries, products, countries, regions, brands, or other categories that suit the company's needs. The general manager of each division is responsible for that division's advertising.

For example, as companies get more involved in foreign markets, they may form joint ventures or invest in foreign sales offices, warehouses, plants, and other facilities. The advertiser typically views such operations as foreign marketing divisions and may use a decentralized **international structure,** in which the divisions are responsible for their own product lines, marketing operations, and profits, and typically create *customized advertising* for each market.[28]

Procter & Gamble, a 160-year-old, $30 billion company, sells more than 2,300 consumer brand varieties internationally in 41 different product categories. These brands include such market leaders as Tide, Ivory soap, Pampers, Duncan Hines, Crisco oils, and Crest toothpaste.[29]

P&G is one of the biggest and most influential consumer advertisers in the world; its expenditures in the U.S. alone approach $2.4 billion annually.[30] Each of the five U.S. consumer product divisions is set up almost like a separate company with its own research and development department, manufacturing plant, advertising department, sales force, and finance and accounting staff. Every brand within a division has a **brand manager** who oversees a brand group and directs his or her own ad agency to create the brand's media advertising. Brand managers work under a marketing manager who reports to a category manager.[31]

Each division also has an advertising department to help coordinate sales promotion and merchandising programs across brands. The corporate advertising department provides statistical information and guidance.

While the brand manager's primary goal is to use advertising and promotion to build market share, the category manager focuses on sharpening overall strategy and building profits.[32] P&G recently streamlined the system by eliminating extra layers of management and redundant facilities. This gives each brand the single-minded drive and personal commitment necessary for success and more authority to the individual responsible for the brand.[33]

For large companies with many divisions like P&G, decentralized advertising is more flexible. Campaigns and media schedules can be adjusted faster. New approaches and creative ideas can be introduced more easily, and sales results can be measured independently of other divisions. In effect, each division is its own marketing department, and the advertising manager reports to each division head (see Exhibit 3–6).

A drawback to decentralized departments is that they often concentrate on their own budgets, problems, and promotions rather than the good of the firm as a whole. Across divisions, ads typically lack uniformity, diminishing the power of repetitive corporate advertising. Rivalry among brand managers may escalate into unhealthy competition or deteriorate into secrecy and jealousy.

Ultimately, the advertising direction a company takes depends on many variables: breadth of product line, quality of management, ability to repeat marketing strategies across countries, costs, and the decision to operate internationally, multinationally, or globally. Every organization operates in a slightly different environment. This alters the search for an *ideal* structure into a search for a "suitable structure."[34] As a result, most companies blend aspects of centralized and decentralized structures to fit their own needs. And when an existing structure shows signs of decay, they must be willing to test new ideas and make changes.

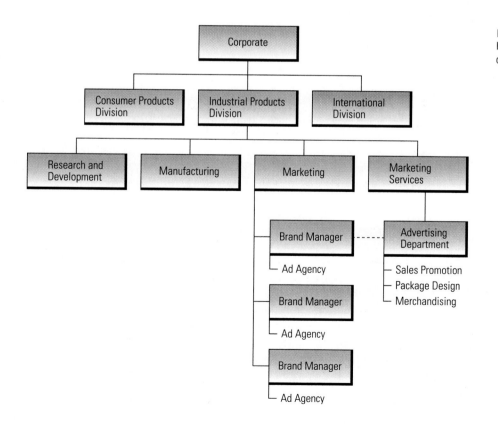

Exhibit • 3–6
In a decentralized department, each division is its own marketing department.

Small Advertisers

A small, local business—say, a hardware, clothing, or electronics store—may have just one person in charge of advertising. That person, the **advertising manager,** performs all the administrative, planning, budgeting, and coordinating functions. He or she may lay out newspaper ads, write ad copy, and select the media. A manager who also has some artistic talent may even design the actual ads and produce them on a desktop computer.

A chainstore operation might maintain a complete advertising department to handle production, media placement, and marketing support services. The department needs artists, copywriters, and production specialists. The department head usually reports to a vice president or marketing manager, as shown in Exhibit 3–7. We cover the subject of local advertising in Chapter 17.

The In-House Agency

To save money and tighten control over their advertising, some companies set up a wholly owned **in-house agency** (or *house agency*). The in-house agency may do all the work of an independent full-service agency, including creative tasks, production, media placement, publicity, and sales promotion.

Advertisers with in-house agencies hope to save money by cutting overhead, keeping the media commission, and avoiding markups on outside purchases. Small, local advertisers especially seek this goal.

Advertisers also expect more attention from their house agencies, which know the company's products and markets better and can focus all their resources to meet deadlines.

Management is often more involved in the advertising when it's done by company people, especially in "single-business" companies. And some in-house advertising is outstanding, especially in the fashion field.

But usually companies sacrifice considerably more than they gain. In-house flexibility is often won at the expense of creativity. Outside agencies typically offer greater experience, versatility, and talent. In-house agencies have difficulty attracting and keeping the best creative people, who tend to prefer the variety and challenge offered by independent agencies. In fact, in Italy, Benetton's stock fell 6 percent in one day when Oliviero Toscani, the company's celebrated in-house ad director, threatened to resign over the issue of creative control.[35]

Exhibit • 3–7
Typical department structure for small advertisers with high volumes of work, such as grocery store chains.

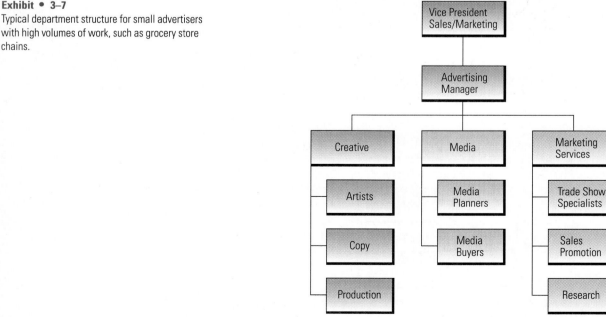

ANNE KLEIN II   MY UNIFORM

● In-house agencies can produce very professional advertising, like this striking ad for Anne Klein II. The company can often save money and tighten control over its advertising and other marketing communications when the work is done in house.

The biggest problem for in-house agencies is loss of objectivity. In the shadow of internal politics, linear-thinking policymakers, and harangues from management, ads may become insipid contemplations of corporate navels rather than relevant messages to customers. In advertising, that's the kiss of death.

Many factors affect the success of a company's advertising program, but one of the most important is the relationship between the advertiser and its agency.

THE CLIENT–AGENCY RELATIONSHIP

How Agencies Get Clients

To succeed, ad agencies need clients. New clients come from personal contact with top management, referrals from satisfied clients, publicity on recent successful campaigns, trade advertising, direct-mail solicitation, or the agency's general reputation.[36] The three most successful ways to develop new business are: having clients who strongly champion the agency, having superior presentation skills, and cultivating a personal relationship with a network of top executives.

Referrals

Most good agencies get clients by referral—from existing clients, friends, advertising consultants, or even other agencies. The head of one company asks another who's doing her ads, and the next week the agency gets a call. If a prospective client presents a conflict of interest with an existing client, the agency may decline the business and refer the prospect to another agency.[37]

Independent advertising consultants often help arrange marriages between agencies and clients. In fact, independent advisers were involved in most of the important recent account shuffles on Madison Avenue: Sears, IBM, BMW, Burger King, and MasterCard, to name a few.[38]

Sales reps for media and suppliers frequently refer local advertisers to an agency they know. So it's important for agencies to maintain cordial relations with the media, suppliers, other agencies, and, of course, with their existing clients.

Presentations

An advertiser may ask an agency to make a presentation—anything from a simple discussion of the agency's philosophy, experience, personnel, and track record to a full-blown audiovisual presentation of a proposed campaign. Successful agencies, therefore, must have excellent presentation skills.

Some advertisers ask for or imply that they want a **speculative presentation,** meaning they want to see what the agency will do for them before they sign on. But most agencies prefer to build their presentations around the work they've already done, to demonstrate their capabilities without giving away their ideas for a new campaign. Invariably, the larger the client, the bigger the presentation.

The presentation process also allows the agency and the advertiser to get to know each other before they agree to work together. Advertising is a people business, so human qualities—mutual regard, trust, and communication—play an important role (see the Ethical Issue box).

Networking and community relations

Agencies frequently find that the best source of new business is people they know socially in the community. Some agencies work *pro bono* (for free) for charities or nonprofit organizations such as the American Indian College Fund. Jo Muse at Muse Cordero Chen contributes time to the Rebuild L.A. campaign, which started after the civil disorders of 1992.

Agencies may help local politicians (a controversial practice in some areas) or contribute to the arts, education, religion, or community. Some agencies sponsor seminars, others assist ad clubs or other professional organizations. All these activities help an agency become known and respected in its community.

Soliciting and advertising for new business

Lesser-known agencies must take a more aggressive approach. An agency may solicit new business by advertising, writing letters, making cold calls, or following up leads from sources in the business. An agency principal usually solicits new business, but staffers may help prepare presentations.

Ethical Issue   Accounting for Account Reviews

Clients periodically review the effectiveness of their advertising agency and invite presentations from other agencies. In 1993, 63 percent of agencies in a survey claimed to be "more customer-focused" than before, but only 26 percent of their clients agreed—a clear indication that agency reviews will continue.

"The tension comes from the fact that the whole business of advertising has had to become more accountable in recent years due to corporate restructuring," states Nancy Salz, president of Nancy L. Salz Consulting, a firm that advises advertisers and agencies how to improve their relationships.

The agency review process is hard on incumbents. An informal survey by *Adweek* revealed that only one incumbent agency out of dozens actually survives a review. "Ninety percent of client-agency breakups happen because the relationship goes bad. If the relationship is bad, nothing will

save the advertising," says Ed Vick, president/CEO of Young & Rubicam, New York.

A number of other temptations encourage advertisers to conduct a review. For one thing, each agency spends thousands of dollars to woo an advertiser, and advertisers usually don't mind a little attention from a new agency. Second, the advertiser has no financial or legal commitment to pay agencies for their presentations (although ethically, one would think they should). Third, some advertisers have been known to view several presentations, incorporate and plagiarize elements from each, redesign the art and script elements, and not reimburse the agencies for their research and creative ideas.

To keep costs low, some advertisers put their agencies on the defensive by threatening to choose other creative sources. "Advertisers have gotten smarter over the years," states James Desrosier, vice president of marketing and product management at Maestro USA, a subsidiary of

MasterCard International. "And they have led the charge that has created the erosion of traditional agency revenue streams. First it was the strategic consultant. Then it was the independent media-buying service. Now it's the external creative resource."

Many advertising professionals insist the process must be changed. But it appears there are no bottom-line incentives to stimulate advertisers to initiate reform, only ethical reasons. So change must come through the actions of agencies and agency associations. As Desrosier says, "The advertising industry wants to be taken more seriously. But so far it has been incapable of conducting itself in the way it wants to be perceived. The only way out of this situation is through change. But rather than playing catch-up, the industry should change the game it plays."

Change may in fact be under way. In February 1994, the CD-i Division of Philips Interactive

"Stephen King" :60

STEPHEN KING: The rats seemed to pour out of the pipe and run down the alley.

PETER THOMAS: Stephen King, author of *Carrie, The Shining,* and *Pet Sematary.*

STEPHEN KING: His legs were too bad to let him move with any speed. He shifted frantically, trying to get up as he watched them come in a seemingly endless wave, past the dumpsters and the barrels. But he couldn't move. And so he sat, against the bags of trash, his face frozen in horror, as they raced toward him, past him, around him, over him, and finally settled on him—diving into his pockets, shredding the bags behind him, ripping at the shopping bag he held, nipping at the exposed skin at his ankles and his wrists. The squealing seemed to fill the sky . . .

(Pause)

STEPHEN KING: The most horrifying part of this story is that I didn't write it. It's the true account of what happened to a homeless man in an alley in Boston's Back Bay. Please. Support the Pine Street Inn. You can't imagine what the homeless go through. Even I can't.

PETER THOMAS: The Pine Street Inn, 444 Harrison Avenue. 482-4944.

• Agencies like Hill, Holliday, Connors, Cosmopulos (Boston) often do public service advertising, such as campaigns like this one featuring Stephen King for the Pine Street Inn, a Boston shelter for the homeless. Pro bono work also helps the ad agency establish good community relations and eventually may lead to new clients.

Today, more agencies are advertising themselves. The Ad Store, a small agency in New York, even advertises on television to reach small, first-time advertisers.[39] Many agencies submit their best ads to competitions around the world to win awards and gain publicity and professional respect for their creative excellence.[40] (Most of the ads in this text are award winners.)

Stages in the Client-Agency Relationship

Just as people and products have life cycles, so do relationships. In the advertising business, the life cycle of the agency-client relationship has four distinct stages: *prerelationship, development, maintenance,* and *termination.*[41]

Media of America initiated an agency review. Cohen/Johnson (Los Angeles) and Woolworth & Partners (San Francisco) were two of the three finalists for the $10 million CD-i account. Suddenly,

---

[Advertisers] have led the charge that has created the erosion of traditional agency revenue streams.

---

in March, the review process was put on hold when Philips Interactive appointed a new senior vice president of sales and marketing, Stephen Race, who decided to "rethink" the list of solicited agencies. The executives at Woolworth and at Cohen/Johnson responded with a lawsuit demanding $20,000 reimbursement for incurred costs and claiming that "Philips has not stood by its good faith commitment." Philips settled out of court, offering to pay $10,000 to each agency.

It is apparently up to agencies to set forth the proper etiquette for an account review and to educate the advertisers. The entire process must rely on the integrity and the good faith of all the parties involved. Observers hope that equitable ethical standards can be established by both agencies and advertisers to make the review process more accountable.

Questions

1. Many advertisers indicate their agencies are not truly customer focused. What can an ad agency do to change this perception—and thus keep its clients from changing agencies?

2. It seems clear that the agency review process is here to stay. What guidelines can advertisers and agencies implement to make this process more equitable and ethical for all parties?

Sources: "Is the Advertiser-Agency Relationship on the Rocks?" *Sales & Marketing Management,* August 1993, p. 13; Noreen O'Leary, "Against All Odds," *Adweek,* August 8, 1994, p. 19; James Desrosier, "How to Repair the Agency-Client Rift," *Adweek,* January 31, 1994, p. 52; Kevin Goldman, "Philips Infomercial Does Its Thing in Popular TV-Watching Hours," *The Wall Street Journal,* September 22, 1993, p. B6; Patrick M. Reilly, "Philips Media Plans Reorganization to Consolidate Its Global Properties," *The Wall Street Journal,* August 16, 1993, p. B4; "Ad Notes: Philips Consumer Electronics Fires DMB&B," *The Wall Street Journal,* July 19, 1994, p. B6; Kathy Tyrer, "Broken Promise," *Adweek,* March 21, 1994, pp. 1, 9; Kathy Tyrer, "Philips Interactive Media Nears Decision among Three Finalists," *Adweek,* February 28, 1994, p. 4; Kathy Tyrer, "Philips Interactive Meets with Four Shops," *Adweek,* February 7, 1994, p. 5; Kathy Tyrer, "RPA Hooks Up with Philips after a Rocky Review," *Adweek,* April 25, 1994, p. 3; Kathy Tyrer and Shelly Garcia, "Philips Reopens Talks on CD-i Biz," *Adweek,* March 28, 1994, p. 3; Tom Weisend, "Riney Out of Philips Review," *Adweek,* February 14, 1994, p. 3.

One way agencies solicit new business is by advertising in trade magazines. A series of ads like this one by Dittler Brothers, an advertising promotions firm, appears in trade magazines such as *Promo,* an international magazine for promotion marketing.

The prerelationship stage

The **prerelationship stage** occurs before an agency and client officially do business. They may know each other by reputation, by previous ads, or through social contact. Initial perceptions usually determine if an agency is invited to "pitch" the account. Through the presentation process, the agency tries to give the best impression it can, because it is selling and the client is buying. (The Checklist for Agency Review offers guidelines for selecting an agency.)

The development stage

Once the agency is appointed, the **development stage** begins. During this honeymoon period, the agency and the client are at the peak of their optimism and eager to develop a mutually profitable relationship. Expectations are at their highest, and both sides are most forgiving. During development, the rules of the relationship are established. The respective roles get set quickly, the true personalities of all the players come out, and the agency creates its first work. At this point, the agency's output is eagerly awaited and then judged very thoroughly. The agency also discovers how receptive the client is to new ideas, how easy the client's staff is to work with, and how well the client pays its bills. During the development stage the first problems in the relationship also occur.

The maintenance and termination stages

The year-in, year-out, day-to-day working relationship is called the **maintenance stage.** When successful, it may go on for many years. Sunkist has used the same

---

Agency Review   *Checklist*

Rate each agency on a scale from 1 (strongly negative) to 10 (strongly positive).

General Information

☐ Size compatible with our needs.

☐ Strength of management.

☐ Financial stability.

☐ Compatibility with other clients.

☐ Range of services.

☐ Cost of services; billing policies.

Marketing Information

☐ Ability to offer marketing counsel.

☐ Understanding of the markets we serve.

☐ Experience dealing in our market.

☐ Success record; case histories.

Creative Abilities

☐ Well-thought-out creativity; relevance to strategy.

☐ Art strength.

☐ Copy strength.

☐ Overall creative quality.

☐ Effectiveness compared to work of competitors.

Production

☐ Faithfulness to creative concept and execution.

☐ Diligence to schedules and budgets.

☐ Ability to control outside services.

Media

☐ Existence and soundness of media research.

☐ Effective and efficient media strategy.

☐ Ability to achieve objectives within budget.

☐ Strength at negotiating and executing schedules.

Personality

☐ Overall personality, philosophy, or position.

☐ Compatibility with client staff and management.

☐ Willingness to assign top people to account.

References

☐ Rating by current clients.

☐ Rating by past clients.

☐ Rating by media and financial sources.

---

agency, Foote, Cone & Belding, for 90 years. Other long-lasting relationships include Unilever/J. Walter Thompson (92 years), Exxon/McCann-Erickson (82 years), and Hammermill Papers/BBDO Worldwide (81 years). Unfortunately, the average client-agency relationship is much shorter—usually seven or eight years.

At some point, an irreconcilable difference may occur, and the relationship must be **terminated,** or ended. Perhaps the agency has acquired a new, competing account, or the agency's creative work doesn't seem to be working. Or perhaps one party or the other simply decides it is time to move on.

In 1993 and 1994 several long-standing client-agency relationships were terminated. After 75 years, AT&T replaced Ayer as the company's lead agency on its $200 million consumer long-distance account, giving the business to FCB/Leber Katz in New York. Ayer retained AT&T's $100 million corporate image business.[42] Seagram fired DDB Needham from its $40 million Chivas Regal account after a 32-year marriage. And Anheuser-Busch dropped a bombshell on D'Arcy Masius Benton & Bowles when it pulled the Budweiser account after 79 years.[43] The way the termination is handled will affect both sides for a long time and is an important factor in whether the two ever get back together. After losing the Apple Computer account, Chiat/Day gave Madison Avenue a lesson in class by placing an ad thanking Apple for their many years together.

Factors Affecting the Client-Agency Relationship

Many forces influence the client-agency relationship. Generally they can be grouped into the four Cs: *chemistry, communication, conduct,* and *changes.*

Chemistry

The most critical factor is the personal chemistry between the client's and the agency's staff.[44] Agencies are very conscious of this factor and wine and dine their clients in hopes of improving it. Smart clients do the same.

Communication

Poor communication, a problem often cited by both agencies and advertisers, leads to misunderstandings about objectives, strategies, roles and expectations—and to poor advertising. Constant, open communication and an explicit agreement on mutual contribution for mutual gain are key to a good relationship.[45]

Checklist   Ways to Be a Better Client

Relationships

☐ **Cultivate honesty.** Be truthful in your meetings and in your ads.

☐ **Be enthusiastic.** When you like the ads, let the agency know.

☐ **Be frank when you don't like the advertising.** Always cite a reason when turning down an idea.

☐ **Be human.** React like a person, not a corporation. Laugh at funny ads even if they won't work.

☐ **Be willing to admit you're unsure.** Don't be pressured. Let your agency know when you need time.

☐ **Allow the agency to feel responsible.** Tell the agency what you feel is wrong, not how to fix it.

☐ **Care about being a client.** Creative people work best for clients they like.

Management

☐ **Don't insulate your top people from creative people.** Agency creative people work best when objectives come from the top, not filtered through layers.

☐ **Set objectives.** For timely and quality service from your agency, establish and openly share your marketing objectives.

☐ **Switch people, not agencies.** When problems arise, agencies often prefer to bring in fresh talent rather than lose you as a client.

☐ **Be sure the agency makes a profit on your account.** Demanding more services from your agency than fees or commissions can cover hurt relationships.

Production

☐ **Avoid nitpicking last-minute changes.** Perfection is important, but waiting until the last moment to make minor changes can damage the client-agency relationship. Agencies see such behavior as indecisive and/or arrogant and lose respect for the client.

☐ **Be aware of the cost of changes (both time and money).** The costs of making major changes at the production stage may be five times greater than in the earlier stages.

☐ **Don't change concepts during the production stage.** Late concept changes can inadvertently change product positioning and personality.

Media

☐ **Understand the economics (and economies) of media.** Be prepared to deal with CPMs, CPPs, and other key elements of media planning and buying so that you can properly understand, evaluate, and appreciate your agency's media strategy.

☐ **Understand the importance of lead time.** Early buys can eliminate late fees, earn discounts, make you eligible for special promotions, strengthen your agency's buying position, and reduce anxiety.

☐ **Avoid interfering with the agency's media relationship.** The stronger your agency's buying position, the greater the discounts available to you. Refrain from cutting deals with media reps directly and plan media well in advance.

☐ **Avoid media arrogance ("they need us").** Some media will deal with clients, and some won't. Misinterpret this relationship and you may either pay more than you should or be too late to get into a medium you need.

☐ **Avoid insularity.** Be willing to let your mind travel beyond your immediate environment and lifestyle.

☐ **Suggest work sessions.** Set up informal give-and-take sessions with creatives and strategists.

☐ **Keep the creative people involved in your business.** Agency creatives do their best work for you when they're in tune with the ups and downs of your business.

Research

☐ **Share information.** Pool information to create new and bigger opportunities.

☐ **Involve the agency in research projects.** An agency's creative talent gets its best ideas from knowledge of your environment.

Creative

☐ **Learn the fine art of conducting the creative meeting.** Deal with the important issues first: strategy, consumer benefits, and reasons why.

☐ **Look for the big idea.** Concentrate on positioning strategy and brand personality. Don't allow a single ad—no matter how brilliant—to change the positioning or personality of the product.

☐ **Insist on creative discipline.** The creative process stimulates concepts and actions. Discipline helps keep focus on those that count the most.

☐ **Don't be afraid to ask for great advertising.** Agencies prefer the high road, but as the client you must be willing to accompany them. If the agency slips, be strong and ask it to try again.

Conduct

Dissatisfaction with agency performance is the most commonly cited reason for agency switches, regardless of country.[46] Services, like products, move through life cycles. The service the agency marketed two years ago may not be perceived by the client in the same way today.[47] And clients change, too. Does the client give the agency timely, accurate information? Does the agency understand the client's marketing problems? Does the client appreciate good work, or does it treat the agency like a vendor?[48] (For more on how clients hold up their end of the relationship, see the Checklist for Ways to Be a Better Client.)

Changes

Changes occur in every relationship. Unfortunately, some of them damage the agency-client partnership. The client's market position or policies may change, or new management may arrive. Agencies may lose key staff people. Client conflicts may arise if one agency buys another that handles competing accounts. Legally, an ad agency cannot represent a client's competition without the client's consent.[49] Saatchi & Saatchi was forced to resign Helene Curtis under pressure from Saatchi's biggest client, Procter & Gamble.[50]

Perhaps the best way to improve understanding between clients and agencies would be to have staff members change places for a while. A Foote, Cone & Belding account executive did just that with great success, filling in temporarily as marketing manager at Levi's Jeans for Women. It gave her a whole new perspective on her agency job and the daily challenges faced by her client.[51]

THE MEDIA OF ADVERTISING

The *medium* that carries the advertiser's message is the vital connection between the company that manufactures a product or offers a service and the customer who might wish to buy it. Although the plural term *media* commonly describes channels of mass communication such as television, radio, newspapers, and magazines, it also refers to other communications vehicles such as direct mail, out-of-home media (transit, billboards, etc.), specialized media (aerial/blimps, inflatables), specialty advertising items (imprinted coffee mugs, balloons), and new communication technologies such as interactive TV, fax, and satellite networks. (Exhibit 3–8 shows the largest U.S. media companies.)

For the student of advertising, it's important to understand the various media, their role in the advertising business, and the significance of current media trends. For a person seeking a career in advertising, the media may offer the first door to employment, and for many they have provided great financial rewards.

Today, we can classify advertising media into six major categories: *print, electronic, out-of-home, direct mail, digital interactive,* and *other media.* Due to recent media trends, there is some overlap. We shall mention these in passing, along with a brief description of each major category.

Print Media

The term **print media** refers to any commercially published, printed medium—such as newspapers and magazines—that sells advertising space to a variety of advertisers. In the U.S. today there are more than 1,700 daily and 8,000 weekly newspapers.[52] Most are local. However, some national newspapers such as *USA Today, The Wall Street Journal, Barron's,* and trade publications like *Electronic News* and *Supermarket News* have become quite successful. Once strictly a local newspaper, the *New York Times* is now distributed to more than a million readers nationwide.[53]

Magazines, on the other hand, have long been national, and some periodicals, like *Elle,* publish editions in many countries. For over a decade, though, the trend has been toward localization and specialization.

Newspapers		Television & Radio	
1. Gannett	$2,844	1. Capital Cities/ABC	$3,882
2. Knight-Ridder	2,069	2. CBS	3,510
3. Times Mirror	1,981	3. General Electric	3,008
4. Advance Publications	1,800	4. News Corp.	1,426
5. New York Times	1,538	5. Tribune Co.	596
Magazines		**Cable**	
1. Time Warner	$2,070	1. Tele-Communications	$4,153
2. Reed Elsevier	1,070	2. Time Warner	3,649
3. Advance Publications	970	3. Turner Broadcasting System	1,762
4. Thomson Corp.	886	4. Viacom International	1,637
5. Reader's Digest	804	5. Continental Cablevision	1,177

Exhibit • 3–8
Top U.S. media companies by category in 1993 ($ millions rounded).

There are nearly 11,000 different magazines published in the United States alone.[54] These include national consumer publications like *Time* and *TV Guide;* national trade publications like *Progressive Grocer* and *Marketing News;* local city magazines like *Palm Springs Life* and *Chicago;* regional consumer magazines like *Sunset;* and local or regional trade or farm publications such as *California Farmer.*

Companies may also publish their own magazines for customers. Examples include CompuServe's *CompuServe Magazine* and Aldus Corp.'s *Aldus Magazine,* both of which are distributed nationally. Likewise, professional associations, fraternal organizations, and national hobbyist clubs also publish nationally distributed magazines, from Lambda Chi Alpha fraternity's *Cross and Crescent* magazine to the American Philatelic Association's *The Philatelist.* A local variation is *AdMonth* magazine, published by the Advertising Club of San Diego and distributed to club members and key businesses in the city.

Print media also include directories such as the Yellow Pages; school or church newspapers and yearbooks; and programs used at sporting events and theatrical performances.

As we shall see in Chapter 12, "Buying Print Media," the vast array of newspapers and magazines makes it possible for both consumer and business advertisers to pinpoint the delivery of their messages to highly select target markets in a variety of fields or geographic locations.

Electronic Media

The **electronic media** of radio and television used to be called the *broadcast media.* But with the advent of cable TV, many programs are now transmitted electronically through wires rather than broadcast through the air.

The U.S. alone has more than 1,000 local commercial TV stations and nearly 10,000 local radio stations as well as major TV and radio networks, including ABC, CBS, NBC, Fox, Westinghouse, and Mutual. More than 11,000 local cable systems blanket the country, serving more than 57 million subscribers.[55] Serving these systems are major cable networks like USA, A&E, and CNN. Cable also provides channels with specialized offerings such as QVC, which offers products that can be purchased by phone; Cinemax, which features only recently released films; and American Movie Classics (AMC), which features only vintage films. We discuss electronic media in Chapter 13, "Buying Electronic and Digital Interactive Media."

Out-of-Home Media

The major categories of out-of-home media are *outdoor advertising* and *transit advertising.* In the U.S., most **outdoor advertising** (billboard) companies are local firms, but most of their revenue comes from national advertisers such as tobacco, liquor, and airline companies. **Transit advertising** (bus, taxi, and subway advertising) is an effective and inexpensive medium for reaching the buying public while they're in the retail neighborhood. Out-of-home media also include posters in bus shelters and train stations, billboards in airport terminals, stadium scoreboard ads, flying banners and lights, skywriting, and kiosk posters.

Direct Mail

When companies mail their advertising directly to prospective customers without using one of the commercial media forms, it's called **direct-mail advertising.** The ad may be a simple sales letter, or it may be a complex package with coupons, brochures, samples, or other devices designed to stimulate a response. Direct mail is the most expensive medium on a cost-per-exposure basis, but also the most effective because advertisers can target customers directly without competition from other advertisers. We discuss direct mail in Chapter 15.

● Bank One advertises its consumer services in a series of humorous TV spots like the one shown here. Electronic media offer an ever-expanding option for advertisers to reach their targeted customers.

"Balloon" :30
(Open on a man standing beside a giant balloon.)
MAN: OK, what we're going to do, I'm going to try to get in this balloon.
SFX: Music starts and plays under the camera cards.
CAMERA CARD: There's a smarter way to get money.

(Man sticks the balloon over his head.)
MAN: I'm going inside. I do accept checks.
CAMERA CARD: A low-interest Bank One Home Equity Loan.

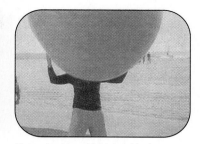

(Cut to the man with his head in the balloon.)
MAN: You know, sometimes I get a headache about this big.
CAMERA CARD: Use it for anything.

(Cut to the man completely inside the balloon.)
MAN: Whooo.
CAMERA CARD: Career counseling, perhaps.

(Man sticks his head out of the balloon and starts jumping around.)
MAN: How about it. Can you dig it? Can you dig it? Can you dig, dig, dig it?

SUPER: Bank One. Whatever it takes.
(Cut back to man still jumping around in the balloon.)

Digital Interactive Media

The advent of the information superhighway has brought a new media form. **Digital interactive media** are channels of communication with which the audience can participate actively and immediately. They are changing the way advertisers and agencies do business.

With a computer keyboard and an electronic credit card reader hooked up to their TVs, audiences can now purchase products via cable TV. They can vote or participate in game shows. And they can manipulate images to better view a scene or seek deeper information about a product or service.

This presents a new challenge to advertisers and agencies to learn new forms of creativity. They have to deal with a whole new environment for their ads. It's an environment where customers may spend 20 minutes or more, not just 30 seconds, and where advertising is a dialog, not a monolog. And on the Internet, they risk getting "flamed" (receiving harsh criticism by e-mail) if the techies don't like their ads.[56]

Technology and competition for viewers have led to tremendous audience fragmentation. Running a spot on network TV used to cover the majority of a market. Now, ad budgets must be bigger to encompass many media. Wherever elusive customers hide, new media forms have arisen to seek them out. But for the big, mass-market advertiser, this represents an enormous financial burden.

● Transit advertising can effectively reach the buying public (in this case, Phoenix Suns fans) in the local area. This award-winning ad depicts the excitement of professional basketball and is a visual reminder to local fans to support their team.

Other Media

Technology has spawned a host of new advertising media to confound even the most knowledgeable media planners and buyers. Advertising appears on videocassettes and computer disks. Computers dial telephones and deliver messages by simulating speech or playing a prerecorded message. Computers can also put callers on hold and play prerecorded sales messages until their line is answered. Business presentations are created on computer and copied to disks that are mailed to prospective customers. As progress continues, so will the proliferation of new media that we can't even imagine today—and so will the opportunities for those seeking careers or fortunes in the media.

Media in Foreign Markets

Many U.S. advertising people get used to foreign styles of advertising faster than they get used to foreign media. In the U.S., if you want to promote a soft drink as a youthful, fun refresher, you use television. In some parts of Europe, Asia, South America, and Africa you may not be able to. Around the world, most broadcast media are owned and controlled by the government, and many governments do not allow commercial advertising on radio or television.

Where countries do allow TV advertising, TV ownership is high, cutting across the spectrum of income groups. In less-developed countries, though, TV sets may be found only among upper-income groups. This means advertisers may need a different media mix in foreign markets.

● Hindustan Lever sells soap in villages with the help of video vans. This one visits Maharashtra.

Virtually every country has access to radio, television, newspapers, magazines, outdoor media, and direct mail. However, the legalities of different media forms vary from country to country. Generally, the media available to the international advertiser can be categorized as either *international media* or *foreign media,* depending on the audience they serve.

International media

In the past, **international media**—which serve several countries, usually without change—have been limited to newspapers and magazines. Several large American publishers like Time, McGraw-Hill, and Scientific American circulate international editions of their magazines abroad. Usually written in English, they tend to be read by well-educated, upper-income consumers and are therefore good vehicles for advertising high-end, brand-name products. *Reader's Digest,* on the other hand, is distributed to 126 foreign countries and printed in the local language of each. Today, television is also a viable international medium. And we are beginning to see the emergence of *global* media.

Foreign media

Advertisers use **foreign media**—the local media of each country—for large campaigns targeted to consumers or businesses within a single country. Since foreign media cater to their own national audience, advertisers must produce their ads in the language of each country. In countries like Belgium and Switzerland, with more than one official language, ads are produced in each language.

Unlike the U.S., most countries have strong national newspapers that are a good medium for national campaigns. Advertisers also get broad penetration of lower-income markets through radio, which enjoys almost universal ownership. And cinema advertising is a viable alternative to TV in markets with low TV penetration or restricted use of commercial TV.

THE SUPPLIERS IN ADVERTISING

The people and organizations that provide specialized services to the advertising business are called **suppliers.** Without their services it would be impossible to produce the billions of dollars' worth of advertising placed every year.

Although we can't mention them all, a few of the important ones include: art studios, printers, film and video production houses, and research companies.

Art Studios

Art studios design and produce artwork and illustrations for advertisements. They may supplement the work of an agency's art department or even take its place for small agencies. Art studios are usually small organizations with as few as three or four employees. Some, though, are large enough to employ several art directors, graphic designers, layout artists, production artists, and sales reps.

Most studios are owned and managed by an artist or art director who calls on agencies and advertising managers to sell the studio's services, takes projects back to the office to be produced, and then delivers them for the client's approval. The work is very time consuming and requires a talent for organization and management as well as a thorough understanding of computer design.

Printers and Related Specialists

The printers who produce brochures, stationery, business cards, sales promotion materials, and point-of-purchase displays are vital to the advertising business. Ranging from small instant-print shops to large web offset operations, printers employ or contract with highly trained specialists who prepare artwork for reproduction, operate digital scanning machines to make color separations and plates, operate presses and collating machines, and run binderies.

As we discuss in Chapter 11, printers may specialize in offset lithography, rotogravure, letterpress, engraving, or other techniques. Their sales reps must be highly skilled, but they often earn very large commissions.

Film and Video Houses

Few agencies have in-house television production capabilities. Small agencies often work with local TV stations to produce commercials. But the large agencies normally work with independent production houses that specialize in film or video production or both.

Research Companies

Advertisers are concerned about the attitudes of their customers, the size of potential markets, and the acceptability of their products. Agencies want to know what advertising approaches to use, which concepts communicate most efficiently, and how effective past campaigns have been.

The media are concerned with the reading and viewing habits of their audiences, the desired markets of their advertiser customers, and public perceptions toward their own particular medium.

● Advertisers and their agencies often need the help of market research companies like Simmons Market Research Bureau to collect information about products, customers, and competition. In this ad, Simmons promises a commitment to meeting its customers' needs.

Research, therefore, is closely allied to advertising and an important tool of the marketing professional. But most firms do not maintain a fully staffed research department. Instead, they use independent research companies or consultants. Research firms come in all sizes and specialties, and they employ staff statisticians, field interviewers, and computer programmers, as well as analysts with degrees in psychology, sociology, and marketing. We discuss research in Chapter 6.

Summary

The advertising business comprises four main groups: advertisers (clients), agencies, media, and suppliers. It employs a wide range of artists and businesspeople, sales reps and engineers, top executives and clerical personnel.

Ad agencies are independent organizations of creative people and businesspeople who specialize in developing and preparing advertising plans, ads, and other promotional tools on behalf of clients.

Agencies can be classified by the range of services they offer and the types of business they handle. The two basic types are full-service agencies and specialized-service agencies such as creative boutiques and media-buying services. Agencies may specialize in either consumer or business-to-business accounts. The people who work in agencies may be involved in account management, research, account planning, creative services, production, traffic, media, new business, administration, or a host of other activities.

Agencies may be organized into departments based on functional specialties or into groups that work as teams on various accounts. Agencies charge fees or retainers, receive commissions from the media, or mark up outside purchases made on behalf of their clients.

A client's advertising department may be centralized or decentralized. Each structure has advantages and disadvantages. The centralized organization is the most typical and may be structured by product, subfunction of advertising, end user, or geography. Decentralized departments are typical of large, farflung organizations with numerous divisions, subsidiaries, products, countries, regions, or brands.

Some advertising departments take responsibility for ad production, media placement, and other marketing support services. Some firms develop in-house agencies to save money by keeping agency commissions for themselves. However, they risk losing objectivity and creativity.

Most agencies get clients through referral, publicity on successful campaigns, advertising or personal solicitation, or through networking. The client–agency relationship goes through four stages: prerelationship, development, maintenance, and termination. Numerous factors affect the relationship, including chemistry, communication, conduct, and changes.

The media of advertising include the traditional mass media of print, electronic, and out-of-home and more specialized channels such as direct mail, digital interactive media, and specialty advertising.

Print media refers to magazines and newspapers as well as directories, Yellow Pages, school yearbooks, and special-event programs. Electronic media includes radio, television, and cable TV. Out-of-home refers to billboard and transit advertising. Direct-mail advertising is the most expensive medium on a cost-per-exposure basis but also typically the most effective at generating inquiries or responses. Interactive media let customers participate, turning advertising from a monolog to a dialog.

In foreign markets, advertisers are faced with different media mixes, different legal constraints, and different economies of advertising.

The suppliers in advertising are all the people and organizations that assist in the business. Examples are art studios, printers, photoengravers, film and video houses, talent agencies, research firms, and consultants.

Questions for Review and Discussion

1. What roles do the major organizations involved in the advertising business perform?

2. What services might a modern full-service advertising agency offer a large business-to-business advertiser?

3. What are the most important things an advertiser should consider when selecting an agency?

4. How does an agency make money? What is the best way to compensate an agency? Explain your answer.

5. If you owned an ad agency, what would you do to attract new business? Be specific.

6. What are the advantages and disadvantages of an in-house agency?

7. What are the major influences on the client–agency relationship? What can clients and agencies do to maintain a good relationship?

8. What structure should international advertisers use to get the best creativity for their target markets?

9. What is meant by the term *interactive media?* Give some examples.

10. If you were planning to advertise your brand of computers in Europe, would you likely use foreign or international media? Why?

CRAFTING MARKETING AND ADVERTISING STRATEGIES

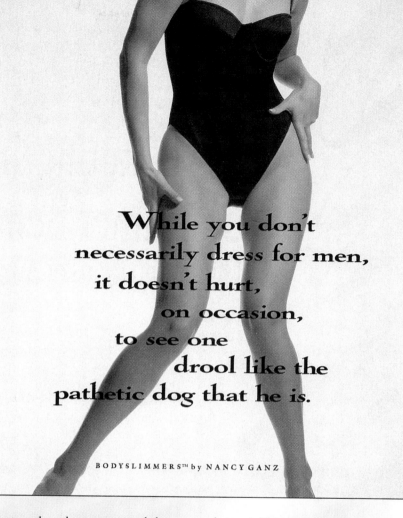

While you don't necessarily dress for men, it doesn't hurt, on occasion, to see one drool like the pathetic dog that he is.

BODYSLIMMERS™ by NANCY GANZ

The success of any business depends on its ability to attract customers willing and able to buy its products and services. To do this, a business must locate, understand, and communicate with potential customers. Part II examines the marketing process, the nature of consumers, the relationship between products and market groups, and the research and planning processes that make for marketing and advertising success. • **Chapter 4,** "Marketing and Consumer Behavior: The Foundations of Advertising," describes products and markets and how advertisers use the marketing process to create effective advertising. The chapter presents the consumer as an acceptor or rejector of products and discusses how the consumer's complex decision-making process affects the design of advertising. • **Chapter 5,** "Using Marketing and Advertising to Link Products to Markets," discusses market segments, the aggregation of segments, and the influence of target marketing on a product company. It presents the elements of the marketing mix and discus-

ses how advertisers use them to understand and improve a product concept. • **Chapter 6,** "Marketing and Advertising Research: Inputs to the Planning Process," points out the value of research in improving marketing and advertising effectiveness. It describes how to organize and gather data and discusses the objectives and techniques of concept testing, pretesting, and post-testing. • **Chapter 7,** "Marketing and Advertising Planning: Top-Down, Bottom-Up, and IMC," details the creation of marketing and advertising plans, particularly setting realistic objectives and developing creative strategies to achieve them. The chapter also presents methods for allocating resources. • **Chapter 8,** "Planning Media Strategy: Finding Links to the Market," introduces the media plan and the changing role of media planners today. It discusses how target audiences are determined and objectives are established for reaching them. The chapter explains the elements of media strategy, how to select specific media vehicles, and how to schedule their use.

4

Marketing and Consumer Behavior
The Foundations of Advertising

Objective: To highlight the significance of the marketing function in business and to define the importance of advertising and other marketing communications tools that present the company and its products to the market. The successful advertising practitioner must understand the relationship between marketing and the way consumers behave. It is that relationship that ideally shapes advertising.

After studying this chapter, you will be able to:

- Define marketing and explain its importance to advertisers.

- Discuss the concept of product utility and the relationship of utility to consumer needs.

- Identify the key participants in the marketing process.

- Outline the consumer perception process and explain why "perception is everything."

- Discuss the various influences on consumer behavior.

- Explain how advertisers deal with cognitive dissonance.

*T*he young audience had come to the screening of a yet-to-be released film. They had no idea of the title or the cast until the National Research Group (NRG) representative announced, "Tonight, we will be showing you a work in progress, Arnold Schwarzenegger's *Last Action Hero.*" They went wild, stomping their feet and applauding.

From the beginning, there had been a giddiness at Columbia Pictures—it had the world's biggest star, an A-list director, and a set of top screenwriters. Along with an experienced, well-funded promotional team, it also had one of the world's most visible promoters, Arnold Schwarzenegger. His last four films had grossed over a billion dollars worldwide.

"When you have Arnold, you have Arnold plus," states Sid Ganis, the head of marketing and distribution for Sony Pictures Entertainment. "Arnold, plus his total understanding of his public."

The *Last Action Hero* represented Schwarzenegger's adjustment to public sentiment. Sensitive to the country's growing antiviolence mood, Schwarzenegger, father of two, was redesigning his Terminator image to a kinder, gentler protagonist—Jack Slater, a hero for a new era. Sony executives pointed to a recent study revealing that the demand for quality family entertainment was high and that a movie with a PG-13 rating would be three times more likely to earn $100 million than an R-rated film. They were optimistic about this blend of political correctness and sound business logic.

Early on, Schwarzenegger, who served as the film's executive producer and had the authority to approve every major decision, said, "I like the idea of putting a new spin on it every month until the movie comes out. To have the rocket out there, then the ride simulator. It makes it look like we are dealing here with a monster movie, a giant monster. And then we will announce the Burger King tie-in."

Unfortunately, however, the screening marked the beginning of the end. The audience—filled with anticipation—saw little more than an editor's first assemblage. The crude film was long, two hours and 18 minutes, and the temporary sound dub made the dialog almost incomprehensible. One scene even featured Arnold falling from a building without the background dubbed over the blue screen behind him. As Schwarzenegger put it, "The movie was shown in the roughest form I've ever seen a movie

screened." The film's director, John McTiernan *(Predator, Die Hard, The Hunt for Red October),* later revealed, "It was literally in a state that you don't even show studio executives." The worry was real—only 45 review cards were turned in, a number too low to record.

Once Hollywood insiders discovered that there were no results from the audience reviews, even the smallest error became lethal evidence of the film's "bad karma." The cancellation of the much-touted NASA rocket launch, with the film's title and Schwarzenegger's name emblazoned on the payload, publicized the downturn. And Sony's inability to install its new digital sound system into more than a handful of theaters fueled the already growing negative press. Columbia's ShoWest reel for exhibitors met with mixed reaction, and the TV spots and trailers left some viewers confused about what type of movie *Last Action Hero* really was. Freelance writer Jeffrey Wells, in an article for the *Los Angeles Times* Sunday Calendar, stated that, according to "actors, directors, film industry executives, social workers, body builders, and dentists," the screening had been a disaster.[1] His claim was vehemently denied by Columbia executives, who threatened to cancel all of Columbia's reported $5 million in advertising with the paper.

While executives wrestled with the media behind the scenes, Schwarzenegger charmed his way through the talk shows. In a last-ditch effort, Sony's Ganis changed the TV and newspaper ads from the original low violence, PG-13 approach to featuring Schwarzenegger delivering Terminator-like damage to the bad guys.

In the end, however, the film flopped big time. Costing an estimated $100 million—with an additional $30 million in marketing costs—it grossed a dismal $15 million in its first weekend and only $8 million the next. By contrast, *Jurassic Park,* which had just opened, earned $50 million in its first weekend alone!

What went wrong? Was it the advertising?

Not really. Even the best advertising cannot overcome a poorly conceived and poorly marketed product. Mark Canton, chair of Columbia Pictures, now concedes that simply having Arnold Schwarzenegger in a film does not make it a blockbuster. And Schwarzenegger acknowledges that the movie was not strong enough to overcome the bad press and bad word of mouth.

The film's poor conception rests on a failure to understand the nature of the people who make up various market segments.

As Schwarzenegger said, "I learned that in my case, if you don't give the people a very clear comedy or a very clear action movie, somehow the two don't mix together. If the kids see PG-13, they say, 'Well, I've heard you talk about that, Arnold, you want to tone down the violence. I'm not interested in that—I want to see limbs come off and bodies flying around.' The hard-core audience that goes for the $25 million opening, they stayed away to some degree."[2] ●

The Assumption Syndrome

The *Last Action Hero* story offers good lessons. To succeed in business, a company's top managers cannot assume anything about their market. Rather, they have to respect the importance of marketing and know how to interpret the data uncovered by their research people. They must know who their customers are, and they must listen and respond to them. Companies that suffer from the assumption syndrome court failure and end up as their own "last action heroes."

The story demonstrates another important principle: even superior advertising can't save a product that isn't marketed correctly. Unfortunately, advertising all too often becomes the scapegoat for management's marketing misfires.

THE IMPORTANCE OF MARKETING TO ADVERTISING

The key to company prosperity is the ability to attract and keep customers who are willing and able to pay for the firm's goods and services. This means being able to locate prospective customers—where they live, work, and play—and then being able to understand and communicate with them.

All advertisers face a perennial challenge: how to present their products, services, and ideas effectively through the media to buyers. To do this, they must comprehend the important relationship between the product and the marketplace. This relationship is the province of marketing. So, to more fully appreciate the role of advertising, we begin by examining the task of marketing in business.

Every business organization performs a number of diverse activities. Management typically classifies these activities into three broad functional divisions:

- Operations (production/manufacturing).
- Administration/finance.
- Marketing.

Students who major in business study a variety of subjects related to one or all of these general functions. For instance, courses in purchasing, quality control, and manufacturing relate to the operations function. Courses in accounting, industrial relations, and business law relate to the administration/finance area. And while many students study advertising in a school of journalism or communications, advertising is actually a specialty within the broad domain of marketing. Other disciplines in the field include market research, transportation and distribution, selling, and promotion management.

Unfortunately, marketing's role is often misunderstood and occasionally overlooked. For example, everybody knows that a business can't survive without proper financing. And many point out that without production, there are no products to sell. But how does a company know what products or services to produce? Or whom to distribute them to, or through what channels? That's where marketing comes in.

Businesspeople use marketing research to determine if a demand even exists for a proposed product. Then, to obtain financing for the endeavor, an entrepreneur must create a *marketing plan* acceptable to financing sources. In short, as important as finance and production are, marketing is still the *only* business function whose primary role is to attract revenues. And without revenue, a company cannot recover its initial investment or earn profits. Advertising helps the organization achieve its marketing goals. So do marketing research, sales, product distribution, and inventory control. These marketing specialties also have an impact on a company's advertising. Thus, an

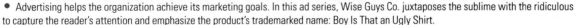

● Advertising helps the organization achieve its marketing goals. In this ad series, Wise Guys Co. juxtaposes the sublime with the ridiculous to capture the reader's attention and emphasize the product's trademarked name: Boy Is That an Ugly Shirt.

advertising specialist must have a broad understanding of the whole marketing environment in which advertising operates.

In the end, customers are people. So advertising professionals must understand how people act and think—and why they buy what they buy. This is the province of another marketing specialty, **consumer behavior.** Understanding consumer buying behavior helps advertisers bring products into the collective consciousness of prospective customers.

This chapter—in fact, this whole unit—defines and outlines marketing to clarify advertising's proper role in the marketing function and to introduce the human factors that ultimately shape advertising. As we shall see, the relationship between advertising and marketing is critical.

✳ WHAT IS MARKETING?

Over the years, marketing has evolved based on the supply of and demand for products. Because we need to understand marketing as it relates to *advertising,* we define the term as follows:

> **Marketing** is the process of planning and executing the conception, pricing, promotion, and distribution of ideas, goods, and services to create exchanges that satisfy the perceived needs, wants, and objectives of individuals and organizations.[3]

The first important element in this definition is that marketing is a *process*—a sequential series of actions or methods. This process includes developing products, pricing them strategically, promoting them through marketing communications, and making them available to customers through a distribution network. In business, the ultimate goal of the marketing process is to earn a profit for the firm by uniting a product or service with customers who need or want it. And advertising informs, persuades, and reminds groups of customers, or markets, about the need-satisfying value of the firm's goods and services. As Chapter 17 explains, even nonprofit organizations use the marketing concept to develop services that satisfy their constituents' needs.

Customer Needs and Product Utility

The second important element in our definition of marketing is the special relationship between a customer's *needs* and a product's *need-satisfying potential,* known as the product's **utility.** Utility is the product's ability to satisfy both functional needs and symbolic (or psychological) wants.[4] Advertising communicates this utility. Thus, some ads promote how well a product works; others tout glamour, sex appeal, or status. Ad Lab 4–A discusses the relationship between needs and utility.

Marketers use research to discover what needs and wants exist in the marketplace and to define a product's general characteristics in the light of economic, social, and political trends. The goal is to use this information for **product shaping**—designing

Ad Lab 4-A   Understanding Needs and Utility

Superior quality will not close a sale by itself. Marketing people must make the product available and promote its advantages, whether it's a graphite tennis racket, a high-performance sports car, or even the prompt, friendly service of a bank.

A key fact in any product's success is that it must satisfy consumers' needs. The capability to satisfy those needs is called *utility*. Five types of *functional utility* are important to consumers: utility of *form, task, possession, time,* and *place*. A product may provide *psychic utility* as well as functional utility.

Companies create *form utility* whenever they produce a tangible good, like a bicycle. They provide *task utility* by performing a task for others. However, merely producing a bicycle—or repairing it—doesn't guarantee consumer satisfaction. Consumers must want the bicycle or require the repair, or no need is satisfied and no utility occurs.

Thus, marketing decisions should guide the production, or operations, side of business too.

Even when a company provides form or task utility, marketers must consider how consumers can take *possession* of the product. This includes distribution, pricing strategies, shelf availability, purchase agreements, delivery, and the like. Money is typically exchanged for *possession utility*. An antique bicycle on display, but not for sale, lacks possession utility because the customer cannot purchase it.

Providing the consumer with the product when he or she wants it is known as *time utility*. Having an ample supply of jam, cars, or bank tellers on hand when the consumer has the need is thus another marketing requirement.

Place utility—having the product available where the customer can get it—is also vital to business success. Customers won't travel very far out of their way to get bicycles or cars. They're

even less likely to travel long distances for everyday needs. That's why banks have branches. And that's why 24-hour convenience markets, which sell gasoline and basic food items, are so popular.

Finally, consumers gain *psychic utility* when a product offers symbolic or psychological need satisfaction such as status or sex appeal. Psychic utility is usually achieved through product promotion (advertising) and may fulfill esteem and self-actualization needs.

Whether it be psychic utility or the functional utilities of form, task, possession, time, and place, product utility is an essential component of marketing success.

Laboratory Application

Select an ad from a weekly newsmagazine and describe in detail what it offers in terms of psychic utility and the functional utilities of form, task, possession, time, and place.

products, through manufacturing, repackaging, or advertising, to satisfy more fully the customer's needs and wants. In England, for example, automakers noted that more women were buying cars. In fact, in 1994, they bought 55 percent of all small cars. Research revealed that women see their cars as a means of independence and status. So Ford launched a soft-focus campaign in women's magazines highlighting features such as superior seat belts and chip-resistant paint. Peugeot ran a campaign starring two sassy women who drive away, in a *Thelma and Louise* parody, to escape their boring lives and two-timing boyfriends.[5]

Businesspeople all too often give the marketing process short shrift. Some companies introduce a product without a clear idea of its utility to the customer, hoping advertising will move the product off the shelf. As Columbia Pictures found out, the consequences of such a short-sighted policy can be severe.

• One of a series of ads aimed at women for GMC's Jimmy truck. In this ad, a businesswoman forgets her coffee cup on the roof of her Jimmy and discovers the benefits of the truck's smooth ride. Another ad features the ease of entry for skirt-wearing women.

"Coffee Cup" : 30 seconds
VO: Along with all the strengths of a GMC truck. The new Jimmy also offers a premium smooth suspension.

No shakes. No jolts. It might just be the perfect way to start your day.

The all-new Jimmy. Drive it at your GMC truck dealer.

Perception, Exchanges, and Satisfaction

Finally, marketing aims "to create exchanges that satisfy the perceived needs, wants, and objectives of individuals and organizations." Three important concepts here are *perception, exchanges,* and *satisfaction.*

Perception is everything

Marketing is concerned with two levels of perception: the perception of the product or service, and the perception of needs, wants, and objectives.

In other words, advertisers must first develop customers' perception of the *product* itself (awareness, attitude, interest) and then a perception of the product's *value* in satisfying a want or need (utility). The greater the customer's need, the greater the potential value or utility of the need-satisfying product. By using mood lighting or appropriate music, for example, a TV commercial might capture customers' attention and stimulate their emotions toward the goal of need or want fulfillment. If customers are aware of the product and its value, and if they decide to satisfy the particular want or need the product addresses, they are more likely to act.[6]

Since it is so important to advertisers, we discuss individual perception more fully later in this chapter.

Exchanges: The purpose of marketing and advertising

Now consider the concept of **exchange,** in which one thing of value is traded for another. Any business transaction in which one person sells something to someone else is an exchange. Advertising facilitates exchanges by making people aware of the availability of products and their selection alternatives. In the case of *direct-response advertising,* it may even close the sale.

People engaging in a business exchange often feel apprehensive. They worry that the exchange may not be equal, even when it is truly fair. The perception of inequity is more likely if the customer has little knowledge of the product. In this case, the more knowledgeable party (the seller) must reassure the buyer—perhaps through advertising—that an equal exchange is possible. If the seller can provide the information and inspiration the buyer seeks, the two may agree that a *perceived equal-value exchange* exists. Without this perception, though, an exchange is unlikely. If people don't believe the *Last Action Hero* is worth the $7 ticket, they won't attend—no matter how much is spent on advertising.

Satisfaction: The goal of the customer

Even after an exchange occurs, *satisfaction* remains an issue. Satisfaction must occur every time customers use the product, or they won't think they got an equal-value exchange. Satisfaction leads to more exchanges—satisfied customers create more sales. Therefore, satisfaction should be the goal of any sophisticated marketer.

Advertising *reinforces* satisfaction by reminding customers why they bought the product, helping them defend the purchase against skepticism, and enabling them to persuade other prospects to buy it. If a product performs poorly, the negative effect will be even more far-reaching. In fact, good advertising for a poor product will quickly ruin a manufacturer. The better the advertising, the more people will try the product once. And the more who try an unsatisfactory product, the more who will reject it—and tell their friends.

In summary, marketing is the process companies use to make a profit by satisfying their customers' needs and desires.

People's needs and wants change daily, and marketers constantly advertise a plethora of products for customer attention and interest. This makes the marketing process very dynamic. At times, it seems like everybody is searching for an exchange. At other

• Promotion for the movie *Last Action Hero* began before the film was completed. Grandiose publicity techniques included emblazoning the film's name on a rocket scheduled for an actual launch and erecting this 50-foot inflatable of the film's star, Arnold Schwarzenegger, in Times Square.

THE KEY PARTICIPANTS IN THE MARKETING PROCESS

● Customers must be satisfied with the products and services they buy. Advertising reinforces customer satisfaction by reminding them why they bought the product in the first place. Photographic manipulation in this ad reminds customers that Wrangler's fade-resistant Checotah shirts are a good value.

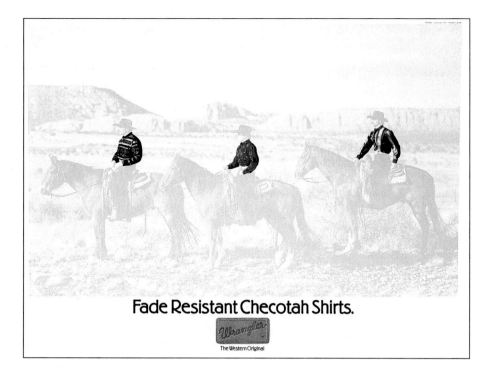

Fade Resistant Checotah Shirts.

The Western Original

times, nobody is. Marketing exchanges depend on three types of participants: *customers, markets* (groups of customers), and *marketers.*

Customers

Customers are the people or organizations who consume products and services. They fall into three general categories: *current customers, prospective customers,* and *centers of influence.*

Current customers have already bought something from a business; in fact, they may buy it regularly. One way to measure a business's success is by calculating the number of current customers it has and their repeat purchases. **Prospective customers** are people about to make an exchange or considering it. **Centers of influence** are customers, prospective customers, or opinion leaders whose opinions and actions others respect. A center of influence is often the link to many prospective customers.

Markets

The second participant in the marketing process is the market, which is simply a group of current and prospective customers who share a common interest, need, or desire, who can use the specific product or service, and who are willing to pay for it.[7] As we discuss more fully in Chapter 5, a market rarely includes everybody. Companies advertise to four broad classifications of markets:

1. **Consumer markets** include people who buy products and services for their own use. Both Nissan and Ford, for example, aim at the consumer market. But they cater to different groups within that market. They advertise some models to single women; others to upscale young families; and still others to retired people. Chapter 5 discusses ways to categorize consumer segments.
2. **Business markets** are composed of organizations that buy natural resources, component products, and services that they resell, use to conduct their business, or use to manufacture another product. There are two subtypes of business markets: reseller markets and industrial markets.

我們的印刷廠

爲 您

擴 展 了

通往世界的路

If you can read the headline above, you don't need the Ringier International Print Group. But if you're like most publishers, chances are it looks a little foreign.

Which is why communication is a major barrier to printing overseas. And why it's just one of the obstacles our team of U.S. based representatives will help you overcome—

from distribution and scheduling to currency conversion. Linking you to our resources on all three key business continents. And helping you take your publication or catalog around the world without leaving home.

You won't find another printer who offers international capabilities with complete domestic accountability.

We'd like to translate this headline for you. And translate all your international printing needs. So call 1-800-RINGIER. Outside the U.S., call 01-708-285-6000.

You'll see we speak your language.

Ringier America
International Print Group
Europe • USA • Asia

Reseller markets buy products to resell them. Ford, for example, aims a portion of its marketing activities at its dealers. Similarly, Sunkist first needs to convince food wholesalers and retail grocers to carry its brand of fruits, or they will never be sold to consumers. Reseller markets, therefore, are extremely important to most companies, even though most consumers are unaware of the marketing or advertising activities aimed at them.

Industrial markets include more than 13 million firms that buy products used to produce other goods and services.[8] Manufacturers of plant equipment and machinery advertise to industrial markets, as do office suppliers, computer companies, and telephone companies. Chapter 5 categorizes types of industrial markets by such factors as their industry segment, geographic location, or size.

3. **Government markets** buy products for municipal, state, federal, and other government activities. Some firms are immensely successful selling only to government markets. They advertise post office vehicles, police and military weapons, and tax collector office equipment in trade magazines read by government buyers.

4. **International** (or **global**) **markets** include any of the other three markets located in foreign countries. Every country has consumers, resellers, industries, and governments. So what's the difference between the foreign market and the domestic U.S. or Canadian market for the same product? Environment. The environment in France differs from that in Japan. The environment in Brazil differs from that in Saudi Arabia. And sometimes, as in the case of Switzerland, environments even vary widely within a single country. Targeting markets across national boundaries presents interesting challenges—and important opportunities—for contemporary advertisers, so we deal with this subject wherever applicable throughout this book.

● Marketers include every person or organization that has products, services, or ideas to sell. This Levis *(not Levi's!)* ad by a Brussels agency is one of a colorful series that advertises its pastel paints for home decorating. The caption says: *Our pastel shades come in all sorts of materials—here, in matte.*

Nos pastels existent dans toutes les matières – ici, en mat.

levis

Marketers

The third participant in the marketing process, **marketers,** includes every person or organization that has products, services, or ideas to sell. Manufacturers market consumer and business products. Farmers market wheat; doctors market medical services; banks market financial products; and political organizations market philosophies and candidates. To be successful, marketers must know their markets intimately—*before* they start advertising.

THE IMPORTANCE OF KNOWING THE CONSUMER

Take a look at your friends in class, or the people you work with. How well do you know them? Could you describe their lifestyles and the kinds of products they prefer? Do they typically eat out or cook for themselves? Do they ski? Play tennis? If so, what brands of equipment do they buy? Do you know which radio stations they listen to? What TV programs? Do they read the daily newspaper? If you wanted to advertise a new soft drink to these people, what type of appeal would you use? What media?

Advertisers spend a lot of money to keep individuals and groups of individuals (markets) interested in their products. To succeed, they need to understand what makes potential customers behave the way they do. The advertiser's goal is to get enough relevant market data to develop accurate profiles of buyers—to find the common ground (and symbols) for communication. This involves the study of **consumer behavior:** the mental and emotional processes and the physical activities of people who purchase and use goods and services to satisfy particular needs and wants.[9] The behavior of **organizational buyers**—the people who purchase products and services for use in business and government—is also very important. We examine this aspect of buying behavior in Chapter 5.

CONSUMER BEHAVIOR FROM THE ADVERTISER'S PERSPECTIVE

Social scientists develop many theories of consumer behavior to explain the process involved in making a purchase decision. Let's look at this information from the viewpoint of the advertiser.

Advertising's primary mission is to reach prospective customers and influence their awareness, attitudes, and buying behavior. To do this, an advertiser must make the marketing communications process, which we discussed in Chapter 1, work very efficiently.

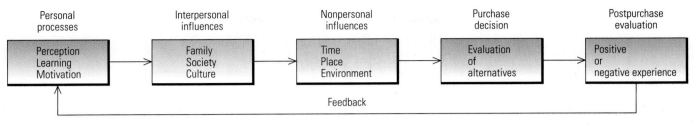

Exhibit • 4–1
The basic consumer decision process comprises a set of fundamental steps that the consumer experiences during and after the purchase process. Advertising can affect the consumer's attitude at any point in this process. For the complete model of the process, see Exhibit 4–6 at the end of this chapter.

The moment a medium delivers an advertising message to us, our mental computer runs a rapid evaluation program called the **consumer decision-making process.** This involves a series of subprocesses that are all affected by many influences. The conceptual model in Exhibit 4–1 presents the fundamental building blocks in the consumer decision-making process.

Note in the first box that three **personal processes** govern the way we discern raw data *(stimuli)* and translate them into feelings, thoughts, beliefs, and actions. These are the *perception,* the *learning,* and the *motivation processes.*

Second, our mental processes and behavior are affected by two sets of influences. **Interpersonal influences** include our *family, society,* and *culture.* **Nonpersonal influences**—factors often outside the consumer's control—include *time, place,* and *environment.* These influences further affect the personal processes of perception, learning, and motivation.

After dealing with these processes and influences, we face the pivotal decision—to buy or not to buy. But taking that final step typically requires yet another process, the **evaluation of alternatives,** in which we choose brands, sizes, styles, and colors. If we do decide to buy, our **postpurchase evaluation** will dramatically affect all our subsequent purchases.

Like the marketing communications process, the decision-making process is circular in nature. The advertiser who understands this process can develop messages more likely to reach and make sense to consumers.

Assume you are the advertising manager launching a new beverage brand for athletes and sports participants. We'll call it MonsterMalt. What's your first objective?

The first task in promoting any new product is to create awareness *(perception)* that the product exists. The second is to provide enough information *(learning)* about the product for prospective customers to make an informed decision. Finally, you want your advertising to be persuasive enough to stimulate customers' desire *(motivation)* to satisfy their needs and wants by trying the product. If they find MonsterMalt satisfying, they likely will continue to purchase it. These three personal processes of consumer behavior—perception, learning, and motivation—are extremely important to advertisers. By studying them, advertisers can better evaluate how people perceive their messages.

PERSONAL PROCESSES IN CONSUMER BEHAVIOR

The Consumer Perception Process

As we mentioned earlier, perception is everything. It guides everything we do, from the activities we enjoy to the people we associate with to the products we buy. How a consumer perceives each of the different brands in a category determines which ones he or she uses.[10] The perception challenge, therefore, is the first and greatest hurdle advertisers must cross. Some marketers spend millions of dollars on national advertising, sales promotion, point-of-purchase displays, and other marketing communications only to discover that many consumers don't remember the product or the promotion. The average adult is exposed to over 1,500 ads every single day but notices only a

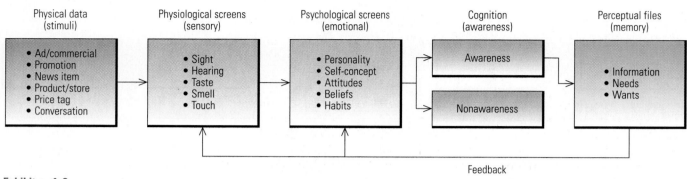

Physical data (stimuli)	Physiological screens (sensory)	Psychological screens (emotional)	Cognition (awareness)	Perceptual files (memory)
• Ad/commercial • Promotion • News item • Product/store • Price tag • Conversation	• Sight • Hearing • Taste • Smell • Touch	• Personality • Self-concept • Attitudes • Beliefs • Habits	Awareness Nonawareness	• Information • Needs • Wants

Feedback

Exhibit • 4–2
The model of the consumer perception process portrays how consumers perceive, accept, and remember an ad or other stimulus to buy.

handful and remembers even fewer.[11] How does this happen? The answer lies in the principle of perception.

Perception is the personalized way we sense, interpret, and comprehend stimuli. This definition suggests several key elements for understanding the consumer perception process, as shown in Exhibit 4–2.

Stimulus

A **stimulus** is the physical data we receive through our senses. When we look at a new car, we receive a number of stimuli. We might note the color of the paint, the smell of the leather, the purr of the engine. When we look at a theater ad in the newspaper, we see a collection of type, art, and photography arranged in a way that we interpret as an ad. That's the stimulus. So, for our purposes, assume that a stimulus is any ad, commercial, or promotion that confronts us.

Advertising stimuli can appear in a variety of forms: a window display at a local department store, the brightly colored labels on cans of Campbell's tomato soup, or even

Any ad, commercial, or promotion is a stimulus. The physical data in an ad—type, art, photography—can create a positive reaction to the product. This ad for Mary J Blige's new album features the personal touch of the star's autograph, complementing the direct invitation that seems to emanate from the photograph.

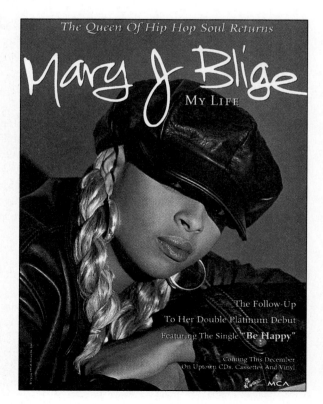

the red price tag on a pair of skis at the Sport Chalet. These objects are all physical in nature; they stimulate our senses—with varying degrees of intensity—in ways that can be measured.

Perceptual screens

The second key element in perception is the personalized way of sensing and interpreting the data—which brings us to *screens*. Before any data can be perceived, they must first penetrate a set of **perceptual screens,** the subconscious filters that shield us from unwanted messages. There are two types of screens, *physiological* and *psychological.*

The **physiological screens** comprise the five senses—sight, hearing, touch, taste, and smell. They detect the incoming data and measure the dimension and intensity of the physical stimuli. A sight-impaired person can't read an ad in *Sports Illustrated.* And if the type in a movie ad is too small for the average reader, it won't be read, and perception will suffer. Similarly, if the music in a TV commercial for a furniture store is not congruent with the message, the viewer may tune out, change channels, or even turn off the TV. The advertiser's message is effectively screened out when the viewer can't interpret it; perception does not occur, and the furniture goes unsold.[12]

We are limited not only by the physical capacity of our senses but also by our feelings and interests. Each consumer uses **psychological screens** to evaluate, filter, and personalize information according to subjective emotional standards. These screens evaluate data based on innate factors, such as the consumer's personality and instinctive human needs, and learned factors, such as self-concept, interests, attitudes, beliefs, past experience, and lifestyle. They help consumers summarize unwieldy or complex data. For example, perceptual screens help us accept or reject symbolic ideas such as the commercial for Nestlé's Aero brand candy bar in which a woman basks in a bathtub of liquid chocolate. The commercial is targeted to women who seek a balance between work and self-indulgence.[13]

After extensive consumer research, Bally's Health & Tennis determined that the perfectly chiseled body, glorified by health club advertising of the 80s and exemplified by such icons as Cher, Victoria Principal, and Don Johnson, wasn't penetrating the psychological screens of its 4.5 million members. That premise no longer fit their **self-concept**—the image we have of who we are and who we want to be. In a major strategy shift, Bally's now relies on customers like Beth from Costa Mesa, California, who is seen rock climbing in a TV commercial while telling viewers, "I think I climb because I'm afraid of heights. . . . There is nothing better than being able to conquer that fear. That's why I work out at Bally's, so I can do more on the rocks." The tagline: "If you can get here [Bally's], you can get there [a mountaintop]."

As the Bally's example shows, advertisers face a major problem dealing with consumers' perceptual screens. As overcommunicated consumers, we unconsciously

BE COMFORTABLE WITH WHO YOU ARE.

Hush Puppies

● Research has shown that consumers screen out commercial messages that conflict with their needs, desires, and self-images. In this ad, Wolverine Worldwide encourages prospective customers to be comfortable with their own self-concepts—and in Hush Puppies.

screen out or modify many of the sensations that bombard us, rejecting those that conflict with our previous experiences, needs, desires, attitudes, and beliefs.[14] We simply focus on some things and ignore others. This is called **selective perception.** Hence, Panasonic may run excellent ads in the daily newspaper, but they won't penetrate the psychological screens of consumers who don't need new camcorders. Later these people won't even remember seeing the ads.

Cognition

The third key element in perception is comprehending the stimulus, or **cognition.** Once we detect the stimulus and allow it through our perceptive screens, we can comprehend and accept it. Now perception has occurred, and the stimulus reaches the consumer's reality zone.

But each of us has his or her own reality. For example, you may consider the tacos advertised by Taco Bell to be "Mexican" food. That perception is your reality. But someone from Mexico might tell you that a fast-food taco bears little resemblance to an authentic Mexican taco. That person's reality, based on another perception, is considerably different. Advertisers thus seek commonly shared perceptions of reality as a basis for their advertising messages.

Mental files

The mind is like a memory bank, and the stored memories in our minds are called the **mental** (or perceptual) **files.**

In today's highly communicative society, stimuli bombard our senses, and information crowds our mental files. To cope with the complexity of stimuli like advertising, we rank products and other data in our files by importance, price, quality, features, or a host of other descriptors. Consumers can rarely hold more than seven brand names in any one file—more often only one or two. The remainder either get discarded to some other file category or rejected altogether.[15] How many brands of running shoes can you name, for example?

Because of our limited memory, we resist opening new mental files, and we avoid accepting new information inconsistent with what is already filed. The experience consumers receive from using a brand solidifies their perceptions of it. These fixed perceptions can rarely be changed through advertising alone.[16] But once a new perception does enter our mental files, the information alters the database on which our psychological screens feed.

• Advertisers must deal with consumers' perceptions of their products, which might not be based in reality. London Fog deals with a perception problem in this ad by reminding potential customers that it makes high-fashion women's coats in addition to its well-known rain gear for men.

You were expecting some middle-aged business guy in a khaki raincoat?

The New Generation of London Fog LONDON FOG

Since perceptual screens are such a major challenge to advertisers, it's important to understand what's in the consumer's mental files and, if possible, modify them in favor of the advertiser's product. That brings us to the second process in consumer behavior—*learning*.

The Consumer Learning Process

Each time we file a new perception in our minds it's a learning process. Like perception, learning works off the mental files and at the same time contributes to them. Learning produces our habits and skills. It also contributes to the development of interests, attitudes, beliefs, preferences, prejudices, emotions, and standards of conduct—all of which affect our perceptual screens and our eventual purchase decisions.

Learning is a relatively permanent change in thought process or behavior that occurs as a result of reinforced experience. Advertisers classify most learning theories into two broad categories—*cognitive theory* and *conditioning theory*—depending on the level of consumer involvement in making a purchase. **Cognitive theory** views learning as a mental process of memory, thinking, and the rational application of knowledge to practical problems. This may be the way people evaluate a complex purchase such as insurance, stocks and bonds, or business products. **Conditioning theory** (also called *stimulus-response theory*) treats learning as a trial-and-error process. A stimulus triggers the consumer's need or want, and this creates the drive to respond. If the consumer's response reduces the drive, then satisfaction occurs, and the response is rewarded or reinforced. That produces repeat behavior the next time the drive is aroused, showing that learning has taken place. Exhibit 4–3 shows simple diagrams of these two theories.

Conditioning theory is more applicable to the simple, basic purchases consumers make every day: soap, cereal, toothpaste, paper towels. And it is here that *reinforcement advertising* plays its most important role—along with superior product performance and good service. If learning is reinforced enough and repeat behavior is produced, a purchasing habit may result.

What if the purchase turns out to be unsatisfactory? Learning still takes place, but with a different result. John O'Toole, former chair of Foote, Cone & Belding and president of the American Association of Advertising Agencies, said, "The mightiest weapon consumers have, and the one manufacturers fear most, is their refusal to repurchase. Advertising is powerful in that it can get them to buy a product once. But if it doesn't please them, the heaviest media budget in the world won't get them to buy again."[17]

Repetition is important to learning. Just as a student prepares for an exam by repeating key information to memorize it, an advertiser must repeat key information to prospective and current customers so they remember the product's name and its benefits. Repeat messages penetrate customers' perceptual screens by rekindling memories of key information from prior ads. Quebec-based Cossette Communications-Marketing used *pairs* of billboards for the Provigo grocery store chain. Each featured a strong visual element similar to the other, and the boards were positioned to be seen in succession. The repetition proved highly successful, producing $100 million in sales in just six months.

Learning produces attitudes and interest

An **attitude** is our acquired mental position regarding some idea or object. It is the positive or negative evaluations, feelings, or action tendencies that we learn and cling to. To advertisers, gaining positive consumer attitudes is critical to success. Attitudes must be either capitalized on or changed. New ads for Grey Poupon mustard, for example, suggest readers "Poupon the potato salad" and "class up the cold cuts." The campaign is aimed at changing the attitude of consumers who view Poupon as a premium brand, reserving it for special occasions.[18]

For mature brands in categories with familiar, frequently purchased products, *brand interest* is even more critical for motivating action. **Brand interest** is an individual's openness or curiosity about a brand.[19] Enjoyable, entertaining advertising can en-

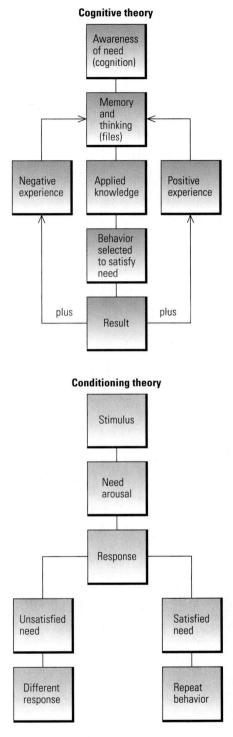

Exhibit • 4–3

Cognitive theory views learning as a mental process; conditioning theory treats learning as a trial-and-error process.

• Repeated messages containing key product information help to break through customers' perceptual screens. This ad doesn't need words to remind customers of Volvo's emphasis on product safety and sturdy construction.

hance interest in the brand and reduce the variety-seeking tendencies of consumers who become bored with using the same old product.[20]

Learning leads to habits and brand loyalty

Attitude is the mental side and habit the behavioral side of the same coin. **Habit**—the acquired behavior pattern that becomes nearly or completely involuntary—is the natural extension of learning. We really are creatures of habit.

Most consumer behavior is habitual for three reasons—it's safe, simple, and essential. First, regardless of how we learned to make our purchase decision (through either a cognitive or conditioning process), if we discover a quality product, brand, or service, we feel *safe* repurchasing it through habit.

Second, habit is *simple*. To consider alternatives we must evaluate, compare, and then decide. This is difficult, time-consuming, and risky.[21]

Finally, because habit is both safe and easy, we rely on it for daily living. Imagine rethinking every purchase decision you make. It would be virtually impossible, not to mention impractical.

The major objective of all brand marketers is to produce *brand loyalty,* a direct result of the habit of repurchasing and the reinforcement of continuous advertising. **Brand loyalty** is the consumer's conscious or unconscious decision—expressed through intention or behavior—to repurchase a brand continually.[22] It occurs because

• Some ads are calculated to create brand interest in customers. Lumex uses an upbeat approach to advertise its Specialty Seating line of chairs. You have to read the small print to realize Lumex products are designed for patients who need special positioning for comfort and support.

the consumer *perceives* that the brand offers the right product features, image, quality, or relationship at the right price.

In the quest for brand loyalty, advertisers have three aims related to habits:

1. **Breaking habits:** Get consumers to unlearn an existing purchase habit—and try something new. Advertisers frequently offer incentives to lure customers away from old brands or stores. Or they may use comparative advertising to demonstrate their product's superiority.

2. **Acquiring habits:** Teach consumers to repurchase their brand or repatronize their establishment. To get you started, Columbia House advertises free CDs when you sign up, tied to a contract to purchase more later on.

3. **Reinforcing habits:** Remind current customers of the value of their original purchase and encourage them to continue purchasing. Many magazines, for example, offer special renewal rates to their regular subscribers.

Developing brand loyalty is much more difficult today due to consumers' increased sophistication and to the legions of habit-breaking, *demarketing* activities of competitive advertisers.[23] Only recently have advertisers come to realize that their years of habit-breaking activities have undermined their own *habit-building* objectives. In the quest for instant results, they shifted much of their advertising budgets to sales promotions (deals, coupons, price cuts). But advertising, unlike sales promotion, is an integral part of what makes a brand saleable. It's advertising that reinforces brand loyalty and maintains market share.[24] We revisit this topic in our discussion of sales promotion in Chapter 15.

Learning defines needs and wants

The learning process is both immediate and long term. The moment we file a perception, some learning takes place. When we see a succulent food ad, we may suddenly feel hungry—we *need* food. As we collate the information in our mental files, comparing new perceptions with old ones, further learning takes place. The need may become a *want*. This leads to the next personal process, motivation.

The Consumer Motivation Process

Motivation refers to the underlying drives that contribute to our purchasing actions. These drives stem from the conscious or unconscious goal of satisfying our needs and wants. Needs are the basic, often instinctive, human forces that motivate us to do something. Wants are "needs" that we learn during our lifetime.[25]

Motivation cannot be observed directly. When we see people eat, we assume they are hungry, but we may be wrong. People eat for a variety of reasons besides hunger: they want to be sociable, it's time to eat, or maybe they're bored.

People are usually motivated by the benefit of satisfying some combination of needs, which may be conscious or unconscious, functional or psychological. *Motivation research* offers some insights into the underlying reasons for unexpected consumer behavior. The reasons (*motives*) some people stop shopping at Lucky Supermarket and switch to Vons may be that the Vons market is closer to home, it has a wider selection of fresh produce, and (most likely) they see other people like themselves shopping at Vons. Any or all of these factors might make the shopper switch even if prices are lower at Lucky.

To better understand what motivates people, Abraham Maslow developed the classic model shown in Exhibit 4–4 called the **hierarchy of needs.** Maslow maintained that the lower, physiological and safety needs dominate human behavior and must be satisfied before the higher, socially acquired needs (or wants) become meaningful. The highest need, self-actualization, is the culmination of fulfilling all the lower needs and reaching to discover the true self.[26]

Exhibit • 4–4

The hierarchy of needs suggests that people resolve their needs according to priorities. Physiological and safety needs carry the greatest priority.

In advertising, the message must match the need of the market or the ad will fail.

Advertisers use marketing research to understand the level of need of their markets and use this information in determining the marketing mix.

Need	Product	Promotional appeal
Self-actualization	Golf clubs	"Time is to enjoy"
Esteem	Luxury car	"Be in control of the road"
Social	Pendant	"Show her you care"
Safety	Tires	"Bounces off hazards"
Physiological	Breakfast cereal	"The natural energy source"

The promise of satisfying a certain level of need is the basic promotional appeal for many advertisements. In such affluent societies as the U.S., Canada, Western Europe, and Japan, most individuals take satisfaction of their physiological needs for granted. So advertising campaigns often portray the fulfillment of social, esteem, and self-actualization needs, and many offer the reward of satisfaction through personal achievement (Apple: "The power to be your best.").

We all have needs and wants, but we are frequently unaware of them. Before the advent of the desktop computer, people were completely unaware of any need for it. But the moment a consumer consciously recognizes a product-related want or need, a dynamic process begins. The consumer first evaluates the need and either accepts it as worthy of action or rejects it. Acceptance converts satisfaction of the need into a *goal,* which creates the dedication (the *motivation*) to reach a particular result. In contrast, rejection removes the necessity for action and thereby eliminates the goal and the motivation to buy.

Advertising should stimulate the decision about wants and needs. An ad that creates interest in a new Microsoft program to expedite writing term papers may stimulate some students to recognize their need for assistance. If they accept this need, they will

---

 *Ethical Issue*   ## Is It Marketing or Is It Exploitation?

A new way to help primary and secondary schools with education funding is commercial sponsorship. San Francisco-based School Properties, Inc., offers various sponsorship programs—including the licensing of school names and mascots, fundraising catalogs, and affinity credit cards—to national, regional, and state marketers. Marketers are guaranteed category exclusivity. They can test products and hold focus groups at schools, display banners at events, and use former student athletes in appearances on behalf of the company. School Properties, aware that extracurricular school activities are in jeopardy because of budget cuts, felt this program was a natural outgrowth of existing athletic and special event sponsorships. Those who like the plan say it will help mobilize resources for schools. But opponents say the funding problem is a state issue, and commercialism has no place in our schools. Others ask: Do commercial product logos belong in the hallways of grammar schools? Does this

allow advertisers to take advantage of captive kids?

The ethical dilemma concerns the point at which marketers can be accused of promoting their products for their own advantage or profit, to the detriment of their customers. Commercial products work only if they meet consumer needs, and advertising is designed to appeal to those needs. But what happens if advertisers overstep a need, especially in a crisis situation, and edge into exploitation? The question has many nuances.

Look at some of the health issues, such as smoking, which are often highly emotional. Tobacco marketers have vigorously defended themselves against a groundswell of antismoking complaints. RJR Nabisco, for one, used newspaper ads to rebut broader charges against the industry. It placed full-page ads that suggested the dangers of secondhand smoke were overdramatized by antismoking forces. In a different health arena, most baby formula companies don't yet ad-

vertise directly to consumers because many doctors think breast feeding is preferable to formula. The companies don't want to be accused of ex-

> Commercial products work only if they meet consumer needs, and advertising is designed to appeal to those needs. But what happens if advertisers overstep a need, especially in a crisis situation, and edge into exploitation?

ploitation; instead, they market their products through health care professionals, hospitals, and new-mother clubs.

When a drastic change occurs in a particular market segment, a new field may become fertile for exploitation. Demographics around the world are changing, and the emerging Third World middle class seems to have an insatiable appetite for

• Advertising must stimulate consumers' decisions about wants and needs. In a market flooded with denim products, Unigroup discovered the most motivating thing it could convey about its Prison Blues was that the jeans are actually made and worn by the inmates in Oregon prisons. This information commands instant attention from consumers looking for a new wrinkle in blue jeans. The tagline—*Real jeans made by real inmates*—also implies that the jeans are sturdy.

formulate a goal: to shop for report-writing software compatible with their computer. If the ad clearly presents the name of the product or store, the advertiser may experience a sales increase.

Before creating messages, advertisers must carefully consider the goals that lead to consumer motivations. Denny's Restaurants would make a costly mistake if its ads portrayed a romantic interlude if the real goal of most Denny's customers is simply to satisfy their need for a filling, low-priced meal.

buying things. Tradition and culture play a big role in what people buy and why, but the evolving role of women, a burgeoning youth culture, and a middle class with higher expectations and more money than ever before are making a whole new group of consumers ripe for the products of major multinationals.

Some critics believe China is especially vulnerable to exploitation. A couple living in a cramped Beijing apartment may have a $270 refrigerator, $700 foreign-made color TV, telephone that had a $600 installation charge, $600 Panasonic VCR, $1,200 Toshiba air conditioner, and $1,200 piano—all bought on a salary of $300 a month. In Mexico, credit cards are pitched to people earning as little as $650 a month. The National Association of Credit Card Holders estimates 5 million Mexicans carry credit cards, but a million of them can't pay their bills.

Critics say that companies act irresponsibly when they target these groups for marketing and advertising activities, because the average consumer can't afford the products being advertised.

On the other hand, how different advertising messages influence people to action has been the subject of much research. One finding holds that people generally believe others are far more influenced by the media than they are themselves. This is called the third-person effect. Perhaps the critics should consider this. They know they have the ability to resist the advertising appeals, but they seem to believe the average consumer lacks their sophistication. Where do you draw the line between what is ethical (marketing) and what is not (exploitation)?

Questions

1. Do you think playing on people's desire for material possessions has a place in advertising? When does this become exploitation?

2. Is it the advertiser's responsibility to determine whether prospective customers can afford a product or service? Why or why not?

3. Do you feel the third-person effect applies to consumers in the developing countries? If so, how can marketers avoid exploiting them?

Source: Rachel Rosenthal, "Program Takes Sponsors to School," *Advertising Age,* September 5, 1994, p. 30; Ira Teinowitz and Steven W. Colford, "RJR, B&W Hit Anti-Smoking Blaze with Ads," *Advertising Age,* May 30, 1994, p. 8; Leah Rickard, "No Brood of New Ads for Baby Formula," *Advertising Age,* April 18, 1994, p. 35; Kathleen Barnes, "Changing Demographics: Middle Class," *Advertising Age International,* October 17, 1994, pp. I-14–16; and Esther Thorson and James Coyle, "The Third-Person Effect in Three Genres of Commercials: Product and Greening Ads and Public Service Announcements," paper presented to the annual conference of the American Academy of Advertising, April 8–11, 1994.

INTERPERSONAL INFLUENCES ON CONSUMER BEHAVIOR

For advertisers, it's not enough just to know the personal processes of perception, learning, and motivation. Important **interpersonal influences** affect—sometimes even dominate—these processes. They also serve as guidelines for consumer behavior. These influences can best be categorized as the *family,* the *society,* and the *cultural environment* of the consumer.

Family Influence

From an early age, family communication affects our socialization as consumers—our attitudes toward many products and our purchasing habits. This influence is usually strong and long lasting. A child who learns that the "right" headache relief is Bayer aspirin and the "right" name for appliances is General Electric has adult purchasing behavior pretty well formed.

Research, however, indicates that family influence is diminishing in the U.S. as working parents take a less active role in raising their children and youngsters look outside the family for social values.[27] As this happens, the influence of the social and cultural environments intensifies.

Society's Influence

The community we live in exerts a strong influence on all of us. When we affiliate with a particular societal division, or identify with some reference group, or value the opinions of certain opinion leaders, it affects our views on life, our perceptual screens, and eventually the products we buy.

Societal divisions: The group we belong to

Sociologists traditionally divided societies into **social classes:** upper, upper-middle, lower-middle, and so on. They believed that people in the same social class tended toward similar attitudes, status symbols, and spending patterns.

But today this doesn't apply to most developed countries. U.S. society, especially, is extremely fluid and mobile—physically, socially, and economically. Americans believe strongly in "getting ahead," "being better than your peers," and "winning greater admiration and self-esteem." As the famous Army campaign illustrates, advertisers often capitalize on this desire to "be all you can be."

Due to this mobility, to dramatic increases in immigration, and to the high divorce rate, social-class boundaries have become quite muddled. Single parents, stockbrokers, immigrant shopkeepers, retired blue-collar workers, and bankers, for example, all see themselves as part of the great middle class. So middle class doesn't mean anything anymore. From the advertiser's point of view, social class seldom represents a functional or operational set of values.

To deal with these often bewildering changes, marketers seek new ways to classify societal divisions and new strategies for advertising to them. We discuss some of these in Chapter 5. Exhibit 4–5 outlines some of the classifications marketers use to describe society today: for example, Mid-Life Success, Movers and Shakers, Stars and Stripes, and University USA. Within each group there are similar patterns of behavior and product usage.

Reference groups: People we relate to

Most of us care how we appear to people whose opinions we value. We may even pattern our behavior after members of some groups we affiliate with. This is the significance of **reference groups**—people we try to emulate or whose approval concerns us. Reference groups can be personal (family, friends, co-workers) or impersonal (film stars, professional athletes, business executives). A special reference group, our peers, exerts tremendous influence on what we believe and how we behave. They determine which brands are cool—and which are not.[28] To win acceptance by our peers (fellow students,

Upper Crust

Metropolitan families, very high income and education, manager/professionals; very high installment activity

Mid-Life Success

Families, very high education, managers/professionals, technical/sales, high income; super-high installment activity

Movers and Shakers

Singles, couples, students, and recent graduates, high education and income, managers/professionals, technical/sales; average credit activity, medium-high installment activity

Successful Singles

Young, single renters, older housing, ethnic mix, high education, medium income, managers/professionals; very high bankcard accounts, very high installment activity, very low retail activity

Stars and Stripes

Young, large school-age families, medium income and education, military, precision/craft; average credit activity

Social Security

Mature/seniors, metro fringe, singles and couples, medium income and education, mixed jobs; very low credit activity

Middle of the Road

School-age families, mixed education, medium income, mixed jobs; very high revolving activity, very high bankcard accounts

Trying Metro Times

Young, seniors, ethnic mix, low income, older housing, low education, renters, mixed jobs; low credit activity, medium-high retail activity

Low-Income Blues

Minorities, singles and families, older housing, low income and education, services, laborers; low credit activity, medium-high retail activity

University USA

Students, singles, dorms/group quarters, very low income, medium-high education, technical/sales; low credit activity, high percent new accounts

Exhibit • 4–5
Contemporary social classes. The groups outlined in this exhibit are just 10 of 50 Microvision lifestyle segments defined by National Decision Systems, a division of Equifax.

co-workers, colleagues), we may purchase a certain style or brand of clothing, choose a particular place to live, and acquire behavioral habits that will earn their approval.

Often an individual is influenced in opposite directions by two reference groups and must choose between them. For example, a college student may feel pressure from some friends to join a Greek house and from others to live independently off campus. In ads targeted to students, a local apartment complex might successfully employ the appeal of reference groups by showing students splashing in the complex's pool.

Opinion leaders: The people we trust

An **opinion leader** is some person or organization whose beliefs or attitudes are respected by people who share an interest in some specific activity. All fields (sports, religion, fashion, politics) have opinion leaders. An opinion leader may be a knowl-

• Advertisers target significant reference groups to encourage customers to purchase certain products. For example, by combining exciting ads like this with cutting-edge technology, Sega has become the "cool" brand with teens.

● Julia Louis-Dreyfus of the TV sitcom "Seinfeld" plays a celebrity endorser from hell who bullies an unwitting passenger into a hair-coloring job—on the bus! The award-winning spot from Clairol Nice 'N Easy allows Louis-Dreyfus to be a refreshing "over-the-top obnoxious" opinion leader in a category that often relies on coyness and anxiety about aging.

SFX: (Moving bus.)
JULIA: You know, you'd look great as a blonde.
WOMAN: Do I know you?
JULIA: Nice 'N Easy 104. It's you.
WOMAN: Well, I've never colored my hair.

JULIA: Ohhh, trust me.
See, Nice 'N Easy works with your hair's own tones and highlights.
Look at mine. Doesn't it look natural?
PASSENGERS: Uh-hmm.

JULIA: Time to rinse.
SFX: (Hair dryer.)

(Both women scream in delight.)

MAN ON BUS: She looks fabulous.
SFX: (Passengers applaud.)

JULIA: She's gonna stop traffic.
AVO: It's Nice 'N Easy. Only from Clairol.

edgeable friend or some expert we find credible. We reason, "If Pikabo Street thinks Marker makes the best ski bindings, then it must be so. She knows more about the sport than I do." Thus the purchasing habits and testimonials of opinion leaders are important to advertisers.

When choosing an opinion leader as a spokesperson for a company or product, advertisers must understand the company's target market thoroughly. For example, even if executives in the company do not relate to the spokesperson, they must follow market tastes and interests. A spokesperson out of sync with the market undermines his or her own credibility—and the company's. On the other hand, an internal person like Dave Thomas, the founder of Wendy's, might turn out to be a highly credible spokesperson without the inherent risks associated with outside celebrities and athletes.[29]

The Influence of Culture and Subculture

Culture has a tenacious influence on the consumer. **Culture** refers to a homogeneous group's whole set of beliefs, attitudes, and ways of doing things, typically handed down from generation to generation.[30] Americans love hot dogs, peanut butter, corn on the cob, and apple pie. Canada, Russia, Germany—every country has its own favorite specialties. And advertisers find it much easier to work with these tastes than try to change them.

The U.S. and Canada embrace many subcultures, some of them quite large. They may be based on race, national origin, religion, language, or geographic proximity. The advertiser must understand these subcultures, for differences among them may affect responses to both products and advertising messages.

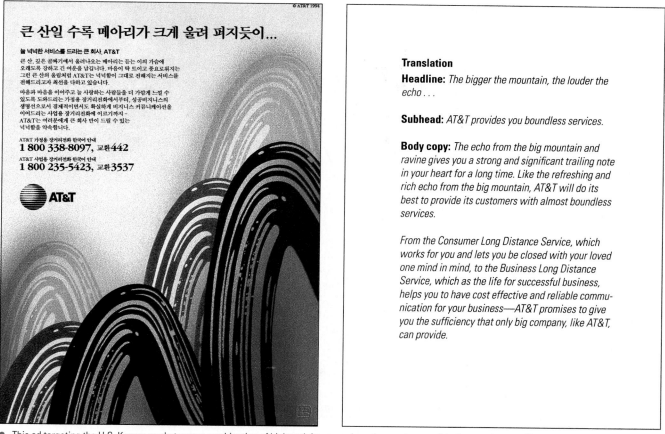

● This ad targeting the U.S. Korean market uses a combination of high-tech image and poetic copy to appeal to these customers. Here you can see the difficulty of translating copy from one language to another. The literal translation is also shown.

The U.S., in particular, is a great melting pot of minority subcultures. A **subculture** is a segment within a culture that shares a set of meanings, values, or activities that differ in certain respects from those of the overall culture.[31] According to the 1990 U.S. Census, 31 million African-Americans, 22 million Hispanics, and 7 million Asians live in the U.S.—plus an unknown number of undocumented foreign nationals. These three minority groups alone account for over 21 percent of the American population, and by the year 2000, they may account for more than 25 percent.[32] Canada has two major subcultures, anglophones and francophones, based on language (English and French), plus a mosaic of many other cultures based on ethnic and national origin.

Subcultures tend to transfer their beliefs and values from generation to generation. Racial, religious, and ethnic backgrounds affect consumers' preferences for styles of dress, food, beverages, transportation, personal care products, and household furnishings, to name a few. As we saw in Chapter 3, many advertising agencies now specialize in minority markets as more advertisers recognize that tailoring appeals to minorities makes good business sense. Recognizing the rapid growth of the Hispanic population, for example, Procter & Gamble spends over $30 million to understand and tap this market. Other major Hispanic marketers include Philip Morris, Anheuser Busch, and Coca-Cola.[33]

Just as in North America, the social environments in countries such as Italy, Indonesia, and Surinam are based on language, culture, literacy rate, religion, and lifestyle. Advertisers who market products globally can't ignore these customs.

In North America, advertising encourages us to keep our mouths clean, our breath fresh, and our teeth scrubbed. On the other hand, people in some southern European countries consider it vain and improper to overindulge in toiletries. Consumers in the

Netherlands and United Kingdom use three times as much toothpaste as those in Spain and Greece. To communicate effectively with Spanish consumers, who view toothpaste as a cosmetic product, advertisers use chic creative executions rather than dry, therapeutic pitches.[34]

In summary, many interpersonal factors influence consumers. They have an important effect on our mental files, screens, and subsequent purchase decisions. Awareness of these interpersonal influences helps marketers—domestic or international—create the strategies on which much advertising is based.

NONPERSONAL INFLUENCES ON CONSUMER BEHAVIOR

Numerous nonpersonal influences may affect a consumer's final purchase decision. The most important **nonpersonal influences**—*time, place,* and *environment*—are typically beyond the consumer's control, but not necessarily the advertiser's.

Time

The old saw, "timing is everything," certainly applies to marketing and advertising. A special weekend sale may provide just the added incentive to penetrate customers' perceptual screens and bring them into a store. But running an ad for that sale on Sunday evening would be a waste of advertising dollars.

Likewise, the consumer's particular need may be a function of time. Forecasts of a frigid winter in the *1995 Old Farmer's Almanac* motivated special ads from Bridgestone Tire, Audi, Jeep, and Cadillac, along with many small retailers of linens, boots, snow shovels, and rock salt.[35] Consumers don't need snow tires and rock salt in the summer (although some off-season promotions do work). But if we unexpectedly get a flat on the highway, tire ads suddenly become timely. As we see in our chapters on media, companies must plan all their marketing activities (including advertising) with the consumer's clock in mind.

Place

Although we may decide to purchase a certain product, we will still hesitate if we don't know where to buy it or if it isn't available in a convenient or preferred location. Similarly, if consumers believe a particular brand is a specialty good but it suddenly appears everywhere, their perception of the product's "specialness" may diminish. Thus, marketers carefully weigh consumer demand when planning distribution strategy, and they devote much advertising to communicating the convenience of location. Distribution is an important element of the marketing mix and will be discussed further in Chapter 5.

Environment

Many **environments**—ecological, social, political, technical, economic, household, and point-of-sale location, to mention a few—can affect the purchase decision. For example, during a recession, advertisers can't expect to penetrate the perceptual screens of consumers who don't have enough money to buy. And no matter how good the advertising or how low the price, NRA memberships aren't likely to be a hot item with members of the Audubon Society. On the other hand, an enticing display next to the cash register can improve sales of low-cost impulse items. Advertisers must consider the influence of the purchase environment on the consumer's decision processes.

International Environments

Global marketers are especially concerned with the purchase environment. Of all business functions, marketing activities are the most susceptible to cultural error.[36] For example, while both demographic and psychographic characteristics figure importantly in U.S. consumer marketing, age and sex are better indicators of consumer behavior and lifestyles in Japan, where income is largely proportional to seniority, and sex roles tend to be standardized.[37] When creating ads for foreign consumption, marketers must consider many environmental factors: cultural trends, social norms, changing fads, market dynamics, product needs, and media channels.[38]

In countries where people earn little income, demand for expensive products is low. So the creative strategy of an automobile advertiser might be to target the small group of wealthy, upper-class consumers. In a country with a large middle class, the same advertiser might be better off mass marketing the car and positioning it as a middle-class product.

Likewise, the state of technological development affects economic and social conditions—and the prospects for advertisers of certain products and services. For example, countries that don't manufacture computers might be poor markets for components such as disk drives and microprocessors. On the other hand, advertisers of low-priced, imported computers might do very well.

Finally, some governments exert far greater control over their citizens and businesses than the U.S. government does. For example, until recently, virtually no American-made products could be sold in many Eastern bloc countries or China. They simply weren't allowed. Political control often extends to which products companies may advertise and sell, which media they use, and what their ads say.

The political environment affects media availability as well. For example, the fall of communism in the Eastern bloc spurred the introduction of a Hungarian edition of *Playboy;* distribution of *The Wall Street Journal/Europe* in Hungary, Poland, and Yugoslavia; and sales of *USA Today International* in Hungary and Poland. Eastern Europeans, hungry for news from the West, provide a motivated market for these types of publications.

● As global markets become more integrated, consistency in advertising across countries becomes more important. This series of commercials for Adidas, featuring tennis star Stefan Edberg, ran in more than 20 countries across Europe, Asia, and the U.S. When asked why he took up tennis, Edberg replies that he could have been a light-bulb tester, an optician, or a bed tester, among other callings.

In the European Union (EU), the Maastricht Treaty fostered a unified system of pan-European trade, finance, labor, and regulatory codes. Barriers to the flow of people, goods, and money within the EU have gradually fallen, making it easier for some advertisers to coordinate pan-European ad campaigns. U.S. and Canadian advertisers are well aware of the opportunity: a barrier-free EU means a $4 trillion market of 320 million consumers.

To better reach the changing European market, IBM started pan-European image advertising in the 1980s and followed up with its first pan-European product ad campaign in 1991. The more Europe becomes integrated, the more important it is to have consistent brands and advertising throughout the European Union. The pan-European approach also saves money. By eliminating duplicate creative and production costs, only the language of the voice-overs has to change—and advertisers can save substantial sums.

THE PURCHASE DECISION AND POSTPURCHASE EVALUATION

Now that we understand the elements in the consumer purchase decision process, let's examine how it might work in a typical situation, the decision to buy a new CD player, made by a hypothetical consumer—Chris. To help follow this process and see the interrelationship of the many behavioral factors we've discussed, study the complete model of the consumer decision-making process shown in Exhibit 4–6.

Enrolled at a state university and financed in part by a small scholarship, Chris also has a part-time job, but must act conservatively when it comes to spending money because tuition, books, and expenses are costly.

One day, thumbing through a consumer electronics magazine, Chris sees an exciting ad for a new top-of-the line CD player. Its new styling, understated design, and special features exude high-tech and class—it's just the right style. The ad's signature: "Exclusively at Tech 2000." (See Ad Lab 4–B: "Applying Consumer Behavior Principles to Ad Making.")

In a split second Chris leaps from perception to motivation. Got to have it!

The next day Chris visits Tech 2000, and while looking for the advertised CD player, encounters a variety of alternative styles and models by well-known manufacturers.

The ad has already done its work; the purchase decision process is well under way. At the point of making a purchase decision, though, consumers typically search, consider, and compare alternative brands.

Consumers evaluate selection alternatives (called the **evoked set**). To do this, they establish **evaluative criteria,** the standards they use to judge the features and benefits of alternative products. Not all brands make it to the evoked set. In fact, based on their mental files, most consumers usually consider only four or five brands—which presents a real challenge to advertisers. If none of the alternatives meets the evaluative criteria, the consumer may reject the purchase entirely or postpone the decision.

Chris finally finds the advertised CD player. It looks smaller on the shelf than it did in the ad, however. Two other good players are also displayed—both attractive, both expensive. While trying out the sound systems, Chris considers other unique qualities of style and design. "This one may be a little too bulky." "This one would fit on my desk." "This one would be okay for me, but I'm not sure about using it for parties."

Chris compares the CD players, considering their style, technology, possible advantages, and price (the models are all within $35 of each other). The advertised player really is the best buy and would be the most satisfying. None of Chris's friends has one like it. The purchase decision is complete when Chris writes out a check for the CD player.

On the way home, the **postpurchase evaluation** *begins. Chris suddenly envisions some friends' possible negative reactions to the purchase. Maybe it wasn't wise to spend so much money on a luxury CD player. Chris starts to worry—and to plan.*

"It's really a great player. It's excellent quality and worth the money. I'll get a lot of use out of it."

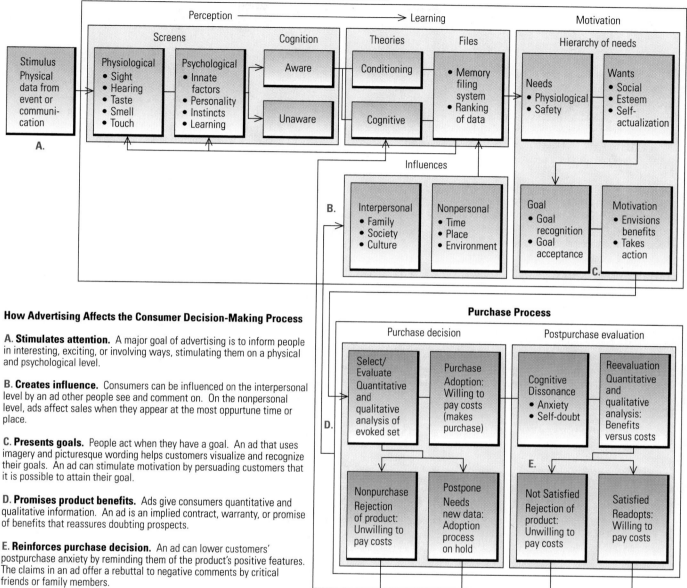

Exhibit • 4–6
The complete model of the consumer decision-making process.

How Advertising Affects the Consumer Decision-Making Process

A. Stimulates attention. A major goal of advertising is to inform people in interesting, exciting, or involving ways, stimulating them on a physical and psychological level.

B. Creates influence. Consumers can be influenced on the interpersonal level by an ad other people see and comment on. On the nonpersonal level, ads affect sales when they appear at the most oppurtune time or place.

C. Presents goals. People act when they have a goal. An ad that uses imagery and picturesque wording helps customers visualize and recognize their goals. An ad can stimulate motivation by persuading customers that it is possible to attain their goal.

D. Promises product benefits. Ads give consumers quantitative and qualitative information. An ad is an implied contract, warranty, or promise of benefits that reassures doubting prospects.

E. Reinforces purchase decision. An ad can lower customers' postpurchase anxiety by reminding them of the product's positive features. The claims in an ad offer a rebuttal to negative comments by critical friends or family members.

A key feature of the postpurchase evaluation is *cognitive dissonance*. The **theory of cognitive dissonance** (also called **postpurchase dissonance**) holds that people strive to justify their behavior by reducing the dissonance, or inconsistency, between their cognitions (their perceptions or beliefs) and reality.[39] In fact, research shows that, to combat dissonance, consumers are more likely to read ads for brands they've already purchased than for new products or competing brands.[40]

Back at the dorm, Chris puts the magazine on the desk with a Post-it marking the ad (for roommate CJ to discover), then phones a friend and describes the purchase, emphasizing its technology, its great design, the enjoyment it will bring, and how expensive it was.

During the postpurchase period, the consumer may enjoy the satisfaction of the purchase and thereby receive reinforcement for the decision. Or the purchase may turn

Ad Lab 4-B   Applying Consumer Behavior Principles to Ad Making

When Norwegian Cruise Line needed to promote its Caribbean cruises, the creatives at the company's agency, Goodby, Berlin & Silverstein, San Francisco, faced a challenge. Essentially, they had to find a simple way to communicate a conflicting, two-part message. The company's name, Norwegian, evoked the image of fjords, icy waters, and snow—anything but the Caribbean. And the concept "Caribbean" stimulated tropical images of palms, beaches, warm waters, and sun—ideas that made the concept of "Norwegian" hardly memorable. They knew consumers may become confused when advertisers try to communicate multiple messages simultaneously.

As with many ad campaigns, creative directors Jeff Goodby, Rich Silverstein, and Steve Stone deliberated over the concept: how could they break through the consumer's resistance—that subtle barrier driven by the perceptual screens? What concepts would penetrate the screens *and* be memorable as well? How could they meld both concepts to create a single "big

Norwegian to the Caribbean.

⊥NORWEGIAN

idea" to keep the message clear, simple, and immediate?

One way to bring together divergent concepts is to employ the power of the metaphor, to portray one idea in terms of another. In this case, words weren't working. "See the Norwegian tropics" and "Norwegibbean" just weren't powerful. So they turned to imagery—and discovered a new continent of meaning.

The ad pictured here shows how the mental files "Norse helmet" and "tropical fruits" overlap to create an effective big idea.

Laboratory Applications

Look closely at the visuals, the words, and the overall design of this ad. How do these elements work together to accomplish the following tasks?

1. Penetrate consumer perceptual screens.
2. Stimulate consumer learning.
3. Utilize the consumer's existing perceptual files.
4. Stimulate consumer wants and needs to affect motivation.

out to be unsatisfactory for some reason. In either case, feedback from the postpurchase evaluation updates the consumer's mental files, affecting perceptions of the brand and similar purchase decisions in the future.

Chris may typify a particular group of consumers. Marketers are interested in defining target markets and developing effective marketing strategies for groups of consumers who share similar characteristics, needs, motives, and buying habits. These are the subjects of market segmentation and the marketing mix, the focus of Chapter 5.

Summary

Marketing is the process companies use to make a profit by satisfying their customers' needs for products. Marketing focuses on the special relationship between a customer's needs and a product's functional or psychic utility. The essence of marketing is the perceived equal-value exchange. Need satisfaction is the goal of the customer and should be the marketer's goal as well.

Advertising is concerned with the promotion aspect of the marketing process. It is one of several tools marketers use to inform, persuade, and remind groups of customers, or markets, about the need-satisfying value of their products and services. Advertising's effectiveness depends on the communication skill of the advertising person. It also depends on the extent to which firms correctly implement other marketing activities, such as market research and distribution.

There are three categories of participants in the marketing process: customers, markets, and marketers. To reach customers and markets, advertisers must effectively blend data from the behavioral sciences with the communicating arts. Advertisers study the behavioral characteristics of large groups of people to create advertising aimed at those groups.

Successful advertising people understand the complexity of consumer behavior, which is governed by three personal processes: perception, learning, and motivation. These processes determine how consumers see the world around them, how they learn information and habits, and how they actualize their personal needs and motives. Two sets of influences also affect consumer behavior. Interpersonal influences include the consumer's family, society, and culture. Nonpersonal influences include time, place, and environment. These factors combine to determine how the consumer behaves, and their influence may differ considerably from one country to another. By evaluating the effect of these factors on groups of consumers, advertisers may determine how best to create their messages.

Once customers or prospects are motivated to satisfy their needs and wants, the purchase process begins. Based on certain standards they have established in their own minds, they evaluate various alternative products—the evoked set. If none of the alternatives meets their evaluative criteria, they may reject or postpone the purchase. If they do buy, they may experience cognitive dissonance in the form of postpurchase doubt and concern. An important role of advertising is to help people cope with dissonance by reinforcing the wisdom of their purchase decision. The result of the postpurchase evaluation will greatly affect the customer's attitude toward future purchases.

Questions for Review and Discussion

1. What is marketing, and what is advertising's role in the marketing process?

2. How does product utility relate to advertising?

3. Why is the perceived equal-value exchange an important advertising issue?

4. What's the difference between a customer and a market, and what are the different types of markets?

5. What does the term *consumer behavior* relate to, and why is it important to advertisers?

6. Which consumer behavior process presents the greatest challenge to advertisers?

7. What are some effects of the learning process on consumers?

8. What is the significance of Maslow's hierarchy of needs to international advertisers?

9. What are some of the environmental influences that affect consumer behavior in international markets?

10. How does the theory of cognitive dissonance relate to advertising?

5

Using Marketing and Advertising to Link Products to Markets

Objective: To describe how marketers use behavioral characteristics to cluster prospective customers into market segments. Since no product or service can please everybody, marketers need to select the specific target markets that offer the greatest potential for sales. By so doing, marketers can fine tune their mix of product-related elements (the 4 Ps), including advertising, to match the needs or wants of the target market.

After studying this chapter, you will be able to:

- Identify the methods used to segment consumer and business markets.

- Explain the process and the importance of aggregation to marketing.

- Discuss the target marketing process.

- Describe the elements of the marketing mix and their roles.

- Explain the role and importance of branding.

all over the west they wear

LEVI STRAUSS & CO'S
COPPER RIVETED
Overalls.

The trip was the most daring of adventures—17,000 miles and five months on a clipper ship from New York around South America to a rowdy frontier town aflame with gold fever. Imagine the awe and the excitement of Mr. Strauss, a young German immigrant, when he stepped off the ship in San Francisco in 1853.

Strauss came to San Francisco at the invitation of his brother-in-law, David Stern. Seeing the city's gold-boom economy, Stern sensed an opportunity for a thriving dry goods business. Strauss brought a variety of supplies for the business with him, including canvas for tents and Conestoga wagon covers.

By the time he reached San Francisco, though, Strauss had sold virtually all his merchandise to the other passengers—everything except the canvas. Before long, the inventive young entrepreneur came up with an idea for selling that as well.

"Should'a brought pants," the prospectors and gold miners told him. "Pants don't wear worth a hoot in the diggins!"

Strauss immediately took the heavy brown canvas to a tailor and created pants that he called "waist-high overalls." These were the world's first jeans, a term derived from the cotton trousers (called *genes* by the French) worn by ancient-day sailors from Genoa, Italy.

Word of the quality of "those pants of Levi's" spread quickly, and young Levi Strauss began turning out dozens of pairs. Exhausting his original supply of canvas, Levi switched to a sturdy serge fabric made in Nimes, France, called serge de Nimes (pronounced *sayrzjh da neem*). Later, the name of the fabric was conveniently shortened to "denim." With the development of an indigo dye, the natural brown color turned to the now familiar deep blue.

While Levi's new product achieved rapid acceptance, prospectors found that the weight of gold nuggets caused the pockets to rip. Ever alert for ways to improve quality, Strauss was quick to adopt—and patent—the idea of riveting the pocket corners for added strength. To this day, rivets remain one of the hallmarks of the stiff, shrink-to-fit, button-fly pants now known as Levi's 501 jeans.

Young Levi achieved success beyond his wildest dreams. His pants, now sold in over 70 countries worldwide, became the flagship product of a diversified global company. Today, almost 150 years later, Levi's worldwide sales exceed $5.5 billion. The family-owned business Levi left to his nephews is the largest apparel company in the world and a recognized trailblazer in corporate social responsibility. Thanks to years of brilliant marketing and advertising on a global scale, virtually everybody in the world knows Mr. Strauss's first name.[1]

THE MARKET SEGMENTATION PROCESS

Marketing and advertising people constantly scan the marketplace to see what various consumer groups need and want and how they might be better satisfied. One technique they use is **market segmentation,** a two-step strategy of *identifying* groups of people (or organizations) with certain shared needs and characteristics within the broad markets for consumer or business products, and *aggregating* (combining) these groups into larger market segments according to their mutual interest in the product's utility. This process gives a company a selection of market segments large enough to target, and lays the foundation for developing a suitable mix of marketing activities—including advertising.

Markets often consist of many segments. A company might differentiate products and marketing strategy for every segment, or it might concentrate all its marketing activities on only one or a few segments. Either task is far from simple. We saw how young Levi Strauss identified and targeted a single market segment and catered to it with specific products and services. The diverse markets Levi's serves today are really combinations of numerous smaller groups that share certain interests or product needs. Catering to all these needs on a global level requires a very sophisticated marketing and communications system. In this chapter, we look first at how marketers identify and categorize *consumer markets* and second at the techniques they use to segment *business markets.* Then we discuss the various strategic options companies might use to match their products with markets and create profitable exchanges.

Segmenting the Consumer Market: Finding the Right Niche

The concept of *shared characteristics* is critical to market segmentation. Marketing and advertising people know that, based on their needs, wants, and mental files, consumers leave many "footprints in the sand"—the tell-tale signs of where they live and work, what they buy, and how they spend their leisure time. By following these foot-

● As the old ad in the chapter opening shows, Levi Strauss originally identified and targeted a single U.S. market segment and catered to it with a specific product. Today, L.S.&Co. has a sophisticated marketing and communications system that targets diverse markets around the world with so many different products they are identified by number. This ad targets the Italian market with the claim: *Levi's. Once put on, never taken off.*

• In local markets, marketing communications are targeted at customers in a fairly limited trading area. Menswear retailer Bigsby & Kruthers uses the outside of its warehouse to target slow-moving commuter traffic on Chicago's Kennedy Expressway. The painting, which features well-known Chicagoans such as actor Joe Mantegna, artist Ed Paschke, and football player Tom Waddle, is a larger-than-life version of the firm's "Suitbook" catalog.

prints, marketers can locate and define groups of consumers with similar needs and wants, create messages for them, and know how and where to send their messages. The goal is to find that particular "niche," or space in the market, where the advertiser's product or service will fit.

Marketers group these characteristics into categories (*geographic, demographic, behavioristic,* and *psychographic*) to identify and segment consumer markets. (RL 5–1 in the Reference Library shows typical breakdowns of the variables.)

Geographic segmentation

One of the simplest ways to segment markets is by **geography.** People in one region of the country—or the world—have needs, wants, and purchasing habits that differ from those in other regions. People in Sunbelt states, for example, buy more suntan lotion. Canadians buy special equipment for dealing with snow and ice—products many Floridians have never seen in stores.

When marketers analyze geographic data, they study sales by region, country size, city size, specific locations, and types of stores. Many products sell well in urban areas but poorly in suburban or rural ones, and vice versa. As we'll see in Chapter 8, this information is critical in developing advertising media schedules because, with limited budgets, marketers want to advertise in those areas where their sales potential is best.

Even in local markets, geographic segmentation is important. For example, a local progressive politician might send a mailer only to precincts where voters typically support liberal causes. And a local retail store rarely draws customers from outside a fairly limited *trading area.*

Demographic segmentation

Demographics refers to a population's statistical characteristics: sex, age, ethnicity, education, occupation, income, and other quantifiable factors. Demographics are often combined with geographic segmentation to select target markets for advertising. This is called **geodemographic segmentation.** For example, research shows that people who identify themselves as "strongly Hispanic" tend to be very loyal to certain brands. And, as Exhibit 5–1 reveals, Hispanic media have recently experienced a boom as many businesses now aim a significant portion of their advertising specifically at this population.[2] To do so efficiently, though, they need to measure the size of the

	1989	1990	1991	1992	1993
Total ad spending	$522.0	$555.0	$610.8	$632.5	$721.5
Percentage growth from previous year	4.7%	5.4%	11.1%	3.6%	14.1%

Exhibit • 5–1
Estimated annual ad spending in U.S. Hispanic market ($ millions).

Exhibit • 5–2
Heavy usage patterns of various age groups.

Age	Name of age group	Merchandise purchased
0–5	Young children	Baby food, toys, nursery furniture, children's wear
6–19	Schoolchildren and teenagers	Clothing, sporting goods, records and tapes, school supplies, fast food, soft drinks, candy, cosmetics, movies
20–34	Young adults	Cars, furniture, housing, food and beer, clothing, diamonds, home entertainment equipment, recreational equipment, purchases for younger age segments
35–49	Younger middle-aged	Larger homes, better cars, second cars, new furniture, computers, recreational equipment, jewelry, clothing, food and wine
50–64	Older middle-aged	Recreational items, purchases for young marrieds and infants, travel
65 and over	Senior adults	Medical services, travel, pharmaceuticals, purchases for younger age groups

"strongly Hispanic" community, as well as its income and age distribution, in each marketing area they plan to target.

As people grow older, their responsibilities and incomes change, and so do their interests in various product categories (see Exhibit 5–2). Buick, for instance, found a huge untapped market of mature single women who were financially secure and good prospects for its brand. The company now sponsors a newsletter specifically targeted to this group.[3]

In the 1960s and 70s, blue jeans were the basic uniform of young males, and Levi's was the "in" brand. In the 80s, the baby boomer population grew older, and the number of young adults dwindled. The big market of men, by then over 25 years old, needed professional clothes for work and wanted looser-fitting clothes for relaxation. So they bought fewer jeans. Levi's needed to evolve the basic blue jean or risk losing this market forever. It responded by targeting its basic, five-pocket, button-fly jeans to 15- to 24-year-olds. Then it developed more comfortable, looser-fitting jeans for men 25 to 34. Finally, Levi's introduced Dockers, cotton casual slacks targeted at men 25 to 54. Dockers soon became the fastest-growing brand in apparel industry history and now includes a whole family of casual clothing for men, women, and boys.

In international markets, the demographics of many populations are changing rapidly. From Kuala Lumpur to Brazil to Poland, middle-class life is becoming available to more people in former Third World countries. And this emerging middle class has an apparently insatiable appetite for consumer goods—everything from color TVs and CD players to video cameras, cars, and refrigerators.[4] In China, for example, only 1 percent of the population has hot running water, but 84 percent have television sets.[5] In Poland, Coca-Cola spent $350 million to build a bottling plant to serve eastern Europe; and Procter & Gamble invested over $10 million advertising its Pampers diapers, Wash & Go shampoo, and Ariel detergents. According to *Advertising Age*, that's about 11 percent of Poland's entire ad spending.[6]

Behavioristic segmentation

Geographic and demographic data provide information about markets but little about the purchase behavior or psychology of the people. Marketers want to reach people who are current or prospective customers, but people in the same demographic or geographic segment have widely differing product preferences and TV viewing habits. Rarely can demographic criteria alone predict purchase behavior.[7]

One of the best ways to segment markets is to group consumers based on their purchase behavior. This is called **behavioristic segmentation.** Behavioral segments are

● Changing demographics in many international markets open up new opportunities for advertisers. This Audi ad, printed in both English and Chinese by Volkswagen Asia-Pacific, targets customers in the Pacific Rim area. The translation reads: *If you could, you would. Where permitted, the Audi Quattro's permanent four-wheel drive system gives you unparalleled road-holding.*

determined by many variables, but the most important are *purchase occasion, benefits sought, user status,* and *usage rate.*

Purchase-occasion variables Buyers can be distinguished by when they buy or use a product or service—the **purchase occasion.** Air travelers, for example, may fly for business or for vacation. So one airline might promote business travel while another promotes tourism. The purchase occasion might be affected by frequency of need (regular or occasional), a fad (candy, computer games), or seasons (water skis, raincoats). The Japan Weather Association tracked buying patterns on 20,000 items and correlated them to the outside temperature. Not surprisingly, when the temperature goes up, people buy more sunshades, air conditioners, watermelons, and swimwear. When there's a chill in the air, sales of suits, sweaters, and heaters take off.[8] A marketer who discovers common purchase occasions for a group has a potential target segment and can better determine when to run specials and how to promote certain product categories.

Benefits-sought variables Consumers seek **benefits** in the products they buy—high quality, low price, status, sex appeal, good taste. For example, people buy Levi's jeans for work, for play, or to make a fashion statement. And often consumers are motivated by symbolism—what the product represents to themselves, to associates, or to some societal reference group.[9] Marketers may segment consumers based on the benefits being sought. **Benefit segmentation** is the prime objective of many consumer attitude studies and the basis for many successful ad campaigns.

Some product categories are characterized by substantial brand switching from one purchase occasion to the next. Researchers have determined that the switching occurs in response to different "need states" consumers experience from one occasion to another. Thus a soft drink company competes not just for *drinkers* (users) but for *drinks* (occasions) based on the benefits the consumer is seeking at that moment. By measuring the importance of occasion-based motives, an advertiser can determine if a campaign needs to reposition the product.[10]

User-status variables Many markets can be segmented by the **user-status** of prospective customers. Stephan and Tannenholz identified six categories of consumers based on user status.

• Customers expect certain benefits from the products and services they buy. This Swissair ad takes the position that customers already know about its outstanding service, good food, and time-efficient terminals, and introduces another benefit to help create brand loyalty: the idea that Swissair is also a fun airline.

An airline for mature travelers. Everyone knows about Swissair's outstanding service, superior food, and civilized terminals. Not everyone has discovered our fun-loving nature. It takes some time. Time is everything.
swissair +

Swissair is a partner in the Delta, USAir and Air Canada frequent flyer programs.

Sole users are the most brand loyal and require the least amount of advertising and promotion. *Semisole* users typically use brand A but have an alternate selection if it is not available or if the alternate is promoted with a discount. *Discount users* are the semisole users of competing brand B. They don't buy brand A at full price but perceive it well enough to buy it at a discount. *Aware nontriers* are category users but haven't bought into brand A's message. A different advertising message could help, but these people rarely offer much potential. *Trial/rejectors* bought brand A's advertising message, but didn't like the product. More advertising won't help. Only a reformulation of brand A will bring them back. *Repertoire users* perceive two or more brands to have superior attributes and will buy at full price. They are the primary brand switchers and respond to persuasive advertising based on their fluctuating wants and desires. They should be the primary target for brand advertising.[11]

Usage-rate variables   It's usually easier to get a heavy user than a light user to increase usage. In **volume segmentation,** marketers measure **usage rates** to define consumers as light, medium, or heavy users of products (see Exhibit 5–3). Often, 20 percent of the population consumes 80 percent of the product. Marketers want to define that 20 percent and aim their advertising at them. For example, one-third of all households purchases 83 percent of Levi's products—worldwide!

By finding common characteristics among heavy users of their products, marketers can define product differences and focus their ad campaigns more effectively. For example, heavy users of bowling alleys tend to be working-class men between 25 and 50 who watch more than three and a half hours of television a day and prefer sports programs. So a bowling equipment company would probably want to advertise on TV sports programs.

Marketers of one product sometimes find that their customers are also heavy users of other products and can define their target markets in terms of the usage rates of the other products. Research indicates that heavy users of home computers are also heavy users of foreign luxury cars, sports cars, backpacking equipment, binoculars, expensive bicycles, and literary magazines.[12]

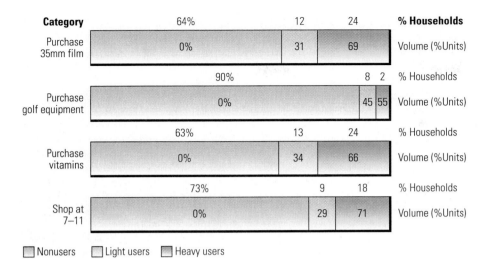

Category			% Households
Purchase 35mm film	64%	12	24	
	0%	31	69	Volume (%Units)

| | 90% | | 8 | 2 | % Households |
| Purchase golf equipment | 0% | | 45 | 55 | Volume (%Units) |

| Purchase vitamins | 63% | 13 | 24 | % Households |
| | 0% | 34 | 66 | Volume (%Units) |

| Shop at 7–11 | 73% | 9 | 18 | % Households |
| | 0% | 29 | 71 | Volume (%Units) |

▨ Nonusers   ☐ Light users   ▨ Heavy users

Exhibit • 5–3

Usage rates vary for different products. For example, of all households, 63 percent never buy vitamins (nonusers), 13 percent account for a third (34 percent) of vitamin sales (light users), and about a quarter of the households (24 percent) make two-thirds (66 percent) of the purchases (heavy users). Note the extreme difference between nonusers and heavy users of golf equipment.

Psychographic segmentation

For certain products, customers are more likely to be swayed by appeals to their emotions and cultural values. So some advertisers use **psychographic segmentation** to define consumer markets. **Psychographics** groups people on the basis of their psychological makeup—their values, attitudes, personality, and lifestyle. It views people as individuals with feelings and tendencies, and it classifies people according to what they feel, what they believe, the way they live, and the products, services, and media they use.[13]

For years, marketers tried to categorize consumers by personality and lifestyle types to determine advertising appeals. One classification system, VALS™, originated by SRI International, was quickly adopted by marketers across the country. In 1989, SRI released VALS2™, a new psychographic profile for segmenting U.S. consumers and predicting their purchase behavior (see Exhibit 5–4).

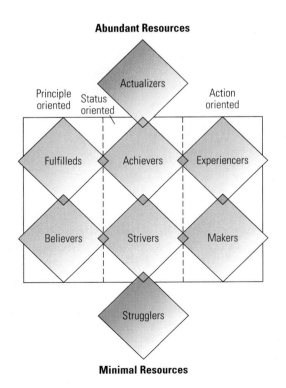

Abundant Resources

Principle oriented   Status oriented   Action oriented

Actualizers

Fulfilleds   Achievers   Experiencers

Believers   Strivers   Makers

Strugglers

Minimal Resources

Exhibit • 5–4

The VALS2™ (Values and Lifestyles) classification system places consumers with abundant resources—psychological, physical, and material means and capacities—near the top of the chart and those with minimal resources near the bottom. The chart segments consumers by their basis for decision making: principles, status, or action. The boxes intersect to indicate that some categories may be considered together. For instance, a marketer may categorize Fulfilleds and Believers together.

Ethical Issue   Niching May Cause Twitching

Revlon tried to strike a note of nostalgia in its perfume commercial by using footage of Nat King Cole crooning "Unforgettable" in praise of a parade of "unforgettable" women—all of whom were white. When Revlon belatedly tried to remedy the gaffe by tacking on a shot of black model Beverly Johnson, the effort seemed clumsy and contrived.

Madison Avenue has been awkward in its efforts to embrace black consumers, and research shows that almost 60 percent of the nation's 31 million African-American consumers feel most commercials and print ads are designed only for white people. Such insensitivity can be downright hazardous to business, as Anheuser-Busch found out.

The "Bud Light Spotlight" commercials showing actual Bud Light drinkers at bars in a dozen cities yucking it up and holding bottles of the brew

were so successful the campaign expanded to include many more cities, including Atlanta. An ensuing flap led to charges of racial insensitivity. Anheuser-Busch wanted the commercial to picture whites in Dugan's, a local tavern, even though its clientele consists overwhelmingly of blacks. The negative reaction of the crowd in the bar when the commercial was shot caused the owner of Dugan's to ask the film crew to leave. They obliged, without incident; but Dugan's no longer serves Bud Light or any other Anheuser-Busch product, and the owner considered yanking those brands out of 22 other establishments in which he has an interest.

Today, advertisers recognize it doesn't pay to alienate or stereotype minorities and women in their ads. Hispanics, African-Americans, Chinese, gays, and other minority group members are portrayed more favorably, not only because of pressure from watchdog groups, but also because it's

good business—these consumers represent sizable target markets.

In efforts to capture similarities and simplify messages, mass marketers may resort to undesirable stereotypes. Portray the traditional "housewife" as agonizing over dirty laundry and you may irritate the two-thirds of American women who work outside the home, other householders who do the laundry, and the more than one-quarter of all households consisting of only one person.

There is often a significant misfit between market segment, program target, and program audience. Take daytime TV, whose audience has greatly changed over the years. At 11 A.M., a spot for Clorox bleach won't necessarily reach people who do laundry. Thus the target of daytime ads is shifting from housewives to the unemployed and underemployed who have bad credit. Ads for personal injury lawyers and car insurance are replac-

---

The **Values and Lifestyles (VALS™)** system breaks consumers into eight groups based on their resources and self-orientation. Each group exhibits distinctive behavior, decision-making patterns, and product/media usage traits.

Radio is a good medium to reach some of the VALS2™ groups. Conservative, blue-collar people with traditional values (the VALS2™ Believer and Maker segments, comprising 29 percent of the U.S. population) often choose country music stations. Higher-income consumers over 45 (the VALS2™ Actualizer, Fulfilled, and Achiever categories) typically listen to news and talk radio. Since radio has only a few formats, SRI's eight typologies fit radio audiences reasonably well.[14]

Numerous advertising agencies jumped on the VALS™ bandwagon. Young & Rubicam used VALS™ for clients Mercury Capri, Dr Pepper, Kodak Instant Cameras, and Merrill Lynch, but then developed its own system, Cross Cultural Consumer Characterization (4Cs). Meanwhile SRI developed Japan VALS™ to determine the consumer effect of changing values and social behavior in Japan. Believing that one segmentation system cannot be applied cross-culturally, SRI is now developing VALS™ systems for Germany, Norway, France, Italy, and the United Kingdom.[15]

Limitations of consumer segmentation methods

Advocates of VALS™ and other psychographic methods claim these methods help them address the emotional factors that motivate consumers. However, since the markets for many products comprise a broad cross section of consumers, psychographics may offer little real value—especially since they oversimplify consumer personalities and purchase behavior. VALS™ is also criticized for being complicated and lacking the proper theoretical underpinnings.[16]

Yet marketers do need to understand and monitor their customers. It helps them select target markets, create ads that match the attributes and image of their products with the types of consumers using the products, develop effective media plans, and budget their marketing dollars wisely. (For an interesting twist on market segmentation, see Ad Lab 5–A.)

ing ads that chided wives for not removing ring around the collar. And today, women are more often portrayed as having an *attitude* about—

One dilemma for advertisers today is recognizing who they might inadvertently insult next.

---

rather than a preoccupation with—perfection in the home. For example, comic Elayne Boozler doesn't fret about kitchen odors for Lemon Fantastik; she wisecracks about them.

One dilemma for advertisers today is recognizing who they might inadvertently insult next. A group of women complained on a nationwide computer network about a commercial for Sony's portable MiniDisc player. The sexist spot depicts a stud, clad in a tight T-shirt, draped over his 1958

Chevrolet Impala convertible. Each time Stud punches buttons on the MiniDisc programmed to display female names, a new leggy lady shows up. In the final shot, all the women are sitting in or lying around the car. The slogan: "If you play it, they will come." The protesters are offended by the blatant objectification of women as automatons that can be ordered up with push-button ease.

While market selection may be a logical consequence of the marketing concept, it raises ethical issues about *which* consumers are included and *how* they are targeted, as well as which consumers are *excluded* and the benefits they are denied. Marketing and advertising managers must be sensitive and balance the rights of different stakeholders.

Questions

1. Is targeting an advertising campaign to a niche market inherently insensitive to other

groups? Do you believe a lack of sensitivity by an ad maker is the same as a bias?

2. How can advertisers avoid using stereotypical images? What are some other ethical problems in targeting minorities as a specific target market?

Sources: Laura Bird, "Marketers Miss Out by Alienating Blacks," *The Wall Street Journal*, April 9, 1993, p. B3; Bob Garfield, "Daytime Audience Does a Makeover," in Special Report: Marketing to Women, *Advertising Age*, October 4, 1993, p. S-11; Kevin Goldman, "Atlanta Tavern Says Budweiser Was Racially Insensitive on Ad," *The Wall Street Journal*, June 4, 1993, p. B6; Kevin Goldman, "Sexy Sony Ad Riles a Network of Women," *The Wall Street Journal*, August 23, 1993, p. B5; N. Craig Smith and John A. Quelch, "Ethical Issues in Researching and Targeting Consumers," in *Ethics in Marketing* (Burr Ridge, IL: Richard D. Irwin, 1993), pp. 188–95.

Segmenting Business and Government Markets: Understanding Organizational Buying Behavior

Business (or *industrial*) **markets** include manufacturers, government agencies, wholesalers, retailers, banks, and institutions that buy goods and services to help them operate. These products may include raw materials, electronic components, mechanical parts, office equipment, vehicles, or services used in conducting the business. Products sold to business markets are often intended for resale to the public, as in the case of Levi's apparel.

Identifying target markets of prospective business customers is just as complex as identifying consumer markets. But many of the variables used to identify consumer markets can also be used for business markets—for example, geography, purchase occasion, benefits sought, user status, and usage rate.

Business markets also have special characteristics. They employ professional buyers and use systematic purchasing procedures. They are categorized by Standard Industrial Classification (SIC) codes. They may be concentrated geographically. And in any single market there may be only a small number of buyers.[17]

Business purchasing procedures

When businesspeople evaluate new products, they use a process far more complex and rigid than the consumer purchase process described in Chapter 4. Business marketers must design their advertising programs with this in mind.

Large firms have purchasing departments that act as professional buyers. They evaluate the need for products, analyze proposed purchases, weigh competitive bids, seek approvals from users and managers, make requisitions, place orders, and supervise all product purchasing. This structured purchase decision process suggests a rational approach. Recent research, however, shows that professional buyers often exhibit significant brand-equity behaviors such as willingness to pay a substantial premium for their favorite brand. This was especially true for buyers concerned about the negative consequences of a product failure. In other words, the buyers perceived well-known brands as a way to reduce risk. Moreover, their feelings about brands tended to transfer from one product category to another, even when the products were very different (for example, fax machines to floppy disks).[18] This suggests that advertising may play a larger role in business-to-business marketing than previously thought.

Making a sale in business markets may take weeks, months, or even years, especially to government agencies. Purchase decisions often depend on factors besides price or quality—product demonstrations, delivery time, terms of sale, dependability of supply, and others. So marketers often emphasize these issues in advertising and promotional appeals.

Business marketers should consider the purchase decision process of various segments before deciding on a target market. New companies, for instance, may target

• In business marketing, product demonstrations and personal service are often important components in making a sale. To drive sales through its dealers, John Deere implemented an award-winning campaign to introduce a new line of agricultural tractors. Deere sent a direct-mail piece and a 10-second message on an electronic chip to 28,000 current Deere tractor users, inviting them to see the new tractors in action. Each message included the name of the local dealer. More than 1,400 dealerships participated, following up with phone calls to schedule demo appointments with the prospective customers.

small firms where the purchase decision can be made quickly. Or they may use commission-only reps to call on the larger prospects that require more time. These decisions dictate where advertising should be placed.

Standard industrial classification

The Department of Commerce classifies all U.S. businesses—and collects and publishes data on them—by **Standard Industrial Classification (SIC) codes.** These codes are based on broad industry categories (food, tobacco, apparel) subdivided into major divisions, subgroups, and then detailed classes of firms in similar lines of business. Exhibit 5–5 breaks down SIC codes in the apparel industry. The federal government reports the number of firms, sales volumes, and number of employees by geographic area for each SIC code. SIC codes help companies segment markets and do research, and advertisers can obtain lists of companies in particular SIC groups for direct mailings.

Market concentration

Many countries' markets for industrial goods are concentrated in one region or several metropolitan areas. In the U.S., for example, the industrial market is heavily concentrated in the Midwest, the South, and California (see Exhibit 5–6). Market concentration reduces the number of geographic targets for an advertiser.

Moreover, business marketers deal with fewer buyers than consumer marketers. Less than 22 percent of U.S. manufacturers employ nearly 70 percent of all production workers and account for over 80 percent of all manufacturing dollars.[19] Customer size is critical for market segmentation. A firm may concentrate its marketing and advertising efforts on a few large customers, many smaller ones, or both.

Levi Strauss markets through three channels: independent department stores; specialty stores (like Miller's Outpost); and chain stores (like Sears and JCPenney). Its top 100 accounts provide 80 percent of the company's annual sales and are made through 13,000 retail outlets. Its remaining accounts (20 percent of sales) represent another 13,000

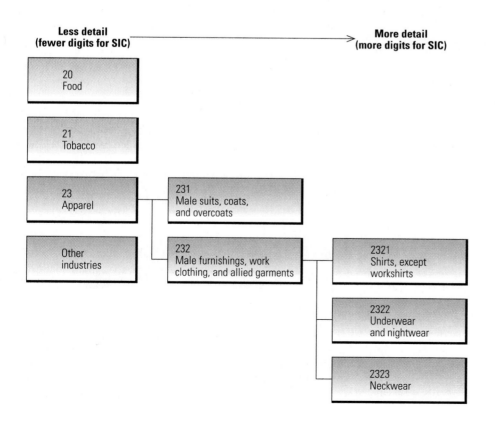

Exhibit • 5–5

A business marketer selling goods or services to firms in the apparel industry can use SIC codes in directories or on subscription databases to locate prospective companies.

Exhibit • 5–6
The states in this map are represented in proportion to the value of their manufactured products.

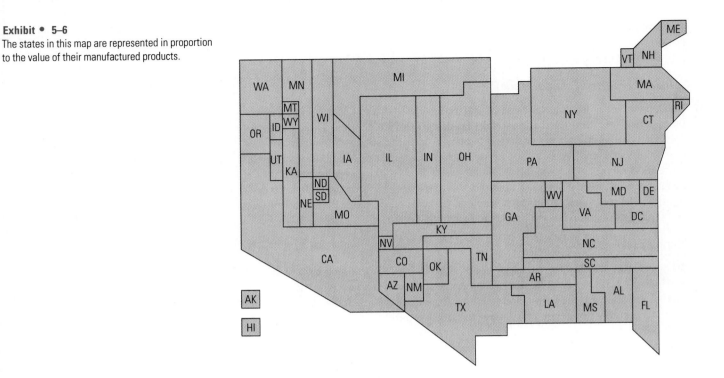

stores. Major accounts are served by sales reps from Levi's various divisions, smaller accounts by telemarketers and pan-divisional sales reps. Foote, Cone & Belding in San Francisco creates and coordinates advertising for all Levi Strauss divisions in the U.S.

Business marketers can also segment by end users. For example, a firm may develop software for one industry, such as banking, or for general use in a variety of industries. That decision, of course, affects ad placement.

Aggregating Market Segments

Once marketers identify and locate broad product-based markets with shared characteristics (geographic, demographic, behavioristic, or psychographic), they can proceed to the next step in the market segmentation process: (1) selecting groups that have a mutual interest in the product's utility and (2) reorganizing and aggregating (combining) them into larger market segments based on their potential for sales and profit. Let's take a look at how this process might work for Levi Strauss & Co. in the U.S. market.

First, the company's management needs to know the market potential for jeans and casual pants in various market areas; that is, it needs to discover the **primary demand trend** of the total U.S. market for its pants. To do this it uses a variety of *marketing research* techniques (discussed in Chapter 6).

Then management has to identify the needs, wants, and shared characteristics of the various groups within the casual apparel marketplace who live near the company's retail outlets. It may use the services of a large market segmentation company like National Decision Systems, which collects data on people's purchasing behavior and creates profiles of geographic markets across the country.

The company finds a huge market of prospective customers throughout the U.S.: students, blue-collar workers, young singles, professional people, homemakers, and so on. It then measures and analyzes household groups in each major retail area by demographic, lifestyle, and purchasing characteristics, sorts them into 50 different geodemographic segments, and refers to them with terms like those in Exhibit 5–7: Established Wealth, Movers & Shakers, Family Ties, Intercity Singles, and others. All

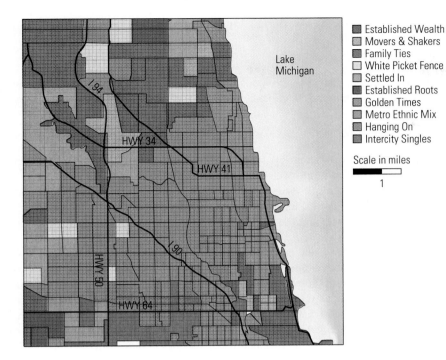

Exhibit • 5–7
National Decision Systems' MicroVision system classifies prospective customers in the Chicago area by census tract and labels each area by the residents' shared characteristics.

these people have apparel needs, and many might be interested in the style, cachet, and durability of the Levi's brand.

Selecting groups interested in product utility

Levi Strauss next selects groups that would like and be able to afford the utilities or benefits of Levi's apparel—suitability for work or play, comfort, style, low cost, durability, and so on. Groups interested in all these features make up the total possible market for Levi's clothes.

Part of the challenge of market segmentation is estimating the profits the company might realize if it (1) aims at the whole market or (2) caters only to a specific market segment. Apparel is a highly competitive market, but 10 percent of 1,000 is always larger than 90 percent of 100. So for a company like Levi Strauss, the target market must be a large mass market or it won't be profitable.[20]

Combining groups to build target market segments

The company needs to find groups that are relatively homogeneous (similar) and offer good potential for profit. Market data turn up a large number of demographic and lifestyle groups, including ethnically diverse families, young singles, and seniors with lower education and income who often live in rented homes or apartments: On Their Own (3.4 percent), Back Country (6.0 percent), and Settled In (5.1 percent). Because of their minimal retail or credit activity, these groups are not prime targets for premium-branded department store products.

But other segments offer greater potential—young to middle-aged households with medium to high incomes and average to high retail activity: Movers & Shakers (2.5 percent), Prosperous Ethnic Mix (2.8 percent), and Home Sweet Home (5.7 percent). By combining these (and similar groups) with the young professionals in the Good Step Forward (2.1 percent) and Great Beginnings segments (3.6 percent), Levi Strauss can target young to middle-aged people on their way up. Nationally, that amounts to 20 million U.S. households. That's not everybody, but it's a large and potentially very profitable mass market segment. These people might like the style and comfort of Levi's 550s as well as the tradition of a brand they know and trust, and the company could develop a campaign to appeal to their particular needs, wants, and self-image.

THE TARGET MARKETING PROCESS

Once this process is complete, a company can proceed to the **target marketing process.** This will determine the content, look, and feel of its advertising.

Target Market Selection

The first step in target marketing is to assess which of the newly created segments offer the greatest profit potential and which can be most successfully penetrated. The company designates one or more segments as a **target market**—that group of segments the company wishes to appeal to, design products for, and aim its marketing activities toward.[21] It may designate another set of segments as a secondary target market and aim some of its resources at it.

Let's look at the most likely target market for loose-fitting jeans: young to middle-aged customers with moderate to high income and education who like the style, comfort, and fashion of Levi's apparel. This group represents a large percentage of the apparel market, and, if won, will generate substantial profits. L.S.&Co. offers what these prospects need and want: the style and fashion of the jeans they grew up with, updated to be more comfortable for the adult body.

If the young, comfort-oriented segment wasn't large enough to be profitable, the company would select a different target market. And its other marketing and advertising activities would have to change as well. For an exercise, look at Ad Lab 5–B and consider how Sears selected its new target market.

The Marketing Mix: A Strategy for Matching Products to Markets

Once a company defines its target market, it knows exactly where to focus its attention and resources. It can shape the product concept and even design special features for its target market (such as certain colors or special sizes). It can establish proper pricing. It can determine the need for locating stores or dealers, and it can prepare the most convincing advertising messages.

As we discussed in Chapter 4, a product offers a number of utilities—perceived by the consumer as a *bundle of values*. With this in mind, marketers and advertisers gener-

• Levi Strauss uncovered a large target market for loose-fitting jeans for both men and women. These customers want the style and fashion—and the label—of the jeans they grew up with, but constructed to fit their adult bodies more comfortably.

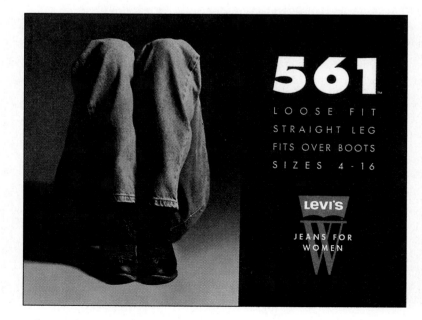

Marketing Sears: Changing Times Call for New Targets and Products

Ad Lab 5-B

Since its first edition in 1886, the Sears catalog has been one of our best records of American culture. Featuring a selection of products far beyond that of any single store, the catalog offered everything from cars and homes to money belts and neckties. It gave Americans a sense of fashion for the times and even taught some how to read. Sears positioned itself as "America's General Store," but the catalog made it even more than that.

For a hundred years, the Sears catalog enjoyed tremendous success, eventually achieving annual sales in excess of $3 billion! However, this very success attracted a lot of competition, and in time major players like JCPenney, Montgomery Ward, Lands' End, and Spiegel were nipping at Sears' heels. By the late 1980s, the competition was hurting Sears badly and it was losing money. Then, in 1992, it suffered its worst year ever. It lost $3.9 billion in total catalog and store sales! Sears had to find a new position in today's marketplace.

After a thorough review of the overall marketing situation, company executives decided to recreate Sears as a "product" and to drastically alter the company's marketing strategy. They closed more than 100 stores, cut some 50,000 jobs, and discontinued the venerable Sears catalog. The company's CEO, Arthur Martinez, decided Sears had to compete in the growing soft merchandise market (apparel and accessories) and immediately launched a $25 million advertising campaign for Sears apparel.

Sears has historically advertised its hard and soft merchandise equally. But with the change in focus, Sears turned to one of the largest advertising agencies in the world, Young & Rubicam in New York, to help refurbish its image. For the new campaign, Y&R targeted young working women with families and Hispanics with the theme, "Come see the softer side of Sears."

At the same time, Sears had to update the image of its stores, so it decided to expand the apparel departments by 30 percent. The refurbishing of 500 mall-based stores should be finished by 1998.

Laboratory Applications

1. What market segment is Sears now appealing to? How is that different from its previous target market?

2. If you were creating a soft goods ad for Sears, what elements would you include to appeal to its new target markets?

---

ally try to shape their basic product into a total **product concept:** the consumer's perception of a product as a bundle of utilitarian and symbolic values that satisfy functional, social, psychological, and other wants and needs.

Companies engage in many activities to enhance the product concept and effect marketing exchanges (sales). These activities can be categorized under four generic functions that must be fulfilled for an exchange to come about: (1) *product,* (2) *price,* (3) *distribution,* and (4) *communication.*[22] For convenience, marketing educators developed a mnemonic device for these four functions: *product, price, place,* and *promotion*—or the **Four Ps (4 Ps).**[23]

The 4 Ps are a simple way to remember the basic elements of the **marketing mix.** But within each element are numerous marketing activities that companies can employ to fine tune its product concept and improve sales. Advertising, for example, is one instrument of the communication (promotion) element. The remainder of this chapter focuses on the relationship between advertising and the other elements of the marketing mix.

ADVERTISING AND THE PRODUCT ELEMENT

In developing a marketing mix, marketers generally start with the **product element.** Major activities typically include the way the product is designed and classified, positioned, branded, and packaged. Each of these affects the way the product is advertised.

Product Life Cycle

Marketers theorize that just as humans pass through stages in life from infancy to death, products (and especially product categories) also pass through a **product life cycle** (see Exhibit 5–8).[24] A product's position in the life cycle influences the kind of advertising used. There are four major stages in the product life cycle: introduction, growth, maturity, and decline.

When a company introduces a new product category, nobody knows about it. To educate consumers, the company has to stimulate **primary demand**—consumer demand for the whole product category, not just its own brand.

Exhibit • 5–8
A product's life cycle curve may vary, depending on the product category. Marketing objectives and strategies also change as the product proceeds from one stage to the next.

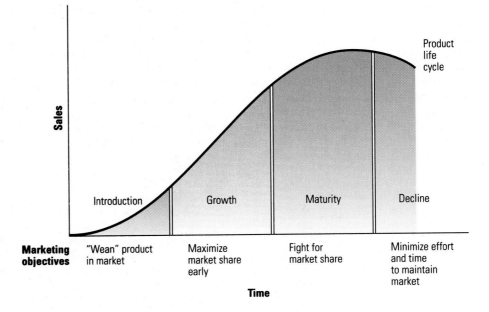

| Marketing objectives | "Wean" product in market | Maximize market share early | Fight for market share | Minimize effort and time to maintain market |

When cellular telephones were introduced in the late 1980s, advertisers had to first create enough consumer demand to *pull* the product through the channels of distribution. Advertising communications educated consumers about the new product and its category, explaining what cellular phones were, how they worked, and the rewards of owning one. Sales promotion efforts aimed at the retail trade—called **push strategy**—encouraged distributors and dealers to stock, display, and advertise the new products (see Chapter 15).

• Advertisers sometimes want to stimulate primary demand for an entire product category rather than for a specific brand. This understated ad, one of a series by the California Fluid Milk Processor Advisory Board, reminds us of the enjoyable sensation of milk and cookies on the taste buds—without even showing the milk, the subject of the campaign.

During the **introductory** (pioneering) **phase** of any new product category, companies incur considerable costs for educating customers, building widespread dealer distribution, and encouraging demand. They must spend significant advertising sums at this stage to establish a position as a market leader and to gain a large share of market before the growth stage begins.

When sales volume begins to rise rapidly, the product enters the **growth stage.** This period is characterized by rapid *market expansion,* as more and more customers, stimulated by mass advertising and word-of-mouth, make their first, second, and third purchases. Competitors jump into the market. But the company that established the early leadership position reaps the biggest rewards. As a percentage of total sales, advertising expenditures should decrease, and individual firms will realize their first substantial profits.

During the early 1990s, the demand for cellular phones exploded, and category sales quadrupled every year. Many competitors suddenly appeared. With increased production and competition, prices started to fall, which brought even more people into the market. By the end of the decade, it's estimated that over 40 percent of all U.S. families will likely own cellular phones.

In the **maturity stage,** as the marketplace becomes saturated with competing products and the number of new customers dwindles, industry sales reach a plateau. Competition intensifies, and profits diminish. Companies increase their promotional efforts but emphasize **selective demand** to impress customers with the subtle advantages of their brand. At this stage, companies increase sales only at the expense of competitors—*conquest sales.* The strategies of market segmentation, product positioning, and price promotion become more important during this shakeout period as weak companies fall by the wayside and those remaining fight for small increases in market share. By 1994, for example, cellular phones that once sold for $1,500 were suddenly advertised regularly for $100 to $200. Ads emphasized features and low prices, and the product became a staple of discount merchandisers.

Late in the maturity stage, companies often scramble to extend the product's life cycle. They may try to find new users, develop new uses for the product, change the size of packages, design new labels, or improve quality. Without innovation, name brands eventually see their sales erode. If the advertised brand is really no better, people will buy whatever's cheapest and most convenient. Gillette realized that and spent 10 years and hundreds of millions of dollars to develop and market Sensor, a breakthrough shaving system, that was successful beyond all expectations.[25] Keds shoes, on the other hand, didn't innovate. During a back-to-basics consumer fad, the brand made a comeback with baby boomers, and the company milked the brand for the windfall

• Advertisers use a variety of strategies to extend the life cycle of a product in its mature stage. Procter & Gamble, testing two new flavors of Crest toothpaste in mass-merchant chains, used Telestar Interactive's MicroTalk shelf units to play audio messages about the products to approaching consumers.

profits. But then the brand suddenly experienced a decline in sales and lost market share in 1993.[26]

Finally, products enter the **decline stage** due to obsolescence, changing technology, or new consumer tastes. Companies may cease all promotion and phase the products out quickly, as in the case of record turntables and LP albums, or let them fade slowly with minimal advertising, like most sheer hosiery brands.[27]

Product Classifications

The way a company classifies its product is important in defining both the product concept and the marketing mix. As Exhibit 5–9 shows, there are many ways to classify tangible goods: by markets, by the purchasing habits of buyers, by the rate of consumption or degree of tangibility, or by physical attributes.

Unlike tangible products, a **service** is a bundle of *intangible* benefits that satisfy some need or want, are temporary in nature, and usually derive from completion of a task.[28] Thus we have *task utility,* as described in Chapter 4. Rail service is transitory—used and priced by time and distance. It offers the functional benefits of transporting people, livestock, and freight. But it can also offer psychological benefits. Just think of the romance and leisure of a train trip across Europe aboard the Orient Express. The railroad relies on the use of *specialized equipment*—vehicles able to pull huge loads over a unique track. This makes it an **equipment-based service.**

In contrast, an ad agency, like a law firm or a bank, is a **people-based service;** it relies on the creative talents and marketing skills of individuals. As one agency CEO said, "My inventory goes up and down the elevators twice a day."[29]

Product Positioning

Once an advertising person understands the product's stage in the life cycle and how it's classified, the first strategic decision can be made—how to **position** the product. The basic goal of positioning strategy is to own a word in the prospect's mind. Levi's owns "jeans." Federal Express owns "overnight." And Volvo owns "safety." At a breakfast celebrating the 25th anniversary of positioning strategy, Al Ries quipped, "What Volvo is exploiting is the fact that the car looks like a tank. They can fire the designers."[30]

Exhibit • 5–9
Product classifications.

By market	By rate of consumption and tangibility	By purchasing habits	By physical description

Consumer goods
  Products and services we use in our daily lives (food, clothing, furniture, automobiles).
 	
Industrial goods
  Products used by companies for the purpose of producing other products (raw materials, agricultural commodities, machinery, tools, equipment).
	Durable goods
	  Tangible products that are long lasting and infrequently replaced (cars, trucks, refrigerators, furniture).
	
	Nondurable goods
	  Tangible products that may be consumed in one or a few uses and usually need to be replaced at regular intervals (food, soap, gasoline, oil).
	
	Services
	  Activities, benefits, or satisfaction offered for sale (travel, haircuts, legal and medical services, massages).
		Convenience goods
		  Purchases made frequently with a minimum of effort (cigarettes, food, newspapers).
		
		Shopping goods
		  Infrequently purchased items for which greater time is spent comparing price, quality, style, warranty (furniture, cars, clothing, tires).
		
		Specialty goods
		  Products with such unique characteristics that consumers will make special efforts to purchase them even if they're more expensive (fancy photographic equipment, special women's fashions, stereo components).
			Packaged goods
			  Cereals, hair tonics, and so forth.
			
			Hard goods
			  Furniture, appliances.
			
			Soft goods
			  Clothing, bedding.
			
			Services
			  Nontangible products.

• In addition to offering functional benefits, an equipment-based service like Amtrak offers psychological benefits, such as providing travelers with a more intimate view of the land.

SONG: by Richie Havens.
The way you see.
The way you see the miles passing by.

The way you look out on life.
Cities and mountains.
Shadows against the sky . . .

There's something about a train that's magic.
All Aboard Amtrak.

Products may be positioned in many different ways. Generally, they are ranked by the way they are differentiated, by the benefits they offer, by the particular market segment to which they appeal, or by the way they are classified. Xerox has repositioned itself as "The Document Company," moving from the narrow, glutted, copier market to the broader, growing, document-handling market. With one stroke, Xerox hopes to redefine the business it is in, differentiate itself from the competition, and create a new number-one position for itself.[31]

Product Differentiation

Product differentiation creates a product difference that appeals to the preferences of a distinct market segment. In advertising, nothing is more important than being able to tell prospects truthfully that your product is new and different. Unfortunately, most "new" products fail to impress consumers.[32] Yet simply adding new colors might differentiate a product enough to attract a new set of customers. Not all product differences need be that obvious. Differences between products may be *perceptible, hidden,* or *induced*. Hank Seiden says every successful product must have a "Unique Advantage." Bob Pritikin humorously calls that differentiating quality the AMAZING NEW![33]

Differences between products that are readily apparent to the consumer are called **perceptible differences.** Snapple, for example, received its initial impetus because of its unique taste, and the company now spends $10 million annually to advertise this difference to consumers nationwide.[34] On the other hand, **hidden differences** are not so readily apparent. Trident gum may look and taste the same as other brands but is differentiated by the use of artificial sweeteners. While hidden differences can enhance a product's desirability, advertising is usually needed to let consumers know about them.

For many product classes, such as aspirin, salt, gasoline, packaged foods, liquor, and financial services, advertising can create **induced differences.** Banks, brokerage houses, and insurance companies, for example, which offer virtually identical services and financial products, use advertising and promotion to differentiate themselves. However, few have yet discovered the image asset of branding as used by the national packaged goods marketers. That is created through the accumulation of consistent advertising campaigns, favorable publicity, and special event sponsorship.[35]

As Sunkist so successfully demonstrated (see Chapter 1), the ability to create the perception of differences in functionally similar products and services depends on the effective use of branding, packaging, and advertising.

Product Branding

The fundamental differentiating device for all products is the **brand**—that combination of name, words, symbols, or design that identifies the product and its source and distinguishes it from competing products. Without brands, consumers couldn't tell one product from another, and advertising them would be nearly impossible.

Branding decisions are difficult. A manufacturer may establish an **individual brand** for each product it produces. Unilever, for example, markets its toothpastes under the individual brand names Aim, Pepsodent, and Close-Up. Such companies designate a distinct target market for each product and develop a separate personality and image for each brand. However, this strategy is very costly.

On the other hand, a company might use a **family brand** and market different products under the same umbrella name. When Heinz promotes its ketchup it hopes to help its relishes too. This decision may be cost effective, but one bad product in a line can hurt the whole family.

Because it is so expensive for manufacturers to market **national brands** (also called *manufacturer's brands*), some companies use a *private-labeling strategy*. They manufacture the product and sell it to **resellers** (distributors or dealers) who put their own brand on the product. **Private labels,** typically sold at lower prices in large retail chain stores, include such familiar names as Kenmore, Craftsman, Cragmont, Kroger, and Party Pride. They now account for 18.7 percent of all grocery-product purchases.[36] The responsibility for creating brand image and familiarity rests with the distributor or retailer, who is also the principal benefactor if the brand is successful. A recent trend has been toward premium private labels, like President's Choice, which has enjoyed immense success. These products feature better packaging, superior quality, and a higher price, comparable to national brands.

Branding decisions are critical because the brands a company owns may be its most important capital asset. Imagine the value of owning a brand name like Coca-Cola, Nike, Porsche, or Levi's. *Financial World's* annual brand value report ranks Coca-Cola as the most valuable brand in the world, followed by Marlboro, Nescafe, Kodak, and Microsoft (see Exhibit 5–10).[37] Some companies pay a substantial fee for the right to use another company's brand name. Thus, we have **licensed brands** like Sunkist vitamins, Coca-Cola clothing, Porsche sunglasses, and Mickey Mouse watches.

Role of branding

For consumers, brands offer instant recognition and identification. They also promise consistent, reliable standards of quality, taste, size, or even psychological satisfaction, which adds value to the product for both the consumer and the manufacturer. In a study by McKinsey & Co., a computer's brand name ranked second, behind performance, in what consumers considered important when choosing a personal computer. Price, by the way, ranked fifth.[38]

Brands must be built on differences in images, meanings, and associations. It's up to manufacturers to differentiate their products clearly and deliver value competitively. The product has to taste better, or get clothes cleaner, or be packaged in a more environmentally friendly container.[39] Advertising for an established brand, particularly a well-differentiated one, is much more effective if it exploits the brand's positioning.[40] Ideally, when consumers see a brand on the shelf, they instantly comprehend the brand's promise and have confidence in its quality. Of course, they must be familiar with and believe in the brand's promise—a function of advertising effectiveness. And

Exhibit • 5–10

Top worldwide brands for 1993.

		Brand value ($ millions)
1.	Coca-Cola	$35,950
2.	Marlboro	33,045
3.	Nescafe	11,549
4.	Kodak	10,020
5.	Microsoft	9,842
6.	Budweiser	9,724
7.	Kellogg's	9,372
8.	Motorola	9,293
9.	Gillette	8,218
10.	Bacardi	7,163

● Coca-Cola's trademark varies from country to country. But the overall look is retained through use of similar letterforms and style, even with different alphabets.

1. Arabic	5. Spanish
2. French	6. Chinese
3. Japanese	7. Hebrew
4. Thai	8. Polish

the advertiser wants to achieve brand preference or, as we pointed out in Chapter 4, *brand loyalty.*

The ultimate goal of all brand advertising and promotion is to build greater **brand equity,** the totality of what consumers, distributors, dealers—even competitors—feel and think about the brand over an extended period of time. In short, it's the value of the brand's capital. Young & Rubicam, the New York ad agency that handles Sears, uses an approach called the BrandAsset Valuator™ to determine brand equity. This model measures a matrix defined by *brand stature* (a blend of familiarity and esteem) and *vitality* (relevance and differentiation). By Y&R's measure, the up-and-coming brands in terms of brand equity are Home Depot, Victoria's Secret, and Snapple—all of which, Y&R says, overshadow more familiar names like Bayer aspirin, Oldsmobile, and Bold detergent.[41]

● Brand equity is the totality of what purchasers, distributors, dealers, and competitors feel and think about the brand over an extended period of time. Snapple is a prime example of a successful, fairly new consumer product achieving brand equity today.

High brand equity offers a host of blessings to the product marketer: customer loyalty, price inelasticity, long-term profits. A loyal customer can be nine times as profitable as a disloyal one.[42] But building brand equity requires time and money. Brand value and preference drive market share, but share points and brand loyalty are usually won by the advertisers who spend the most. And increasing brand loyalty requires a spending increase of 200 percent to 300 percent to affect loyalty dramatically.[43] Charlotte Beers, the head of Ogilvy & Mather, points out the importance of "brand stewardship." She believes companies must maintain consistency in their message by integrating all their marketing communications—from packaging and advertising to sales promotion and publicity—to maintain and reinforce the brand's personality in a real-life context and avoid doing something stupid like changing the distinctive color of a Ryder rental truck.[44]

Product Packaging

The product's package is a component of the product element. But it is also an exhibitive *medium* that can determine the outcome of retail shelf competition.

Package designers (who sometimes work in agencies) must make the package exciting, appealing, and at the same time functional. The five considerations in package design are *identification, containment and protection, convenience, consumer appeal,* and *economy.* These functions may even become **copy points**—copywriting themes—in the product's advertising (see Chapter 14).

Identification

Packaging is such an important identification device that some companies use the same package and label design for years. Why? Because the unique combination of trade name, trademark, or trade character, reinforced by the package design, quickly identifies the product's brand and differentiates it from competitors. For example, the traditional contoured Coca-Cola bottle was so unusual and popular that in 1992 the company began reintroducing it to U.S. markets. The company never stopped using it in many international markets, since it differentiated Coke so well from other cola products.

Packages must offer high visibility and legibility just to penetrate shoppers' *physiological* screens. Product features must be easy to read and color combinations must provide high contrast to differentiate the product. To penetrate the consumer's *psychological* screens, the package design must reflect the tone, image, and personality of the product concept. In many product categories (wine, cosmetics), the quality of the package largely determines the consumer's perception of the product's quality.

Containment, protection, and convenience

The basic purpose of any package is to hold and protect the product and make it easy to use. While marketers must design an interesting package, they must also make sure it will keep the product fresh and protect its contents from shipping damage, water vapor (for frozen goods), grease, infestation, and odors. And packages must adhere to legal protection requirements.

Retailers want packages that are easy to stack and display; they also want a full range of sizes to fit their customers' needs. Consumers want packages that are easy to carry, open, and store. So these are important design considerations. But convenience can't interfere with protection. Spouts make pouring easier, but they may also limit a package's physical strength.

Consumer appeal

Consumer appeal in packaging is the result of many factors—size, color, material, and shape. Certain colors have special meanings to consumers. It's not uncommon for even a subtle change in color to result in as much as a 20 percent change in sales.[45]

● Some marketers today use packaging to demonstrate their environmental awareness. Here Coca-Cola uses a bold red outdoor ad with the slogan *Bounces back like a yo-yo* to tell Czech customers about Coke's returnable plastic bottles. A similar Coke campaign in Hungary uses a boomerang.

In this age of environmental awareness, *green marketing* is an important issue for many companies and consumers alike. New technology has made ecologically safe packaging available and affordable for many product categories. And many companies now advertise their packages as environmentally responsible.

A package's shape also offers an opportunity for consumer appeal based on whimsy, humor, or romance. Heart-shaped packages of Valentine's Day candy instantly tell what the product is. Some companies design packages with a secondary use in mind. Kraft's cheese jar, once emptied, can be used for serving fruit juice. Some tins and bottles even become collectibles (Chivas Regal). These packages are really premiums that give buyers extra value for the dollars they spend.

Economy

The costs of protection, identification, convenience, and consumer appeal add to basic production costs, but this increase may be more than offset by increased customer appeal. These benefits may make a considerable difference to the consumer and affect both the product concept and the way it is advertised.

Many companies, especially small ones, request input from their advertising people about pricing strategies. That's because the **price element** of the marketing mix influences consumer perceptions so dramatically.

ADVERTISING AND THE PRICE ELEMENT

Key Factors Influencing Price

Companies typically set their prices based on market demand for the product, costs of production and distribution, competition, and corporate objectives. However, a company often has relatively few options for determining its price strategy, depending on the desired product concept.

Market demand

If the supply of a product is static but the desire (or demand) for it increases, the price tends to rise. If demand drops below available supply, the price tends to fall. This may dramatically affect advertising messages. See Exhibit 5–11.

Exhibit • 5–11
This graph plots demand versus price and supply versus price. The demand curve shows the amounts purchased at various prices. The supply curve shows the amounts offered for sale at various prices. The point where the two curves cross is called the market clearing price, where demand and supply balance. It is the price that theoretically sells out the product.

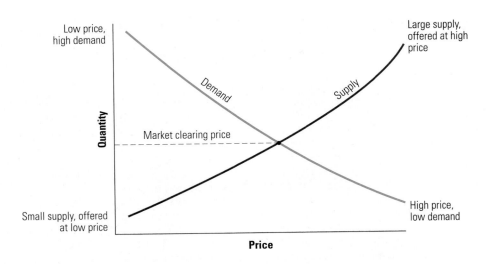

In the 1991 recession, many auto manufacturers faced a glut of unsold new cars and declining demand. Several companies offered substantial factory rebates—price cuts—to motivate prospective buyers. Dealers immediately sold more cars. No amount of image or awareness advertising would have had the same effect. But, of course, advertising was essential to communicate the price cut.

Some marketing researchers theorize that for new durable-good products, advertising works with word-of-mouth communication to generate awareness of and belief in the product's attributes. Once consumers perceive that the product's value warrants the purchase price, sales occur. As product experience and information spread, the risks typically associated with new products diminish, which effectively increases the consumer's willingness to purchase at a higher price.[46]

Production and distribution costs

The price of goods depends to some extent on the costs of production and distribution. As these costs increase, they must be passed on to the consumer, or the company will be unable to meet its overhead and be forced out of business.

Competition

Marketers believe that, in many product categories, consumers are less concerned with a product's actual price than with its perceived price relative to competitors. For the advertiser, maintaining that perception during periods of intense price competition and fluctuation is challenging and critically important.[47]

Corporate objectives and strategies

A company's objectives also influence price. When introducing new products, companies often set a high price initially to recover development and start-up costs. On the other hand, the objective may be to position the product as an inexpensive convenience item aimed at a broad target market. In this case, ads stress the product's economy.

Price also depends on the company's marketing strategy, and image advertising may be used to justify a higher price. Many premium-priced products, like L'Oréal, are touted for the very fact that they do cost more.

As products enter the maturity stage of their life cycle, corporate objectives tend to aim at increasing, or at least maintaining, market share. To accomplish this, competitive advertising and promotion heat up, and prices tend to drop.

Variable influences

Economic conditions, consumer income and tastes, government regulations, marketing costs, and other factors also influence prices and thus advertising. Marketing manage-

Marketing Sears: Changing Times Mean Changing Prices   *Ad Lab 5-C*

Sears, for a century one of the most trusted companies in America, found itself out of step and losing money in the 1980s. By 1990 it was working to resolve the problem. Sears discontinued its catalog, closed some unprofitable stores, and stocked the remaining ones with new, brand-name merchandise. By 1994, it had modified its marketing emphasis from hard goods to soft merchandise.

Changes in the Sears product element of the marketing mix led to changes in the pricing element. A key change included being in line with the prices of competitive department stores. To be successful, companies in the fashion industry must reach people on an emotional level. Products that evoke emotions often sell for higher prices, compared to products with prices based

on manufacturing costs. Thus, the new emphasis on fashion at Sears enabled it to move away from the promotional pricing strategy of paint and tools to a strategy more in keeping with the subjective value perception of fashion customers. If the consumer feels the product or the store suits his or her style, then the value goes up along with the customer's willingness to pay a little more.

At the same time, Sears improved the company's credibility in the eyes of consumers by adopting the Council of Better Business Bureau's proposed code for comparative price advertising. This ethics code was established in response to increased investigation and tougher legislation by state and local authorities. The code provides guidelines for a range of comparative pricing tac-

tics, including comparisons with former selling prices, list prices, and prices of competitors. The code also discusses price matching and lowest-price claims.

Laboratory Applications

1. How would you describe the new image Sears is trying to build? What advertising headlines can you think of that would communicate this image to the higher end of the market?

2. Visit a Sears store in your area and examine the prices. How would you describe the pricing strategy Sears is using? How do Sears' prices compare to similar department stores'?

ment must consider all these to determine an appropriate pricing strategy and then create advertising that justifies the product's price. Consider the alternatives listed in RL 5–2, Checklist of Strategies for Setting Prices, in the Reference Library. Each strategy will have a different effect on the advertising a company employs. To understand Sears' pricing strategy, see Ad Lab 5–C, "Marketing Sears: Changing Times Mean Changing Prices."

Before the first ad can be created, the **distribution element,** or place, must be decided. Companies use two basic methods of distribution: *direct* or *indirect*.

ADVERTISING AND THE DISTRIBUTION (PLACE) ELEMENT

Direct Distribution

When companies sell directly to end users or consumers, they use **direct distribution.** Avon, for example, employs sales reps who work for the factory rather than a retailer and sell directly to consumers. Encyclopedia publishers and insurance companies often sell and distribute their products and services directly to customers without the use of wholesalers or retailers. In these cases, the advertising burden is carried entirely by the manufacturer.

One of the fastest-growing methods of direct distribution today is **network marketing** in which individuals act as independent distributors for a manufacturer or private-label marketer. These individuals sign up friends and relatives to consume the company's products and recruit others to join. Through a gradual, word-of-mouth process, they form a "buying club" of independent distributors who buy the products wholesale direct from the company, use them, and tout them to more and more friends and acquaintances.

If successful, the rewards for the network marketing company (and many of the distributors) can be staggering. Amway International, the granddaddy of network marketing, now boasts international sales in excess of $5 billion, and many of its longtime distributors became multimillionaires in the process. Other companies have broken the billion-dollar sales mark, too, among them Nikken (Japan), Herbalife, and Shaklee.[48] These companies brag about the fact that they do *no media advertising*. Since they usually sell consumer products (that would typically carry a heavy advertising and sales promotion burden), they save a tremendous amount of money. Most marketing communications are simply word-of-mouth. The companies do provide attractive product packaging, catalogs, brochures, and other sales material—which the distributors typically pay for at cost. Today, companies using this distribution method include subsidiaries or spinoffs of well-known public corporations—such as Gillette, U.S. Sprint, and Rexall Sundown.

Indirect Distribution

Manufacturers usually don't sell directly to end users or consumers. Most companies market their products through a *distribution channel* that includes a network of *resellers*. A **reseller** (also called a *middleman*) is a business firm that operates between the producer and the consumer or industrial purchaser. It deals in trade rather than production.[49] Resellers include both wholesalers and retailers, as well as manufacturers' representatives, brokers, jobbers, and distributors. A **distribution channel** comprises all the firms and individuals that take title, or assist in taking title, to the product as it moves from the producer to the consumer.

Indirect distribution channels make the flow of products available to customers conveniently and economically. Appliance companies, for example, contract with exclusive regional distributors who buy the products from the factory and resell them to local dealers, who then resell them to consumers. Many industrial companies market their products through reps or distributors to *original-equipment manufacturers (OEMs)*. These OEMs may use the product as a component in their own product, which is then sold to their customers.

The advertising a company uses depends on the product's method of distribution. Much of the advertising we see is not prepared or paid for by the manufacturer but by the distributor or retailer. Members of a distribution channel give enormous promotional support to the manufacturers they represent.

A part of marketing strategy is determining the amount of coverage necessary for a product. Procter & Gamble, for example, distributes Crest toothpaste to virtually every supermarket, discount store, drug, and variety store. Other products might need only one dealer for every 50,000 people. Consumer goods manufacturers traditionally use three distribution strategies: *intensive, selective,* and *exclusive.*

Intensive distribution

Soft drinks, candy, Timex watches, and other convenience goods are available at every possible location because of **intensive distribution.** In fact, consumers can buy them with a minimum of effort. The profit on each unit is usually very low, but the volume of sales is high. The sales burden is usually carried by the manufacturer's national ad-

● With a little bit of humor, Staples gives tremendous promotional support to the brands it carries without ever mentioning a single one by name.

MUSIC: (Stirring throughout.)
ANNCR: To succeed in business, you don't need to be big. All you need is a dream. Just a dream and the passion to pursue it. And the dedication to see it through. And the talent to build on it. And the opportunity to use your talent. And a little luck. And some pencils. And pens. Maybe some typewriter ribbon and correction fluid. And some of those little yellow note pads with the sticky stuff on the back. And some computer paper. And some laser printers to put it in. And some desks to put the prints on. And a fax machine. And some of those #10 envelopes with the little windows in them so you can send out bills. And you can save a bundle on all of these things at Staples, The Office Superstore. Because Staples offers guaranteed lowest prices on over 5,000 basic business necessities. With such incredibly low prices, you can take all that money you save and put it into your dream, instead. Staples. The Office Superstore. Conveniently located in Cincinnati and Springdale or call for delivery at 1-800-333-3330. Dreams sold separately.

vertising. Ads in trade magazines **push** the product into the retail "pipeline," and in mass media they stimulate consumers to **pull** the products through the pipeline. As a manufacturer modifies its strategy to more push or more pull, special promotions may be directed at the trade or at consumers to build brand volume (see Chapter 15).

Selective distribution

By limiting the number of outlets through **selective distribution,** manufacturers can cut their distribution and promotion costs. Many hardware tools are sold selectively through discount chains, home-improvement centers, and hardware stores. Levi Strauss sells through better department and chain stores. Manufacturers may use national advertising, but the sales burden is normally carried by the retailer. The manufacturer may share part of the retailer's advertising costs through a **cooperative advertising** program. For example, a Levi's retailer may receive substantial allowances from the manufacturer for advertising Levi's clothing in its local area. In return, the retailer agrees to display the manufacturer's products prominently.

Exclusive distribution

Some manufacturers grant **exclusive distribution** rights to a wholesaler or retailer in one geographic region. For example, a town of 50,000 to 100,000 people will have only one Chrysler dealer and no Mercedes dealer. This is also common in high fashion, major appliances, and furniture lines. What is lost in market coverage is often gained in the ability to maintain a prestige image and premium prices. Exclusive distribution agreements also force manufacturers and retailers to cooperate closely in advertising and promotion programs.

Vertical Marketing Systems: The Growth of Franchising

To be efficient, members of a distribution channel need to cooperate closely with one another. This need gave rise to the **vertical marketing system (VMS),** a centrally programmed and managed distribution system that supplies or otherwise serves a group of stores or other businesses.

There are many types of vertical marketing systems. Today, the greatest growth is in **franchising**—like McDonald's or Mailboxes, Etc.—in which dealers (or *franchisees*) pay a fee to operate under the guidelines and direction of the parent company or manufacturer (the *franchisor*). An estimated 33 percent of all retail sales in the United States are made through franchise outlets.[50] There are only 4,500 franchisors throughout the U.S. and Canada, compared to some 20 million businesses in the United States alone.[51]

Franchising and other vertical marketing systems offer both manufacturers and retailers numerous advantages, not the least of which are centralized coordination of marketing efforts and substantial savings and continuity in advertising. Perhaps most important is consumer recognition: the moment a new McDonald's opens, the franchisee has instant customers. Moreover, a single newspaper ad can promote all of a chain's retailers in a particular trading area.

Many marketers find that franchising is the best way to introduce their services into global markets. Subway sandwich shops, for example, is the fastest-growing franchise operation in North America with a total of 7,000 stores (400 in Canada). With a solid base at home, the company entered the 90s by aggressively approaching new markets in Australia, Japan, Israel, Ireland, Mexico, Portugal, and South Korea.[52]

The European Union, a market of 340 million people, is now opening to innovative marketers. As a result, franchising is starting to grow rapidly, especially in the United Kingdom, France, Germany, Spain, Belgium, and the Netherlands. Though franchising is less regulated in Europe, advertising is more regulated. This again points out the need for local experts to manage the advertising function in foreign markets.[53]

● McDonald's is one of the best-known franchisors in the world. The Swedish ad *(left)* emphasizes value: *McDonald's = 39 Swedish crowns. Our three Extra Value Meals still do not cost more.* The ad from South Korea *(right)* encourages family dining with its headline: *A place where eating enjoyment leads to an even bigger enjoyment. McDonald's.*

ADVERTISING'S ROLE IN THE COMMUNICATION (PROMOTION) ELEMENT

Once it determines product, price, and distribution, a company is ready to plan its marketing communications, of which advertising is just one component. (See Ad Lab 5–D, "Marketing Sears: Soft Sell for Soft Goods.")

The **communication element** includes all marketing-related communications between the seller and the buyer. A variety of marketing communications tools comprise the **communications mix.** These tools can be grouped into *personal selling* and *nonpersonal selling* activities.

Personal selling includes all person-to-person contact with customers. **Nonpersonal selling** activities—which use some medium as an intermediary for communications—include *advertising, direct marketing, public relations, collateral materials,* and *sales promotion.* Today, successful marketing managers blend all these elements into an *integrated marketing communications program.*

Personal Selling

Some consumer products are sold by clerks in retail stores, others by salespeople who call on customers directly. Personal selling is very important in business-to-business marketing. It establishes a face-to-face situation in which the marketer can learn firsthand about customer wants and needs and customers find it harder to say no.

Advertising

Advertising is sometimes called mass or nonpersonal selling. Its usual purpose is to inform, persuade, and remind customers about particular products and services. In some cases, like mail order, advertising even closes the sale.

Marketing Sears: Soft Sell for Soft Goods   *Ad Lab 5-D*

For a hundred years, Sears was known as the general store where you could get everything from washing machines to car batteries. But now that Sears is establishing a new image, it needs to position itself differently in the marketplace. Sears is communicating its new image through advertising—a lot of it. In 1995, the company planned to spend about $23.5 million on advertising, a 30 percent increase from 1994.

To help customers alter their perception of Sears, a new campaign from Young & Rubicam promotes the new soft merchandise by using what Sears is best known for, its hard goods. TV jingles state, "Come on in, see what's new. Sears has got the softest hardware for you." Y&R has

also developed ads for Sears' exclusive new line of fragrances and beauty products under the theme line: "The many sides of Sears."

At the same time, the company is trying to raise its perception on other levels. In a 45-second TV spot during the Winter Olympics, a rock star described how he felt about Sears working with him to raise funds for the homeless. The senior executive VP of marketing explained that Sears likes to combine the excitement of high-profile events with the image of its stores. Events are an important way to capture change and put its brand in front of consumers in new ways. Using a rock star also reaches people who like the entertainer but might not normally shop at Sears.

By using broad areas of communication to reach consumers, Sears is positioning itself to be seen. And if being seen results in awareness, that in turn may increase sales.

Laboratory Applications

1. Do you think the "softer" side of Sears will be more profitable than the "harder" side? If you were the ad agency working for Sears, what campaign would you come up with to position Sears in the softer marketplace?

2. What types of events do you think Sears should sponsor to help unify its new softer image? What kinds of celebrities should it use?

Certain products lend themselves to advertising so much that it plays the dominant communications role. The following factors are particularly important for advertising success:

- High primary demand trend.
- Chance for significant product differentiation.
- Hidden qualities highly important to consumers.
- Opportunity to use strong emotional appeals.
- Substantial sums available to support advertising.

Where these conditions exist, as in the cosmetics industry, companies spend large amounts on advertising, and the ratio of advertising to sales dollars is often quite high. For completely undifferentiated products, such as sugar, salt, and other raw materials or commodities, price is usually the primary influence, and advertising is minimally important. Sunkist is an interesting exception. As we saw in Chapter 1, this farmers' cooperative successfully brands an undifferentiated commodity (citrus fruit) and markets it internationally.

Direct Marketing

Direct marketing is like taking the store to the customer. A mail-order house that communicates directly with consumers through ads and catalogs is one type of company engaged in direct marketing. It builds its own database of customers and uses a variety of media to communicate with them.

Today, the field of direct marketing is growing rapidly as companies discover the benefits of control, cost efficiency, and accountability. For example, many companies like Levi Strauss use **telemarketing** (a direct-marketing technique) to increase productivity through person-to-person phone contact. By using the phone to follow up direct-mail advertising, companies can increase the response rate substantially. Moreover, through telemarketing, a company like Levi Strauss can develop a valuable database of customers and prospects to use in future mailings and promotions.[54] We discuss this topic more thoroughly in Chapter 15.

Public Relations

Many firms supplement (or replace) their advertising with various public relations activities such as publicity (news releases, media advisements, feature stories) and special events (open houses, factory tours, VIP parties, grand openings) to inform various audiences about the company and its products and build corporate credibility and image. Public relations activities, as we discuss in Chapter 16, are extremely powerful tools that should always be integrated into a company's communications mix.

Collateral Materials

As mentioned in Chapter 3, **collateral** refers to the many accessory advertising materials companies produce to integrate and supplement their advertising or public relations activities. These include booklets, catalogs, brochures, films, sales kits, and annual reports. Collateral materials should always be designed to reinforce the company's image or the brand's position in the minds of customers.

Sales Promotion

As we discuss in Chapter 15, **sales promotion** is a category of demand-influencing instruments and activities that supplement the basic instruments of the marketing mix for short periods of time by stimulating channel members or prospective customers to some immediate, overt behavior.[55] This broad category includes trade deals, free samples, displays, trading stamps, sweepstakes, cents-off coupons, and premiums, among others. *Reader's Digest,* for example, is famous for its annual sweepstakes designed to increase circulation. And grocery manufacturers print and distribute over 322 billion coupons per year, saving consumers $2.5 to $3 billion annually.[56]

Some promotions are linked mainly to the communications function of the marketing mix (displays, events, trade shows). Others are linked more to the product element (free samples, premiums) or the price element (coupons, volume discounts, end-of-

• Checkout Coupon is an electronic in-store sales promotion that delivers incentives to shoppers at the checkout counter, based on what they buy. Catalina Marketing Network helps the retailer coordinate the campaigns with tie-in of the coupons to in-store posters, shelf-talkers, savings on related store products, and newspaper ads.

month sales). And some complement the distribution element (trade deals, sales contests). Sales promotion (often referred to simply as *promotion*) is used primarily as a tactical adaptation to some external situation such as competitive pressure, changing seasons, declining sales, or new product introductions.[57] As advertising people are frequently called upon to solve a variety of marketing problems, it is critical that they understand and know how to integrate the whole mix of communications techniques.

With the target market designated and the elements of the marketing mix determined, the company has a complete product concept and a strategic basis for marketing to that target. Now it can formalize its strategies and tactics in a written marketing and advertising plan. As part of the planning process, companies use marketing and advertising research. We discuss this in Chapter 6 before dealing with the formal planning process in Chapter 7.

THE MARKETING MIX IN PERSPECTIVE

Summary

Market segmentation is the process of identifying groups of people with certain shared characteristics within a broad product market and aggregating these groups into larger market segments according to their mutual interest in the product's utility. From these segments, companies can then select a target market. Marketers use a number of methods to identify behavioral groups and segment markets. The most common are geographic, demographic, behavioristic, and psychographic.

Business markets are often segmented in the same way as consumer markets. They may also be grouped by business purchasing procedures, by SIC code, or by market concentration.

In the target marketing process, companies designate specific segments to target and develop their mix of marketing activities. The product concept is the consumer's perception of the product as a bundle of utilitarian and symbolic need-satisfying values.

Every company can add, subtract, or modify four major elements in its marketing program to achieve a desired marketing mix. These elements are product, price, distribution (place), and communications (promotion)—the 4 Ps.

The *product* element includes the way the product is designed and classified, positioned, branded, and packaged. Just as humans pass through a life cycle, so do products—and product categories. The stage of a product's life cycle may determine how it is advertised.

To satisfy the variety of consumer tastes and achieve competitive advantages, marketers build differences into their products. Even the product's package is part of the product concept. The product concept may also be developed through unique positioning against competitive products.

Price refers to what and how a customer pays for a product. Companies use many common pricing strategies. Some products compete on the basis of price, but many do not.

Distribution refers to how the product is placed at the disposal of the customer—where the product is distributed, how it is bought, and how it is sold. Companies may use direct or indirect methods of distribution. Consumer goods manufacturers use several types of distribution strategies.

Communications refers to all marketing-related communications between the seller and the buyer. Tools of the communications element include personal selling, advertising, direct marketing, public relations, collateral materials, and sales promotion. Marketers try to integrate all their marketing communications programs for greater effectiveness and consistency.

Questions for Review and Discussion

1. How does the concept of *shared characteristics* relate to the market segmentation process?

2. How could you use VALS™ to develop the marketing strategy for a product of your choice?

3. How does the segmentation of business markets differ from that of consumer markets?

4. What is the most important factor to consider when determining the elements of the marketing mix?

5. What is the difference between a product and a product concept?

6. What are some examples of product positioning not discussed in this chapter?

7. What effect does the product life cycle have on the advertising a company employs?

8. What factors influence the price of a product?

9. How do the basic methods of distribution affect advertising?

10. What product characteristics encourage heavy advertising? Little advertising? Why?

6

Marketing and Advertising Research
Inputs to the Planning Process

Objective: To examine how advertisers gain information about the marketplace and how they apply their findings to marketing and advertising decision making.

After studying this chapter, you will be able to:

- Discuss how research helps advertisers locate market segments and identify target markets.

- Explain the basic steps in the research process.

- Discuss the differences between formal and informal research and primary and secondary data.

- Explain the methods used in quantitative and qualitative research.

- Debate the pros and cons of advertising testing.

- Define and explain the concepts of validity and reliability.

- Recognize the issues in creating survey questionnaires.

- Explain the challenges international advertisers face in collecting research data abroad.

 t was an unusual commercial for an antihistamine. But Dan believed it was what the client needed to break through viewer boredom. The product—Claritin—was new to Canada's over-the-counter (OTC) market. People didn't know the name, they didn't know the product, and they certainly didn't know the benefits it offered—effective allergy relief with no drowsiness. Moreover, Claritin faced two major, established competitors (Seldane and Hismanal) that already dominated the nondrowsy antihistamine market.

Fortunately, in its two years on the market as a prescription drug, Claritin had sold well. And the client and agency had done a lot of research. They knew Claritin had the features allergy sufferers wanted: fast, effective, nondrowsy relief at an affordable price. From extensive clinical tests, they also knew Claritin didn't have the pharmacological problems of some of its competitors (although Canadian law, as well as business ethics, did not permit them to advertise this fact). They had to get people to try Claritin.

Claritin's agency was Cossette Communication-Marketing in Montreal, the largest domestically owned agency in Canada. And Daniel Rabinowicz was the agency's key person for Schering Canada, the giant pharmaceutical company that developed Claritin and was preparing to launch it nationally. Dan marshalled the agency's top research, creative, and media people to come up with an unusual campaign for Claritin—one that would quickly penetrate consumers' perceptual screens and create instant awareness of the new product.

Chuck McDonald, Schering's vice president of sales and marketing, and Elyse Rowen, the OTC product manager in charge of Claritin, agreed with Dan. Going up against a half dozen competitive products led by two market leaders, they had to use an unconventional approach and make an unprecedented assault on the marketplace—or they would never recoup the millions invested in research and development for Claritin.

They agreed to use TV. Media research convinced them that no other medium could get the product into the consumer's consciousness as fast.

The creative approach was, well, different. Instead of employing the typical "doctor" testimonial, Cossette used a heavy-metal rock singer as a metaphor for the misery of allergies. The commercial showed the singer contorting his face while twanging discordant "music" on his guitar. When Claritin came to the rescue, the singer's image and sound disappeared.

Awareness they got, but Chuck McDonald was not prepared for the barrage of letters. Half the viewers loved the commercials; the other half thought they were incredibly irritating. Schering debated whether to pull them.

Cossette's Impact Research division quickly ran a telephone posttest of 200 consumers to measure market reactions. Results were indeed negative. But rather than pulling the commercials, Cossette showed its creative moxie by using the research to spawn a new commercial: real allergy sufferers talking about how much they hated the Claritin commercials—but loved the product.

Awareness and trial soared. Schering and Cossette's research led to even more creative ads. Claritin's sales rose; competitors' plummeted. Within two years, Claritin was number two, and by 1993, it led the market. By continuously researching the market and integrating that information with outstanding advertising creativity, Schering made Claritin second to none.[1] •

• Claritin's first commercial of a heavy metal rock musician was very memorable but received mixed reactions from the public, so the agency created new testimonial spots spoofing its own commercials.

"There's this TV ad that's driving me nuts."
SFX: Heavy metal guitar.
"It's this new antihistamine . . .
Uh . . . Claritin."
"He does something with his face . . ."

SFX: Heavy metal guitar.
"Claritin's great . . . it's the ad."
SFX: Heavy metal guitar.
"I think I'm allergic to the commercial . . .
Quick, gimme a Claritin."

AVO: New Claritin. Fast, 24-hour relief of seasonal allergies that lets you stay alert. From the makers of ChlorTrippolon.

THE NEED FOR RESEARCH IN MARKETING AND ADVERTISING

Companies don't want to spend millions of dollars on advertising that their customers won't notice or respond to or in media their customers don't watch or read. Advertising is expensive. In the United States in 1995, for example, the cost of a single 30-second commercial on prime-time network TV averaged $97,200. Likewise, a single, full-page color ad in a national business magazine averaged $150 to reach a thousand prospects.[2] That's too much money to risk on speculative information; and that's why advertisers need research. Without it, they're forced to use intuition or guesswork. In today's fast-changing, highly competitive, global economy, this invites failure.

Marketing Research

The systematic procedure used to gather, record, and analyze new information to help managers make marketing decisions is called **marketing research.**[3] (It should not be confused with *market research,* which is information gathering about a *particular* market or market segment.) For firms that use the marketing concept (discussed in Chapter 4), marketing research helps identify consumer needs and market segments, develop new products and marketing strategies, and assess the effectiveness of marketing programs and promotional activities. It is also useful in financial planning, economic forecasting, and quality control as well as in traditional marketing areas like advertising.

Companies spend millions of dollars developing new products and bringing them to market. In the pharmaceutical business, for instance, a company like Schering may spend as much as $200 million on R&D before it can even bring a new drug to market. Major advertisers can't afford to risk that kind of money by ignoring the findings of marketing research. They depend on sophisticated information. Worldwide, companies currently spend over $4 billion per year on marketing, advertising, and public opinion research. Research has become big business. In fact, the top 50 U.S. research organizations, led by the global D&B Marketing Information Services, account for $3.7 billion—over 60 percent of the worldwide total—much of it coming from foreign clients.[4] Exhibit 6–1 lists the top 10 research companies by U.S. research revenues.

Marketing research gives the advertiser and its agency the information they need to decide which strategies will enhance the brand's image and lead to higher revenues and profits. Good research enables the company to devise a sophisticated, integrated mix of product, price, distribution, and communication elements, all committed to the three Rs of marketing: *recruiting* new customers, *retaining* current customers, and *regaining* lost customers.[5]

To *recruit* new customers, researchers study market segments and create product attribute models to match buyers with the right products and services. Advertisers need the answers to a lot of questions: What are the most important product benefits to our cus-

• Cossette likened the distress of allergy sufferers to the misery of a jackhammer operator in one of its highly creative spots for Claritin.

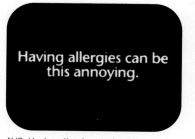

AVO: Having allergies can be this annoying.

SFX: Pneumatic jackhammer throughout.

AVO: Taking Claritin is this effective.

SFX: Sound of jackhammer . . .
. . . diminishes.

SFX: Truck horn.
AVO: New Claritin. Fast, 24-hour relief of

seasonal allergies that lets you stay alert.
From the makers of ChlorTrippolon.

tomers? What changes in the product's appearance and performance will increase sales? What price will maintain the brand's image, create profits, and still be attractive and affordable to consumers? Answers may lead to product design and marketing decisions that directly affect the product's nature, content, packaging, pricing—and advertising.

Customer satisfaction studies are used to *retain* existing customers. In addition, databases of customer transactions identify reasons for customer satisfaction—or dissatisfaction.[6] Today, companies realize that the best sales go to those who develop good relationships with individual customers.[7] And customer satisfaction is now the fastest-growing field in marketing research.

Information gained for the first two Rs helps the third, *regaining* lost customers. If an office equipment manufacturer finds through research that an increase in service calls typically precedes cancellation of a service contract, it can watch for that pattern with current customers and then take preventive action. Likewise, it can review service records of former customers and—if the pattern holds true—devise some marketing action or advertising appeal to win them back.[8]

Rank	Company	U.S. research revenues
1.	D&B Marketing Information	$2,043
2.	Information Resources	377
3.	Arbitron	121
4.	Westat	119
5.	Maritz Marketing Research	107
6.	Walsh International	105
7.	The NPD Group	81
8.	NFO Research Inc.	62
9.	Market Facts Inc.	56
10.	M/A/R/C Group	51

Exhibit • 6–1
Top research companies by U.S. research revenues in 1994 ($ millions).

• PacTel Cellular of San Diego understands the need to develop good customer relations, as shown in this unique billboard. PacTel wanted to tell people that cellular phones are handy and can go anywhere, so it put a real person up on the billboard who actually answered calls. Morning disc jockeys called live on the air. As the Franklin Stoorza agency noted, it worked great until the highway patrol made them take it down because it was causing traffic jams.

Advertising Research

Before developing any campaign, an agency needs to know how consumers perceive the client's product, how they view its competitors, and what image would be most credible. Advertising research provides this information.

A subset of marketing research, **advertising research** is the systematic gathering and analysis of information to help develop or evaluate advertising strategies, ads and commercials, and media campaigns.

In this chapter, we consider the importance of research to the development of advertising plans and strategies, look at how research can be used to test the effectiveness of ads before and after they run, and explore specific research techniques.

APPLYING RESEARCH TO ADVERTISING SITUATIONS

Advertising research serves various purposes, but most falls into four categories, as shown in Exhibit 6–2:

1. Advertising strategy research (to define the product concept or to select the target market, the advertising message, or the media to be used).
2. Creative concept research (to measure the target audience's acceptance of different creative ideas at the concept stage).
3. Pretesting of ads and commercials (to diagnose possible communication problems before a campaign begins).
4. Posttesting of ads (to evaluate a campaign after it runs).

As Exhibit 6–2 shows, the different categories are used at different stages of ad or campaign development, and the techniques also vary considerably.

Advertising Strategy Research

Companies develop advertising strategies by blending elements of the *creative mix:* the *product concept,* the *target audience,* the *communication media,* and the *creative message.* Advertising strategy research answers questions about these elements.

	Category 1: Advertising Strategy Research	Category 2: Creative Concept Research	Category 3: Pretesting	Category 4: Posttesting
Timing	Before creative work begins	Before agency production begins	Before finished artwork and photography	After campaign has run
Research problem	Product concept definition Target audience selection Message-element selection	Concept testing Name testing Slogan testing	Print testing TV storyboard pretesting Radio commercial pretesting	Advertising effectiveness Consumer attitude change Sales increases
Techniques	Consumer-attitude and usage studies	Free-association tests Qualitative interviews Statement-comparison tests	Consumer juries Matched samples Portfolio tests Storyboard test Mechanical devices Psychological rating scales	Aided recall Unaided recall Sales tests Inquiry tests Attitude tests

Exhibit • 6–2
Categories of research in advertising development.

Product concept definition

From their extensive consumer surveys and focus groups, Schering and Cossette determined that most Canadian allergy sufferers weren't completely satisfied with available antihistamines. Some had a sedating side effect that made them difficult to use during the workday. Some of the nondrowsy products had other problems: slowness in clearing from the body, weight gain, and dry mouth.

Research showed Claritin did not have the same negative side effects. Schering therefore positioned Claritin as a fast-acting, long-lasting, effective medication. And consumer use bore out the integrity of this product concept. Schering reps successfully informed physicians throughout Canada about Claritin, and more doctors started prescribing it. By 1990, Claritin's prescription sales surpassed both Seldane and Hismanal. By 1994, the product concept for Claritin included that it was "the antihistamine most recommended by doctors."

Advertisers want to know how consumers perceive their brands and what qualities lead to initial purchases and eventually brand loyalty. Young & Rubicam, for example, developed the BrandAsset Valuator™ to determine how brands are built and derive their strength. This model measures brands in terms of familiarity, relevance, differentiation, and esteem. During a 1994 study in 19 countries, Y&R found that one of the

• Research showed that Schering's Claritin did not have the negative side effects found in most antihistamines. As its prescription sales increased, Schering positioned Claritin as the antihistimine most recommended by doctors.

highest-valued brands around the world was Disney—even in France, home of the troubled EuroDisney theme park.[9]

Target audience selection

Allergy sufferers comprise approximately 25 percent of the population. Schering's research showed that the most attractive market of antihistamine users was 18 to 49 years old, a large target market in Canada.

With any new product, the biggest problem is invariably the budget. There is never enough money to attack all geographic markets effectively at the same time. So Cossette recommended the *dominance concept*—researching which markets are most important to product sales and selecting those where Schering could focus its resources to achieve advertising dominance.

As a result, Schering introduced Claritin first in the provinces of Alberta, British Columbia, Ontario, and the Maritimes, which accounted for approximately 67 percent of the Canadian population but 75 percent of the allergy market. After succeeding there, they introduced Claritin to the rest of Canada.

Media selection

To develop media strategies, select media vehicles, and evaluate their results, advertisers use a subset of advertising research called **media research.** Agencies subscribe to **syndicated research services** (A. C. Nielsen, Arbitron, Simmons, Standard Rate & Data Service) that monitor and publish information on the reach and effectiveness of media vehicles—radio, TV, newspapers, and so on—in every major geographic market in the United States and Canada. (We'll discuss these in Part IV: "Buying Media Space and Time.") Cossette's media research indicated that TV would have the greatest impact for the introduction of Claritin.

Message-element determination

Companies can find promising advertising messages by studying consumers' likes and dislikes in relation to brands and products.

For example, in 1993 AT&T created a corporate campaign to tell consumers how the company was developing high-tech products and services to improve people's lives. The company's agency, N. W. Ayer, conducted a series of qualitative consumer attitude studies and discovered numerous potential themes. Next, the agency used concept testing to determine which message-element options might prove most successful. This was now category 2 research aimed at developing creative advertising concepts.

Creative Concept Research

Ayer prepared several tentative ad concepts in the form of *animatics,* rough commercials using stills instead of action. Each scene stressed a different service AT&T would offer consumers in the future, such as sending faxes from the beach with a personal communi-

● AT&T developed animatic commercials to test the appeal of various future services it planned to advertise in its corporate campaign.

AVO: Have you ever paid a toll without slowing down?

AVO: Read a book from 1,000 miles away? Given dictation to a computer?

AVO: Or tucked your kid in from a phone booth?

● The "You will" campaign from AT&T received high marks from advertising critics—a result of good creativity and adequate testing.

AVO: Have you ever paid a toll . . . without slowing down?

AVO: Bought concert tickets . . .
FIRST GIRL: "There we go."

SECOND GIRL: "Yeah, perfect."

AVO: Or tucked your baby in . . . from a phone booth?

MOTHER: "Hi, pretty girl."
AVO: You will.

AVO: And the company that will bring it to you . . . AT&T.

cator, paying road tolls without slowing down, or buying concert tickets with a "smart" card. The agency then conducted focus groups in its unique developmental lab, which combines intensive qualitative interviews with quantitative techniques. While a discussion leader moderated the conversation, each group viewed the animatics. The groups' reactions were measured, taped, and observed by Ayer staff behind a one-way mirror.

Once the most appealing products and services were determined, Ayer developed a campaign to verbally and nonverbally express AT&T's benefits to the consumer. The theme was simply: "YOU WILL." The commercials posed questions such as "Have you ever tucked your baby in from a phone booth?" Answer: "You will. And the company that will bring it to you . . . AT&T." This embodied the company's mission of being the world's leader in bringing people together, giving them easy access to each other and to the information and services they want and need—anytime, anywhere.

The campaign was so successful that the Advertising Research Foundation named Ayer a finalist for its prestigious David Ogilvy Award, given to the most effective ad campaign supported by research.[10]

Testing and Evaluating Advertising

Advertising is often the largest single cost in a company's marketing budget. No wonder its effectiveness is a major concern! Companies want to know what they are getting for their money—and whether their advertising is working.

Testing is the primary tool advertisers use to ensure their advertising dollars are being spent wisely. Testing can prevent costly errors, especially in judging which advertising strategy or medium is most effective. And it can give the advertiser some measure (besides sales results) of a campaign's value.

Objectives of testing

Pretesting increases the likelihood of preparing the most effective advertising messages. Some agencies, like DDB Needham, pretest all ad copy for communication gaps or flaws in message content before recommending it to clients.[11] As we saw earlier,

Schering didn't pretest its launch ads for Claritin and encountered a surprising reaction from the marketplace. But most negative response is more insidious: consumers simply turn the page or change the channel.

Posttesting evaluates the effectiveness of an ad or campaign *after* it runs and provides the advertiser with useful guidelines for future advertising. Several variables are evaluated in pretesting, including merchandise, markets, motives, messages, media, budgeting, and scheduling (5Ms+B+S). Many of these can be posttested too. However, in posttesting, the objective is to evaluate, not diagnose.

Merchandise For purposes of alliteration, this is the product concept. Advertisers may pretest the package design or how advertising positions the brand. One company, MarketWare Simulation Services, has introduced a virtual-reality testing program called Visionary Shopper which allows test subjects to "shop" on a realistic on-screen shelf, using a touch-sensitive monitor and a track ball. They can "pull" products off the shelf, study them in 3-D, and rotate them to read side and back panels. They select items by touching an on-screen shopping cart, and the computer tracks the products examined and/or chosen, instantly gauging the impact of whatever the client is testing.[12]

Markets Advertisers may pretest advertising strategy and commercials with various market segments or audience groups. They may even decide to alter the strategy and target the campaign to a different market. In posttesting, advertisers want to know if the campaign succeeded in reaching its target markets. Changes in awareness and increases in market share are two indicators.

Motives Consumers' motives are outside advertisers' control, but the messages they create to appeal to those motives are not. Pretesting helps advertisers find better ways to appeal to consumers' needs and motives.

Messages Pretesting helps determine what a message says (from the customer's point of view) and how well it says it. Advertisers might test the headline, the text, the illustration, the typography—or the message concept.

Through posttesting, the advertiser can determine to what extent the advertising message was seen, remembered, and believed. Changes in consumer attitude, perception, or brand interest indicate success as does consumers' ability to remember a campaign slogan or identify the sponsor.

Media The cost of media advertising is soaring, and advertisers today demand greater accountability. Pretesting can influence four types of media decisions: classes

• The Visionary Shopper, a virtual-reality product-testing program, allows subjects to "shop" as in a real store. A computer tracks items "shoppers" examine or select, providing instant feedback about the product being tested.

of media, media subclasses, specific media vehicles, and media units of space and time.

Media classes are the broad media categories such as print, electronic, outdoor, and direct mail. **Media subclasses** are radio or TV, newsmagazines or business publications, and so on. The specific **media vehicle** is the particular program or publication. **Media units** are the size or length of an ad: half-page or full-page ads, 15- or 30-second spots, 60-second commercials, and so forth.

After the campaign runs, posttesting can determine how effectively the media mix reached the target audience and communicated the desired message. Audience measurement is discussed further in Chapters 12 through 14.

Budgeting How large should a company's advertising budget be? How much should be allocated to various markets and media? To specific products? Advertisers use pretesting techniques to determine optimum spending levels before introducing national campaigns. (Chapter 7, "Marketing and Advertising Planning," provides further information on budgeting.)

Scheduling Advertisers can test consumer response to a product ad during different seasons of the year or days of the week. They can test whether frequent advertising is more effective than occasional or one-time insertions, or whether year-round advertising is more effective than advertising concentrated during a gift-buying season. (Chapter 8, "Media Strategy and Planning," discusses the most common types of media schedules.)

Overall results Finally, advertisers want to measure overall results to evaluate how well they accomplished their objectives. Posttesting helps determine whether and how to continue, what to change, and how much to spend in the future.

● How much should a company spend to advertise its products? National advertisers like HealthTex use pretesting techniques before introducing ads like these with national campaigns.

STEPS IN THE RESEARCH PROCESS

Now let's explore some of the specific techniques used in marketing and advertising research. There are five basic steps in the research process: situation analysis and problem definition, informal (exploratory) research, construction of research objectives, formal research, and interpretation and reporting of findings (see Exhibit 6–3).

Analyzing the Situation and Defining the Problem

The first step in the marketing research process is to *analyze the situation* and *define the problem*. Many large firms have in-house research departments. At Schering Canada, for example, the manager of marketing and sales services maintains a **marketing information system (MIS)**—a set of procedures for generating a continuous, orderly flow of information for use in making marketing decisions. These systems ensure managers get the information they need when they need it.[13]

Most smaller firms don't have dedicated research departments, and their methods for obtaining marketing information are frequently inadequate. These firms often find the situation analysis difficult and time-consuming. Yet good research on the wrong problem is a waste of effort.

Conducting Informal (Exploratory) Research

The second step in the process is to use **informal** (or *exploratory*) **research** to learn more about the market, the competition, and the business environment, and to better define the problem. Researchers may discuss the problem with informed sources inside the firm; with wholesalers, distributors, or retailers outside the firm; with customers; or even with competitors. They look for whoever has the most information to offer.

There are two types of research data: primary and secondary. Information collected from the marketplace about a specific problem is called **primary data**—and acquiring it is expensive and time-consuming. So during the exploratory stage, researchers usually use **secondary data**—information previously collected or published, usually for some other purpose, by the firm or by some other organization. This information is readily available, either internally or externally, and can be gathered more quickly and inexpensively than primary data.

Assembling internal secondary data

Company records are often a valuable source of secondary information. Useful internal data include product shipment figures, billings, warranty-card records, advertising expenditures, sales expenses, customer correspondence, and records of meetings with sales staffs.

A well-developed marketing information system can help researchers analyze sales data, review past tracking studies, and examine previous marketing research data. This information might point the way toward an interesting headline or positioning statement such as Claritin's: "The antihistamine most recommended by doctors." Another example is Jiffy Lube: "America's favorite oil change."

Gathering external secondary data

Much information is available, usually at little or no cost, from the government, market research companies, trade associations, various trade publications, or even computerized databases. For example, as the advertising manager for a large nutritional com-

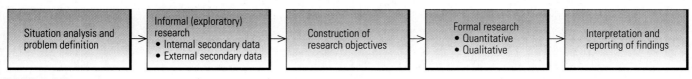

Exhibit • 6–3
The marketing research process begins with evaluation of the company's situation and definition of the problem.

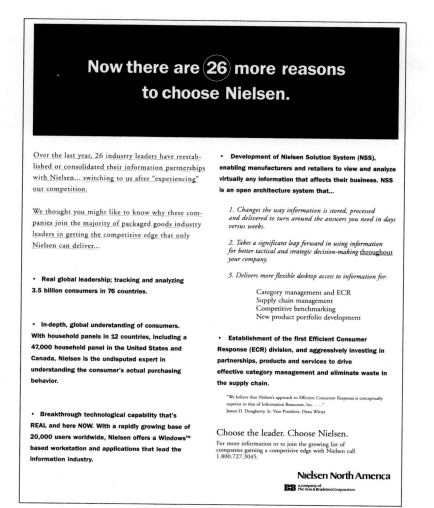

pany introducing a new line of vitamins, you might need to know the current demand for vitamins and food supplements, the number of competitors in the marketplace, the amount of advertising each was doing, and the challenges and opportunities the industry faced. RL 6–1 in the Reference Library lists sources of information on the vitamin market. Many of these sources apply to other markets as well.

In the U.S., frequently used sources of secondary data include:

- Library reference materials (*Business Periodicals Index* for business magazines, *Reader's Guide to Periodical Literature* for consumer magazines, *Public Information Service Bulletin,* the *New York Times Index,* and the *World Almanac and Book of Facts*).

- Government publications (*Statistical Abstract of the United States*).

- Trade association publications (annual fact books containing government data gathered by various industry groups listed in the *Directory of National Trade Associations*).

- Research organization publications (literature from university bureaus of business research, Nielsen retail store audits, MRCA consumer purchase diaries, and Standard Rate & Data Service).

- Consumer/business publications (*Business Week, Forbes, Fortune, American Demographics, Advertising Age, Computer Marketing,* and thousands more).

- Computer database services (DIALOG Information Service, IQuest and Knowledge Index from CompuServe, and Dow Jones News Retrieval Service).

Secondary data carries potential problems: information may be obsolete, irrelevant, invalid, unreliable, or just overwhelming in amount.

Using secondary data for international markets

In developing countries the research profession is not so sophisticated or organized as in North America and Europe.[14] The available secondary research statistics may be outdated or invalid. When evaluating secondary data, advertising managers should ask: Who collected the data and why? What research techniques did they use? Would the source have any reason to bias the data? When was the data collected? International advertising managers should exercise caution when dealing with "facts" about foreign markets.

Establishing Research Objectives

Once the exploratory research phase is completed, the company may need additional information. For example, it may want to identify exactly who its customers are and clarify their perceptions of the company and the competition. To do so, the company first must establish specific research objectives.

A concise, written statement of the research problem and objectives should be formulated at the beginning of any research project. A company must decide what it's after and correlate these objectives with its marketing and advertising plans. For example, a department store, noticing that it is losing market share, might write its problem statement and research objectives as follows:

Market Share:
Our company's sales, while still increasing, seem to have lost momentum and are not producing the profit our shareholders expect. In the last year, our market share slipped 10 percent in the men's footwear department and 7 percent in the women's fine apparel department. Our studies indicate we are losing sales to other department stores in the same malls and that customers are confused about our position in the market.

Research Objectives:
We must answer the following questions: (1) Who are our customers? (2) Who are the customers of other department stores? (3) What do these customers like and dislike about us and about our competitors? (4) How are we currently perceived? and (5) What do we have to do to clarify and improve that perception?

This statement of the problem is specific and measurable, and the questions are related and relevant. The answers might provide a basis for developing a new positioning strategy for the company. The positioning strategy, in turn, facilitates the development of marketing and advertising plans that will set the company's course for years to come.

Conducting Formal Research

When a company wants to collect primary data directly from the marketplace about a specific problem or issue, it uses **formal research.** The two types of formal research are *quantitative* and *qualitative*.

Basic methods of quantitative research

Advertisers use **quantitative research** to gain hard numbers about market situations. There are three basic research methods used to collect quantitative data: *observation, experiment,* and *survey.*

Observation In the **observation method,** researchers monitor people's actions. They may count the traffic that passes by a billboard, count a TV audience through instruments hooked to TV sets, or study consumer reactions to products displayed in the supermarket.

Technology has greatly facilitated the observation method. One example is the Universal Product Code (UPC) label—an identifying series of vertical bars with a 10-digit number—that adorns every consumer packaged good. By reading the codes with optical scanners, stores can tell which products are selling and how well. The UPC label not only increases speed and accuracy at the checkout counter; it also enables timely inventory control and gives stores and manufacturers accurate point-of-purchase data sensitive to the impact of price, in-store promotion, couponing, and advertising. Suddenly marketers have reliable data on the effectiveness of the tools they have been using to influence consumers. And with that information, they can develop empirical models to evaluate alternative marketing plans, media vehicles, and promotional campaigns.[15]

In one case, data indicated that a 40-cent coupon for toothpaste could create $147,000 in profits, but a 50-cent coupon on the same item would create a $348,000 loss.[16]

Advertisers used to assume that changes in market share and brand position happen slowly. But observation shows that the packaged-goods market is complex and volatile. At the local level, weekly sales figures may fluctuate considerably, making it difficult to measure advertising's short-term effectiveness.

Video cameras have also affected observation techniques. Envirosell, a New York–based research company, uses security-type cameras to capture consumer in-store shopping habits. The company analyzes how much time people spend with an item and how they read the label to determine the effectiveness of packaging and displays.[17]

Experiment   To measure actual cause-and-effect relationships, researchers use the **experimental method.** An experiment is a scientific investigation in which a researcher alters the stimulus received by a *test group* and compares the results with that of a *control group* that did not receive the altered stimulus. This type of research is used primarily for test-marketing new products in isolated geographic areas and for testing new ad campaigns prior to national introduction. For example, a new campaign might run in one geographic area but not another. Sales in the two areas are then compared to determine the campaign's effectiveness. However, researchers must use strict controls so the variable that causes the effect can be accurately determined. And because it's hard to control every marketing variable, this method is difficult and expensive to use.

Survey   The most common method of gathering primary research data is the **survey,** in which the researcher gains information on attitudes, opinions, or motivations by questioning current or prospective customers. (Political polls are a common type of survey.) Surveys can be conducted by *personal interview, telephone,* and *mail.* Each has distinct advantages and disadvantages (see Exhibit 6–4).

• The Universal Product Code on packaging is scanned at checkout counters. It improves checkout time and inventory control, and provides a wealth of accessible data for use in measuring advertising response.

• This video frame from Envirosell shows how the company uses security-type cameras to capture in-store consumer shopping habits.

Exhibit • 6–4
Comparison of data collection methods.

	Personal	Telephone	Mail
Data collection costs	High	Medium	Low
Data collection time required	Medium	Low	High
Sample size for a given budget	Small	Medium	Large
Data quantity per respondent	High	Medium	Low
Reaches widely dispersed sample	No	Maybe	Yes
Reaches special locations	Yes	Maybe	No
Interaction with respondents	Yes	Yes	No
Degree of interviewer bias	High	Medium	None
Severity of nonresponse bias	Low	Low	High
Presentation of visual stimuli	Yes	No	Maybe
Fieldworker training required	Yes	Yes	No

Basic methods of qualitative research

To get people to share their thoughts and feelings, researchers use **qualitative research** that elicits in-depth, open-ended responses rather than yes or no answers. Unfortunately, no matter how skillfully posed, some questions are uncomfortable for consumers to answer. When asked why they bought a particular status car, for instance, consumers might reply that it handles well or is economical or dependable, but they rarely admit that it makes them feel important.

Qualitative research is used more often to give advertisers a general impression of the market, the consumer, or the product. Some advertisers refer to it as **motivation research.** Sophisticated agencies use a balance of both qualitative and quantitative methods, understanding the limits of each and how they work together (see Exhibit 6–5).[18] The methods used in qualitative research are usually described as projective or intensive techniques.

Exhibit • 6–5
Differences between qualitative and quantitative research.

	Qualitative	Quantitative
Main techniques for gathering data	Focus groups and in-depth interviews.	Surveys and scientific samples.
Kinds of questions asked	Why? Through what thought process? In what way? In connection with what other behavior or thoughts?	How many? How much?
Role of interviewer	Critical: interviewer must think on feet and frame questions and probes in response to whatever respondents say. A highly trained professional is advisable.	Important, but interviewers need only be able to read scripts. They should not improvise. Minimally trained, responsible employees are suitable.
Questions asked	Questions vary in order and phrasing from group to group and interview to interview. New questions are added, old ones dropped.	Should be (ideally) exactly the same for each interview. Order and phrasing of questions carefully controlled.
Number of interviews	Fewer interviews tending to last a longer time.	Many interviews in order to give a projectable scientific sample.
Kinds of findings	Develop hypotheses, gain insights, explore language options, refine concepts, flesh out numerical data, provide diagnostics on advertising copy.	Test hypotheses, prioritize factors, provide data for mathematical modeling and projections.

Projective techniques Advertisers use **projective techniques** to understand people's underlying or subconscious feelings, attitudes, interests, opinions, needs, and motives. By asking indirect questions (such as, "What kind of people do you think shop here?"), the researcher tries to involve consumers in a situation where they can express feelings about the problem or product.

Projective techniques were adapted for marketing research after their use by psychologists in clinical diagnosis. But such techniques require highly experienced researchers.

Intensive techniques **Intensive techniques** such as in-depth interviews also require great care to administer properly. In the **in-depth interview,** carefully planned but loosely structured questions help the interviewer probe respondents' deeper feelings. Schering, for example, uses in-depth interviews with physicians to find out what attributes doctors consider most important in the drugs they prescribe and to identify which brands the doctors associate with different attributes.[19]

While in-depth interviews help reveal individual motivations, they are also expensive and time-consuming. And skilled interviewers are in short supply.

The **focus group** is one of the most common intensive research techniques. The company invites four or more people typical of the target market to a group session to discuss the product, the service, or the marketing situation. The session may last an hour or more. A trained moderator guides the often freewheeling discussion, and the group interaction reveals the participants' true feelings or behavior toward the product. Focus-group meetings are usually recorded and often viewed or videotaped from behind a one-way mirror. Focus groups don't represent a valid sample of the population, but participants' responses are useful for several purposes. They can provide input about the viability of prospective spokespeople, determine the effectiveness of visuals and strategies, and identify elements in ads that are unclear or claims that don't seem plausible. Focus groups are best used in conjunction with surveys. In fact, focus-group responses often help design questions for a formal survey.[20] And following a survey, focus groups can put flesh on the skeleton of raw data.[21]

In a series of focus-group studies, American Express learned that its two-decade-old campaign for American Express Traveler's Cheques featuring the traveler as victim was no longer effective because it reminded people of an unpleasant event. The company tested several new concepts and, in 1994, changed the campaign to humorous spots of travelers losing things—like traveler's checks—which consumers liked better.[22]

Methods used to pretest ads

Although there is no infallible way to predict advertising success or failure, pretesting gives the advertiser useful insights if properly applied. Advertisers often pretest for likability and perception analysis using both qualitative and quantitative techniques.

• A focus group is an intensive research technique used to evaluate the effectiveness of the various elements of a sponsor's ad or advertising campaign. Focus groups are especially effective used in conjunction with market surveys.

Checklist   Models for Pretesting Advertisements

Print Advertising

- **Direct questioning.** Asks specific questions about ads. Often used to test alternative ads in early stages of development.

- **Focus group.** A moderated but freewheeling discussion and interview conducted with four or more people.

- **Order-of-merit test.** Respondents see two or more ads and arrange them in rank order.

- **Paired-comparison method.** Respondents compare each ad in a group.

- **Portfolio test.** One group sees a portfolio of test ads interspersed among other ads and editorial matter. Another group sees the portfolio without the test ads.

- **Mock magazine.** Test ads are "stripped into" a magazine, which is left with respondents for a specified time. (Also used as a posttesting technique.)

- **Perceptual meaning study.** Respondents see ads in timed exposures.

- **Direct-mail test.** Two or more alternative ads are mailed to different prospects on a mailing list to test which ad generates the largest volume of orders.

Broadcast Advertising

- **Central location projection test.** Respondents see test commercial films in a central location like a shopping center.

- **Trailer test.** Respondents see TV commercials in trailers at shopping centers and receive coupons for the advertised products; a matched sample of consumers just get the coupons. Researchers measure the difference in coupon redemption.

- **Theater test.** Electronic equipment enables respondents to indicate what they like and dislike as they view TV commercials in a theater setting.

- **Live telecast test.** Test commercials are shown on closed-circuit or cable TV. Respondents are interviewed by phone and/or sales audits are conducted at stores in the viewing areas.

- **Sales experiment.** Alternative commercials run in two or more market areas.

Physiological Testing

- **Pupilometric device.** Dilation of the subject's pupils is measured, presumably to indicate the subject's reaction.

- **Eye-movement camera.** The route the subject's eyes traveled is superimposed over an ad to show the paths they take and the areas that attracted and held attention.

- **Galvanometer.** Measures subject's sweat gland activity with a mild electrical current; presumably the more tension an ad creates, the more effective it is likely to be.

- **Voice-pitch analysis.** A consumer's response is taped and a computer used to measure changes in voice pitch caused by emotional responses.

- **Brain-pattern analysis.** A scanner monitors the reaction of the subject's brain.

When pretesting print ads, advertisers often ask direct questions: What does the advertising say to you? Does the advertising tell you anything new or different about the company? If so, what? Does the advertising reflect activities you would like to participate in? Is the advertising believable? What effect does it have on your perception of the merchandise offered? Do you like the ads?

Direct questioning elicits a full range of responses from which researchers can infer how well advertising messages convey key copy points. It is especially effective for testing alternative ads in the early stages of development when respondents' reactions and input can best be acted on. In addition to direct questioning and focus groups, techniques for pretesting print ads include order-of-merit tests, paired comparisons, portfolio tests, mock magazines, perceptual meaning studies, and direct-mail tests. (See the Checklist of Models for Pretesting Advertisements.)

Several methods are used specifically to pretest radio and TV commercials. In **central location tests,** respondents are shown videotapes of test commercials, usually in shopping centers, and questions are asked before and after exposure. In **clutter tests,** test commercials are shown with noncompetitive control commercials to determine their effectiveness, measure comprehension and attitude shifts, and detect weaknesses.

Many companies' own employees are an important constituency. FedEx, for example, pretests new commercials by prescreening them on its in-house cable-TV system for its 90,000 employees and soliciting feedback.[23]

The challenge of pretesting

There is no best way to pretest advertising variables. Different methods test different aspects, and each has its own advantages and disadvantages—a formidable challenge for the advertiser.

Methods for Posttesting Advertisements   *Checklist*

□ **Aided recall (recognition-readership).** To jog their memories, respondents are shown certain ads and then questioned whether their previous exposure was through reading, viewing, or listening.

□ **Unaided recall.** Respondents are asked, without prompting, whether they saw or heard advertising messages.

□ **Attitude tests.** Direct questions, semantic differential tests, or unstructured questions measure changes in respondents' attitudes after a campaign.

□ **Inquiry tests.** Additional product information, product samples, or premiums are given to readers or viewers of an ad; ads generating the most responses are presumed to be the most effective.

□ **Sales tests.** Measures of past sales compare advertising efforts with sales. Controlled experiments test different media in different markets. Consumer purchase tests measure retail sales from a given campaign. Store inventory audits measure retailers' stocks before and after a campaign.

Pretesting helps distinguish strong ads from weak ones. But since the test occurs in an artificial setting, respondents may assume the role of expert or critic and give answers that don't reflect their real buying behavior. They may invent opinions to satisfy the interviewer, or be reluctant to admit they are influenced, or vote for the ads they think they *should* like.

Researchers encounter problems when asking people to rank ads. Respondents often rate the ones that make the best first impression as the highest in all categories (the **halo effect**). Also, questions about the respondent's buying behavior may be invalid. Behavior *intent* may not become behavior *fact*. And some creative people mistrust ad testing because they believe it stifles creativity.

Despite these challenges, the issue comes down to dollars. Small advertisers rarely pretest—but their risk isn't as great, either. When advertisers risk millions of dollars on a new campaign, they *must* pretest to be sure the ad or commercial is interesting, believable, likable, and memorable—and that it reinforces the brand image.

Methods used for posttesting

Following the launch campaign for Claritin, Schering was anxious to know to what extent people saw and paid attention to the campaign and how effectively it communicated the product story. So Impact Research began posttesting.

Posttesting is generally more costly and time-consuming than pretesting, but it can test ads under actual market conditions. Some advertisers benefit from pretesting *and* posttesting by running ads in select markets before launching a campaign nationwide.

Advertisers use both quantitative and qualitative methods in posttesting. Most posttesting techniques fall into five broad categories: *aided recall, unaided recall, attitude tests, inquiry tests,* and *sales tests.* (See the Checklist of Methods for Posttesting Advertisements.)

To measure a campaign's effectiveness in creating a favorable image for a company, its brand, or its products, some advertisers use **attitude tests.** Presumably, favorable changes in attitude predispose consumers to buy the company's product.

Impact Research developed a proprietary posttest called TES (Tracking Efficiency Study) that it administers regularly for clients.[24] Using a random sample of 200 people in each market, Impact researchers phone or visit respondents and ask 8 to 10 questions to determine what ads or commercials they remember seeing, if they can identify the sponsor, which message elements they remember, and how well they liked the ads. Then, Impact develops statistics on the real reach and frequency of the campaign—that is, how many people *actually* saw the ads or commercials and how often.

Similarly, Nissan interviews 1,000 consumers every month to track brand awareness, familiarity with vehicle models, recall of commercials, and shifts in attitude or image perception. If a commercial fails, it can be pulled quickly.[25]

• Starch Readership Reports posttest magazine ad effectiveness by interviewing readers. The summary tab at the top of this ad indicates that 51 percent of women readers noted the ad; 49 percent associated the ad with the advertiser (Hanes); and 27 percent read most of the copy.

The challenge of posttesting

Each posttesting method has limitations. **Recall tests** reveal the effectiveness of ad components, such as size, color, or themes. But they measure what respondents noticed, *not* whether they actually buy the product.

Attitude tests often measure sales effectiveness better than recall tests. An attitude change relates more closely to product purchase, and a measured change in attitude gives management the confidence to make informed decisions about advertising plans. Unfortunately, many people find it difficult to determine and express their attitudes. For mature brands, *brand interest* may be a better sales indicator, and advertisers now measure that phenomenon.[26]

Inquiry tests—in which consumers respond to an ad for information or free samples—can test an ad's attention-getting value, readability, and understandability. They also permit fairly good control of the variables that motivate reader action, particularly if a *split-run test* is used (split runs are covered in Chapter 12). The inquiry test is also effective for testing small-space ads.

Unfortunately, inquiries may not reflect a sincere interest in the product, and responses may take months to receive. **Sales tests** are a useful measure of advertising effectiveness when advertising is the dominant element, or the only variable, in the company's marketing plan. However, many other variables also affect sales (competitors' activities, the season of the year, and even the weather). Sales response may not be immediate, and sales tests, particularly field studies, are often costly and time-consuming. Finally, sales tests are more suited for gauging the effectiveness of campaigns than of individual ads or components of ads.

Type of research	Features	Cost
Telephone	500 20-minute interviews, with report	$15,000–$18,000
Mail	500 returns, with report (33 percent response rate)	$8,000–$10,000
Intercept	500 interviews, four or five questions, with report	$15,000
Executive interviews (talking to business administrators)	20 interviews, with report	$2,500–$7,500
Focus group	One group, 8 to 10 people, with report and videotape	$2,500–$3,800

Exhibit • 6–6
The cost of professional research.

Interpreting and Reporting the Findings

The final step in the research process involves interpreting and reporting the data. Research is very costly (see Exhibit 6–6), and its main purpose is to help solve problems. The final report must be comprehensible to the company's managers and relevant to their needs.

Tables and graphs are helpful, but they must be explained in words management can understand. Technical jargon (such as "multivariate analysis of variance model") should be avoided, and descriptions of the methodology, statistical analysis, and raw data should be confined to an appendix. The report should state the problem and research objective, summarize the findings, and draw conclusions. The researcher should make recommendations for management action, and the report should be discussed in a formal presentation to allow management feedback and to highlight important points.

CONSIDERATIONS IN CONDUCTING FORMAL QUANTITATIVE RESEARCH

Quantitative research requires formal design and rigorous standards for collecting and tabulating data to ensure its accuracy and usability. When conducting formal research, advertisers must consider certain issues carefully, especially whether the research is *valid* and *reliable*.

Validity and Reliability

Assume you want to determine a market's attitude toward a proposed new toy. The market consists of 10 million individuals. You show a prototype of the toy to five people, and four say they like it, an 80 percent favorable attitude. Is that test valid? Hardly. For a test to be **valid,** results must be free of bias and reflect the true status of the market.[27] Five people aren't enough for a minimum sample, and the fact that *you* showed a prototype of *your* toy to these people would probably bias their response.

Moreover, if you repeated the test with five more people, you might get an entirely different response. So your test also lacks reliability. For a test to be **reliable,** it must be repeatable—it must produce approximately the same result each time it is administered (see Exhibit 6–7).

Validity and reliability depend on several key elements: the sampling methods, the survey questionnaire design, and the data tabulation and analysis methods.

Sampling Methods

When a company wants to know what consumers think, it can't ask just everybody. But its research must reflect the **universe** (the entire target population) of prospective customers. Researchers select from that population a **sample** that they expect will represent the population's characteristics.[28] To accomplish this, they must decide who to

Ethical Issue   Research Statistics Can Be Friends or Foes

Research—the systematic gathering of facts and statistics—is the basis for most advertising claims. Marketing research gives the advertiser and its agency the data they need to identify consumer needs, develop new products and communication strategies, and assess the effectiveness of marketing programs.

But how research is used is at the heart of many an ethical dilemma. Statistics can be hidden, shaped, and manipulated in many ways. Companies have deliberately withheld information, falsified figures, altered results, misused or ignored pertinent data, compromised the research design, and misinterpreted the results to support their point of view.

TRIUMPH BEATS MERIT. Triumph, at less than half the tar, preferred over Merit. In fact, an amazing 60% said 3 mg. Triumph tastes as good or better than 8 mg. Merit.

Lorillard, the manufacturer of Triumph cigarettes, obtained the data for this claim from a survey. But in a classic illustration of selective facts and omissions, the ads did not say how Lorillard arrived at the 60 percent figure.

But industry regulators contradicted Triumph's claim. Thirty-six percent of respondents had preferred Triumph; 24 percent said the two were equal; the remaining 40 percent preferred Merit. So an even more "amazing" 64 percent (40 plus 24) said Merit tasted as good as or better than Triumph. Philip Morris's Merit was the real winner of Lorillard's survey. Philip Morris sued Lorillard and won a prohibition of false claims.

Consider the Joe Camel controversy. The Coalition on Smoking OR Health petitioned the FTC to prohibit the use of the cartoon trade character Joe Camel in RJR Nabisco's advertising for Camel cigarettes. Its petition was based on three articles in the *Journal of the American Medical Association (JAMA)*. The articles claimed the Camel ads were targeted at minors.

After many months of study, the FTC "acquitted" Joe Camel due to lack of evidence. The FTC case files included several briefs from marketing and advertising professors who challenged the validity of the studies cited in the *JAMA* articles.

One brief pointed out that, on the charge of inducing minors to smoke, the *JAMA* articles used the wrong measure. The charge required data addressing *primary demand*, the use of the whole product category. But the articles examined only brand share data, a measure of *selective demand* for brands within a category. And the University of Michigan's "Monitoring the Future" study, an annual survey of high school seniors, showed no change in the level of smoking after the Joe Camel campaign debuted.

A brief filed by University of Michigan professor Claude Martin found a gross misquotation in one *JAMA* reference. In an attempt to prove RJR's intent to target minors, coauthor Dr. Joseph DiFranza quoted from an RJR document—except that he omitted key words, as well as parentheses around the words "new users." The RJR statement follows, with the words that DiFranza deleted underlined. (First read the quote without the underlined portions; then go back and read it in its entirety.)

Whose behavior are we trying to affect?: <u>Demographics: adults—male (predominantly), females (must not be excluded), 18–34; emphasis 18–24</u> (new users). The goal is optimizing product and user imagery of Export A [Camels] against young starter smokers.

Exhibit • 6–7

The reliability/validity diagram. Using the analogy of a dart board, the bull's-eye is the actual average of a value among a population (say, the average age in the community). The **top row** shows high reliability—or *repeatability*—because the darts are closely clustered. When reliability drops, the darts land more randomly and spread across a wider area, as in both examples in the **bottom row.** The **left column** demonstrates high validity because in both examples the darts center around the bull's-eye. The **right column** represents low validity because a bias in the testing process drew all the darts to one side. In the **upper-right quadrant,** members of a fraternity are in the same age group (high reliability or repeatability), but their ages do not reflect the average of the community (low validity). The **lower-left quadrant** suggests the testing of our average age sample is highly valid; but it is not reliable because it includes people with a wide range of ages. The **upper-left quadrant** reflects the truest picture of the data.

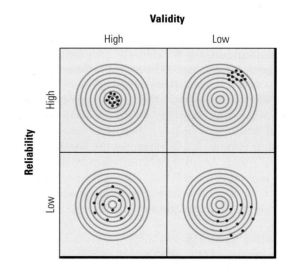

The *Washington Times* alleged that DiFranza had not conducted an objective study. Based on memos he wrote in pursuit of funding, the *Times* charged that DiFranza had set out to develop evidence that would prove his predetermined conclusion.

Consumer goodwill is vital for most marketing research. In an activity that rarely yields any direct benefit to the individual respondent, unethical practices lessen the likelihood of consumer cooperation.

In another critique, St. Joseph's University professor Joel Dubow asked, "Was Joe Camel Framed?" Dubow obtained DiFranza's original data and discovered that DiFranza had actually deleted from his article data that contradicted the charge that Joe Camel's maximum appeal was to "children." Dubow (himself an advocate of tobacco control) reported that when the critical data were reentered into the study and the advertising data then broken out by age, the

maximum appeal of Joe Camel was among 18-to-24-year-olds—just the market RJR said it was targeting. He concluded that Joe Camel had indeed been framed. In a simultaneously published response to Dubow's article, DiFranza did not deny the charge.

Consumer goodwill is vital for most marketing research. In an activity that rarely yields any direct benefit to the individual respondent, unethical practices lessen the likelihood of consumer cooperation.

Honest surveys provide excellent consumer information. They can also give advertisers legitimate selling points. As the FTC noted, "The existence of a survey as support for a claim of superiority may well imply to many consumers a measure of precision and accuracy that they would be less willing to attribute to the same claim made without reference to any statistical support. We assume this is why advertisers wish to use surveys."

Questions

1. Do you feel that DiFranza, in pursuing his "noble" purpose, was justified in his actions? How do you feel about the misquote of the

RJR document? What about the manner in which he reported his data?
2. Are there any circumstances that might justify a portrayal of research findings in a biased or distorted fashion?
3. Why is it so important when discussing marketing research results with a client to report all results—not just those that put the client in a good light?

Sources: Ivan L. Preston, *The Tangled Web They Weave: Truth, Falsity and Advertisers* (Madison, WI: The University of Wisconsin Press, 1994), pp. 142, 143, 145; Ira Teinowitz, "Nielsen in Turmoil," *Advertising Age,* November 15, 1993, pp. 21, 24; N. Craig Smith and John A. Quelch, "Ethical Issues in Researching and Targeting Consumers," in *Ethics in Marketing* (Burr Ridge, IL: Richard D. Irwin, 1993), pp. 145, 177; University of Michigan, "Monitoring the Future Study," *News and Information Services,* January 27, 1994; "Now All We Need Is Some Data," *The Washington Times,* August 4, 1992; Claude R. Martin, "Research Validity and Resulting Public Policy: The Case of the DiFranza 'Old Joe' Cigarette Study," Annual Conference of the American Association of Public Opinion Research, May 1993; Joel S. Dubow, "Was Joe Camel Framed?" *Food & Beverage Marketing,* July 1993, pp. 28–30.

survey, how many to survey, and how to choose the respondents. Defining **sample units**—the individuals, families, or companies being surveyed—is very important.

A sample must be large enough to achieve precision and stability. The larger the sample, the more reliable the results. However, adequate sample size has nothing to do with the size of the population. Reliability can be obtained with very small samples, a fraction of 1 percent of the population. There are two types of samples: random probability samples and nonprobability samples. Both are derived from mathematical *theories of probability*.

Random probability samples offer greater accuracy because everyone in the universe has an equal chance of being selected.[29] For example, a researcher who wants to know a community's opinion on an issue selects members of the community at random. But this method has difficulties. Every unit (person) must be known, listed, and numbered so each has an equal chance of being selected, an often prohibitively expensive and sometimes impossible task, especially with customers of nationally distributed products.

Nonprobability samples, on the other hand, don't give every unit in the universe an equal chance of being included, so there's no guarantee the sample is representative. As a result, researchers can't be as confident in the validity of the responses.[30] Nonetheless, researchers use nonprobability samples extensively because they're easier as well as less expensive and time-consuming. Most marketing and advertising research needs general measures of the data. For example, the nonprobability method of interviewing shoppers in malls may be sufficient to determine the shopping preferences, image perceptions, and attitudes of customers.

How Questionnaires Are Designed

Constructing a good questionnaire requires considerable expertise. Much bias in research is blamed on poorly designed questionnaires. Typical problems include asking the wrong types of questions, asking too many questions, using the wrong form for a question (which makes it too difficult to answer or tabulate), and using the wrong choice of words. Exhibit 6–8 shows some typical questions that might be used in a survey for a retail store.

Consider the simple question: "What kind of soap do you use?" The respondent doesn't know what *soap* means. Hand soap, shampoo, laundry detergent, or dishwashing soap? Does *kind* mean brand, size, or type? Finally, what constitutes *use?* What a person buys (perhaps for someone else) or uses personally—and for what purpose? In fact, one person probably uses several different kinds of soap, depending on the occasion. It's impossible to answer this question accurately. Worse, if the consumer does answer it, the researcher doesn't know what the answer means and will likely draw an incorrect conclusion. For these reasons, questionnaires *must* be pretested. (See the Checklist for Developing an Effective Questionnaire.)

Exhibit • 6–8
A personal questionnaire like this helps determine shoppers' feelings toward a chain of stores, its merchandise, and its advertising.

1. Do you intend to shop at _(Store name)_ between now and Sunday?
   Yes 1   No 2   (If no, skip to question 5)

2. Do you intend to buy something in particular or just to browse?
   Buy 1   Browse 2

3. Have you seen any of the items you intend to buy advertised by _(Store name)_ ?
   Yes 1   (continue)   No 2   (skip to question 5)

4. Where did you see these items advertised? Was it in a _(Store name)_ advertising flyer included with your newspaper, a _(Store name)_ flyer you received in the mail, the pages of the newspaper itself, on TV, or somewhere else?
   - ☐ Flyer in newspaper   ☐ On TV
   - ☐ Flyer in mail   ☐ Somewhere else (specify)
   - ☐ Pages of newspaper   ☐ Don't recall

5. Please rate the _(Store name)_ advertising insert on the attributes listed below. Place an X in the box at the position that best reflects your opinion of how the insert rates on each attribute. Placing an X in the middle box usually means you are neutral. The closer you place the X to the left or right phrase or word, the more you believe it desribes the _(Store name)_ insert.

Looks cheap							Looks expensive
Unskillful							Cleverly done
Unappealing							Appealing
Does not show clothing in an attractive manner	1	2	3	4	5	6	7	Shows clothing in an attractive manner

6. Please indicate all of the different types of people listed below you feel this _(Store name)_ advertising insert is appealing to.
   - ☐ Young people   ☐ Quality-conscious people
   - ☐ Bargain hunters   ☐ Low-income people
   - ☐ Conservative dressers   ☐ Budget watchers
   - ☐ Fashion-conscious people ☐ Older people
   - ☐ Rich people   ☐ Middle-income people
   - ☐ Professionals   ☐ Blue-collar people
   - ☐ High-income people   ☐ Women
   - ☐ Men   ☐ Office workers
   - ☐ Someone like me   ☐ Smart dressers
   - ☐ Career-oriented women   ☐ Other (specify) _____

Developing an Effective Questionnaire | *Checklist*

☐ **List specific research objectives.** Don't spend money collecting irrelevant data.

☐ **Write short questionnaires.** Don't tax the respondent's patience; you may get careless or flip answers.

☐ **State questions clearly** so there is no chance for misunderstanding. Avoid generalities and ambiguities.

☐ **Write a rough draft first,** then polish it.

☐ **Use a short opening statement.** Include the interviewer's name, the name of the orga-

nization, and the purpose of the questionnaire.

☐ **Put the respondent at ease** by opening with one or two inoffensive, easily answered questions.

☐ **Ask general questions before more detailed ones.** Structure questions so they flow logically.

☐ **Avoid questions that suggest an answer or could be considered leading.** They bias the results.

☐ **Include a few questions that cross-check earlier answers.** This helps ensure validity.

☐ **Put the demographic questions (age, income, education) and any other personal questions at the end of the questionnaire.**

☐ **Pretest the questionnaire** with 20 to 30 people to be sure they interpret the questions correctly and that all the information sought is included.

Effective survey questions have three important attributes: *focus, brevity,* and *clarity.* They focus on the topic of the survey. They are as brief as possible. And they are expressed simply and clearly.[31]

The four most common types of questions are *open-ended, dichotomous, multiple choice,* and *semantic differential* (see Exhibit 6–9). But there are many ways to ask questions within these four types. Additional choices, for example, can be added to the multiple-choice format. Neutral responses can be removed from the semantic differential question so the respondent must answer either positively or negatively. And there is obvious bias in the dichotomous question.

Questions should elicit a response that is both accurate and useful. By testing questionnaires on a small subsample, researchers can detect any confusion, bias, or ambiguities.

Data Tabulation and Analysis

Collected data must be validated, edited, coded, and tabulated. Answers must be checked to eliminate errors or inconsistencies. For example, one person might answer two years, while another says 24 months; such responses must be changed to the same units for correct tabulation. Some questionnaires may be rejected because respondents'

Type	Questions
Open-ended	How would you describe (Store name) advertising?
Dichotomous	Do you think (Store name) advertising is too attractive? _____ Yes _____ No
Multiple choice	What description best fits your opinion of (Store name) advertising? _____ Modern _____ Unconvincing _____ Well done _____ Old-fashioned _____ Believable
Semantic differential (scale)	Please indicate on the scale how you rate the quality of (Store name) advertising. ___ ___ ___ ___ ___ 1 2 3 4 5 Poor Excellent

Exhibit • 6–9
Different ways to phrase research questions.

• Release 8 of MINITAB® Statistical Software features a menu interface and advanced statistical capabilities. Such programs make it possible for small advertisers and large companies to analyze research data.

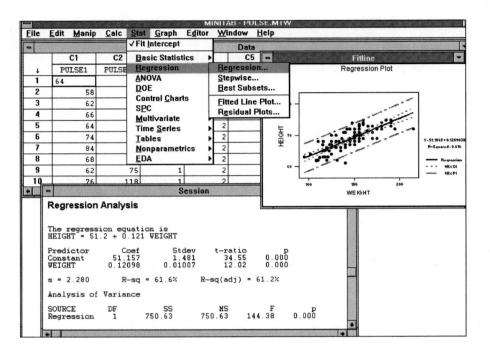

answers indicate they misunderstood the questions. Finally, the data must be counted and summarized, usually by computers.

Many researchers want *cross-tabulations*—for example, product use by age group or education. Software programs such as MINITAB® Statistical Software make it possible for small advertisers as well as large corporations to tabulate data on a personal computer and apply advanced statistical techniques.[32] Many cross-tabulations are possible, but researchers must use skill and imagination to select only those that show significant relationships. On small samples, using additional cross-tabs dramatically reduces the level of confidence. (For information on PC software for research analysis, see RL 6–2 in the Reference Library.)

Collecting Primary Data in International Markets

International marketers face a number of challenges when they collect primary data. For one thing, research overseas is often more expensive than domestic research. Many marketers are surprised to learn that research in five countries costs five times as much as research in one country.[33]

But advertisers must determine whether their messages will work in foreign markets. (Maxwell House, for example, had to change its "great American coffee" campaign when it discovered that Germans have little respect for U.S. coffee.)

Control and direction of the research is another problem. Some companies want to direct research from their headquarters but charge it to the subsidiary's budget. This creates an instant turf battle. It also means that people less familiar with the country—and therefore less sensitive to local cultural issues—might be in charge of the project, which could flaw data. Advertisers need more than just facts about a country's culture. They need to understand and appreciate the nuances of the its cultural traits and habits, a difficult task for people who don't live there or speak the language. Knowledgeable international advertisers like Colgate-Palmolive work in partnership with their local offices and use local bilingual marketing people when conducting primary research abroad.[34]

For years, Mattel tried unsuccessfully to market the Barbie doll in Japan. It finally sold the manufacturing license to a Japanese company, Takara, which did its own research. Takara found that most Japanese girls and their parents thought Barbie's breasts were too big and her legs too long. It modified the doll accordingly, changed the blue eyes to brown, and sold 2 million dolls in two years.

Conducting original research abroad can be fraught with problems. First, the researcher must use the local language, and translating questionnaires can be tricky. Second, many cultures view strangers suspiciously and don't wish to talk about their personal lives. U.S. companies found that mail surveys and phone interviews don't work in Japan; they have to use expensive, time-consuming personal interviews.[35]

Despite these problems—or perhaps because of them—it's important for global advertisers to perform research. Competent researchers are available in all developed countries, and major international research firms have local offices in most developing countries. The largest of these companies, which serve the largest multinational clients, organize their services globally based on the type of specialized research they regularly conduct. Research International Group, for instance, has global research directors for advertising research and for customer satisfaction research and global account directors for their clients' projects worldwide.[36]

Two goals for international research are flexibility and standardization, and both are necessary for the best results. Flexibility means using the best approach in each market. If you're studying the use of laundry products, it's just as irrelevant to ask Mexicans about soy sauce stains as it is to ask Thais how they get *mole* out of their clothes.[37]

On the other hand, standardization is important so information from different countries can be compared.[38] Otherwise the study will be meaningless. Balance is required to get the best of flexibility and standardization.

Summary

Marketing research is the systematic procedure used to gather, record, and analyze new information to help managers make decisions about the marketing of goods and services. Marketing research helps management identify consumer needs, develop new products and communication strategies, and assess the effectiveness of marketing programs and promotional activities.

Advertising research, a subset of marketing research, is used to gather and analyze information for developing or evaluating advertising. It helps advertisers develop strategies and test concepts. The results of research help define the product concept, select the target market, and develop the primary advertising message elements.

Advertisers use testing to make sure their advertising dollars are spent wisely. Pretesting helps detect and eliminate weaknesses before a campaign runs. Posttesting helps evaluate the effectiveness of an ad or campaign after it runs. Testing is used to evaluate several variables including markets, motives, messages, media, budgets, and schedules.

Research involves several steps: analyzing the situation and defining the problem, conducting exploratory research by analyzing internal data and collecting external secondary data, setting research objectives, conducting research using quantitative or qualitative methods, and finally, interpreting and reporting the findings.

Quantitative techniques include observation, experiment, and survey. Marketers use qualitative research to get a general impression of the market. The methods used may be projective or intensive.

Techniques used in pretesting include central location tests, clutter tests, and direct questioning. Pretesting has numerous problems, including artificiality, consumer inaccuracy, and the halo effect of consumer responses. The most commonly used posttesting techniques are aided recall, unaided recall, attitude tests, inquiry tests, and sales tests.

The validity and reliability of quantitative surveys depend on the sampling methods used and the design of the survey questionnaire. The two sampling procedures are random probability and nonprobability. Survey questions require focus, brevity, and simplicity.

In international markets, research is often more expensive and less reliable. But advertisers must use research to understand cultural traits and habits in overseas markets.

Questions for Review and Discussion

1. How does research help advertisers meet the challenge of the 3 Rs of marketing?
2. Give an example that demonstrates the difference between marketing research and market research.
3. Which kind of research data is more expensive to collect, primary or secondary? Why?
4. How have you personally used observational research?
5. Do people use quantitative or qualitative research to evaluate movies? Explain.
6. Which of the major surveying methods is most costly? Why?
7. When might research offer validity but not reliability?
8. When could research help in the development of advertising strategy for an international advertiser? Give an example.
9. How could the halo effect bias a pretest for a soft drink ad?
10. How would you design a controlled experiment to test the advertising for a chain of men's stores?

7

Marketing and Advertising Planning
Top-Down, Bottom-Up, and IMC

Objective: To describe the process of marketing and advertising planning. Marketers and advertisers need to understand the various ways plans are created, and they must know how to analyze situations; set realistic, attainable objectives; develop strategies to achieve them; and establish budgets for marketing communications.

After studying this chapter, you will be able to:

- Explain the role and importance of a marketing plan.

- Describe how marketing and advertising plans are related.

- Explain the difference between objectives and strategies in marketing and advertising plans.

- Give examples of need-satisfying and sales-target objectives.

- Discuss the suitability of top-down, bottom-up, and integrated marketing communications planning.

- Explain how advertising budgets are determined.

- Describe how share-of-market/share-of-voice budgeting can be used for new product introductions.

decade ago, Japanese cars were the stars of the automotive world. But in the 90s, a player as down-home American as fried chicken entered the scene.

It all started in the mid-80s when then-chair of GM Roger Smith vowed to find a better way to manufacture and market cars by building partnerships between management and labor, company and supplier. GM's mission was to produce a car that would be a powerful import fighter and to build the best-liked automotive company in America.[1]

The company eschewed its Detroit roots for the rural foothills of Spring Hill, Tennessee, where it built the most modern auto plant in America. Working with its target market of typical import buyers, the company designed the vehicle they wanted: small, economical, safe, attractive, comfortable, and affordable: the Saturn.

In partnership with its employees, the company discarded assembly line methods and developed teams to build its cars. Quality was paramount.

By 1987, Saturn officials started looking for an ad agency to introduce the first all-new American car since the Edsel. After an exhaustive search, they selected a San Francisco shop—Hal Riney & Partners—29 months before the first car would go on sale. Riney executives immediately traveled to Saturn's headquarters to immerse themselves in the product plans and to undergo the orientation to Saturn culture given to all new employees.

Many key brand-building decisions were made well before the launch with contributions from Riney and a panel of 16 dealer advisers. "Most people start and stop with the car," says Donald Hudler, Saturn VP of sales, service, and marketing. But to Saturn, the product concept included not just the car's but the company's image, the customers' perceptions, and the whole shopping, buying, and owning experience. With Riney's help,

the company meticulously crafted Saturn's brand image.

Saturn emphasized straight talk. Red cars would be called red, not "raspberry red." Customers would not have to haggle over price, and dealers would be called retailers ("we're not in the deal business"). Even the models would be designated by letters or numbers rather than names that might detract from the Saturn image. "The truth," Riney says, "is far better than anything we can make up. Saturn has to represent honesty and directness." Moreover, all communications had to be integrated and consistent.

Before producing any consumer advertising, the agency created several internal communications pieces about the company. A short film documented the plant start-up and the workers' incredible commitment. The company used the film to train new employees and help introduce itself to suppliers and the press. Retailers used it in presentations for bank loans and zoning variances. After the launch, Riney even ran it as a "documercial" on cable TV. The film showed Saturn team members explaining in their own words, often emotionally, what the project meant to them.

When the agency began creating consumer ads, it took the same tack: "A different kind of company. A different kind of car."

The cars were such an immediate success that production couldn't keep up with demand. Riney had to create ads apologizing for delivery delays. In 1992, despite production restraints, Saturn sold 196,126 cars—more than twice as many as the year before—outselling Hyundai, Subaru, Mitsubishi, and Volkswagen. Touted by the critics for its high quality-to-price ratio, the company also finished third in the J. D. Power & Associates survey of new-car buyer satisfaction, right behind Lexus and In-

• This 26-minute film entitled "Spring, in Spring Hill" used actual comments from real employees to tell what Saturn meant to them. The film was first used as an internal communication piece and later as a 30-minute infomercial.

finiti, which cost several times more than Saturn's frugal $10,000. With its fanatic devotion to integrated marketing communications, Riney helped Saturn build a brand.[2] And in 1993, thanks largely to its work on the Saturn account, Hal Riney & Partners was named agency of the year by *Advertising Age.* •

THE MARKETING PLAN

The Saturn story demonstrates that business success depends more on careful marketing and advertising planning than on advertising creativity. Yet, many companies waste millions of dollars on ineffectual advertising due to a woeful lack of prior planning.

The Importance of Marketing Planning

Since marketing is typically a company's *only* source of income, the marketing plan may well be a company's most important document.

The **marketing plan** assembles all the pertinent facts about the organization, the markets it serves, and its products, services, customers, competition, and so on. It forces all departments—product development, production, selling, advertising, credit, transportation—to focus on the customer. Finally, it sets goals and objectives for specified periods of time and lays out the precise strategies and tactics to achieve them.

The written marketing plan must reflect the goals of the company's top management and be consistent with the company's capabilities. Depending on its scope, the plan may be long and complex or, in the case of a small firm or a single product line, very brief. Formal marketing plans are typically reviewed and revised yearly, but planning is not a one-time event; it's a continuous process that includes research, formulation, implementation, evaluation, review, and reformulation.

The Effect of the Marketing Plan on Advertising

The marketing plan has a profound effect on an organization's advertising program. It helps managers analyze and improve all company operations, including marketing and advertising programs. It dictates the role of advertising in the marketing mix. It enables better implementation, control, and continuity of advertising programs, and it ensures the most efficient allocation of advertising dollars.

Successful organizations do not separate advertising plans from marketing. They view each as a vital building block for success. Companies employ three types of marketing planning models today: top-down, bottom-up, and integrated marketing communications (IMC) planning.

Top-Down Marketing Planning

The traditional **top-down marketing plan** is the most common planning format. It has been used for over 30 years and fits with the hierarchical way most companies are organized. It is also appropriate for companies planning to launch completely new products. As Exhibit 7–1 shows, the top-down plan has four main elements: *situation analysis, marketing objectives, marketing strategy,* and *tactics* (or *action programs*).

Extended marketing plans for large companies may also include additional sections. Appendix A at the end of the book outlines a complete top-down marketing plan.

Situation analysis

The **situation analysis** section is a *factual* statement of the organization's current situation and how it got there. It presents all relevant facts about the company's history, growth, products and services, sales volume, share of market, competitive status, markets served, distribution system, past advertising programs, results of marketing research studies, company capabilities, strengths and weaknesses, and any other pertinent information. To plan successfully for the future, company executives must agree on the accuracy of the data and its interpretation. See RL 7–1, Checklist for Situation Analysis in the Reference Library, for the most important elements to consider.

Once the historical information is gathered, the focus changes to potential threats and opportunities based on key factors outside the company's control—for example, the economic, political, social, technological, or commercial environments the company operates in.[3]

Look at the situation GM faced at the beginning of the 90s. American cars were perceived as lacking the quality or value of Japanese and German competitors. Detroit's management and manufacturing systems were considered outmoded bureaucracies, and people questioned the productivity of the American worker.[4] Roger Smith believed that Americans wanted to buy domestic cars but had to be given a good reason.

Marketing objectives

The organization's next step is to determine specific marketing objectives. These must consider the amount of money the company has to invest in marketing and production, its knowledge of the marketplace, and the competitive environment. General Motors, for example, invested $5 billion in the Saturn project before the first car ever rolled out.[5]

Marketing objectives follow logically from a review of the company's current situation, management's prediction of future trends, and the hierarchy of company objec-

Exhibit • 7–1
Traditional top-down marketing plan.

• Some sales and marketing objectives are quite short range. To celebrate Father's Day in Singapore, Hagemeyer Electronics, a distributor of Japanese electronic products, ran this newspaper ad for the National brand wet and dry shaver. The ad, aimed at young adults looking for Father's Day gifts, appeared in Singapore's afternoon tabloid. *(Turn the ad upside down to get the full effect of the advertiser's message.)*

tives. For example, **corporate objectives** are stated in terms of profit or return on investment—or net worth, earnings ratios, growth, or corporate reputation. **Marketing objectives,** which derive from corporate objectives, relate to the needs of target markets and to specific sales goals. These are called general *need-satisfying objectives* and specific *sales-target objectives.*

Need-satisfying objectives shift management's view of the organization from a producer of products or services to a satisfier of target market needs. They enable the firm to view its business broadly. Since customer needs change, too narrow a view may lead the company into markets in which its products are obsolete.[6] Revlon founder Charles Revson once said a cosmetic company's product is hope, not lipstick. An insurance company sells financial security, not policies.

Sales-target objectives are specific, quantitative, realistic marketing goals to be achieved within a specified time period. Saturn defined its goal as selling 75,000 cars nationwide in 1991, and 196,000 in 1992. These objectives were specific as to product and market, quantified as to time and amount, and—judging by the results—fairly realistic. In 1991, Saturn sold 74,493 cars; in 1992, it sold 196,126. Only by setting specific objectives can management measure its marketing success. Saturn's objectives for 1993 and 1994 were 235,000 and 300,000 respectively. Their sales for those two years were 229,356 and 286,003.[7]

Sales-target objectives may be expressed in several ways: total sales volume; sales volume by product, market segment, customer type; market share in total or by product line; growth rate of sales volume in total or by product line; and gross profit in total or by product line.

Marketing strategy

The **marketing strategy** describes how the company plans to meet its marketing objectives. (See Ad Lab 7–A, "The Strategies of Marketing Warfare.") In a top-down situation, the way objectives and strategies are set frequently depends on the corporate hierarchy. For example, the company CEO might set an objective of increasing the stock dividend. The strategy for this is to increase sales. To the marketing director, the CEO's strategy (increased sales) becomes an objective. The marketing director's strategy is to use advertising to persuade current customers to use the product more. That becomes the advertising agency's objective. The agency's strategy, then, may be to make the product more appealing to regular buyers by defining more use occasions.

A company's marketing strategy has a dramatic impact on its advertising. It determines the role of advertising in the marketing mix and the amount to be used, its creative thrust, and the media employed.

Selecting the target market   In top-down marketing, the first step in strategy development is to define and select the target market using the processes of market segmentation and research discussed in Chapters 5 and 6.

Saturn, for instance, defined its target market as "college-educated import owners and intenders"—highly educated young adults (18 to 34) considering their first or second car purchase. They were further defined as 60 percent female, living in one- or two-person households, and seeking a vehicle with sporty styling, fun performance, fuel economy, a good warranty, and sound quality/reliability/dependability.[8] They typically drive a Honda Civic, Toyota Corolla, or Nissan 240SX.

Determining the marketing mix   The second step in developing the marketing strategy is to determine a cost-effective marketing mix for *each* target market the company pursues. As we discussed in Chapter 5, the mix blends the various marketing elements the company controls: *product, price, distribution,* and *communication.*

Saturn manufactured a solidly engineered, driver-oriented product and supported it with a 24-hour roadside assistance program and a money-back guarantee for dissatisfied customers who returned their cars within 30 days or 1,500 miles. Then, to reinforce its

• As a part of its integrated marketing strategy, Saturn places this brochure in dealer showrooms for prospective and current customers.

The Strategies of Marketing Warfare   *Ad Lab 7-A*

Jack Trout and Al Ries's *Marketing Warfare* is based on the classic book on military strategy, *On War*, written by Prussian general Carl von Clausewitz and published in 1832. The book outlines the principles behind all successful wars, and two simple ideas dominate: *force* and the *superiority of the defense.*

The Strategic Square

How do the principles of warfare apply to marketing? It comes down to the "strategic square":

Out of every 100 companies:
One should play defense;
Two should play offense;
Three should flank;
And 94 should be guerrillas.

Defensive Warfare

Datril opened its war on Tylenol with a price attack. Johnson & Johnson immediately cut Tylenol's price, even before Datril started its price advertising. Result: It repelled the Datril attacks and inflicted heavy losses on the Bristol-Myers entry.

Here are the rules for defensive marketing warfare:

1. Participate only if you are a market leader.
2. Introduce new products and services before the competition does.
3. Block strong competitive moves by copying them rapidly.

Offensive Warfare

Colgate had a strong number-one position in toothpaste. But rival Procter & Gamble knew a thing or two about Carl von Clausewitz.

P&G launched Crest toothpaste with not only a massive $20 million advertising budget but also the American Dental Association "seal of approval." Crest went over the top and is now the best-selling toothpaste in the country.

But overtaking the leader is not that common. Most companies are happy if they can establish a profitable number-two position.

There are rules for waging offensive marketing warfare:

1. Consider the strength of the leader's position.
2. Launch the attack on as narrow a front as possible, preferably with single products.
3. Launch the attack at the leader's weakest position.

Flanking Warfare

The third type of marketing warfare is where the action is for many companies. In practice, it means launching products where there is no competition. Unilever introduced Mentadent, the first baking soda/peroxide toothpaste, which became a very successful brand.

Here are the principles of flanking marketing warfare:

1. Make good flanking moves into uncontested areas.
2. Use surprise. Too much research often wastes precious time.
3. Keep up the pursuit; too many companies quit after they're ahead.

Guerrilla Warfare

Most of America's companies should be waging guerrilla warfare. The key to success in guerrilla wars is flexibility. A guerrilla should abandon any product or market if the tide of battle changes.

Here are the principles of guerrilla marketing warfare:

1. Find a market segment small enough to defend.
2. No matter how successful you become, never act like the leader.
3. Be prepared to "bug out" at a moment's notice.

Bottom Up

Trout and Ries's later book, *Bottom-Up Marketing* (discussed later in this chapter), continues the military analogy.

"Deep penetration on a narrow front is the key to winning a marketing war," they say. By this they mean that smaller companies should keep their product narrowly focused on a single concept. Too many companies spread their forces over a wide front. In fact, most large corporations today must fend off focused attacks by smaller companies.

Laboratory Applications

1. Think of a successful product and explain its success in terms of marketing warfare.
2. Select a product and explain how marketing warfare strategy might be used to gain greater success.

---

commitment to doing business differently, it established an MSRP (manufacturer's suggested retail price) well below Honda Civic and Toyota Corolla, and does not employ factory rebates or dealer incentives.[9]

GM created a completely new wholly owned subsidiary and nationwide retail distribution system for Saturn, separate from the GM network. Finally, Saturn initiated an integrated marketing communications program that included extensive training programs for retailer sales and service staffs (personal selling), innovative Media Days at the Spring Hill factory (public relations), and a full TV, magazine, and radio ad campaign to develop a distinct Saturn personality—not just for the car, but also for the company.

Companies have a wide variety of marketing strategy options. They might increase distribution, initiate new uses for a product, change a product line, develop entirely new markets, or start discount pricing. Each option emphasizes one or more marketing mix elements. The choice depends on the product's position in the market and its stage in the product life cycle.

● "How should we position this product?" is a question every marketer must ask. The Puget Sound Volvo Dealers group ran transit ads and TV spots with a "Buy safely" theme, a play on Volvo's national "Drive safely" program. The dealers wanted to highlight Volvo's number-one safety record. Other ads feature babies and copy lines such as, "The best reason for buying a Volvo can't talk."

Positioning strategies   David Ogilvy says the first decision in marketing and advertising is also the most important: how to position the product. To Ogilvy, positioning means "what the product does and who it is for."[10] His agency (Ogilvy & Mather), for example, differentiated Dove soap in 1957 by positioning it as a *complexion bar for women with dry skin*. Now, some 40 years later, every commercial still uses the same cleansing cream demonstration, and Dove is consistently the number-one brand, spending over $20 million in advertising annually to maintain its 14 percent share of the $1.5 billion bar soap market.[11]

Companies usually have a number of positioning options. They might pick a position similar to a competitor's and fight for the same customers. Or they might find a position not held by a competitor—a hole in the market—and fill it quickly, perhaps through product differentiation or market segmentation.

Ethical Issue   ## The Winds of Ad Wars

Across the advertising battlefield a war is being waged. It's called comparative advertising. More frequently than ever, charges and countercharges are appearing in ads. And the main players are no longer just second-rate brands looking to make their mark. Now dominant but vulnerable marketers, once content simply to ignore their smaller competitors, are increasingly fighting back with comparisons of their own. Unfortunately, such advertising may muddy the issues more than illuminate them.

"It almost becomes defensive communications," says Jim Arnold, chairman of Arnold & Truitt, a New York management consultancy. "The benefit message is so clouded in irritable language and . . . bullying tactics that I just think most people tune it out."

Most notably, American Express and Visa have ping-ponged one another with hard-hitting ads that emphasize the other's weakness. An American Express Optima True Grace Card ad read:

QUESTION: Why is Visa incorrectly claiming 7 million more merchants than American Express? (We challenge Visa to name them.)

ANSWER: So you won't notice the $1.5 BILLION unnecessary interest they charge you.

The tagline mocked Visa's long-running slogan: "Visa. It's everywhere you want to pay more interest charges."

Visa USA retaliated by pointing out AmEx's lower merchant acceptance:

American Express is offering you a new credit card, but you don't have to accept it. Heck, 7 million merchants don't.

While American Express snipes at Visa, AT&T goes after MCI. American Home Products attacks Procter & Gamble. IBM fires back at Hewlett-Packard. Name-calling, finger-pointing, taunting, insulting—they're all contemporary weapons of the marketing wars between virtually identical brands desperate to differentiate themselves from the competition.

But lingering behind the scenes are three important issues: effectiveness, legality, and ethics. Product differentiation certainly has its place in competitive strategy because imperceptible differences *can* enhance a product's desirability. Moreover, the Supreme Court and the FTC encourage comparative advertising. They believe it gives consumers more information to consider in their purchase decisions. But does it really?

Research shows that direct product comparisons do create awareness for low-share brands. But established products and services may actually lose sales because consumers often confuse brands. Worse, negative ad campaigns may decrease the sponsor's credibility in the public's mind.

And if taken too far, comparative advertising can be *illegal*—if the comparison is false, misleading, or deceptive. Even ads that are literally correct can be found liable. According to one court, "innuendo, indirect intimations, and ambiguous suggestions" can unjustly injure a com-

Saturn positioned its car as an American alternative to the Japanese imports, offering comparable styling, performance, and quality at a lower price, and its company as the "caring" car company.[12]

Customer perception of many big, older brands (Chevrolet, Budweiser, VW) has gotten badly out of focus. Trout suggests that "repositioning" is the solution when customer attitudes have changed or technology has overtaken existing products.[13]

There are so many types of product differentiation, price/quality, positioning, and segmentation strategies that it's difficult to find the best one. Marketing and advertising managers need to work together to develop creative alternatives.

Exhibit • 7–2
Bottom-up marketing plan.

Marketing tactics (action programs)

A company's objectives indicate where it wants to go; the strategy indicates the intended route; and the **tactics** (or **action programs**) determine the specific short-term actions to be taken—internally and externally—by whom and when. Advertising campaigns live in the world of marketing tactics. And tactics are the key to *bottom-up marketing*.

Bottom-Up Marketing: How Small Companies Plan

In a small company, everybody is both player and coach, and the day-to-day details seem to come first, leaving little or no time for formal planning. However, there is a solution to this dilemma: **bottom-up marketing** (see Exhibit 7–2).

Trout and Ries think the best way for a company to develop a competitive advantage is to focus on an ingenious tactic first and then develop that tactic into a strategy. By reversing the normal process, advertisers sometimes make important discoveries.[14] Researchers at Vicks developed an effective liquid cold remedy but discovered that it put people to sleep. Rather than throw out the research, Vicks positioned the formula

---

petitor. McNeil Lab's Extra-Strength Tylenol, for example, successfully sued American Home Products' Maximum Strength Anacin even though

> The ethical problem is even stickier, because moral beliefs are typically personal. Many consumers just don't like advertising that names competitors. And many in the industry feel similarly.

Anacin's ad was literally true. Anacin had implied superiority over Tylenol when in fact both products contain the same amount of pain reliever.

The ethical problem is even stickier, because moral beliefs are typically personal. Many consumers just don't like advertising that names competitors. And many in the industry feel similarly. In an effort to keep the comparison battles from getting out of hand, numerous groups including the American Association of

Advertising Agencies, the National Association of Broadcasters, the FTC, and the TV networks have issued their own guidelines for comparative ads, often stricter than current laws. NBC, for example, insists that "advertisers shall refrain from discrediting, disparaging, or unfairly attacking competitors, competing products, or other industries."

This is a good step. But the legal language governing comparisons is vague, obscuring the line between healthy one-upmanship and illegal behavior. As competition continues to increase, and ethical and legal guidelines remain fuzzy, the public will no doubt continue to be blitzed by comparative ads. The responsibility falls on consumers to sift the facts and figures and to separate truth from fiction.

Questions

1. How do you feel about ads that compare the features and benefits of competitive products and services? Do you believe they

are unethical even if the comparisons are honest? Why or why not?

2. Select a comparative ad and study the copy. What points of comparison does the ad make? Are the points made honestly and directly, or are they masked by innuendo and implication? Is the ad literally true but still potentially misleading? Do you feel the ad is ethical or not?

Sources: Gary Levin, "Marketers Get Really Nasty with In-Your-Face Advertising," *Advertising Age,* October 17, 1994, p. 2; Jim Henry, "Comparative Ads Speed Ahead for Luxury Imports," *Advertising Age,* September 12, 1994, p. 10; Thomas E. Barry, "Comparative Advertising: What Have We Learned in Two Decades?" *Journal of Advertising Research,* March/April 1993, pp. 19–29; A. Andrew Gallo, "False and Comparative Advertising under Section 43(a) of the Lanham Trademark Act," in Theodore R. Kupferman, ed., *Advertising and Commercial Speech* (CN: Meckler Corp., 1990), pp. 49–76; Steven A. Meyerowitz, *Marketing, Sales, and Advertising Law* (Detroit: Visible Ink Press, 1994).

as a nighttime cold remedy. NyQuil went on to become the number-one cold remedy and the most successful new product in Vicks' history.

The tactic: A singular, competitive mental angle

By planning from the bottom up, entrepreneurs can find unique tactics to exploit. But advertisers should find just *one* tactic, not two or three. Once a tactic is discovered, the advertiser can build a strategy around it, focusing all elements of the marketing mix on it. The tactic becomes the nail, and the strategy is the hammer that drives it home.

The combination of tactic and strategy creates a position in the consumer's mind. When Tom Monaghan thought of the tactic of delivering pizza to customers' homes, he focused his whole strategy on this singular idea and ended up making a fortune with Domino's Pizza.

The company's advertising plan is an excellent place to discover a competitive tactic. But opportunities are hard to spot because they often don't look like opportunities—they look like angles or gimmicks.

Managers of small companies actually have an advantage. Surrounded by the details of the business, they are more likely to discover a good tactic that can be developed into a powerful strategy.

Integrated Marketing Communications (IMC) Planning

In recent years, the customer's role has become so dominant that companies have gone beyond marketing oriented to *market driven*. Technology has enabled marketers to adopt flexible manufacturing—customizing products for customized markets. It means bundling more services with products to create a "unique product experience." As with Saturn, it means companies and customers working together to find solutions.[15]

The counterpart to flexible manufacturing is flexible marketing—and integrated marketing communications to reach customers at different levels in new and better ways.

How the customer sees marketing communications

In one study, consumers identified 102 different media as "advertising"—everything from TV to shopping bags to sponsored community events.[16] Customers also develop perceptions of the company or brand through news reports, word-of-mouth, experts' opinions, financial reports, even the CEO's personality. All these communications or brand contacts—sponsored or not—create an *integrated product* in the consumer's mind.[17]

The evolution of the IMC concept

Along with technological change came a host of new, specialized media and the fragmentation of the mass market. Suddenly companies needed to coordinate the multiplicity of company and product messages being issued, many of which lacked consistency.

Companies initially took a narrow, inside-out view of IMC; they saw it as a way to coordinate and manage their marketing communications (advertising, sales promotion, public relations, personal selling, and direct marketing) to give the audience a consistent message about the company.[18]

A broader, more sophisticated, outside-in perspective of IMC views customers as partners in an ongoing relationship, recognizes the references they use, acknowledges the importance of the whole communications system, and accepts the many ways they come in contact with the company or the brand. Companies committed to IMC realize their biggest asset is not their products or their plants or even their employees, but their customers.[19]

Defined broadly, **integrated marketing communications** is the process of building and reinforcing mutually profitable relationships with employees, customers, other stakeholders, and the general public by developing and coordinating a strategic com-

• A broad perspective of integrated marketing communications (IMC) views customers as partners in an ongoing relationship. This promotional brochure designed to launch Aveda natural color cosmetics serves the advertiser's trade as a selling piece and introduced the new product to consumers.

munications program that enables them to make constructive contact with the company/brand through a variety of media.

Whether a company employs the narrow view or the broad view depends to a great extent on its corporate culture. Some companies have enjoyed rapid growth and strong customer relationships because they intuitively integrated and focused all corporate and marketing activities—Saturn, Apple, Honda, Nike, and Banana Republic are just a few.

Tom Duncan, director of the IMC graduate program at the University of Colorado, has identified four distinct levels of integration for companies' use (see Exhibit 7–3). These levels demonstrate how IMC programs range from narrowly focused corporate monologs to broad, interactive dialogs resulting in a corporate culture that permeates an organization and drives everything it does, internally and externally.[20]

The IMC process

Using the outside-in process, the integrated marketing communications approach starts with the customer. Marketers study what media customers use, the relevance of the marketer's message to the customer, and when customers and prospects are most *receptive* to the message. In short, marketers begin with the customer and work back to the brand.[21]

The IMC process can be viewed as an inverted pyramid (see Exhibit 7–4). At its simplest level, IMC starts with a single customer, allowing the company to discover and serve the customer's needs and wants. If the experience is positive for both parties, a relationship develops, and the company has a very narrow specialty: serving *that* customer's needs. But that customer now becomes a reference for other potential customers.

Next, by coordinating database research, media advertising, sales promotion, direct-marketing, personal selling, and public relations, the company locates other customers

Level	Name	Description/focus	Examples
1	Unified image	One look, one voice; strong brand image focus	3M
2	Consistent voice	Consistent tone and look; coordinated messages to various audiences (customers, trade, suppliers, etc.)	Hallmark, Coca-Cola
3	Good listener	Solicits two-way communication, enabling feedback through 800 numbers, surveys, trade shows, etc.; focus on long-term relationships	Andersen windows, Saturn
4	World-class citizen	Social, environmental consciousness, strong company culture; focus on wider community	Ben & Jerry's, Apple, Honda

Exhibit • 7–3
Levels of integration.

Exhibit • 7–4
A successful business often begins by serving a single customer. At this point, limited marketing communications are needed. Once the product or service
grows in popularity to fill broader market needs, the
company must expand and integrate the marketing
communications to keep up momentum.

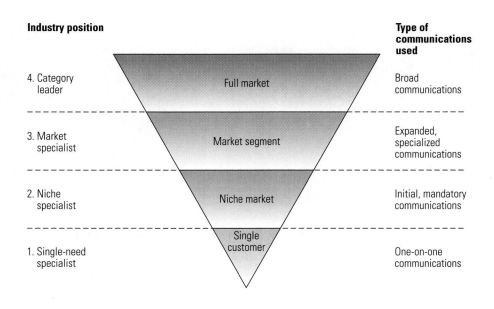

(and their references) with similar needs. As the company develops more experience,
soliciting constant feedback from its customers, it eventually becomes a specialist in
that niche of customers. Finally, the company uses the same techniques to expand its
specialty niche into a full market in which it also enjoys leadership. Most large markets
evolve from niches.

The goal is market dominance—owning the market.[22] That is precisely how Apple
Computer became the leader in desktop publishing. Customers discovered the application. Apple listened and then developed the niche into market leadership.[23]

The IMC Approach to Marketing and Advertising Planning

The inverted pyramid suggests a new approach to planning marketing and communications activities—one that differs substantially from the traditional process discussed
earlier—by mixing marketing and communications planning together rather than sepa-
rating them.

Thanks to computer technology, marketers of mass merchandise today have a
wealth of information at their fingertips. With supermarket scanner data, for instance,
packaged-goods marketers can (1) identify specific users of products and services; (2)
measure their actual purchase behavior and relate that to specific brand and product
categories; (3) measure the impact of various advertising and marketing communications activities and determine their value in influencing the actual purchase; and (4)
capture and evaluate this information over time.[24]

This ever-expanding database of customer behavior can become the basis for planning all future marketing and communications activities—especially if the database
contains information on customer demographics, psychographics, purchase data, and
brand or product category attitudes (see Exhibit 7–5).

Starting the whole planning process with the database forces the company to focus
on the consumer, business customer, or prospect, not on the company's sales or profit
goals. These marketing objectives are moved farther down in the planning process.[25]

The first step in Wang and Schultz's seven-step IMC planning model is to segment
the customers and prospects in the database—either by brand loyalty, as illustrated, or
by some other measurable purchase behavior—heavy usage, for instance.

The second step is to analyze the information on customers to understand their attitudes, their history, and how they came (or come) into contact with the brand or product—in other words, determining the best time, place, and situation to communicate
with them.

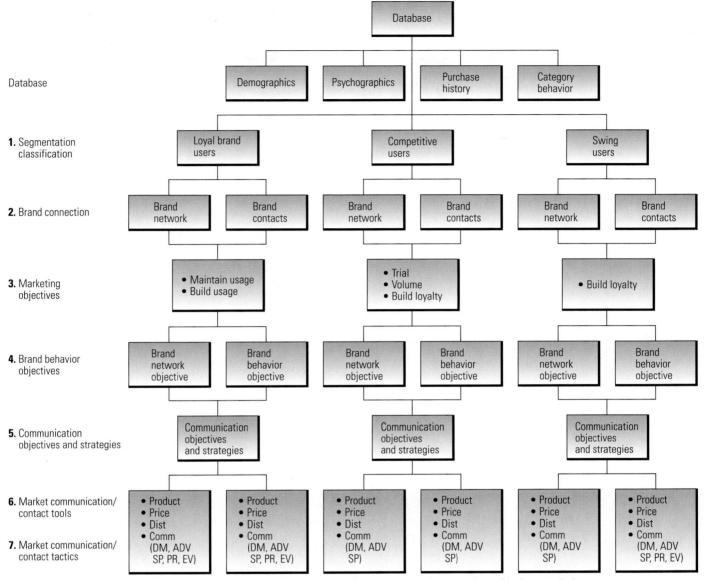

DM = Direct marketing   ADV = Advertising   SP = Sales promotion   PR = Public relations   EV = Event marketing
Dist = Distribution   Comm = Marketing communications

Exhibit • 7–5
Integrated marketing communications planning process.

Next, based on this analysis, the planner sets marketing objectives. In the illustrated example, the marketing objectives relate to building and maintaining usage or nurturing brand loyalty.

Then the marketer identifies what brand contacts and what changes in attitude will be required to support the consumer's continuance or change of purchase behavior.

The fifth step is to set communications objectives and strategies for making contact with the consumer and influencing his or her attitudes, beliefs, and purchase behavior.

Next, the marketer decides what other elements of the marketing mix (product, price, distribution) can be used to further encourage the desired behavior. And finally, the planner determines what communications tactics to use—media advertising, direct marketing, publicity, sales promotion, special events, and so on—to make contact and influence the consumer's behavior.[26]

• The IMC planner must decide which communications tactics to use to reach customers and encourage desired purchase behavior. Kodak opened up new territory with a display-based promotion that targeted moviegoers in more than 4,500 movie theaters across the U.S. It offered free movie tickets in exchange for proofs of purchase from specially marked Kodak products. The over-sized three-dimensional displays offered mail-in forms that doubled as sweepstakes entries for a Universal Studios "Backlot Bash" for the winner and 10 friends.

By following this model, the marketer sets objectives based on an understanding of the customer or prospect and on what must be communicated. All forms of marketing are turned into communication, and all forms of communication into marketing.[27]

The Importance of IMC to the Study of Advertising

Since customers see all sponsored communications as advertising, advertising people—account managers, creatives, media planners—must grow beyond their traditional specialty to become enlightened generalists, familiar with and able to integrate all types of marketing communications.

In a survey of 100 company marketing executives, most respondents thought integration of advertising, promotion, public relations, and other communications activities would influence companies' marketing strategies more in the next three to five years than economic trends, globalization, and even pricing (see Exhibit 7–6).[28] However,

Exhibit • 7–6
Factors influencing marketing strategies.

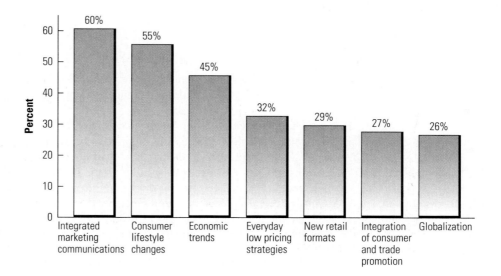

studies also suggest that most practitioners today lack the broad knowledge required to develop, supervise, and execute full IMC programs.[29]

The **advertising plan** is a natural outgrowth of the marketing plan and is prepared in much the same way. In IMC planning, in fact, the advertising plan is an integral part of the overall procedure. Appendix B at the end of the book outlines a top-down advertising plan.

THE ADVERTISING PLAN

Reviewing the Marketing Plan

The advertising manager first reviews the marketing plan to understand where the company is going, how it intends to get there, and what role advertising will play in the marketing mix. The first section of the advertising plan is a situation analysis that briefly restates the company's current situation, reviews the target market segments, itemizes the long- and short-term marketing objectives, and cites decisions regarding market positioning and the marketing mix.

Setting Advertising Objectives

The advertising manager then determines what tasks advertising must take on. Unfortunately, some corporate executives (and advertising managers) state vague goals for advertising, like "creating a favorable impression of the product in the marketplace in order to increase sales and maximize profits." When this happens, no one understands what the advertising is intended to do, how much it costs to do it, or how to measure the results. Advertising objectives should be specific and measurable.

Understanding what advertising can do

Most advertising programs encourage prospects to take some action. However, it is usually unrealistic to assign advertising the whole responsibility for achieving sales. Sales goals are marketing objectives, not advertising objectives. Before an advertiser can persuade customers to buy, it must inform, persuade, or remind its intended audience over time about the company, product, service, or issue. A simple adage for setting objectives is: "Marketing sells, advertising tells."

● Most advertising has a communications goal—to inform, persuade, or remind its audience about the company over an extended time. In this ad, Sico, a Canadian paint manufacturer, uses outdoor advertising to remind prospects about the product's use and brand name.

Exhibit • 7–7
The advertising pyramid depicts the progression of effects advertising has on mass audiences—especially for new products. Compared to the large number of people aware of the product (the base of the pyramid), the number actually motivated to action is usually quite small.

The advertising pyramid: A guide to setting objectives

Suppose you're advertising a new product, but you're not sure what kind of results to expect. The pyramid in Exhibit 7–7 shows some of the tasks advertising can perform. Before your product is introduced, prospective customers are totally unaware of it. Your first advertising objective therefore might be to create *awareness*—to acquaint people with the company, product, service, or brand.

The next task is to develop *comprehension*—to communicate enough information so some percentage of the aware group recognizes the product's purpose, image or position, and perhaps some of its features.

Next, advertising needs to communicate enough information to develop *conviction*—to persuade a certain number of people to believe in the product's value. Of those who become convinced, some can be moved to *desire* the product. Finally, some percentage of those who desire the product will take *action*—request additional information, send in a coupon, visit a store, or buy it.

The pyramid works in three dimensions: time, dollars, and people. Advertising results take time, especially if the product is expensive or not purchased regularly. Over time, as a company continues advertising, the number of people who become aware of the product increases. As more people comprehend the product, believe in it, and desire it, more take the final action of buying it.

Let's apply these principles to Saturn's advertising pyramid. In 1992, Saturn introduced an entry level 2 + 2 coupe, the SC1. Specific advertising objectives for this car might have read as follows:

1. Within two years, communicate the existence of the Saturn SC1 to half of the more than 500,000 people who annually buy foreign economy cars.
2. Inform two-thirds of this "aware" group that the Saturn is a technologically superior economy car with many design, safety, and performance features; that it is a brand new nameplate backed up with unmatched service, quality, and value; and that it is sold only through dedicated Saturn dealers.
3. Convince two-thirds of the "informed" group that the Saturn is a high-quality car, reliable, economical, and fun to drive.
4. Stimulate desire within two-thirds of the "convinced" group for a test drive.
5. Motivate two-thirds of the "desire" group to visit a retailer for a test drive.

These advertising objectives are specific as to time and degree and are quantified like marketing objectives. Theoretically, at the end of the first year, a consumer attitude study could determine how many people are aware of the Saturn SC1, how many people understand the car's primary features, and so on, measuring the program's effectiveness.

Saturn's advertising accomplishes the objectives of creating awareness, comprehension, conviction, desire, and action. But once the customer is in the store, it's the retailer's responsibility to close the sale with effective selling and service.

The old model versus the new

The advertising pyramid represents the *learn-feel-do* model of advertising effects. That is, it assumes that people rationally consider a prospective purchase, and once they feel good about it, they act. The theory is that advertising affects attitude, and attitude leads to behavior. That may be true for certain expensive products that require a lot of consideration. But other purchases may follow a different pattern. For example, impulse purchases at the checkout counter may involve a *do-feel-learn* model in which behavior leads to attitude. Other purchases may follow some other pattern. Thus, there are many marketing considerations when setting advertising objectives, and they must be thought out carefully. (For more ideas on this, see RL 7–2, Checklist for Developing Advertising Objectives in the Reference Library.)

The advertising pyramid also reflects the traditional mass marketing monolog. The advertiser talks, the customer listens.[30] That was appropriate before the advent of computers and databases; and it may still be appropriate in those categories where the marketer has no choice.

But today, as the IMC model shows, many marketers have databases of information on who their customers are, where they live, what they buy, and what they like and dislike. When marketers can have a dialog and establish a relationship, the model is no longer a pyramid but a circle (see Exhibit 7–8). Consumers and business customers can send messages back to the marketer in the form of coupons, phone calls, surveys, and database information on purchases. And with interactive media, the responses will be in real time. This feedback can help the marketer's product, service, and messages evolve.[31] And reinforcement advertising, designed to build brand loyalty, will remind people of their successful experience with the product and suggest reuse.

By starting with the customer and then integrating all aspects of their marketing communications—from package and store design to personal selling, advertising, public relations activities, special events, and sales promotions—companies hope to accelerate the communications process, make it more efficient, and achieve lasting loyalty from *good* prospects, not just prospects.[32]

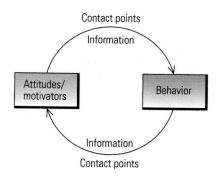

Exhibit • 7–8
Messages go to the customer through advertising and other communication channels. Messages come back via direct response, surveys, and a purchase behavior database. The marketer's message can evolve based on this feedback.

Advertising Strategy and the Creative Mix

The advertising (or communications) *objective* declares where the advertiser wants to be with respect to consumer awareness, attitude, and preference; the advertising (or creative) *strategy* describes how to get there.

Advertising strategy blends the elements of the **creative mix:** target audience, product concept, communications media, and advertising message.

The target audience: Everyone who should know

The **target audience,** the specific people the advertising will address, is typically larger than the target market. Advertisers need to know who the end user is, who makes the purchase, and who influences the purchasing decision. Children, for example, often exert a strong influence on where the family eats. So while McDonald's target market is adults, its target audience also includes children, and it spends much of its advertising budget on campaigns directed at kids.

The product concept: Presenting the product

The "bundle of values" the advertiser presents to the consumer is the **product concept.** Quaker Oats Life cereal and Plus Fiber are similarly priced brands aimed at the U.S. ready-to-eat breakfast cereal market. However, Life is presented as a cereal kids will like, Plus Fiber as a healthy cereal for adult needs.

When writing the advertising plan, the advertising manager must develop a simple statement to describe the product concept—that is, how the advertising will present the product. To create this statement, the advertiser first considers how the consumer perceives the product and then weighs this against the company's marketing strategy.

The Kim-Lord grid, shown in Exhibit 7–9, can help with this process. It depicts the degree and the kind of involvement the consumer brings to the purchase decision for different products.[33] Some purchases, like cars, require a high degree of personal involvement on both the *cognitive* (think) and *affective* (feel) levels. For others, like detergent, involvement is low on both axes. Sometimes a marketer uses an advertising strategy aimed at shifting the product within the grid to higher involvement on either axis. A product's location on the grid also indicates how the product is purchased (learn-feel-do; feel-learn-do) and how advertising copy should be written (more emotional or more rational).[34]

Exhibit • 7–9
The Kim-Lord grid.

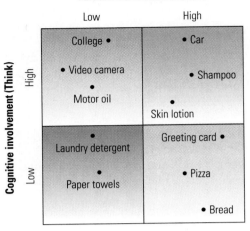

The communications media: The message delivery system

As an element of creative strategy, the **communications media** are all the vehicles that might transmit the advertiser's message. They include traditional media such as radio, TV, newspapers, magazines, and billboards and, in an integrated communications program, direct marketing, public relations, special events, and sales promotion.

Introducing a new product is a daunting task, particularly if the advertiser's budget is lower than competitors'—as was the case with Saturn. Hal Riney & Partners invited the media to build a relationship with Saturn and then limited advertising media purchases to those that responded. As a result, Saturn got choice back-cover positions with magazines, received economical placements on the Fox TV network, and—in a single deal with Patrick Media Group—became the largest brand advertiser on outdoor boards in California.[35]

• From the beginning, Saturn's advertising messages featured employees and customers to symbolize the company and its philosophy. Later, General Motors applied the Saturn Excel training program of cooperation, quality, and customer relationships throughout the company. GM, like Saturn, uses employees to send this advertising message to customers.

The advertising message: What the advertising communicates

What the company plans to say in its ads and how it plans to say it, verbally and non-verbally, make up the **advertising message.** As we discuss in Chapter 9, the combination of copy, art, and production elements forms the message, and there are infinite ways to combine these elements. (See Portfolio: Strategic Use of the Creative Mix.)

Riney broke new creative ground for Saturn. Rather than focusing on product features—standard fare in automotive advertising—Riney used Saturn employees and customers to symbolize the company and its philosophy.[36]

The Secret to Successful Planning

Whether the advertiser is a large corporation or small company, the key to successful planning is information. But the genius of business is in interpreting what the information means. This leads to direction, which makes planning easier and more rewarding.

In 1990, after eight years of unprecedented growth, the U.S. and Canada experienced the first throes of a recession. Interest rates were high, real estate sales dropped, construction of new homes slowed, defense spending was cut, and unemployment began to rise. To make matters worse, threats of war in the Mideast caused fear of higher fuel prices. Consumer confidence sank and with it sank retail sales.

As sales dropped, many executives cut back their advertising budgets, some to zero. Two years later, when the government announced the recession was over, these executives wondered why sales were still down and how their companies had lost so much market share.

Money is the motor that drives every marketing and advertising plan. If you suddenly shut the motor off, the car may coast for a while, but before long it will stop running. The marketing department has to convince management that advertising spending makes good business sense, even in an adverse economic climate.

ALLOCATING FUNDS FOR ADVERTISING

Advertising Is an Investment in Future Sales

Accountants and the Internal Revenue Service consider advertising a current business expense. Consequently, many executives treat advertising as a budget item to be trimmed or eliminated like other expense items when sales are either extremely high or extremely low. This is understandable but shortsighted.

The cost of a new plant or distribution warehouse is an investment in the company's future ability to produce and distribute products. Similarly, advertising—as one element of the communication mix—is an investment in future sales. While advertising is often used to stimulate immediate sales, its greatest power is in its cumulative, long-range, reinforcement effect.

Advertising builds consumer preference and promotes goodwill. This, in turn, enhances the reputation and value of the company name and brand. And it encourages customers to make repeat purchases.

So while advertising is a current expense for accounting purposes, it is also a long-term capital investment. For management to see advertising as an investment, however, it must understand how advertising relates to sales and profits.

The relationship of advertising to sales and profits

Many variables—both internal and external—influence the effectiveness of a company's marketing and advertising efforts. Methods to measure the relationships between advertising and sales, as well as sales and profits, are far from perfect. However, research does verify the following.

(continued on page 214)

Strategic Use of the Creative Mix

Where marketing strategy blends elements of the marketing mix (product, price, distribution, communications), **advertising strategy** blends the elements of the **creative mix:** the target audience, the product concept, the communications media, and the advertising message. The ads in this Portfolio show how some advertisers use the elements of the creative mix to promote their products.

The target audience: Everyone who should know

The target audience includes not only the target market (the end users or buyers) but others who might influence the purchase of products and services. This ad for Cremes Unlimited was placed in *Baking Buyer,* a trade magazine circulated to supermarket delis and bakeries, food service chains and restaurants, retail bakeries, specialty wholesalers, and distributors.

The product concept: Presenting the product

Marketers, in trying to deal with the never-ending array of new and established products on the market, must first catch targeted customers' attention and then convince them to try—or remain loyal to—their product. The Buick ad for its established Regal brand is an example of this type of product presentation.

Buick presents the 1995 Regal with a play on words about changes on the instrument panel, and reminds consumers that dual air bags and antilock brakes are standard safety equipment. The 800 number encourages customers to call for more information.

The communications media: The message delivery system

Advertising messages can be delivered to the target audience in a variety of ways, including TV commercials, packaging, and direct mail.

AUDIO: Jolly Norwegian folk music throughout the entire film.

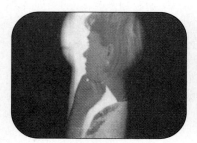

SUPER: Warning: We're flying your in-laws at half price.

Braathens SAFE, the Norwegian airline.

Braathens SAFE, the Norwegian Airline, produced this hilarious commercial about a man who thinks he'll surprise his wife, only to be surprised by her parents—who had flown in for a visit on the airline's half-price fare promotion.

Packaging often helps deliver the advertiser's message. The creative package for this Soapstone Carving Kit by Natural Wonders was designed to hold carving tools, soapstone pieces, and instructions for using Native American motifs in creating sculptures. The printing is two-color on a corrugated box, which presented many technical challenges for the design firm.

Right now, there is no other organization focused on you –the designer using computers. Some other design groups have computer sections. But, you need more than just basic information on electronic design. In today's constantly–changing climate, you need what only IDEA offers–help in using your computer as a design tool and a business partner. As an IDEA member, you'll receive a unique–and extensive–package of benefits. At a lower price, IDEA offers more than many other non-technical design groups. Our discounts alone can more than repay the cost of your membership the first time out.

A 1-of-a-kind Idea!

Direct mail is the fastest-growing advertising medium today. Marketers send direct-mail messages about myriad consumer and business products and services to their target audiences. This direct-mail piece from IDEA (International Design by Electronics Association) encourages professional designers to join the association. The large type embedded in the copy gives a short, attention-getting message that previews the benefits discussed in the small print.

The advertising message: What the advertising communicates

Print ads use both images and words to convey the advertiser's message, as shown in these two ads.

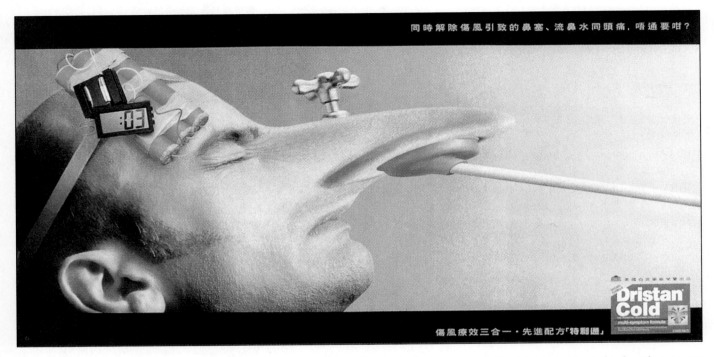

This Dristan ad from Hong Kong uses humor to portray one way to relieve the misery of cold symptoms. The brief copy asks: *Is this the only way to get rid of a stuffed-up and runny nose and the headaches a cold can bring?* The succinct tagline gives a better alternative: *Dristan. Three remedies in one.*

STRATEGIC ALTERATION *of* REALITY.

ADOBE PHOTOSHOP

Reality is fine, except when it's limited by budget, backgrounds, lighting or even the occasional blemish. These situations needn't stop the intrepid photographer, because now there's Adobe Photoshop.™ Welcome to photography without limits. Scan a simple portrait into Photoshop™ and what was once impossible becomes gloriously possible. Use its amazing features to alter reality, add tone and color to the skin, create dazzling effects and other subtleties too numerous to name. Enter the world of Photoshop on Macintosh®, Windows™, Silicon Graphics® or Sun™, and leave harsh reality at the door. For more information and your nearest Adobe™ Authorized Reseller, call 1-800-833-6687, Dept. E, Ext. 7125.

IF YOU CAN *dream* IT, YOU CAN *do* IT.™

In this ad, Adobe Photoshop offers photographers a way to manipulate their work digitally for a "strategic alteration of reality." The image attracts readers' attention and draws them into the advertiser's extensive message, which highlights Adobe Photoshop features, offers an 800 number for information and dealer locations, and ends with its encouraging trademarked tagline. *If you can dream it, you can do it.*

Ad Lab 7-B   How Economists View the Effect of Advertising on Sales

Normally, quantity sold depends on the number of dollars the company spends advertising the product. And within reasonable limits (if its advertising program is not too repugnant), the more dollars spent on advertising, the more a company will sell—up to a point. Yet, even the most enthusiastic ad agency admits, reluctantly, that it is possible to spend too much.

Management needs to know how much more it will be able to sell per additional dollar of advertising and when additional advertising dollars cease being effective. It doesn't need a fixed number representing potential demand, but a graph or a statistical equation describing the relationship between sales and advertising.

In our illustration, most of the curve goes uphill as we move to the right (it has a positive slope). This means that additional advertising will continue to bring in business until (at a budget of x million dollars) people become so saturated by the message that it begins to repel them and turn them away from the product.

Even if the saturation level cannot be reached within the range of outlays the firm can afford, the curve is likely to level off, becoming flatter and flatter as the amount spent on advertising

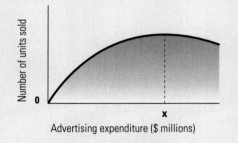

Advertising expenditure ($ millions)

gets larger and larger and saturation is approached. The point at which the curve begins to flatten is the point at which returns from advertising begin to diminish. When the total advertising budget is small, even a $1 addition to the campaign may bring in as much as $10 in new sales. But when the market approaches saturation, each additional dollar may contribute only 30 cents in new sales.

Laboratory Applications

1. When would an advertising expenditure curve have a negative slope?

2. Economists suggest that the quantity sold depends on the number of dollars the company spends on advertising. Is that a safe assumption? Discuss.

In consumer goods marketing, increases in market share are more closely related to increases in the marketing budget than to price reductions, and market share is a prime indicator of profitability.[37]

- Sales normally increase with additional advertising. At some point, however, the rate of return declines. (See Ad Lab 7–B, "How Economists View the Effect of Advertising on Sales.")

- Sales response to advertising may build over time, but the durability of advertising is brief, so a consistent investment is important.[38]

- There are minimum levels below which advertising expenditures have no effect on sales.

- There will be some sales even if there is no advertising.

- There are saturation limits imposed by culture and competition above which no amount of advertising can increase sales.

To management, these facts might mean: Spend more until it stops working. In reality, the issue isn't that simple. Advertising isn't the only marketing activity that affects sales. A change in market share may occur because of quality perceptions, word-of-mouth, the introduction of new products, the opening of more attractive outlets, better personal selling, or seasonal changes in the business cycle.

Furthermore, most companies don't have a clear-cut way to determine the relationship between sales and profit. What if the company sells a variety of products? Which advertising contributes to which sales?

One thing remains clear. Since the response to advertising is spread out over an extended time, advertising should be viewed as a long-term investment in future profits. Like all expenditures, advertising should be evaluated for wastefulness. But historically, companies that make advertising the scapegoat during tough times end up losing substantial market share before the economy starts growing again.[39]

The corollary is also true. Sustained ad spending during difficult times protects, and in some cases even increases, market share and builds brands. During the last global recession, the leading European marketers recognized this fact, and less than 40 percent of the top spenders in Italy, Austria, Germany, France, and Spain cut their budgets.[40]

• One environment an advertiser must deal with is customer attitude toward a product category in general and the advertiser's brand in particular. Health-conscious customers today look for fat-reduced food products without preservatives or artificial ingredients. Tyson reassures consumers its chicken meets these standards and that Tyson is "feeding you like family."

The variable environments of business

Before attempting to determine advertising allocations, the advertising manager must consider the company's economic, political, social, and legal situation. These factors affect total industry sales and corporate profits on sales.

The manager must consider the institutional and competitive environments. What is the level of sales within the industry? How much are competitors spending? And what are they doing that might either help or hinder the company's marketing efforts?

Finally, the manager must consider the internal environment. Do the company's current policies and procedures allow it to fulfill the promises its advertising intends to make?

Methods of Allocating Funds

Most business executives will spend more money on advertising as long as they are assured it will mean more profit. However, the point of equilibrium is hard to predict when advertising budgets are being developed.

Companies use a number of methods to determine how much to spend on advertising, including the *percentage-of-sales, percentage-of-profit, unit-of-sale, competitive-parity, share-of-market,* and *task methods.* (See the Checklist of Ways to Set Advertising Budgets.)

No technique is adequate for all situations. The three methods discussed here are used primarily for national advertising budgets. Retailers use other techniques that we discuss in Chapter 17.

Percentage-of-sales method

The **percentage-of-sales method** is one of the most popular techniques for setting advertising budgets. It may be based on a percentage of last year's sales, anticipated sales for next year, or a combination of the two. Businesspeople like this method be-

Checklist   Ways to Set Advertising Budgets

☐ **Percentage of sales.** Advertising budget determined by allocating a percentage of last year's sales, anticipated sales for next year, or a combination of the two. The percentage is usually based on an industry average, company experience, or an arbitrary figure.

☐ **Percentage of profit.** Percentage is applied to profit, either past years' or anticipated.

☐ **Unit of sale.** Also called the *case-rate method.* A specific dollar amount is set for each box, case, barrel, or carton produced. Used primarily in assessing members of horizontal cooperatives or trade associations.

☐ **Competitive parity.** Also called *self-defense method.* Allocates dollars according to the amounts spent by major competitors.

☐ **Share of market/share of voice.** Allocates dollars by maintaining a percentage share of total industry advertising comparable to or somewhat ahead of desired share of market. Often used for new-product introductions.

☐ **Objective/task.** Also referred to as the *budget buildup method,* this method has three steps: defining objectives, determining strategy, and estimating the cost to execute that strategy.

☐ **Empirical research.** By running experimental tests in different markets with different budgets, companies determine which is the most efficient level.

☐ **Quantitative mathematical models.** Computer-based programs developed by major advertisers and agencies that rely on input of sophisticated data, history, and assumptions.

☐ **All available funds.** Go-for-broke technique generally used by small firms with limited capital trying to introduce new products or services.

cause it is the simplest, it doesn't cost them anything, it is related to revenue, and it is considered safe. The problem is knowing what percentage to use. As Exhibit 7–10 shows, even leaders in the same industry use different percentages.

Usually, the percentage is based on an industry average or on company experience. Unfortunately, it is too often determined arbitrarily. An industry average assumes that every company in the industry has similar objectives and faces the same marketing problems. Company experience assumes that the market is highly static, which is rarely the case.

However, when applied against future sales, this method often works well. It assumes that a certain number of dollars will be needed to sell a certain number of units. If the advertiser knows what the percentage is, the correlation between advertising and sales should remain constant, assuming the market is stable and competitors' advertising remains unchanged. And since this method is common in the industry, it diminishes the likelihood of competitive warfare.

Exhibit • 7–10
Advertising expenditures by the top 15 leading advertisers in 1993 ($ millions, rounded).

Rank	Company	U.S. advertising expenditures	U.S. sales	Advertising as percentage of U.S. sales
1	Procter & Gamble	$2,398	$ 15,579	7.3
2	Philip Morris	1,844	38,387	5.1
3	General Motors	1,539	109,668	1.8
4	Sears Roebuck	1,311	50,838	4.7
5	PepsiCo	1,039	18,309	6.3
6	Ford Motor	958	75,661	2.3
7	AT&T	812	61,580	*
8	Nestlé	794	*	5.0
9	Johnson & Johnson	763	7,203	12.6
10	Chrysler	762	37,847	*
11	Warner-Lambert	751	2,747	5.7
12	Unilever	738	8,550	3.4
13	McDonald's	737	3,931	14.6
14	Time Warner	695	4,414	*
15	Toyota Motor	690	*	1.3

*Figures not provided.

The greatest shortcoming of the percentage-of-sales method is that it violates a basic marketing principle. Marketing activities are supposed to *stimulate* demand and thus sales; marketing activities aren't supposed to occur as a *result* of sales. And if advertising automatically increases when sales increase and declines when sales decline, it ignores all other factors that might encourage an opposite move. It may also become a self-fulfilling prophecy.

Share-of-market/share-of-voice method

In markets with similar products, a high correlation usually exists between a company's share of the market and its share of industry advertising.

The **share-of-market/share-of-voice method** is a bold attempt to link advertising dollars with sales objectives.[41] It holds that a company's best chance of maintaining its share of market is to keep a share of advertising (voice) somewhat ahead of its market share. For example, a company with a 30 percent share of the market should spend 35 percent of the industry's advertising dollars.

The share-of-market/share-of-voice method is commonly used for new products.[42] According to this formula, when a new brand is introduced, the advertising budget for the first two years should be about one and a half times the brand's targeted share of the market in two years. This means that if the company's two-year sales goal is 10 percent of the market, it should spend about 15 percent of total industry advertising during the first two years.

One hazard of this method is the tendency to become complacent. Simply maintaining a higher percentage of media exposure usually isn't enough to accomplish the desired results. The top national packaged goods marketers still spend 25 percent of their marketing budgets on consumer and trade promotion rather than consumer advertising.[43] Companies must be aware of all their competitors' marketing activities, not just advertising.

Objective/task method

The **objective/task method,** also known as the **budget buildup method,** is used by the majority of U.S. major national advertisers. It considers advertising a marketing tool to generate sales.

• National packaged-goods marketers spend most of their marketing budgets on consumer and trade sales promotion rather than on advertising. In this example, Mattel introduces Revealers, a new line of Hot Wheels, with on-pack coupons for a free Kid's Cone at Dairy Queen. Mattel supported the promotion with a national TV campaign aimed at kids, and Dairy Queen featured in-store posters telling them to "redeem your Revealers coupons here."

The task method has three steps: defining objectives, determining strategy, and estimating cost. After setting specific, quantitative marketing objectives, the advertiser develops programs to attain them. If the objective is to increase the number of coffee cases sold by 10 percent, the advertiser determines which advertising approach will work best, how often ads must run, and which media to use. The estimated cost of the program becomes the basis for the advertising budget. Of course, the company's financial position is always a consideration. If the cost is too high, objectives may have to be scaled back. After the campaign runs, if results are better or worse than anticipated, the next budget may need revision.

The task method forces companies to think in terms of accomplishing goals. Its effectiveness is most apparent when the results of particular ads or campaigns can be readily measured. The task method is adaptable to changing market conditions and can be easily revised.

However, it is often difficult to determine in advance the amount of money needed to reach a specific goal. And techniques for measuring advertising effectiveness still have many weaknesses.

Additional methods

Advertisers also use several other methods. In the **empirical research method,** a company runs a series of tests in different markets with different budgets to determine the best level of advertising expenditure.

Computers can generate quantitative mathematical models for budgeting and allocating advertising dollars. Foote, Cone & Belding developed a response-curve database from tracking studies on more than 40 clients' products and services. The program analyzes media programs and estimates customer response.[44] Many other sophisticated techniques facilitate marketing and advertising planning, budget allocation, new-product introductions, and media analysis.[45] However, most are not easily understood by line executives, and each relies on data that may be unavailable or estimated.[46] While widely employed by major national advertisers, they require very sophisticated users and, for the most part, are still too expensive for the average business.

The Bottom Line

Unfortunately, all these methods rely on one of two fallacies. The first is that advertising is a *result* of sales. Advertisers know this is not true, yet they continue to use the percentage-of-sales method.

The second fallacy is that advertising *creates* sales. In certain circumstances (where direct-action advertising is used), advertising closes the sale. But advertising's real role is to locate prospects, build brand equity, and stimulate demand. It may even stimulate inquiries.

The job of advertising is to influence perception by informing, persuading, and reminding. Advertising *affects* sales, but it is just one of many influences on consumer perception. And advertising managers must keep this in mind when preparing their plans and budgets.

Summary

The marketing plan may be the most important document a company possesses. It assembles all the pertinent and current facts about a company, the markets it serves, its products, and its competition. It sets specific goals and objectives to be attained and describes the precise strategies that will be used to achieve them. It musters the company's forces for the marketing battlefield and, in so doing, dictates the role of advertising in the marketing mix and provides focus for advertising creativity.

There are three types of marketing planning models: top-down, bottom-up, and integrated marketing communications planning.

The top-down marketing plan contains four principal sections: situation analysis, marketing objectives, marketing strategy, and action programs. A company's marketing objectives should be logical deductions from an analysis of its current situation, its prediction of future trends, and its understanding of corporate objectives. They should relate to the needs of specific target markets and specify sales objectives. Sales-target objectives should be specific, quantitative, and realistic.

The first step in developing a marketing strategy is to select the target market. The second step is to determine a cost-effective marketing mix for each target market the company pursues. The marketing mix is determined by how the company blends the elements it controls—product, price, distribution, and communications. Advertising is a communications tool.

One way for small companies to accomplish the marketing and advertising planning task is to work from the bottom up, taking an ingenious tactic and building a strategy around it.

Integrated marketing communications planning is driven by technology. Thanks to computers and databases, marketers can learn more about their customers' wants and needs, likes and dislikes. IMC offers the synergy of various communications media strategically managed to positively affect the relationship between the customer and the brand or company. Starting with the customer, the IMC planning model utilizes seven steps to segment the customer database by product-purchase-related attributes; determine the best place, situation, and time to reach the prospect; develop behavior-related marketing and communications objectives and strategies; and develop specific communications tactics to implement the plan. In the IMC model all marketing becomes communications and all communications become marketing.

Advertising is a natural outgrowth of the marketing plan, and the advertising plan is prepared in much the same way as the top-down marketing plan. It includes a section on analysis, advertising objectives, and strategy.

In some cases, advertising objectives may be expressed in terms of moving prospective customers up through the advertising pyramid (awareness, comprehension, conviction, desire, action). Or they may be expressed in terms of generating inquiries, coupon response, or attitude change.

The advertising (or creative) strategy is determined by the advertiser's use of the creative mix. The creative mix is composed of the target audience, product concept, communications media, and advertising message. The target audience includes the specific groups of people the advertising will address. The product concept refers to the bundle of product-related values the advertiser presents to the customer. The communications media are the vehicles used to transmit the advertiser's message. The advertising message is what the company plans to say and how it plans to say it.

Several methods are used to allocate advertising funds. The most popular methods are the percentage-of-sales approach and the objective/task method. The share-of-market/share-of-voice method is also used.

Questions for Review and Discussion

1. What is a marketing plan and why is it a company's most important document?
2. What examples illustrate the difference between need-satisfying objectives and sales-target objectives?
3. What are the three types of marketing plans? How do they differ?
4. What basic elements should be included in a top-down marketing plan?
5. How does one person's strategy become another person's objective? Give examples.
6. How can small companies use bottom-up marketing to become big companies?
7. What are the elements of an advertising plan and an advertising strategy?
8. What is the best method of allocating advertising funds for a real estate development? Why?
9. What types of companies tend to use the percentage-of-sales method? Why?
10. How could a packaged-foods manufacturer use the share-of-market/share-of-voice method to determine its advertising budget?

8

Planning Media Strategy
Finding Links to the Market

Objective: To show how communication media help advertisers achieve marketing and advertising objectives. To get their messages to the right people in the right place at the right time, media planners follow the same procedures as marketing and advertising planners: setting objectives, formulating strategies, and devising tactics. To make sound decisions, media planners must possess marketing savvy, analytical skill, and creativity.

After studying this chapter, you will be able to:

- Describe how a media plan helps accomplish marketing and advertising objectives.

- Explain the importance of creativity in media planning.

- Define reach and frequency and debate the controversy surrounding effective frequency.

- Discuss how reach, frequency, and continuity are related.

- Calculate gross rating points and cost per thousand.

- Name some of the secondary research sources available to planners and describe how they are used.

- Describe different types of advertising schedules and the purpose for each.

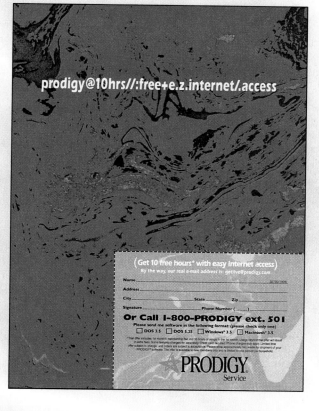

s a 21-year old senior at the University of North Carolina, Chapel Hill, Kelly Clark was majoring in economics and journalism. He had no background in advertising. In fact, he aspired to be a reporter for *The Wall Street Journal*. But when they met him at J. Walter Thompson (JWT) in New York, they wanted him. He was articulate, bright, and obviously capable. With his business and writing background, advertising looked like a natural fit.

It was. They got him, and it's been raining promotions ever since. Within six months he went from assistant media planner to media planner. A year later he became media supervisor on several of the agency's major accounts: Prodigy, Benetton, and (ironically) *The Wall Street Journal*. Vice president a year after that and then JWT's group media director on Kellogg and Citibank—all by the age of 27. That's when *Mediaweek* magazine named him one of 1993's Media All-Stars.

Said Emily Swartzentruber, senior VP/New York media director, "Kelly's never stopped excelling. He's on the fastest track we've ever experienced."

His can-do, low-key style nabbed Clark's Prodigy media team the agency's annual North American White Pea award, which celebrates practical innovations in the use of media to solve client problems. (An innovative media plan stands out like a white pea in a pod of green ones.)

Clark immersed himself in Prodigy to better understand the people using the online service. Then he walked into the Prodigy meeting and introduced the idea of target marketing so well the clients ended up understanding their own customers better.

The beauty of the Prodigy plan was that, with a very limited budget, it created a major marketing event. Working with Time-Warner magazines, JWT developed preprinted inserts with personalized ink-jet messages to subscribers, along with the promise of free software and videotape gifts if they went to their nearest Prodigy dealer for a demonstration of the software. Once they got people to the demonstration, the system was so user friendly customers would be able to navigate it themselves. And that would pique interest and build desire.

The basic media plan was augmented by direct mail, cable TV, and space ads in the magazines to guide people to the ink-jet inserts. Point-of-purchase displays at the newsstands created more interest in the Prodigy push.

It worked—to the tune of over 50,000 individual customer presentations. Plus, it created such enthusiasm and support from the trade that Prodigy's retailer base expanded from 3,000 to over 9,000!

In short, by carefully studying the customer and skillfully using modern technology, Clark and his team were able to match Prodigy's leading-edge image with a leading-edge media plan, despite the limited budget.[1]

That's creativity. •

MEDIA PLANNING: AN OVERVIEW

In an overcommunicated society, advertising media planners need to exercise as much creativity as senior art directors and copywriters. Solid media decisions are a critical element of the overall marketing communications plan.

The purpose of **media planning** is to conceive, analyze, and select channels of communication that will direct advertising messages to the right people in the right place at the right time. It involves many decisions:

- Where should we advertise? (In what countries, states, or parts of town?)
- Which media vehicles should we use?
- When during the year should we concentrate our advertising?
- How often should we run the advertising?
- What opportunities are there for integrating other communications?

The Challenge

People who plan and buy media have historically had low profiles compared to the "stars" in the creative and account service departments. But their assignment is just as critical: One media planner can be responsible for millions of client dollars. The planner's work attests to an agency's strategic ability to negotiate the best price and effectively use the incredible array of media choices available today. Jack Klues, the senior VP/director of U.S. media services for Leo Burnett USA, says, "Our mission is to buy and plan media so effectively that our clients obtain an unfair advantage versus their competitors."[2]

In the 90s, the media department has gained prominence as agencies compete for media buying assignments as well as the creative business.[3] It's big news when an agency such as Young & Rubicam loses the $200 million Johnson & Johnson network television media account to McCann-Erickson, or when Chrysler taps BBDO to handle its $400 million media planning and buying account, which was previously handled by three agencies.[4]

As the complexity of the field increases, media decisions become more critical and clients more demanding. Advertisers want agencies to be more than efficient. They want creative buys.[5]

What makes media planning today so much more complicated than it was just a few years ago?

Increasing media options

Today, there are more media to choose from, and each offers more choices. It used to be that major advertisers could ensure a big audience by simply advertising on network television. Not anymore. Today it's very difficult to reach a big audience. As Stacey Lippman, director of corporate media at TBWA Chiat/Day, says, "There's too much to keep track of and too many things to explore."[6]

TV is now fragmented into network, syndicated, and local television, as well as network and local cable. Specialized magazines now aim at every possible population segment. Even national magazines publish editions for particular regions or demographic groups. Exhibit 8–1 shows local and national advertising expenditures for traditional media in the U.S.

Nontraditional media—from videotape and movie advertising to computer online services, electronic kiosks, and even shopping carts—also expand the menu of choices. Ad Lab 8–A describes some nontraditional media.

Increasing fragmentation of the audience

Audience fragmentation also complicates the media planner's job. Readers and viewers have scattered to many media, selectively reading only parts of magazines or newspapers, watching only segments of programs, and listening to many different radio sta-

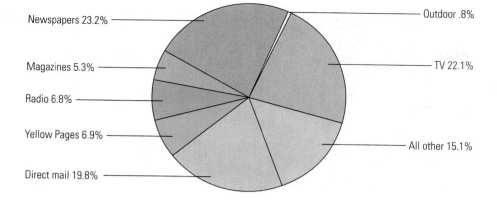

Exhibit • 8–1
U.S. ad spending by medium.

Newspapers 23.2%

Magazines 5.3%

Radio 6.8%

Yellow Pages 6.9%

Direct mail 19.8%

Outdoor .8%

TV 22.1%

All other 15.1%

Off-the-Wall Media That Pull Customers Off the Fence   *Ad Lab 8-A*

Advertising can be found everywhere these days, even places where we least expect it.

Videotapes

Advertisers either sponsor videos, such as Mr. Boston's *Official Bartender's Guide* and Red Lobster Inns' *Eat to Win,* or place ads on videos of popular films.

Aerial Banners and Lights

Banners carrying ad messages can be pulled by low-flying planes. After dark, traveling aerial lights can display messages of up to 90 characters. Slow-flying helicopters can carry 40'-by-80' signs lit by thousands of bulbs.

Blimps

In addition to Goodyear, blimps now carry ads for Citibank, Coca-Cola, and Fuji Film, among others. Computer-run lighting systems allow the blimps to advertise at night.

In-Flight Ads

Many airlines' in-flight audio and video entertainment runs ads. The travel industry and advertisers that want to reach business fliers are the primary users.

Parking Meters

In Calgary, Alberta, or Baltimore, Maryland, parking meters carry signs on top advertising national products and local businesses. Newer versions are solar-powered meters with liquid crystal displays for ad messages.

Electronic Billboards

Most modern sports stadiums and arenas sell ad space on giant electronic displays.

Inflatables

Giant inflatable beer cans, mascots, cereal boxes, and other items are used for advertising purposes.

Taxicab Advertising

In addition to the familiar ads on the roofs and backs of taxis, some companies sell ad space inside, facing the riders. In one sophisticated system, an electronic message scrolls across a screen in the rider's view.

Painted Vehicles

Buses, trucks, and cars are completely decorated with patterns, bigger-than-life illustrations, and messages to attract attention.

Trash Receptacles

Uniquely designed and decorated trash bins, boxes, and baskets bear the advertiser's logo and message. Some major cities offer ad space on concrete litter receptacles at major commercial intersections.

Kiosks

Stand-alone kiosks can be painted with eye-catching designs and messages. Unique constructions can be attached to the top and sides to draw attention. Electronic displays running presentation software can show colorful fast-action video clips, slide images, and interactive text. These systems can also play synchronized sounds and music.

Laboratory Applications

1. How effective are off-the-wall media?
2. What other off-the-wall media can you think of?

The *San Diego Union Tribune* uses painted trucks to deliver newspapers and its advertising message.

Exhibit • 8–2

Hours per person per year using media.

	TV	Radio	Recorded music	Daily newspapers	Consumer magazines	Consumer books	Home videos*	Home video games
1988	1,490	1,165	215	178	110	90	35	4
1989	1,485	1,155	220	175	90	96	39	6
1990	1,470	1,135	235	175	90	95	42	12
1991	1,513	1,115	219	169	88	98	43	18
1992	1,550	1,150	233	172	85	100	46	19
1993	1,529	1,082	248	170	85	99	49	19
1994	1,539	1,061	261	168	84	99	51	21
1995	1,525	1,047	274	166	84	100	54	23
1996	1,552	1,054	287	164	84	101	55	24
1997	1,540	1,040	295	163	83	103	56	25
1998	1,544	1,034	305	162	83	105	57	26
Compound annual growth in %								
1988–93	0.5	–1.5	2.9	–0.9	–5.0	1.9	7.0	36.6
1993–98	0.2	–0.9	4.2	–1.0	–0.5	1.2	3.1	6.5

*Playback of prerecorded tapes only.

Note: Data from 1995–98 are projected.

tions. This makes it very difficult to find the prospect in the marketplace, even though consumers are spending more time with media than ever before—an average of over 3,300 hours in 1994![7] (See Exhibit 8–2.)

Increasing costs

Costs are increasing for almost all media. In the last decade, the cost of exposing 1,000 people to each of the major media (called **cost per thousand**) rose faster than inflation. Rising costs make media planning more challenging than ever, especially for advertisers with small budgets. Clients want proof that planners are squeezing the most out of every media dollar.[8]

Increasing complexity in media buying

Buying and selling media is not the straightforward process it once was. In the battle for additional sales, many print and broadcast media companies developed "value-added" programs to provide extra benefits.[9] Besides selling space or time at rate-card prices or below, these companies now offer reprints, merchandising services, special sections, even sponsorships and mailing lists (see Exhibit 8–3). To get a bigger share of the advertiser's budget, larger media companies are bundling the various stations, publications, or properties they own and offering them in integrated combos as further incentives. International Data Group (IDG), for example, which publishes *PC World* and *Computer World* magazines, offers a marketing access program (MAP) that gives major business-to-business advertisers access to IDG's research subsidiary, its world exposition unit (for trade shows), and its book company.[10]

Television networks work with professional sports associations to develop integrated marketing "partnerships" for sports and event sponsors.[11] And CBS developed a strategic affiliation with Kmart to cross-promote one another. The result was a win–win case history: CBS's new shows got a whopping 28 percent ratings increase over the previous year, and Kmart got a dramatically larger audience for its ads than it had paid for.[12]

Value-added packages often employ communications vehicles outside traditional media planning, such as public relations, sales promotion, and direct marketing. With BMW, for instance, *Yachting* magazine sponsors sailing weeks in various markets and

According to advertisers	According to agencies
1. Targeted promotional mailings	1. Research surveys
2. Research surveys	2. Free list rental
3. Advertorials	3. Targeted promotional mailings
4. Free list rental	4. Special editorial sections
5. Focus groups	5. Postcard mailings
6. Special editorial sections	6. Advertorials
7. Postcard mailings	7. Exclusive event sponsorship
8. Telemarketing services	8. Convention, seminar, or trade show tie-ins

Exhibit • 8–3
The most attractive value-added options.

displays the advertiser's cars on site. So people who can afford expensive sailboats are also exposed to the cars, to BMW signage at the event, and to any premium giveaways the sponsors might offer.[13] Integrated events like these help advertisers build relationships with their customers and prospects. And that's a major goal today. But placing a value on these deals is difficult because the nonmedia elements are hard to quantify.

This trend toward integrating marketing communications and *relationship marketing* is creating a new breed of media planner—younger, computer literate, and schooled in marketing disciplines beyond traditional media. George Hayes, McCann-Erickson's senior VP/media director, points out that the good media specialist today is actually "a real advertising generalist."[14] And with many of the biggest client billing changes happening in *media-only* agency reviews, it's apparent that the media professionals have finally come into their own.[15]

Increasing competition

Independent media buying services have grown dramatically in the last decade, attracting some of the best and brightest talent in the business to compete with agencies for what was once a private domain (see Exhibit 8–4). The independents buy advertising space and time at lower bulk rates and then sell it, at a higher rate or for a handling commission, to advertisers or ad agencies that don't have a fully staffed media department. Recent surveys indicate that independents now handle over a quarter of all national advertising media accounts.[16]

In this chapter, we examine how media planners develop a basic plan, devise strategies to carry out the plan, and schedule media buys. But first we need to see how media planning fits into the overall marketing plan.

Exhibit • 8–4
Top accounts that independent media-buying services won from ad agencies in 1992–1993 ($ millions).

Advertiser	Buying service	Previous ad agency	Estimated billings
1992			
American Isuzu Motors	SFM Media	Della Femina, McNamee	$75
MasterCard International	DeWitt Media	Lintas New York	$55
G. Heileman Brewing Co.	SFM Media	Della Femina, McNamee	$30
Chi-Chi's	International Communications Group	Cohen/Johnson	$20
1993			
BMW of North America	DeWitt Media	Ammirati & Puris	$80
Home Depot	Western International	Admarketing	$45
Northwest Airlines	Media First International	JWT	$25
National Presto Industries	SFM Media	Bozell	$15.5

THE ROLE OF MEDIA IN THE MARKETING FRAMEWORK

Before media planning begins—indeed, before advertising is even considered—companies must establish an overall marketing plan for their products.

Marketing Objectives and Strategy

As we saw in Chapter 7, the top-down marketing plan defines the market need and the company's sales objectives and details strategies for attaining those objectives. As Exhibit 8–5 shows, objectives and strategies result from a marketing situation analysis, which uncovers both strengths and weaknesses, threats and opportunities. Marketing objectives may focus on solving a problem ("regaining sales volume lost to major competitive introductions over the past year") or seizing an opportunity ("increasing share in the male buyer segment of the frozen food market").

Marketing strategies lay out the steps for meeting these objectives by blending the four elements of the marketing mix. A company whose marketing objective is to increase sales of a particular brand in a certain part of the country has many options. For example, it can adapt the product to suit regional tastes (product); it can lower the price to compete with local brands (price); it can devise deals to gain additional shelf space in retail outlets (distribution); and it can reposition the product through intensive trade and consumer advertising (communication). Thus, advertising is just one of the many strategic tools a company may use to achieve its marketing objectives.

Advertising Objectives and Strategy

The objectives and strategies of an advertising plan unfold from the marketing plan. But advertising objectives focus on communication goals, such as:

- Increasing brand preference by 8 percent in the South during the next year.
- Increasing intent of men ages 18 to 24 to purchase the brand by 10 percent within the next year.

To achieve these objectives, companies devise advertising strategies that employ the elements of the **creative mix:** the product concept, target audience, advertising message, and communications media.

The media department makes sure the advertising message (developed by the creative department) gets to the correct target audience (established by the marketing managers and account executives) effectively (as measured by the research department). Media planners go through the same process of setting objectives, devising strategies, and defining tactics.

DEFINING MEDIA OBJECTIVES

Media objectives translate the advertising strategy into goals that media can accomplish. Exhibit 8–6 shows general media objectives for a new food product. They explain who the target audience is and why, where messages will be delivered and when, and how much advertising weight needs to be delivered.

Media objectives have two major components: *audience objectives* and *message-distribution objectives*.

Audience Objectives

Audience objectives define the specific types of people the advertiser wants to reach. Top-down planners typically use geodemographic classifications to define their target audiences. In Exhibit 8–6, for example, the target audience is food purchasers for large families who live in urban areas across the country.

The target audience may consist of people in a specific income, educational, occupational, or social group—any of the segments we discussed in Chapter 5. And the target audience is not necessarily the product's actual consumers.

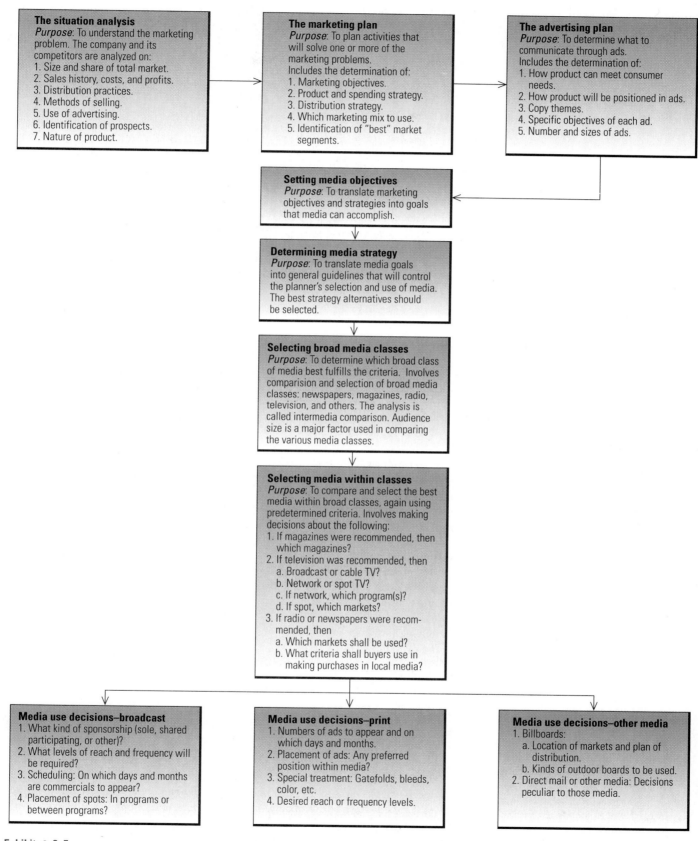

The situation analysis
Purpose: To understand the marketing problem. The company and its competitors are analyzed on:
1. Size and share of total market.
2. Sales history, costs, and profits.
3. Distribution practices.
4. Methods of selling.
5. Use of advertising.
6. Identification of prospects.
7. Nature of product.

The marketing plan
Purpose: To plan activities that will solve one or more of the marketing problems.
Includes the determination of:
1. Marketing objectives.
2. Product and spending strategy.
3. Distribution strategy.
4. Which marketing mix to use.
5. Identification of "best" market segments.

The advertising plan
Purpose: To determine what to communicate through ads.
Includes the determination of:
1. How product can meet consumer needs.
2. How product will be positioned in ads.
3. Copy themes.
4. Specific objectives of each ad.
5. Number and sizes of ads.

Setting media objectives
Purpose: To translate marketing objectives and strategies into goals that media can accomplish.

Determining media strategy
Purpose: To translate media goals into general guidelines that will control the planner's selection and use of media. The best strategy alternatives should be selected.

Selecting broad media classes
Purpose: To determine which broad class of media best fulfills the criteria. Involves comparision and selection of broad media classes: newspapers, magazines, radio, television, and others. The analysis is called intermedia comparison. Audience size is a major factor used in comparing the various media classes.

Selecting media within classes
Purpose: To compare and select the best media within broad classes, again using predetermined criteria. Involves making decisions about the following:
1. If magazines were recommended, then which magazines?
2. If television was recommended, then
   a. Broadcast or cable TV?
   b. Network or spot TV?
   c. If network, which program(s)?
   d. If spot, which markets?
3. If radio or newspapers were recommended, then
   a. Which markets shall be used?
   b. What criteria shall buyers use in making purchases in local media?

Media use decisions–broadcast
1. What kind of sponsorship (sole, shared participating, or other)?
2. What levels of reach and frequency will be required?
3. Scheduling: On which days and months are commercials to appear?
4. Placement of spots: In programs or between programs?

Media use decisions–print
1. Numbers of ads to appear and on which days and months.
2. Placement of ads: Any preferred position within media?
3. Special treatment: Gatefolds, bleeds, color, etc.
4. Desired reach or frequency levels.

Media use decisions–other media
1. Billboards:
   a. Location of markets and plan of distribution.
   b. Kinds of outdoor boards to be used.
2. Direct mail or other media: Decisions peculiar to those media.

Exhibit • 8–5
This diagram outlines the scope of media planning activities.

Exhibit • 8–6
How media objectives are expressed.

ACME Advertising
Client: Econo Foods
Product/Brand: Chirpee's Cheap Chips
Project: Media plan, first year introduction

Media Objectives

1. To target large families with emphasis on the family's food purchaser.
2. To concentrate the greatest weight of advertising in urban areas where prepared foods traditionally have greater sales and where new ideas normally gain quicker acceptance.
3. To provide extra weight during the announcement period and then continuity throughout the year with a fairly consistent level of advertising impressions.
4. To deliver advertising impressions to every region in relation to regional food store sales.
5. To use media that will reinforce the copy strategy's emphasis on convenience, ease of preparation, taste, and economy.
6. To attain the highest advertising frequency possible once the need for broad coverage and the demands of the copy platform have been met.

Many advertisers, for example, have to defend their media decisions with the retailers who stock and resell their products. Why? If these people construed a change in media strategy as a loss of advertising support, they might reduce the shelf space for the advertiser's products.

The consumer target audience is often determined from the marketer's research. Planners also rely on secondary research such as Simmons Market Research Bureau (SMRB) or Mediamark Research, Inc. (MRI) (see Exhibit 8–7). These syndicated reports give demographic profiles of heavy and light users of various products and enable planners to define the target audience. The reports also specify which TV programs or magazines heavy and light users watch and read, which helps planners select media with large audiences of heavy users. Planners select **media vehicles**—particular magazines or broadcast programs—according to how well they "deliver" or expose the message to the desired target audience.

Advertisers using the integrated marketing communications (IMC) planning model start by segmenting their target audiences according to brand-purchasing behavior (for example, loyal users, brand switchers, new prospects), and then ranking them by profit to the brand.[17] Communications objectives are then stated in terms of reinforcing or modifying customer purchasing behavior or creating a perceptual change about the brand over time.[18]

Message-Distribution Objectives

Distribution objectives define where, when, and how often advertising should appear. To answer these questions, a media planner must understand *reach, frequency, message weight,* and *continuity.*

Reach ✓

The term **reach** refers to the total number of *different* people or households exposed at least once to an ad or campaign during a given period of time, usually four weeks. For example, if 40 percent of 100,000 people in a target market hear a commercial on radio station WKKO at least once during a four-week period, the reach is 40,000 people. Reach may be expressed as a percentage of the total market (40 percent) or as a raw number (40,000).

Exhibit • 8–7
A media planner's toolbox.

Secondary sources of information help media planners do their jobs. Some examples:

- Simmons Market Research Bureau (SMRB) and Mediamark Research, Inc. (MRI): report data on product, brand, and media usage by both demographic and lifestyle characteristics.
- Broadcast Advertisers Reports (BAR), Leading National Advertisers (LNA), and Media Records: report advertisers' expenditures by brand, media type, market, and time period.
- Standard Rate & Data Service (SRDS): provides information on media rates, format, production requirements, and audience.
- Audit Bureau of Circulations (ABC): verifies circulation figures of publishers.

Introducing a little gourmet for your store.

This number, however, doesn't take into account the *quality* of the exposure. Some people exposed to the message still won't be aware of it. So reach isn't the best measure of media success. The term **effective reach** describes the quality of exposure. It measures the number or percentage of the audience who receive enough exposures for the message to have the desired effect.[19]

Frequency ✓

Frequency refers to the number of times the same person or household is exposed to a message—a radio spot, for example—in a specified time span. It measures the *intensity* of a media schedule, based on repeated exposures to the message. Repetition is the key to memory.

(Jingle set to music)

FEMALE SINGER: When you walk into Behemoth Bank, don't expect a smile . . .

MALE SINGER: Or a friendly "How do you do". . .

TOGETHER: 'Cause that's just not our style.

FEMALE: We treat you like a number . . .

TOGETHER: Like the worm you are to us. We'll just laugh in your face, if you ever start to fuss. We're Behemoth Bank and Trust and we don't care, we don't care. About you or your family or the great big world out there. We've got a ton of money, so why should we give a hoot? We're Behemoth Bank and Trust and we don't care about you.

ANNCR: If you're tired of big banks making you feel small, call First Commercial, member FDIC.

Frequency is calculated as the *average* number of times individuals or homes are exposed to the communication. For instance, suppose in the example above that 20,000 people hear a commercial on WKKO three times during a four-week period, and another 20,000 people hear it five times. Calculate the *average frequency* by dividing the total number of exposures by the total reach:

$$\begin{aligned} \text{Average frequency} &= \text{Total exposures} \div \text{Audience reach} \\ &= (20{,}000 \times 3) + (20{,}000 \times 5) \div 40{,}000 \\ &= 160{,}000 \div 40{,}000 \\ &= 4 \end{aligned}$$

For the 40,000 listeners reached, the average frequency or number of exposures was four.

Similar to the concept of effective reach is **effective frequency**—the average number of times a person must see or hear a message before it becomes effective. Effective frequency falls between a minimum level that achieves message awareness and a maximum level that becomes overexposure, which leads to "wearout" (starts to irritate consumers).

Conventional wisdom considers effective frequency to be three or more **opportunities-to-see (OTS)** over a four-week period, but no magic number works for every commercial and every product. There are many factors to consider, among them credibility and relevance of the advertiser, popularity of the product, quality of the commercial, competitive noise, and timing.

The concepts of effective reach and frequency are controversial, but virtually all agencies use them. Cannon and Riordan point out that conventional media planning is based on *media vehicle exposure* (the number of people in a medium's audience), but effectiveness should relate to *advertising message exposure*. For example, only 20 percent of viewers may pay attention when a commercial runs. It may take 10 OTS to reach an average frequency of one! Cannon and Riordan would replace effective frequency with *optimal frequency*. Most studies of the **advertising response curve** indicate that incremental response to advertising actually diminishes—rather than builds—with repeated exposures (see Exhibit 8–8). The optimal frequency concept moves the focus of media planning from exposure effectiveness to *effective exposures per dollar*.

> With a response curve that is characterized by continually diminishing returns, the first ad will be the most profitable. But subsequent exposures—advertising frequency—are still important. How important depends on the slope of the response curve and the cost of advertising. Obviously, the less money it costs per exposure to advertise, the more the firm can afford to advertise. The profit-maximizing firm will continue to spend until the revenue resulting from an additional advertisement placed is offset by its cost.[20]

The implications of Cannon and Riordan's theory are immense. Historically, media planning has emphasized frequency as the most important media objective. This assumes an S-shaped advertising response curve in which the first two or three exposures don't count. But Cannon and Riordan's analysis indicates that response curves are convex. The first exposure is the most effective, followed by diminishing returns. If that's

Exhibit • 8–8
Two advertising response curves.

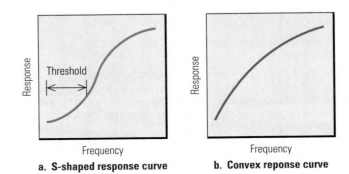

a. **S-shaped response curve**   b. **Convex reponse curve**

the case, then the basic emphasis in advertising should switch from maximizing frequency to maximizing target market reach, adding less profitable second exposures only as the budget permits[21]

The only solution to this dilemma is for the media planner to establish which response curve is most likely to apply to the particular situation and then to develop media objectives accordingly.

Message weight

Media planners often define media objectives by the schedule's **message weight,** the total size of the audience for a set of ads or an entire campaign. Advertisers calculate message weight by totaling the gross audience size for each ad or commercial, disregarding any overlap or duplication. There are two ways to express message weight: *gross impressions* and *gross rating points*.

One OTS is counted as one impression. So the **gross impressions** are the total number of potential exposures. The number of people reached (as estimated by media research companies) is multiplied by the number of times the ad runs. In the radio example used earlier, there were 160,000 gross impressions.

With large media schedules, gross impressions can run into the millions, so they are often converted into percentages called **gross rating points (GRPs).** A single rating point represents 1 percent of the potential audience, so when we hear a particular TV show garnered a 20 rating, it means 20 percent of the households with TV sets (**television households** or **TVHH**) were tuned in to that show.

A simple way to calculate GRPs is to multiply a show's reach, expressed as a rating percentage, by the average frequency. In our radio example 40 percent of the radio households heard the commercial an average of four times during the four-week period:

$$\text{Reach} \times \text{Frequency} = \text{GRPs}$$
$$40 \times 4 = 160 \text{ GRPs}$$

Another way is to divide the total number of impressions by the size of the target population and multiply by 100. In our radio example, the total gross impressions were 160,000, and the target audience was 100,000 people.

$$\text{Gross rating points} = (\text{Total gross impressions} \div \text{Target audience}) \times 100$$
$$= (160,000 \div 100,000) \times 100$$
$$= 1.6 \times 100$$
$$= 160 \text{ GRPs}$$

When we see 160 GRPs, we know that the gross impressions generated by our schedule equaled 160 percent of the target market population. For broadcast media, GRPs are often calculated for a week or a month. In print media, they're calculated for the number of ads in a campaign. For outdoor advertising, they're calculated on the basis of daily exposure.

Media planners use GRPs to determine the optimal level of spending for a campaign. The more GRPs they buy, the more it costs. However, because of discounting, the unit cost of GRPs will decrease as more GRPs are bought. Beyond a certain point, the effectiveness of additional GRPs also diminishes. Through the use of computer models and certain assumptions based on experience, planners can determine the optimal objective based on *return on investment (ROI)* and frequently save their clients substantial sums.[22]

Continuity ✓

Continuity refers to the duration of an advertising message or campaign over a given period of time. A media planner for a new product might decide that after a heavy introduction period of, say, four weeks, a radio campaign needs to maintain continuity for an additional 16 weeks but on fewer stations. While frequency is important to *create* memory, continuity is important to *sustain* it.

Once the media objectives have been determined—that is, the optimum levels of reach, frequency, message weight, and continuity—the media planner can develop the strategy for achieving them.

DEVELOPING A MEDIA STRATEGY: THE MEDIA MIX

The media strategy describes how the advertiser will achieve the stated media objectives: which media will be used, where, how often, and when. Advertisers develop media strategies by blending the elements of the media mix.

Elements of the Media Mix: The 5Ms

Media planners use the Five Ms (5Ms) of the media mix—markets, money, media, mechanics, and methodology—to develop an effective media strategy.

Markets refers to the various targets of a media plan: trade and consumer audiences; global, national, or regional audiences; or certain ethnic or socioeconomic groups. In an integrated marketing communications plan, the IMC planner wants to find the reasons and motivations for the prospect's purchase and usage patterns and then create a media plan based on those findings.[23]

Using intuition, marketing savvy, and analytical skill, the media planner determines how much money to budget and where to allocate funds: how much for print media, how much in TV, how much to nontraditional or supplemental media, how much to each geographic area. We discuss this issue in depth in the chapters on media selection and buying (Chapters 12–14).

Today, **media** include all communications vehicles available to a marketer, such as radio, TV, newspapers, magazines, outdoor, and direct mail, plus sales promotion, direct marketing, public relations and publicity, special events, and collateral materials.[24] Good media planners champion the integration of all marketing communications to help achieve their companies' marketing and advertising objectives. And they look at the media element not just analytically but creatively as well.

The media planner deals with the complex **mechanics** of advertising media and messages. Electronic commercials come in a variety of time units; and print ads are created in a

---

 Ethical Issue   ## The Ethical Cost of Gifts and Commissions

Advertising agencies have long accepted commissions as remuneration and advised clients to distribute gifts and specialty items to reinforce the marketing message. These exchanges are sometimes criticized, though, as being unethical.

Ad agencies traditionally make money from three sources: media commissions, markups, and fees or retainers. Of the three, agency commissions generate the most income, but also a lot of criticism. Just one ad with national exposure can yield a huge commission and generous profits to an agency—especially compared to the amount of time directly spent generating that income. Because ad agencies realize greater profits when their clients buy additional advertising space or time from the media, some observers regard an agency's so-called expert and impartial advice to the advertiser on spending for commissionable

media as tainted. And some agency critics see commissions as kickbacks.

It might be helpful to understand where the commission system originated. In 1843, when the advertising industry was young and formless, the very first advertising agent, Volney Palmer, solicited orders as an agent for the media, not for the advertisers. He was paid a commission on what he sold. Later, when advertising agents began working for the clients, the commission system remained. So the tradition is now over 150 years old, but the legions of its detractors are growing.

Some clients balk at the system. Most large national accounts now negotiate the commission with their agencies, which may receive substantially less than the standard 15 percent commission. Others negotiate a fee against which commissions are credited. And some now use an incentive system—

a base fee supplemented by bonuses for meeting specific goals. Both of these latter approaches help answer the ethical question.

But the whole area of promotions, gifts, and premiums raises some people's hackles. From advertising's earliest days, agency and media people have presented gifts, offered special incentives, and wined and dined prospects. They also recommended that their clients do the same. For example, it has been common practice for brewery executives to accept gifts from outside suppliers. When Anheuser-Busch (A-B) investigated senior executives to see if they had accepted gifts from companies handling A-B's sales promotion, the gifts were so numerous at headquarters that they lined both sides of the corridors.

Some of the sales promotion and advertising agencies involved contended that the gifts were

variety of sizes and styles. IMC planners may also deal with the mechanics of nontraditional media: everything from shopping bags to multimedia kiosks to the Internet. The myriad media options now available offer exciting, creative ways to enhance consumer acceptance of the advertiser's message and offer the consumer a relevant purchase incentive.[25]

Methodology refers to the overall strategy of selecting and scheduling media vehicles to achieve the desired reach, frequency, and continuity objectives. It offers the opportunity for creativity in planning, negotiating, and buying.[26]

Influencing Factors in Media Strategy Decisions

Media decisions are greatly influenced by factors over which the media planner has little or no control. These include the scope of the media plan, the sales potential of different markets, competitive strategies and budget considerations, the availability of different media vehicles, the nature of the medium, the mood of the message, message size and length, and buyer purchase patterns.

Scope of the media plan

The location and makeup of the target audience strongly influence the breadth of the media plan, thereby affecting decisions regarding the *market,* the *money,* and the *media* elements.

Domestic markets A media planner normally limits advertising to areas where the product is available. If a store serves only one town, or if a city has been chosen to test market a new product, then the advertiser will use a *local* plan. We explore the subject of local advertising further in Chapter 17.

A *regional* plan may cover several adjoining metropolitan areas, an entire state or province, or several neighboring states. Regional plans typically employ a combination of local media, regional editions of national magazines, or spot TV and radio.

Advertisers who want to reach several regions or an entire country use a *national* plan. This may call for network TV and radio, full-circulation national magazines and newspapers, and nationally syndicated Sunday newspaper supplements.

---

needed for obtaining business and that the brewers didn't dissuade them in their gift-giving practices.

> **The purpose of gifts and favors is generally to create goodwill. If they do more than that, and unduly influence judgment or create a feeling of obligation, we should not give or accept them.**

But in today's highly competitive atmosphere, business ethics in general have come under increased scrutiny, especially since the insider trading and savings and loan scandals.

Now, agencies are very cautious when advising clients about incentive programs. They could lose an account by suggesting practices that conflict with their client's ethical code. An excerpt from NCR's code of ethics on "gifts and favors," for example, offers guidelines useful to advertising people as well as clients: "Giving and receiving gifts in our business dealings can create conflicts of interest; such situations require careful thought. The purpose of gifts and favors is generally to create goodwill. If they do more than that, and unduly influence judgment or create a feeling of obligation, we should not give or accept them."

Fortunately, advertising agencies today are becoming more sensitive to the issue of questionable exchanges—particularly regarding the commission system and the giving of gifts—that could lead people to question the industry's integrity.

Questions

1. Compare the advantages and disadvantages of the commission system versus those of the fee or incentive system.

2. When, if ever, is it appropriate for companies to give gifts to customers? Should some limit be placed on the value of gifts given or received? Who should make that judgment call?

Sources: Jonathan D. Hibbard, "Anheuser-Busch," in N. Craig Smith and John A. Quelch, eds., *Ethics in Marketing* (Homewood, IL: Richard D. Irwin, 1993), pp. 651–54; Robert J. Kopp, "Ethical Issues in Personal Selling and Sales Force Management," in N. Craig Smith and John A. Quelch, eds., *Ethics in Marketing,* pp. 539–54; Steven Fox, *The Mirror Makers* (New York: Vintage Books, 1985), pp. 14–17.

International markets Foreign media can be a challenge for U.S. advertisers. While many broadcast stations, for example, are being privatized in countries as diverse as Israel and Russia, governments around the world still control most broadcast media, and many do not permit commercials. Others limit advertising to a certain number of minutes per hour or per day.[27]

In countries that do allow TV advertising, advertisers face other problems: how many people own TV sets, who they are, and what channels they receive. While this is not an issue in Europe and is becoming less so in Latin America, it is still a problem in many of the less-developed nations of Africa and Asia.[28] There, TV ownership may be limited to upper-income consumers, or the availability of commercial channels may be severely limited. In those markets, advertisers must use a different media mix.

Even in Europe, over 60 percent of total advertising expenditures are still spent in print media versus 25 percent on television. However, like the U.S., Europe and Asia are experiencing a virtual explosion of new media and technology, and advertisers and agencies alike are realizing the importance of developing integrated marketing communications plans to build their brands and establish long-term relationships with their customers.[29]

Most marketers develop an international media plan by formulating individual national plans first. But it's not as simple as it sounds. Precise media information isn't so available overseas, circulation figures aren't necessarily audited, audience demographics may be sketchy, and even ad rates may be unreliable. Finally, the methodology used in media research may be considerably different from one market to another, making comparisons virtually impossible.[30]

Because of the media variations from country to country, most international and global advertisers entrust national media plans to in-country foreign media specialists rather than risk faulty centralized media planning.[31]

Sales potential of different markets

The *market* and *money* elements of the media mix also depend on the sales potential of each area. National advertisers use this factor to determine where to allocate their advertising dollars. Planners can determine an area's sales potential in several ways.

The brand development index (BDI) The **brand development index (BDI)** indicates the sales potential of a particular brand in a specific market area. It compares the percentage of the brand's total U.S. sales in an area to the percentage of the total U.S. population in that area. The larger the brand's sales relative to the area's percentage of U.S. population, the higher the BDI and the greater the brand's sales potential. BDI is calculated as:

$$BDI = \frac{\text{Percent of the brand's total U.S. sales in the area}}{\text{Percent of total U.S. population in the area}} \times 100$$

Suppose sales of a brand in Los Angeles are 1.58 percent of the brand's total U.S. sales and the population of Los Angeles is 2 percent of the U.S. total. The BDI for Los Angeles is:

$$BDI = \frac{1.58}{2} \times 100 = 79$$

An index number of 100 means the brand's performance balances with the size of the area's population. A low BDI index number (below 100) indicates potential for the brand is not strong.

The category development index (CDI) To determine the potential of the whole product category, media planners use the **category development index (CDI),** which works on the same concept as the BDI and is calculated in much the same way.

$$CDI = \frac{\text{Percent of the product category's total U.S. sales in the area}}{\text{Percent of total U.S. population in the area}} \times 100$$

	Low BDI	High BDI
High CDI	Low market share *but* Good market potential	High market share *and* Good market potential
Low CDI	Low market share *and* Poor market potential	High market share *but* Monitor for sales decline

If category sales in Los Angeles are 4.92 percent of total U.S. category sales, the CDI in Los Angeles is:

$$CDI = \frac{4.92}{2} \times 100 = 246$$

The combination of BDI and CDI can help the planner determine a media strategy for the market. (See Exhibit 8–9.) In our example, low BDI (under 100) and high CDI (over 100) in Los Angeles indicate that the product category has high potential but the brand is not selling well. This may represent a problem or an opportunity. If the brand has been on the market for some time, the low BDI raises a red flag—some problem is standing in the way of brand sales. But if the brand is new, the low BDI may not be alarming. In fact, the high CDI may indicate the brand can grow substantially, given more time and greater media and marketing support. At this point, the media planner should assess the company's share of voice (discussed in Chapter 7) and budget accordingly.

Competitive strategies and budget considerations

Advertisers always consider what competitors are doing, particularly those that have larger advertising budgets. This will affect the *media, mechanics,* and *methodology* elements of the media mix. Several services, like the A. C. Nielsen Co. and Leading National Advertisers (LNA), report competitive advertising expenditures in the different media. By knowing the size of competitors' budgets, what media they're using, the regionality or seasonality of their sales, and any new product tests and introductions, advertisers can better plan a counterstrategy.[32]

Again, the media planner should analyze the company's share of voice in the marketplace. If an advertiser's budget is much smaller than the competition's, the brand could get lost in the shuffle. Advertisers should bypass media that competitors dominate and choose other media that offer a strong position.

When Karen Ritchie, senior vice president/director of media services at McCann-Erickson, Detroit, had to develop a media plan for the introduction of Buick's Roadmaster Wagon, she didn't have the budget of Honda Accord or Ford Mustang to work with. So she didn't want to place her ads where theirs were. Ritchie and her team creatively fashioned a targeted media plan that included preprinted inserts in seven national magazines, ads in other magazines featuring special ink-jet printing of the subscriber's name, national cable TV on A&E and Discovery, and outdoor advertising and network radio targeted to affluent suburban car buyers. The response was excellent.[33]

It sometimes makes sense to use media similar to the competition's if the target audiences are the same or if competitors are not using their media effectively.

Media availability and economics: The global marketer's headache

North American advertisers are blessed—or cursed—with an incredible array of media choices, locally and nationally. Such is not always the case in other areas of the world, which is one reason their per capita advertising expenditures are so much lower than

Exhibit • 8–10

The big 12 in advertising spending ($ millions).

Country	1993 ad spending
U.S.	$134,000
Japan	30,500
Germany	18,000
U.K.	14,000
France	9,000
Spain	8,500
Italy	7,000
Canada	6,500
Australia	4,000
South Korea	4,000
Brazil	3,500
Netherlands	3,500

in the U.S. (Exhibit 8–10 shows the total ad spending for the top 12 advertising countries in the world.)

Every country has communications media, but they are not always available for commercial use—especially radio and television—and coverage may be limited. Lower literacy rates and education levels in some countries restrict the coverage of print media. Where income levels are low, TV ownership is also low. These factors tend to segment markets by media coverage.

To reach lower-income markets, radio is the medium of choice, as both Coke and Pepsi have demonstrated successfully for years. Auto manufacturers make good use of TV and magazine advertising to reach the upper class. And movie advertising can reach whole urban populations where TV ownership is low because motion picture attendance in such countries is very high. The Checklist for International Media Planning outlines some basic considerations for media buyers entering international markets.

Some companies are attempting to become true global marketers of their brands with centralized control of media and standardized creative. As a group, global media are growing, which is good news for global marketers.[34] However, there are still few true global media (see Exhibit 8–11). So these major advertisers must continue to use local foreign media in the countries where they do business and localize their campaigns for language and cultural differences.

Exhibit • 8–11

Leading global media distribution by circulation and household reach.

Media	Total distribution 1994	North America	Central/ South America	Europe	Middle East/ Africa	Asia	Australia/ New Zealand
Dailies							
Financial Times (London)	297,463	29,748	1,299	255,246	3,000	7,689	301
International Herald Tribune (Neuilly, France)	190,705	10,867	1,436	129,577	5,204	42,984	362
USA Today (Arlington, VA)*	2,108,830	2,038,830	—	[48,317	]	19,349	—
The Wall Street Journal (New York)	2,937,059	1,854,901	977,000	59,201	—	45,957	—
Weeklies							
Business Week (New York)	1,006,762	886,326	19,710	62,981	—	37,745	—
The Economist (London)	568,683	258,698	10,927	224,225	16,108	45,925	12,800
The Guardian Weekly (Manchester, England)	102,221	26,994	3,043	22,253	32,178	8,303	15,000
Newsweek (New York)	4,108,000	3,100,000	73,000	290,000	50,000	225,000	110,000
Paris Match (Paris)	194,434	32,395	1,399	121,894	16,833	649	—
Monthlies							
Cosmopolitan (New York)	5,755,795	2,528,280	636,343	1,781,489	110,272	398,000	301,411
Esquire (New York)	1,207,478	739,828	—	112,650	—	355,000	—
Good Housekeeping (New York)	5,715,865	5,056,700	203,129	456,036	—	—	—
Harper's Bazaar (New York)	1,056,711	738,647	77,652	158,035	—	82,377	—
National Geographic (Washington)	9,367,954	7,942,463	101,654	911,605	—	158,933	229,958
TV							
BBC Worldwide TV (London)	23,800,000	7,000,000+	—	2,000,000+	—	7,200,000+	—
CMT: Country Music Television (New York)	34,900,000	26,800,000	—	8,000,000	—	3,236	400
CNN (Atlanta)*	143,000,000	62,000,000+	1,600,000	[50,000,000+	]	[4,400,000	]
Cartoon Network (Atlanta)*	34,400,000	12,000,000	1,500,000	[20,400,000	]	[500,000	]
The Discovery Channel (Bethesda, MD)	85,000,000	67,100,000	5,000,000	10,000,000	—	2,800,000	—

*Europe includes Middle East. Asia includes Australia.

International Media Planning   *Checklist*

Basic Considerations (Who Does What?)

☐ **What is the client's policy regarding supervision and placement of advertising?** When, where, and to what degree is client and/or client branch office abroad involved?

☐ **Which client office is in charge of the campaign?** North American headquarters or foreign office or both? Who else has to be consulted? In what areas (creative or media selection and so forth)?

☐ **Is there a predetermined media mix?** Can international as well as foreign media be used?

☐ **Who arranges for translation of copy if foreign media are to be used?**

  ☐ Client headquarters in North America.

  ☐ Client office in foreign country.

  ☐ Agency headquarters in North America.

  ☐ Foreign media rep in North America.

☐ **Who approves translated copy?**

☐ **Who checks on acceptability of ad copy in foreign country?** Certain ads need approval by foreign governments.

☐ **What is the advertising placement procedure?**

  ☐ From agency branch office in foreign country directly to foreign media.

  ☐ From North American agency to American-based foreign media rep to foreign media.

  ☐ From North American agency to American-based international media.

  ☐ From North American agency to affiliated agency abroad to foreign media.

☐ **What are the pros and cons of each approach?** Is media commission to be split with foreign agency branch or affiliate office? Can campaign be run from North America? Does the client save ad taxes by placing from North America? In what currency does client want to pay?

☐ **Who receives checking copies?**

☐ **Will advance payment be made to avoid currency fluctuation?**

☐ **Who bills?** What currency? Who approves payment?

Budget Considerations

☐ **Is budget predetermined by client?**

☐ **Is budget based on local branch or distributor recommendation?**

☐ **Is budget based on agency recommendation?**

☐ **Is budget related to sales in the foreign market?**

☐ **What is the budget period?**

☐ **What is the budget breakdown for media,** including ad taxes, translation, production, and research costs?

☐ **What are the tie-ins with local distributors, if any?**

Market Considerations

☐ **What is the geographic target area?**

  ☐ Africa and Middle East.

  ☐ Asia, including Australasia.

  ☐ Europe, including Eastern Europe.

  ☐ Latin America.

☐ **What are the major market factors in these areas?**

  ☐ Local competition.

  ☐ GDP growth over past four years and expected future growth.

  ☐ Membership of country in a common market or free trade association.

  ☐ Literacy rate.

  ☐ Attitude toward North American products or services.

  ☐ Social and religious customs.

☐ **What is the basic target audience?**

  ☐ Management executives in business and industry.

  ☐ Managers and buyers in certain businesses.

  ☐ Military and government officials.

  ☐ Consumers; potential buyers of foreign market goods.

Media Considerations

☐ **Availability of media to cover market:** Are the desired media available in the particular area?

☐ **Foreign media and/or international media:** Should the campaign be in the press and language of a particular country, or should it be a combination of the two types?

☐ **What media does the competition use?**

☐ **Does the medium fit?**

  ☐ Optimum audience quality and quantity.

  ☐ Desired image, editorial content, and design.

  ☐ Suitable paper and color availability.

  ☐ Justifiable rates and CPM (do not forget taxes on advertising, which can vary by medium).

  ☐ Discount availability.

  ☐ Type of circulation audit.

  ☐ Availability of special issues or editorial tie-ins.

☐ **What are the closing dates at North American rep and at the publication headquarters abroad?**

☐ **What is the agency commission?** (When placed locally abroad at the agency, commission is sometimes less than when placed in North America.)

☐ **For how long are contracted rates protected?**

☐ **Does the publication have a North American rep** to help with media evaluation and ad placement?

Finally, there's the problem of **spillover media**—local media that many consumers in a neighboring country inadvertently receive. For example, media from Luxembourg regularly spill over into France, Belgium, and Holland. Media often spill over into countries lacking indigenous-language publications, particularly specialty publications. English and German business media enjoy a large circulation in Scandinavian countries, for example, where there are relatively few specialized trade publications written in Swedish, Danish, or Norwegian.

Spillover media pose a threat for the multinational advertiser because they expose readers to multiple ad campaigns. If the advertiser runs both international and local campaigns for the same products, discrepancies in product positioning, pricing, or advertising messages could confuse potential buyers. Advertisers' local subsidiaries or distributors need to coordinate local and international ad campaigns to preclude such confusion. On the positive side, spillover media offer potential cost savings through regional campaigns.

Nature of the medium and mood of the message

An important influence on the *media* element of the mix is how well a medium works with the style or mood of the particular message.

Advertising messages differ in many ways. Some are simple messages: "Just do it" (Nike). Others make emotional or sensual appeals to people's needs and wants: "The great taste of fruit squared" (Jolly Rancher candies). Many advertisers use a reason-why approach to explain their product's advantages: "Twice the Room. Twice the Comfort. Twice the Value. Embassy Suites. Twice the Hotel."

Complex messages, such as ads announcing a new product or concept, require more space or time for explanation. Each circumstance affects the media selection as well as the *methodology* of the media mix.

A new or highly complex message may require greater frequency and exposure to be understood and remembered. A dogmatic message like Nike's may require a surge at the beginning, then low frequency and greater reach.

Once consumers understand reason-why messages, pulsing advertising exposures at irregular intervals is often sufficient. Emotionally oriented messages are usually more effective when spaced at regular intervals to create enduring feelings about the product. We discuss these scheduling methods further in the next section on media tactics.

Message size, length, and position considerations

The particular characteristics of different media, over which the media planner has no control, affect the *mechanics* element of the media mix. For example, in print, a full-

● This TV campaign for Norfolk Southern, titled "Horse of a Different Color," is a complex message. Computer-generated images of the horse—the key element of the logo—pass through several transformations to symbolize the variety of services and benefits offered. Understated or complex commercials such as this must be aired with greater frequency than simple, bold messages.

MUSIC & SFX: To grow stronger, America depends on its bounty.

Both natural and manmade.

Finding new ways to get these goods to market more efficiently and reliably is the

noble pursuit of Norfolk Southern. The Thoroughbred of Transportation.

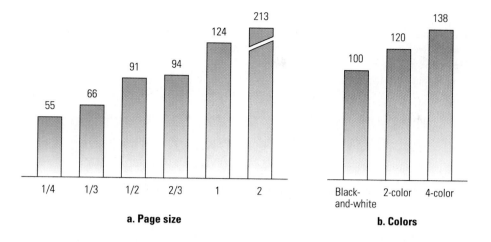

a. **Page size**

b. **Colors**

Exhibit • 8–12
a. Readership scores for ads of various sizes. Readership is the greatest for four-color, two-page ads, but increased readership may not offset the additional cost in some publications.
b. Readership scores for ads with various degrees of color.

page ad attracts more attention than a quarter-page ad and a full-color ad more than a black-and-white one. Color and larger units of space or time cost dearly in terms of reach and frequency (see Exhibit 8–12).

Should a small advertiser run a full-page ad once a month or a quarter-page ad once a week? Is it better to use a few 60-second commercials or many 15- and 30-second ones? The planner has to consider the nature of the advertising message: some simply require more time and space to explain. Competitive activity often dictates more message units. The product itself may demand the prestige of a full page or full color. However, it's often better to run small ads consistently rather than one large ad occasionally. Unfortunately, space and time units may be determined by someone other than the media planner—creative or account service, for example—in which case the planner's options are limited.

The position of an ad is another consideration. Preferred positions for magazine ads are front and back covers; for TV, sponsorship of prime-time shows. Special positions and sponsorships cost more, so the media planner must weigh the additional costs against increased reach and frequency.

Buyer Purchase Patterns

Finally, the customer's product purchasing behavior affects every element of the media mix. The media planner must consider how, when, and where the product is typically purchased and repurchased. Products with short purchase cycles (convenience foods and paper towels) require more constant levels of advertising than products purchased infrequently (refrigerators and furniture).

Stating the Media Strategy

A written rationale for the media strategy is an integral part of any media plan. Without one, it's difficult for client and agency management to analyze the logic and consistency of the recommended media schedule.

Generally, the strategy statement starts with a brief definition of target audiences (the market element) and the priorities for weighting them. It explains the nature of the message and indicates which media types will be used and why (the media element). It outlines specific reach and frequency goals and how they are to be achieved (methodology element). It provides a budget for each medium (the money element) including the cost of production and any collateral materials. Finally, it states the intended size of message units, any position or timing considerations (the mechanics element), and the effect of budget restrictions.

Once the strategy is delineated, the plan will detail the tactics to be employed (discussed in the next section). Then, the media planner creates a flowchart of the plan. The **flowchart** is a graphic presentation of the total campaign to let the creative department, media department, account services, and the client see the pattern of media events that will occur throughout the period—usually one year.

• The planning and buying of media is usually done by computer and involves graphing or listing the data in easy-to-understand arrays such as this list from Capener, Mathews, Walcher, a San Diego agency that serves clients nationwide.

• The media plan flowchart such as this computerized printout by MediaPlan, Inc., gives a bird's-eye view of the major media purchases and where and when they will appear over a specified period of time.

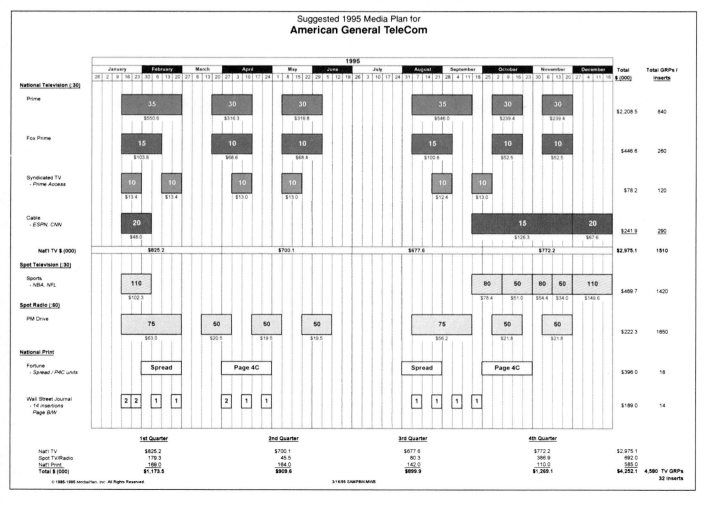

Suggested 1995 Media Plan for
American General TeleCom

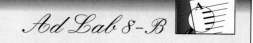

Media Selection: Quicklist of Advantages — Ad Lab 8–B

Medium	Advantages	Medium	Advantages
Newspapers	Many ad sizes available. Quick placement, local targeting.	Radio	Intimacy. Loyal following. Ability to change message quickly.
Magazines	High-quality graphics/reproduction. Prestige factor. Color.	Direct mail	Measurable. Graphics, color. Three-dimensional. Highly personal.
Television	Combines sight, sound, movement. A single message. Demonstration.	Outdoor/Transit	Local targeting. Graphics, color. Simple message. Larger than life.

An extensive list of media appears as RL 8–1 in the Reference Library.

Laboratory Applications

1. If you wanted a set of complementary media to cover all the creative advantages, which mix would you select?
2. What creative advantages can you add to the list?

Once the general media strategy is determined, the media planner can select and schedule particular media vehicles. The planner usually considers each medium's value on a set of specific criteria (see Ad Lab 8–B).

Criteria for Selecting Individual Media Vehicles

In evaluating specific media vehicles, the planner considers several factors: overall campaign objectives and strategy; size and characteristics of each medium's audience; attention, exposure, and motivational value of each medium; and cost efficiency. (For a comparative evaluation of various media types, see RL 8–1 in the Reference Library.)

Overall campaign objectives and strategy

The media planner's first job is to review the nature of the product or service, the intended objectives and strategies, and the primary and secondary target markets and audiences. The characteristics of the product often suggest a suitable choice. A product with a distinct personality or image, such as a fine perfume, might be advertised in media that reinforce this image. The media planner considers how consumers regard various magazines and TV programs—feminine or masculine, highbrow or lowbrow, serious or frivolous—and determines whether they're appropriate for the brand.

The content and editorial policy of the media vehicle and its compatibility with the product are important considerations. *Tennis* magazine is a poor vehicle for cigarette or alcohol ads even though its demographic profile and image might match the desired target audience.

Consumers choose a particular media vehicle because they gain some "reward": self-improvement, financial advice, career guidance, or simply news and entertainment. Advertising is most effective when it positions a product as part of the solution the consumer seeks. Otherwise, consumers may see it as an intrusion.[35]

If the marketing objective is to gain greater product distribution, the planner should select media that influence potential dealers. If the goal is to stimulate sales of a nationally distributed product in isolated markets, ads should be placed in local and regional media that penetrate those markets. Pricing strategy influences media choices too. A premium-priced product should use prestigious or "class" media to support its market image.

Characteristics of media audiences

An **audience** is the total number of people or households exposed to a medium. The planner needs to know how closely the medium's audience matches the profile of the

MEDIA TACTICS: SELECTING AND SCHEDULING MEDIA VEHICLES

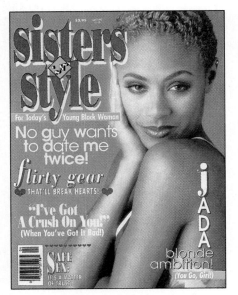

• *Content* of a medium usually determines the type of people in the audience. *Sisters in Style* magazine is aimed at African-American teen-aged girls, and its articles and advertising are tailored to their interests.

target market and how interested such people are in the publication or program. A product intended for a Latino audience, for example, would likely appear in specific media directed toward Hispanics. Simmons Market Research Bureau provides research data on age, income, occupational status, and other characteristics of magazine readers. Simmons also publishes demographic and psychographic data on product usage of consumers. Likewise, Arbitron and Nielsen provide audience statistics for radio stations and TV programs.

The *content* of the medium usually determines the type of people in the audience. Some radio stations emphasize in-depth news or sports; others feature jazz, rock, or classical music. Each type of programming attracts a different audience.

Exposure, attention, and motivation value of media vehicles

The media planner has to select media that will not only achieve the desired *exposure* to the target audience, but also attract *attention* and *motivate* people to act.

Exposure To understand the concept of **exposure value,** think of how many people an ad "sees" rather than the other way around. How many of a magazine's 3 million readers will an ad actually see? How many of a TV program's 10 million viewers will a commercial actually see?

As we discussed earlier, just because someone reads a particular magazine or watches a certain program doesn't mean he or she sees the ads. Some people read only one article, set the magazine aside, and never pick it up again. Many people change channels during commercial breaks or leave to get a snack. Comparing the exposure value of different media vehicles is very difficult. Without statistics, media planners have to use their best judgment based on experience.

Five factors that affect the probability of ad exposure are:[36]

1. The senses used to perceive messages from the medium.
2. How much and what kind of attention the medium requires.
3. Whether the medium is an information source or a diversion.
4. Whether the medium or program aims at a general or a specialized audience.
5. The placement of the ad in the vehicle (within or between broadcast programs; adjacent to editorial material or other print ads).[37]

Attention Degree of attention is another consideration. Consumers with no interest in motorcycles or cosmetics won't remember ads for those products. But someone in the market for a new car tends to notice every car ad.

Exposure value relates only to the medium; **attention value** concerns the advertising message and copy, as well as the medium. Special-interest media, such as boating magazines, offer good attention value to a marine product. But what kind of attention value does the daily newspaper offer such a product? Do sailors think about boats while reading the newspaper? Much research still needs to be done, but six factors are known to increase attention value:[38]

1. Audience involvement with editorial content or program material.
2. Specialization of audience interest or identification.
3. Number of competitive advertisers (the fewer, the better).
4. Audience familiarity with the advertiser's campaign.
5. Quality of advertising reproduction.
6. Timeliness of advertising exposure.

Motivation These same factors affect a medium's **motivation value,** but in different ways. Familiarity with the advertiser's campaign may affect attention significantly but motivation very little. The attention factors of quality reproduction and timeliness can motivate someone.

• The quality and presentation of advertising messages affect the consumer's degree of attention and motivation to respond. This Italian in-your-face anti-smoking ad certainly captures the consumer's attention. And the fact that the sponsor is an undertaker who includes his telephone number adds credibility and urgency to the message. Translation: *How much of you goes up in smoke every day?—Eugenio Fabozzi, Undertaker. Telephone: 23 23 23 23.*

Media planners analyze these values by assigning numerical ratings to their judgments of a medium's strengths and weaknesses. Then, using a weighting formula, they add them up. Planners use similar weighting methods to evaluate other factors, such as the relative importance of age versus income.

Cost efficiency of media vehicles

Finally, media planners analyze the cost efficiency of each medium. A common term used in media planning and buying is **cost per thousand,** or **CPM** (M is the Roman numeral for 1,000). If a daily newspaper has 300,000 subscribers and charges $5,000 for a full-page ad, the cost per thousand is the cost divided by the number of thousands of people in the audience. Since there are 300 *thousands* of subscribers, you divide $5,000 by 300:

$$\text{CPM} = \frac{5,000}{300,000 \div 1,000} = \frac{5,000}{300} = \$16.67$$

However, media planners are more interested in **cost efficiency**—the cost of exposing the message to the target audience rather than to the total circulation. Let's say the target audience is males ages 18 to 49, and 40 percent of a weekly newspaper's subscriber base of 250,000 fits this category. If the paper charges $3,000 for a full-page ad, the CPM is computed as follows:

$$\text{Target audience} = 0.40 \times 250,000 = 100,000$$

$$\text{CPM} = \frac{3,000}{100,000 \div 1,000} = \$30$$

The daily newspaper, on the other hand, might turn out to be more cost-efficient if 60 percent of its readers (180,000) belong to the target audience:

$$\text{CPM} = \frac{5,000}{180,000 \div 1,000} = \$27.78$$

Comparing different media by CPMs is important but does not take into account each medium's other advantages and disadvantages. The media planner must evaluate all the criteria to determine:

1. How much of each medium's audience matches the target audience;
2. How each medium satisfies the campaign's objectives and strategy; and
3. How well each medium offers attention, exposure, and motivation.

Economics of Foreign Media

The main purpose of media advertising is to communicate with customers more efficiently than through personal selling. In some developing countries, though, it's cheaper to send people out with baskets of samples. For mass marketers in the U.S., this kind of personal contact is virtually impossible.

In many foreign markets, outdoor advertising enjoys far greater coverage than in the U.S. because it costs less to have people paint the signs and there is also less government restriction.

Cost inhibits the growth of broadcast media in some foreign markets, but most countries now sell advertising time to help foot the bill. China and Vietnam, for example, have recently become booming markets for advertising.[39] As more countries allow commercial broadcasts and international satellite channels gain a greater foothold, TV advertising will continue to grow.

The Synergy of Mixed Media

A combination of media is called a **mixed media approach.** There are numerous reasons for using mixed media:

- To reach people unavailable through only one medium.
- To provide repeat exposure in a less expensive secondary medium after attaining optimum reach in the first.
- To use the intrinsic value of an additional medium to extend the creative effectiveness of the ad campaign (such as music on radio along with long copy in print).
- To deliver coupons in print media when the primary vehicle is broadcast.
- To produce **synergy,** where the total effect is greater than the sum of its parts.

Newspapers, for example, can be used to introduce a new product and give immediacy to the message. Magazine ads can then follow up for greater detail, image enhancement, longevity, and memory improvement.

A mixed media campaign was effective for General Electric's lighting products. The promotion used a combination of network TV spots, print advertising, Sunday supplement inserts, in-store displays in over 150,000 stores, and a highly creative publicity

● Outdoor advertising enjoys wide coverage in many foreign markets. Here Kodak invites comparison by putting pictures of this park in Amsterdam in front of the actual park. The tagline translates as *Kodacolor Gold. True-to-life colors.*

• This mixed media advertising campaign for Alka-Seltzer was custom designed to create customer excitement and increase retail floor traffic. The Feel Better Fast Fest generated sales through local radio personalities piggy-backed with 30-second national advertising, local event sponsorships and radio tie-ins, in-store display headers, mini-remotes, and coupon distribution.

program. By using an integrated, mixed media approach, the campaign produced "unprecedented" consumer awareness and dealer support. It had synergy.[40]

Methods for Scheduling Media

After selecting the appropriate media vehicles, the media planner decides how many space or time units of each vehicle to buy and schedules them for release over a period of time when consumers are most apt to buy.

Continuous, flighting, and pulsing schedules

To build continuity in a campaign, planners use three principal scheduling methods: *continuous, flighting,* and *pulsing.* See Exhibit 8–13.

In a **continuous** schedule, advertising runs steadily and varies little over the campaign period. It's the best way to build continuity. Advertisers use this scheduling pattern for products consumers purchase regularly. For example, a commercial is scheduled on radio stations WTKO and WRBI for an initial four-week period. Then, to maintain continuity in the campaign, additional spots run continuously every week throughout the year on station WRBI.

Flighting alternates periods of advertising with periods of no advertising. This intermittent schedule makes sense for products and services that experience large fluctuations in demand throughout the year (tax services, lawn care products, cold remedies). The advertiser might introduce the product with a four-week flight and then schedule three additional four-week flights to run during seasonal periods later in the year.

The third alternative, **pulsing,** mixes continuous and flighting strategies. As the consumer's purchasing cycle gets longer, pulsing becomes more appropriate. The advertiser maintains a low level of advertising all year but uses periodic pulses to "heavy up" during peak selling periods. This strategy is appropriate for products like soft drinks, which are consumed all year but more heavily in the summer.

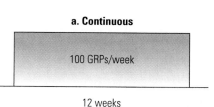

a. Continuous

100 GRPs/week

12 weeks

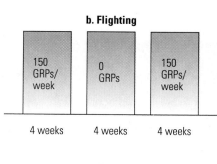

b. Flighting

150 GRPs/week	0 GRPs	150 GRPs/week
4 weeks	4 weeks	4 weeks

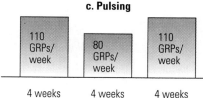

c. Pulsing

110 GRPs/week	80 GRPs/week	110 GRPs/week
4 weeks	4 weeks	4 weeks

Exhibit • 8–13

Three ways to schedule the same number of total GRPs: continuous, flighting, and pulsing.

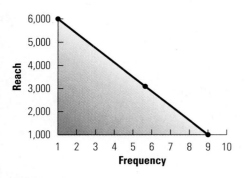

Exhibit • 8–14
Reach and frequency have an inverse relationship. For the same budget, an advertiser can reach 6,000 people once, 3,000 people 5.5 times, or 1,000 people 9 times.

Additional scheduling patterns

For high-ticket items that require careful consideration, **bursting**—running the same commercial every half hour on the same network during prime time—can be effective. A variation is **roadblocking,** buying air time on all three networks simultaneously. Chrysler used this technique to give viewers the impression that the advertiser was everywhere, even if the ad showed for only a few nights. Digital Equipment used a scheduling tactic called **blinking** to stretch its slim ad budget. To reach business executives, it flooded the airwaves on Sundays—on both cable and network channels—to make it virtually impossible to miss the ads.[41]

Maximizing reach, frequency, and continuity: The art of media planning

Good media planning is an art. The media planner must get the most effective exposure on a limited budget. As Exhibit 8–14 shows, the objectives of reach, frequency, and continuity have an inverse relationship. To achieve greater reach, some frequency has to be sacrificed, and so on. Research shows that all three are critical. (For guidelines on determining the best reach, frequency, continuity, and pulsing combinations, study RL 8–2 in the Reference Library.)

Computers in Media Selection and Scheduling

The last decade has seen a profusion of new desktop computer software to assist media planners. Computers perform the tedious number crunching needed to compute GRPs, CPMs, reach, frequency, and the like. They also save time and money. One agency found it could plan the entire TV, radio, and print co-op budgets for one of its largest clients in two days with only three people and one software system. Previously, that task required 70 staffers working manually for a week and a half.

Advertising executives may now gather information from their media directories electronically and then create timely budgets for their clients. Standard Rate & Data Service's program, called Media-Scope, includes monthly updates. Planners can reconfigure budgets on screen according to circulation, CPM, or other variables using any of the 7,000 publications in the SRDS database.[42]

Similarly, Interactive Market Systems (IMS) has introduced PC software and online data for the business-to-business computer marketplace. The software analyzes readership of various business publications for the customized target audience and ranks the publications on any of ten variables. Additionally, the program creates an optimized schedule within the parameters specified by the user.[43]

Many other programs calculate reach, frequency, and GRPs of broadcast and print schedules using sophisticated mathematical models. These are typically known by acronyms such as CANEX, MEDIAC, ADMOD, or VIDEAC, and each touts features or areas of accuracy that the others don't have.[44]

In Europe, two of the most widely known simulation models are the CAM model of the London Press Exchange and the Simulmatics model out of New York. Both have been in use for almost 20 years. More recent models are TOM, developed by CMC in Paris, and Ecotel's model, developed by Ecotel S.A. in Spain—the same company that operates the Spanish People Meter for measuring TV audiences. With any of these models, the computer instantly recalculates results whenever the planner changes one of the basic factors in the program. That enables the planner to perform what-ifs on the schedule.[45]

But even with technological timesavers and shortcuts, it's still up to the media planner to know the product, the market, and the media, and make the call. Computers can't decide which medium or environment is best for the message. They can't evaluate the content of a magazine or the image of a TV program. They can't judge whether the numbers they're fed are valid or reliable, and they can't interpret the meaning of the numbers. What they can do is help the process along.

Summary

Media planning directs the advertising message to the right people at the right time. It involves many decisions: where to advertise and when, which media to use, and how often to use them. Media planners need as much creativity as art directors and copywriters. And like good art and copy ideas, media decisions should be based on sound marketing principles and research.

Media planners work in several kinds of department structures, including advertising agency media departments, independent media-buying services, and company in-house media departments.

The task of media planners has become more complicated and competitive in recent years due to the dramatic increase in media options, the continuing fragmentation of media audiences, the rising cost of media space and time, and the increasing complexity in the way media buys are made. But this has also given the professionals who work in media departments new prominence.

The media function involves two basic processes: planning media strategy and selecting media vehicles. Media planning begins with defining audience objectives—the specific types of people the advertising message will be directed to—and then setting the goals for communicating with those audiences. The target audience is often determined from the marketer's past experience, through special research studies, or through secondary research sources such as Simmons Market Research Bureau and Mediamark Research. Planners who follow an IMC model start by segmenting their audiences according to brand purchasing behavior and then ranking these segments by profit to the brand. Once the target audience is determined, the planner sets the message distribution objectives. These specify where, when, and how often the advertising should appear. They may be expressed in terms of reach, frequency, message weight, and continuity. In this process, the planner considers the amount of advertising necessary for achieving effectiveness.

To create the appropriate media strategy, the planner develops the best blend of the 5Ms—markets, money, media, mechanics, and methodology. The planner must also consider many uncontrollable variables: the scope of the media plan, which is determined by the location and makeup of the target audience; the sales potential of different markets for both the brand and the product category; competitive strategies and budget considerations; media availability and economics; the nature of the medium and the mood of the message; the size, length, and position of the message in the selected media; and buyer purchase patterns. IMC planners try to discover the reasons and motivations for people's purchase and usage patterns and then create media plans based on those findings.

For international markets, media planners have to consider the availability and cost structure of foreign media and the differing cultural markets they serve. Some advertisers attempt to standardize their messages through the use of global media, but these media are still quite limited.

After the media strategy is developed, the planner selects specific media vehicles. Both the quantitative and qualitative criteria used to make this decision are important in the evaluation process. Factors that influence the selection process include campaign objectives and strategy; the size and characteristics of each medium's audience; geographic coverage; the exposure, attention, and motivation value of each medium; cost efficiency; and the advisability of a mixed media approach.

Once media vehicles are selected, the media planner decides on scheduling—how many of each medium's space or time units to buy over what period of time. A media campaign can run continuously or in erratic pulses. These decisions are affected by consumer purchase patterns, the product's seasonality, and the balance of reach, frequency, and continuity that meets the planner's media objectives and budget.

The media planner must spend money wisely to maximize the campaign's effectiveness. To that end, many computer models have been developed both in the U.S. and overseas to help planners determine optimum levels of expenditure or compare alternative media schedules.

Questions for Review and Discussion

1. What major factors contribute to the increased complexity of media planning?
2. What must media planners consider before they begin?
3. What secondary research sources are available to planners?
4. How does the IMC approach differ from the top-down media planning approach?
5. What is the "right" reach and frequency for a given message?
6. How are GRPs and CPMs calculated?
7. What are the 5Ms of the media mix, and how are they determined?
8. What major factors influence the choice of individual media vehicles?
9. Why might an advertiser use a mixed media approach?
10. What are the principal methods used to schedule media?

Part

III

CREATING ADVERTISEMENTS AND COMMERCIALS

Minnesota celebrates Matisse.

An exhibit of selected works of Henri Matisse pulled entirely from collections within Minnesota. October 10th through January 9th.
THE MINNEAPOLIS INSTITUTE OF ARTS

⊙ **TARGET**

Once advertising objectives and strategies have been set, the advertiser prepares a creative brief for the creative department, which in turn develops a message strategy to guide the conception and production of ads and commercials. Part III looks at this process in detail, examining how the creative process works, how we apply creativity to ad making, and how advertisers adapt their message strategies to a variety of print and electronic media. • *Chapter 9,* "Creative Strategy and the Creative Process," examines the development of advertising strategies, creative briefs, message strategies, and advertising concepts, including the "big idea." It explains how our preferred style of thinking modifies the creativity within all of us and presents a simple, flexible, four-step model of the creative process that can be used in all walks of life. • *Chapter 10,* "Creative Execution:

Art and Copy," depicts the complexity of preparing copy and art for a variety of media forms. Discussion includes common copy and art terminology, as well as the typical formats used by art directors and copywriters in creating print ads and radio and TV commercials. • *Chapter 11,* "Producing Ads for Print, Electronic, and Digital Media," presents an overview of how advertisers create ads and commercials for the print, broadcast, and digital media. The chapter discusses the techniques and equipment used in the process and the dynamic impact of computerization. It explores the printing process and the advantages and limitations of various print media. And it concludes by examining in detail how a print ad and a TV commercial were created from initial concept through final production.

9

Creative Strategy and the Creative Process

Objective: To show how advertising strategies are translated into creative briefs and message strategies that guide the creative process. The chapter examines styles of thinking, the nature of creativity, its importance in advertising, and the role of the agency creative team. We discuss how research serves as the foundation for creative development and planning, and we review common problems and pitfalls faced by members of the creative team.

After studying this chapter, you will be able to:

- State the meaning and the importance of creativity.

- Identify the members of the creative team and their primary responsibilities.

- Explain the role of the creative brief and its affect on the artistic expression in an ad or commercial.

- Enumerate the principal elements that should be included in a creative brief.

- Explain the purpose of the message strategy and how it differs from the creative strategy.

- Discuss the relevance of thinking styles to creativity.

- Define the four roles in the creative process.

- List several techniques creatives can use to enhance their productivity.

IN ITS SIMPLEST
FORM, A GUITAR IS
JUST A HOLLOW BOX
MADE OF WOOD.
IT'S UP TO YOU
TO DECIDE HOW TO
FILL IT.

When you think about it, it's amazing that those sweet sounds can come from a wooden box. But quit thinking about it. And play. Write us at 1940 Gillespie Way, El Cajon, CA 92020 for the dealer near you.

ob Taylor has designed and assembled guitars for more than two decades. He's an artisan, and his instruments show it. The average Taylor guitar sells for around $2,000 dollars, some for as much as $7,000. The company makes some of the best guitars in the world. But its sales volume didn't reflect that fact.

So Taylor and Kurt Lustig, the company's CEO, put in a call to John and John—Vitro and Robertson, that is. John Vitro had been an outstanding art director for some time, and John Robertson was a great copywriter. But when they got together, they were even better. Call it *creative synergy*. The two Johns had been the principal creative team at Taylor Guitar's previous ad agency but had gone out on their own. Now, not only Taylor Guitar but also AirTouch Cellular (formerly PacTel) and Thermoscan wanted them back. And Chiat/Day, the L.A. agency they had worked for prior to moving to San Diego, wanted them to do some freelance work.

What did these guys have that everybody wanted?

For starters, they were winning more awards than any creative team around. And not just local medals, but major national honors from the New York Art Director's Club, the One Show, and the leading trade press. Vitro and Robertson never had great notions about owning an agency of their own, but with clients knocking their doors down, there seemed little choice. They formed VitroRobertson, and the clients started coming.

The first meetings with Taylor Guitar were successful. The agency and the client saw eye to eye and seemed to share similar values. Lustig and Taylor both understood marketing and advertising. They wanted advertising that would make a statement about the company and its ideals—not just words and pictures, but something genuine and visceral, yet subtle.

Their marketing problem was clear. In limited circles, people recognized the Taylor guitar as a quality instrument. But to the vast majority of amateur guitar enthusiasts, Taylor was completely unknown. Dealers told Rick Fagan, Taylor's national sales rep, "We know Taylor makes a great guitar, but our customers have never heard of it. Nobody knows the name." Vitro and Robertson had to develop a creative strategy that would put the Taylor name on the tongue of every serious guitarist. If the campaign was successful, these people would *ask* to strum a Taylor when considering their next instrument.

"We had plenty of research data to give them," said Fagan. The Johns looked at the research, listened to the founders, and reviewed guitar publications. Competitors used two general approaches, feature comparisons or celebrity artist endorsements.

Vitro and Robertson understood the parameters. To increase name recognition, Taylor's ads had to be completely different. They had to stand out, and they had to reflect the quality that goes into every Taylor guitar. Moreover, they had to appeal to the sensibilities of today's musicians. The ads should talk *to* them, not *at* them.

The creative process began. VitroRobertson started playing with ideas, putting them down on paper. "A lot of times, it's based on their gut instinct," says AirTouch/San Diego's marketing manager Mary Bianchetti, "and their gut instinct is usually very good."

The challenge was to integrate all the concepts into a single *big idea*. If they could accomplish that, they could develop individual messages for a series of ads. Unfortunately, finding the big idea is rarely a simple task. It's usually a frustrating, laborious process of developing an initial stream of concepts—5, 10, 20, whatever it takes. Sifting, sorting, evaluating, throwing them out and starting over again—90 percent perspiration, 10 percent inspiration.

Vitro and Robertson plugged away, discarding one concept after another. And then suddenly it came. The big idea was *trees.* Because *wood* came from trees.

They would use magnificent photos of trees—trees alone, trees in a forest, trees in the fog. Big photos. Not just a full-page ad but a *spread,* two full pages. And they would use very short, slightly humorous copy lines to speak about wood's subtle relationship with people's lives. In contrast to Taylor's competitors, they would appeal to the sensitive, emotional side of the marketplace *and* make their prospects think.

They prepared two-page, horizontal layouts of their ideas for Taylor and Lustig to evaluate. One ad featured a lone tree in a barren landscape. The headline read: "In its simplest form, a guitar is just a hollow box made of wood. It's up to you to decide how to fill it." Taylor and Lustig loved it. The proposed campaign passed the review, and the rest is history.

"The recognition has been fantastic," reports Rick Fagan. "No one mentions the name problem since these ads have appeared. And sales are up."

The recognition has also been good for VitroRobertson. The Taylor Guitar campaign has won national awards and been applauded in *Advertising Age* and *Adweek.* And when the Magazine Publishers of America invited Ken Mandelbaum, CEO of the New York agency Mandelbaum Mooney Ashley, to choose a favorite ad for its "I wish I'd done that ad" series, he chose a VitroRobertson ad for Taylor Guitars.[1] •

THE CREATIVE TEAM: THE AUTHORS AND ENCODERS OF ADVERTISING

In Chapter 1 we discussed the marketing communication process, in which a source encodes a message that is sent through a channel to be decoded by a receiver. The source is multidimensional, comprising a sponsor, an author, and a persona. In advertising, the *encoding* of messages—the conversion of mental concepts into symbols—is the responsibility of the creative team. While the client is the sponsor of the advertising, the creative team is the *author.*

Each member of the creative team plays an essential role. The team's **copywriter** develops the verbal message—the copy (words) within the ad spoken by the imaginary persona. The copywriter typically works with an **art director** who is responsible for the *nonverbal* aspect of the message—the design—that determines the visual look and intuitive feel of the ad. Together, they work under the supervision of a **creative director** (often a former copywriter) who is ultimately responsible for the creative product—the form the final ad takes. As a group, the people who work in the creative department are typically referred to as **creatives,** regardless of their specialty.

In the Taylor Guitar ads, we see how the creative team's taste, talent, and conceptual skill determine an ad's overall character and its ability to communicate.

This chapter focuses on the creative process—where it comes from, how it's developed, and its relationship to a company's marketing and advertising strategy. To get a proper perspective on creativity, we deal with strategy first.

FORMULATING ADVERTISING STRATEGY: THE KEY TO GREAT CREATIVE

While the text and the visual carry the ad message, behind the creative team's choice of tone, words, and ideas lies an advertising strategy. Let's look at the *advertising* (or *creative*) *strategy* Vitro and Robertson developed for Taylor Guitar. Then we'll see how they translated that into a *message strategy* and a big idea and, finally, into effective ads.

Recall from Chapter 7 that advertising strategy consists of four elements: the *target audience,* the *product concept,* the *communications media,* and the *advertising message.*

What is Taylor Guitar's target audience? Taylor's target audience comprises resellers, consumers, and centers of influence. Resellers (or retailers) are Taylor's *primary market*—that's who it sells to. So the company definitely wants them to see its advertising. Since they are hand-crafted from the highest quality materials, Taylor guitars command premium prices. Therefore, the primary target audience also includes a segment of the retailer's customers—serious musical enthusiasts who play acoustic guitars and are willing to spend between $2,000 and $5,000 for a superior instrument. Professional guitarists typically circumvent the normal distribution channels, so there was no reason to include them in the target market. However, they might act as *centers of influence* (or *key influentials*), in which case they would be a secondary target audience for the advertising.

What is Taylor Guitar's product concept? Taylor's acoustic guitars are top-quality, handcrafted musical instruments made from the finest woods available. They are designed and constructed differently from other guitars for a unique, distinguishable sound quality—a certain ring in the tone—that customers like. In other words, there is something special about a Taylor guitar that makes it worth more.

What communications media does Taylor use? The company has a small budget and uses limited media. It advertises in special-interest consumer magazines targeted to well-defined segments of the guitar enthusiast market. The magazines offer high-quality reproduction and color and are read by members of the trade as well as professional musicians. The company produces high-quality brochures and price lists that detail the instruments' features and construction.

What is Taylor Guitar's advertising message? In its simplest terms, **message strategy** is determined by what a company wants to say and how it wants to say it. Although Taylor was well known in the trade for its quality guitars, the word was not filtering down to the larger guitar-buying public. The goal (or message objective) was to get prospective customers to ask for the Taylor name when they shopped for a guitar. To accomplish this, the ads had to exude an aura of quality. So the agency creative team chose a message strategy that was simple yet thoughtful, entertaining, credible, and most of all, distinctive.

The agency and client team must understand and agree to these four elements of the advertising strategy—target, product, media, and message—before any creative work begins. In most agencies, the account management group is responsible for developing the advertising strategy. When that task is completed, it communicates the strategy to the creative department by preparing the *creative brief.*

Writing the Creative Brief (Copy Platform)

With the overall advertising objectives and strategy determined, the account managers (account planners in some agencies) write a brief statement of the intended advertising strategy. The **creative brief** serves as the creative team's guide for writing and producing the ad. In some agencies it may be referred to as a *copy platform,* a *work plan,* or a *copy* (or *creative*) *strategy* document. In all cases, though, it is a simple written statement of the most important issues to consider in the development of the ad or campaign—the who, why, what, where, and when.

- **Who?** Who is the prospect in terms of geographic, demographic, psychographic, and/or behavioristic qualities? What is the typical prospect's personality?
- **Why?** Does the consumer have specific wants or needs the ad should appeal to? Advertisers use two broad categories of appeals. Rational appeals are directed at the consumer's practical, functional need for the product or service; emotional appeals at the consumer's psychological, social, or symbolic needs. For a sampling of specific appeals within these categories, see Exhibit 9–1.
- **What?** Does the product have special features to satisfy the consumer's needs? What factors support the product claim? What is the product's position? What personality or image—of the product or the company—can be or has been created? What perceived strengths or weaknesses need to be dealt with?
- **Where and when will these messages be communicated?** Through what medium? What time of year? What area of the country?
- **Finally, what style, approach, or tone will the campaign use?** And, generally, what will the copy say?

Approach / Needs	Selected advertising appeals		
	Rational	Emotional	
Self-actualization	Opportunity for more leisure Efficiency in operation or use	Ambition Avoidance of laborious task Curiosity Entertainment	Pleasure of reaction Simplicity Sport/play/physical activity
Esteem	Dependability in quality Dependability in use Enhancement of earnings Variety of selection	Pride of personal appearance Pride of possession	Style/beauty Taste
Social	Cleanliness Economy in purchase	Cooperation Devotion to others Guilt Humor Home comfort	Romance Sex attraction Social achievement Social approval Sympathy for others
Safety	Durability Protection of others Safety	Fear Health	Security
Physiological	Rest or sleep	Appetite	Personal comfort

Exhibit • 9–1
Selected advertising appeals.

The creative brief identifies the benefits to be presented to consumers, but it avoids executional issues. *How* the benefits will be presented is the creative team's job.

Procter & Gamble and Leo Burnett use a simple creative brief with three parts:[2]

1. **An objective statement.** A specific, concise description of what the advertising is supposed to accomplish or what problem it is supposed to solve. The objective statement also includes the name of the brand and a brief, specific description of the target consumer. For example:

   Advertising will convince serious guitar players that the Taylor guitar is a distinctive, high-value instrument and persuade them to consider it the next time they are in the market for an acoustic guitar.

2. **A support statement.** A brief description of the evidence that backs up the product promise; the reason for the benefit. For example:

   Support is that Taylor guitars are handcrafted from the finest woods available, which gives the instrument a distinctive sweet sound.

3. **A tone or brand character statement.** A brief statement of either the advertising's tone or the long-term character of the brand. Tone statements are short-term emotional descriptions of the advertising strategy. Brand character statements are long-term descriptions of the enduring values of the brand—things that give the product brand equity. A tone statement might be phrased:

   The tone of Taylor Guitar advertising should convey beauty, quality, sophistication, and value, with just a touch of good-natured humor.

   On the other hand, a brand character statement might be phrased:

   Taylor Guitars — handcrafted from the finest materials to give the sweetest sound.

The delivery of the creative brief to the creative department concludes the process of developing an advertising strategy. It also marks the beginning of the next step: the *advertising creative process,* in which the creative team develops a *message strategy* and begins the search for the *big idea.* After writing the first ad, the copywriter should review the copy platform to see if the ad measures up. If it doesn't, the team must start again.

Elements of Message Strategy

The creative team is responsible for developing creative ideas for ads, commercials, and campaigns and for executing them. From the information given by the account team (in the creative brief) and any additional research it might perform, the creative team develops the message strategy. This may occur before, during, or after the creative process of searching for the big idea.

The **message strategy** (or **rationale**) is a simple description and explanation of an ad campaign's overall creative approach—what the advertising says, how it says it, and why. The message strategy has three components:

- **Verbal**—guidelines for what the advertising should say; considerations that affect the choice of words; and the relationship of the copy approach to the type of medium (or media) that will carry the message.

- **Nonverbal**—overall nature of the ad's graphics; any visuals that must be used; and the relationship of the graphics to the media in which the ad will appear.

- **Technical**—preferred execution approach and mechanical outcome including budget and scheduling limitations (often governed by the media involved); also any **mandatories**—specific requirements for every ad such as addresses, logos, slogans, and so on.

Because all these elements of the message strategy intertwine, they typically evolve simultaneously. Language affects imagery, and vice versa. However, the verbal elements are the starting point for most advertising campaigns.

The message strategy helps the creative team sell the ad or the campaign concept to the account managers and helps the managers explain and defend the creative work to the client. Of course, the message strategy must conform to the advertising strategy outlined in the creative brief or it will probably be rejected.

In the development of message strategy, certain basic questions need to be answered: How is the market segmented? How will the product be positioned? Who are the best prospects for the product? Is the target audience different from the target market? What is the key consumer benefit? What is the product's (or company's) current image? And what is the product's unique advantage?[3] At this point, research data is important. Research helps the creative team answer these questions.

HOW CREATIVITY ENHANCES ADVERTISING

The powerful use of imagery, copy, and even humor in the Taylor Guitar campaign demonstrates how creativity enhances advertising. But what exactly is creativity or the creative process? What is the role of creativity in advertising? And where does creativity come from?

What Is Creativity?

To create means to originate, to conceive a thing or idea that did not exist before. Typically, though, **creativity** involves combining two or more previously unconnected objects or ideas into something new. As Voltaire said, "Originality is nothing but judicious imitation."

Many people think creativity springs directly from human intuition. But as we'll see in this chapter, the creative process is a step-by-step procedure that can be learned and used to generate original ideas.

The Role of Creativity in Advertising

Advertisers often select an agency specifically for its creative style and its reputation for achieving original concepts. Creativity is vital to advertising's basic mission of informing, persuading, and reminding.

Creativity helps advertising inform

Advertising's responsibility to inform is greatly enhanced by creativity. Good creative work makes advertising more vivid, and many researchers believe vividness attracts attention, maintains interest, and stimulates consumers' thinking.[4] A common technique is to use plays on words and verbal or visual metaphors, such as "Put a tiger in your tank," "Fly the friendly skies," or "Own a piece of the rock." The metaphor describes one concept in terms of another, helping the reader or viewer learn about the product.[5]

Other creative techniques can also improve an ad's ability to inform. Advertising writers and artists must arrange visual and verbal message components according to a genre of social meaning so that readers or viewers can easily interpret an ad using commonly accepted symbols. For example, esthetic cues such as lighting, pose of the model, setting, and clothing style can signal viewers nonverbally whether a fashion ad reflects a romantic adventure or a sporting event.[6]

Creativity helps advertising persuade

The ancients created legends and myths about gods and heroes—symbols for humankind's instinctive, primordial longings and fears—to affect human behavior and thought. To motivate people to some action or attitude, advertising copywriters have created new myths and heroes, like the Jolly Green Giant and the Energizer Bunny. A creative story or persona can establish an original identity for the product in the collective mindset—a key factor in helping a product beat the competition.

Creativity also helps position a product on the top rung of consumers' mental ladders. The Taylor Guitar ads, for example, suggest metaphorically that the personal touch of Taylor's artisans can caress trees into making beautiful music. The higher form

SShhh. Listen real closely and you can hear the sound of handcrafted guitars being shaped from special woods. Oddly enough, the sound's coming from El Cajon, California. Write us: 1940 Gillespie Way, El Cajon, CA 92020.

● Taylor creatively suggests its artisans can coax trees into making beautiful music. The small print reinforces the concept and invites prospective customers to write in: *Sshhh. Listen real closely and you can hear the sound of handcrafted guitars being shaped from special woods. Oddly enough, the sound's coming from El Cajon, California. Write us: 1940 Gillespie Way, El Cajon, CA 92020.*

The Psychological Impact of Color   *Ad Lab 9–A*

National origin or culture can play a role in color preferences. For example, warm colors—red, yellow, and orange—tend to stimulate, excite, and create an active response. People from warmer climes, apparently, are most responsive to these colors. Certain color combinations stimulate ethnic connotations. Metallic golds with reds, for example, are associated with China. Turquoise and beige are associated with the Indian tribes of the American Southwest.

Colors can impart lifestyle preferences. Vivid primary colors (red, blue, yellow) juxtaposed with white stripes exude decisiveness and are often used in sporting events as team colors. Thus, they are associated with a sporting lifestyle.

The colors we experience during the four seasons often serve as guides for combining colors and for guessing the temperaments of individuals who dress themselves or decorate their house in specific seasonal colors. Spring colors such as yellows, greens, and light blues, for example, suggest a fresh, exuberant character. Winter colors such as dark blues, deep violets, and black are associated with cool, chilly attitudes.

Because we usually feel refreshed from sleeping, we associate the colors of the morning—emerald green, raspberry, and pale yellow—with exuberance. And because the mellow colors of sunset predominate when we're usually home relaxing after work, we may associate sunset colors—peach, turquoise, and red-orange—with relaxation and reflective moods.

Some colors are ambiguous. Violet and leaf green fall on the line between warm and cool. They can be either, depending on the shade.

Here are some more observations:

 Red

Symbol of blood and fire. Second to blue as people's favorite color but more versatile, the hottest color with highest "action quotient." Appropriate for soups, frozen foods, and meats. Conveys strong masculine appeal, so is often used for shaving cream containers.

Brown

Another masculine color associated with earth, woods, mellowness, age, warmth, comfort. Used to sell anything, even cosmetics (Revlon's Braggi). *Concerned w/ bodily function.*

Yellow

High impact to catch consumer's eye, particularly when used with black. Good for corn, lemon, or suntan products.

 Green

Symbol of health and freshness; popular for mint products and soft drinks (7UP). *earthy, money*

 Blue

Coldest color with most appeal; effective for frozen foods (ice impression); if used with lighter tints becomes "sweet" (Yoplait yogurt, Lowenbrau beer, Wondra flour).

Black

Conveys sophistication and high-end merchandise, and is used to stimulate purchase of expensive products. Good as background and foil for other colors.

 Orange

Most "edible" color, especially in brown-tinged shades; evokes autumn and good things to eat. *Hostile*

Laboratory Application

Explain the moods or feelings that are stimulated by two color ads or packages illustrated in this text.

---

of expression creates a grander impression. And when such an impression spreads through the market, the product's perceived value also rises.

To be persuasive, an ad's verbal message must be reinforced by the creative use of nonverbal message elements. Artists govern the use of these elements—color, layout, and illustration, for example—to increase vividness. Research suggests that, in print media, *information graphics* (colorful explanatory charts, tables, etc.) can raise the perception of quality for some readers.[7] Artwork can also stimulate emotions. Color, for example, can often motivate consumers depending on their cultural background and personal experiences (see Ad Lab 9–A, The Psychological Impact of Color).

Creativity helps advertising remind

Imagine using the same invitation, without any innovation, to ask people to try your product again and again, year after year. Your invitation would become stale very quickly—worse, it would become tiresome. Only creativity can transform your boring reminders into interesting, entertaining advertisements. Nike is proof. Several commercials in a Nike campaign never mentioned the company name or even spelled it on the screen. The ads told stories. And the only on-screen cue identifying the sponsor was the single, elongated "swoosh" logo inscribed on the final scene. A Nike spokesperson said the ads weren't risky "given the context that the Nike logo is so well known."[8] We are entertained daily by creative ads—for soft drinks, snacks, and cereals—whose primary mission is simply to remind us to indulge again.

• Nike creatives believe the product's name is so well known that reminder ads like these using only the Nike logo and the "Just do it" slogan are sufficient product identifiers.

Women's Aerobics/Dance
This is for every boy who didn't ask me to dance

This is for relatives who said I probably just had big bones
This is because I can scream, and no one will think I'm hysterical,

Maybe
This is because there's music and crowds
Because if my body's a temple,
This temple is going to move.

Understanding Creative Thinking

Some people exhibit more of it than others, but creativity lives within all of us. Human creativity, developed over millions of years, enabled our ancestors to survive. Without creativity we wouldn't have discovered how to harness fire, domesticate animals, irrigate fields, or manufacture tools. As individuals, we use our natural creativity every time we select a wardrobe in the morning, style our hair, contrive an excuse, decorate our home, cook a meal, or choose a costume for a party.

Styles of thinking

At the turn of the century, the German sociologist Max Weber determined that people think in two ways: in an objective, rational, fact-based manner and in a qualitative, intuitive, value-based manner. For example, in studying for a test, we use our rational, fact-based style of thinking. On the other hand, when we buy a car, we call on taste, intuition, and knowledge to make a qualitative value judgment of the car's features, styling, and performance weighed against its price.

In the late 1950s, the theories of convergent and divergent thinking described how one can process concepts by narrowing or expanding one's assortment of ideas.[9] In the late 1970s, researchers discovered the left side of the brain controls logical functions and the right controls intuitive functions. In the 1980s, social scientists Allen Harrison and Robert Bramson defined five categories of thinking: the synthesist, the idealist, the pragmatist, the analyst, and the realist. They concluded that the analyst and realist fit Max Weber's fact category and the synthesist and idealist fit his value category.[10]

Roger von Oech defined this dichotomy as hard and soft thinking. *Hard thinking* refers to concepts like logic, reason, precision, consistency, work, reality, analysis, and specificity. *Soft thinking* refers to less tangible concepts: metaphor, dream, humor, ambiguity, play, fantasy, hunch. On the hard side, things are right or wrong, black or white. On the soft side, there may be many right answers and many shades of gray.[11]

Also in the 80s, Alessandra and Wexler developed a model featuring four types of personalities and relationship behaviors based on assertiveness and responsiveness factors (the relater, the socializer, the director, and the thinker).[12] The relater and the socializer exhibit value-based characteristics and the director and the thinker display fact-based traits.

Fact-based versus value-based thinking

Most theories of thinking fit into two general categories: value-based or fact-based. Let's examine these styles of thinking more closely.

People whose preferred style of thinking is **fact-based** tend to fragment concepts into components and to analyze situations to discover the one best solution. Although fact-based people can be creative, they tend to be linear thinkers and prefer to have facts and figures—hard data—they can analyze and control. They are not comfortable with ambiguous situations. They like logic, structure, and efficiency.[13]

In contrast, **value-based** thinkers make decisions based on intuition, values, and ethical judgments. They are better able to embrace change, conflict, and paradox. This style fundamentally relies on melding concepts together. Value-based thinkers, for example, attempt to integrate the divergent ideas of a group into an arrangement that lets everyone win. They are good at using their imagination to produce a flow of new ideas and at synthesizing existing concepts to create something new.[14]

How styles of thinking affect creativity

If the creative team prefers a value-based thinking style, it tends to produce ads like those in the Taylor Guitar and Nike campaigns—soft, subtle, intuitive, metaphorical. That's fine if the client also prefers that style of thinking.

On the other hand, clients who prefer a fact-based style often seek agencies that produce practical, hard-edged work characterized by simple, straightforward layouts, rational appeals, and lots of data. In fact, a value-based campaign may be unsettling to a fact-based client.

The Saatchi & Saatchi ad campaign for Hewlett-Packard's laser printers, for example, created a stir at Hewlett-Packard. The ads simulated interviews. The actors portrayed harried customers, talking about how they didn't have time to think about their printers. "Some people within Hewlett-Packard are somewhat uncomfortable with the direction of the campaign," reported Arlene King, a marketing communications man-

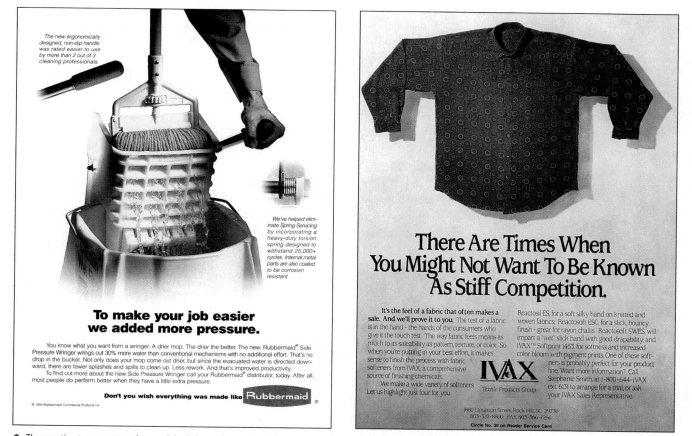

● The creative team must understand the information needs of the target audience. Fact-based business-to-business ads like these use straightforward layouts, rational appeals, and pertinent data. The Rubbermaid ad appeared in *Cleaning and Maintenance Management* magazine; the IVAX ad to clothing manufacturers ran in *Apparel Industry* magazine.

ager for H-P, "because we are a high-tech company and the ads don't focus on any aspect of the technology."[15]

The creative team needs to understand the campaign's target audience. In some market segments—computers, for example—customers may tend toward one style of thinking more than another. And that could dictate which approach to use.

As we shall see in the next section, the best art directors and copywriters use both styles to accomplish the necessary task. In the creative process, they need to use their imagination (value-based thinking) to develop a variety of concepts. But to select the best alternative and get the job done, they probably have to use the fact-based style.

THE CREATIVE PROCESS: DIFFERING VIEWS

The **creative process** is the step-by-step procedure used to discover original ideas and reorganize existing concepts in new ways. By following it people can improve their ability to unearth possibilities, cross-associate concepts, and select winning ideas.

Over the years, many notions of the creative process have been proposed (see Exhibit 9–2). Although similar, each format has unique merits. In 1926, British sociologist Graham Wallas published his view that the creative process involved four steps: preparation, incubation, illumination, and verification.[16] In 1963, Alex Osborn, the former head of BBDO, published a seven-step model: orientation, preparation, analysis, ideation, incubation, synthesis, and evaluation.[17] Twenty years later, an even more comprehensive model by James Young was published in *Marketing News* (see RL 9–1 in the Reference Library).[18] Then, in 1986, Roger von Oech published a four-step creative model used today by many Fortune 100 companies. Each step in the process is a role: the Explorer, the Artist, the Judge, and the Warrior.[19]

Any of these models can be effective depending on your style of thinking. The more complex models appeal to fact-based thinkers. The simpler four-step models are preferred by the value-based thinkers.

The new generation of advertising creatives will face a world of ever-growing complexity. They must handle the many challenges of integrated marketing communications (IMC) as they help their clients build relationships with highly fragmented target markets. They will need to understand the wide range of new technologies affecting advertising (new computer hardware and software, electronic networking, high-definition television, etc.). And they will have to learn how to advertise to emerging international markets. To do this, they need a model that handles many situations simply.

Hence, we use von Oech's four-step model. It offers flexibility for fact-based thinkers and value-based thinkers alike. Von Oech describes four distinct roles in the creative process:

1. **The Explorer**—searches for new information, paying attention to unusual patterns.
2. **The Artist**—experiments and plays with a variety of approaches, looking for an original idea.

Exhibit • 9–2
The creative process: A comparison.

Roger von Oech model 1986	Graham Wallas model 1926	Alex Osborn model 1963	James Young model 1983
1. Explorer	1. Preparation	1. Orientation 2. Preparation	1. Problem definition 2. Perception
2. Artist	2. Incubation 3. Illumination	3. Analysis 4. Ideation 5. Incubation 6. Synthesis	3. Confrontation with the problem 4. Incubation and illumination
3. Judge			5. Concept(s)
4. Warrior	4. Verification	7. Evaluation	6. Execution 7. Run ad or campaign 8. Outcome

3. **The Judge**—evaluates the results of experimentation and decides which approach is most practical.
4. **The Warrior**—overcomes excuses, idea killers, setbacks, and obstacles to bring a creative concept to realization.

Copywriters and art directors thrive on the challenge of creating advertising messages—the encoding process. But first they need the raw materials for ideas: facts, experiences, history, knowledge, feelings. That's the role of the **Explorer.**

The creatives start by examining the information they have. They review the creative brief and the marketing and advertising plan; they study the market, the product, and the competition. (See RL 9–2, Checklist of Product Marketing Facts for Creatives in the Reference Library.) They may seek additional input from the agency's account managers and from the client side (sales, marketing, product, or research managers).

When John Vitro and John Robertson began work for Taylor Guitar, they first assumed the Explorer role. They spoke with people about the nature of the company, its products, its marketing history, its competitors, and the competitors' styles of advertising. They reviewed all appropriate sources of advertising for acoustic guitars and studied the company's marketing environment.

THE EXPLORER'S ROLE: GATHERING INFORMATION

Develop an Insight Outlook

In advertising, the Explorer gets off the beaten path to look in new and uncommon places for information—to discover new ideas and to identify unusual patterns. Vitro and Robertson might have hiked in the wilderness to spark a new idea for Taylor Guitar. Or they could have opened a book on national parks and experienced the same flash.

Von Oech suggests adopting an "insight outlook" (a positive belief that good information is available and that you have the skills to find and use it). This means opening up to the outside world to receive new knowledge. Ideas are everywhere: visit a museum, an art gallery, a hardware store, the airport. The more divergent the sources, the greater your chance of uncovering an original concept.

Know the Objective

If people know what they're looking for, they have a better chance of finding it. Think about the color blue. Now look around you. Note how blue suddenly jumps out at you. If you hadn't been looking for it, you probably wouldn't have noticed it.

Philosopher John Dewey said, "A problem well-stated is a problem half-solved." This is why the creative brief is so important. It helps define what the creatives are looking for. The creatives typically start working on the message strategy during the Explorer stage because it, too, helps them define what they're looking for.

To get their creative juices flowing, most copywriters and art directors maintain an extensive library of advertising award books and trade magazines. Many also keep a tickler (or *swipe*) file of ads they like that might give them direction.

Brainstorm

As Explorers, the art director and copywriter look first for lots of ideas. One technique is **brainstorming,** a process (invented by Alex Osborn of BBDO) in which two or more people get together to generate new ideas. A brainstorming session is often a source of sudden inspirations. To succeed, it must follow a couple of rules: all ideas are above criticism (no idea is "wrong") and all ideas are written down for later review. The goal is to record any inspiration that comes to mind, a process that psychologists call *free association,* allowing each new idea an opportunity to stimulate another.

Von Oech suggests other techniques for Explorers: leave your own turf (look in outside fields and industries for ideas that could be transferred); shift your focus (pay attention to a variety of information); look at the big picture (stand back and see what it all means); don't overlook the obvious (the best ideas are right in front of your nose); don't be afraid to stray (you might find something you weren't looking for); and stake your claim to new territory (write down any new ideas or they will be lost).

The Explorer's job is to find new information for the Artist to use. But to be effective, explorers must exercise flexibility, courage, and openness.[20]

THE ARTIST'S ROLE I: DEVELOPING THE BIG IDEA

For creative people, the role of the **Artist** is both the toughest and the most rewarding. It's the long, tedious, difficult task of reviewing all the pertinent information gathered by the Explorer, analyzing the problem, and searching for a key verbal or visual concept to communicate what needs to be said. It means creating a mental picture of the ad or commercial before any copy is written or artwork begun.

This step (also called **visualization** or **conceptualization**) is the most important in creating the advertisement. It's where the search for the *big idea*—that flash of insight—takes place. The **big idea** is a bold, creative initiative that builds on the strategy, joins the product benefit with consumer desire in a fresh involving way, brings the subject to life, and makes the reader or the audience stop, look, and listen.[21]

What's the difference between a strategy and a big idea? A strategy describes the direction the message should take. A big idea gives it life. For example, the creative brief discussed earlier for the Taylor Guitar campaign contains a strategic brand character statement:

Taylor Guitars—handcrafted from the finest materials to give the sweetest sound.

Vitro and Robertson could have used that strategy statement as a headline. But it would have been dreadfully dull for an ad aimed at musicians. It lacks what a big idea

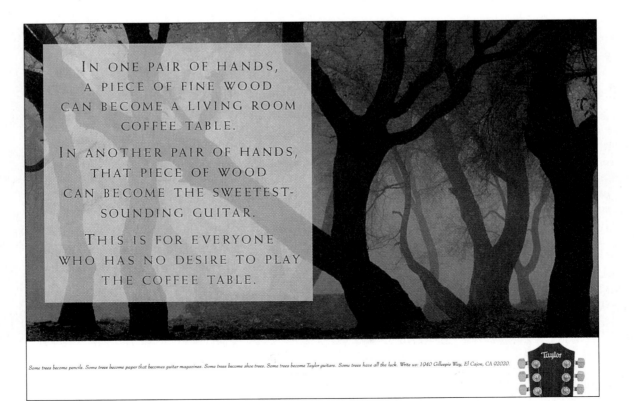

• Taylor Guitar ads run as large, high-quality two-page spreads in guitar magazines. The small print in this reduced reproduction continues the witty approach of the headline: *Some trees become pencils. Some trees become paper that becomes guitar magazines. Some trees become shoe trees. Some trees become Taylor guitars. Some trees have all the luck. Write us: 1940 Gillespie Way, El Cajon, CA 92020.*

headline delivers: a set of multiple meanings that create interest, memorability, and, in some cases, drama. Note the long, provocative, slightly poetic, and very witty headline that Vitro and Robertson chose to convey the same strategic concept:

> In one pair of hands, a piece of wood can become a living room coffee table.
>
> In another pair of hands, that piece of wood can become the sweetest-sounding guitar.
>
> This is for everyone who has no desire to play the coffee table.

John O'Toole said, "While strategy requires deduction, a big idea requires inspiration."[22] The big idea in advertising is almost invariably expressed through a combination of art and copy. And most ads use a specific word or phrase to connect the text to the images, like "wood" in the Taylor Guitar ad. Think what this ad would look like without the beautiful visual of the trees in the background, with just the headline and body copy on an otherwise bare page. They could have saved a lot of money. But how much would they have lost because of low readership?

Transforming Concepts: Do Something to It

Creative ideas come from manipulating and transforming resources. Von Oech points out that the Artist has to do something to the materials the Explorer has collected to give them value. That means asking lots of questions: What if I added this? Or took that away? Or looked at it backwards? Or compared it to something else? The Artist has to change patterns and experiment with various approaches.

Vitro and Robertson had two concepts to begin with: "guitar" and "music." Looking at the guitar, they noted it was made of wood—special wood. So "wood" became a third concept. Thinking about wood led them to "trees." Interesting notion. But now they had to determine how they could turn these four concepts into a "big idea."

A good Artist has many strategies for transforming things. Von Oech suggests several techniques for manipulating ideas:[23]

1. **Adapt.** Change contexts. Think what else the product might be besides the obvious. A Campbell's Soup ad showed a steaming bowl of tomato soup with a bold headline underneath: "HEALTH INSURANCE."

2. **Imagine.** Ask what if. Let your imagination fly. Be zany. What if people could do their chores in their sleep? What if animals drank in saloons? Clyde's Bar in Georgetown actually used that idea. The ad showed a beautifully illustrated elephant and donkey dressed in business suits and seated at a table toasting one another. The headline: "Clyde's. The People's Choice."

3. **Reverse.** Look at it backward. Sometimes the opposite of what is expected has great impact and memorability. A cosmetics company ran an ad for its moisturizing cream under the line: "Introduce your husband to a younger woman." A vintage Volkswagen ad used the line: "Ugly is only skin deep."

4. **Connect.** Join two unrelated ideas together. Ask yourself: What ideas can I connect to my concept? A Sunkist billboard showed a salt shaker cap on a lemon. The headline: "S'alternative." To get people to send for its catalog, Royal Caribbean Cruises ran an ad that showed the catalog cover under the simple headline: "Sail by Mail."

5. **Compare.** Take one idea and use it to describe another. Ever notice how bankers talk like plumbers? "Flood the market, laundered money, liquid assets, cash flow, take a bath, float a loan." The English language is awash in metaphors because they help people understand. Jack in the Box advertised its onion rings by picturing them on a billboard and inviting motorists to "Drive thru for a ring job." An elegant magazine ad for the Parker Premier fountain pen used this sterling metaphor: "It's wrought from pure silver and writes like pure silk."

6. **Eliminate.** Subtract something. Or break the rules. In advertising, there's little virtue in doing things the way they've always been done. Seven-Up became fa-

● Creative humor and parody in ads can catch the attention of the prospective customer. This outdoor ad for Mattel's Frisbee® discs relies on role reversal and off-the-board layout to intrigue viewers, and gets the message across with minimum copy to boot.

mous by advertising what it wasn't ("the Uncola") and succeeded in positioning itself as a refreshing alternative. And Federal Express exceeded all the guidelines for length of copy in a TV commercial with its famous fast-talking Mr. Spleen. It also won all the advertising awards that year, and business skyrocketed.

7. **Parody.** Fool around. Have some fun. Tell some jokes—especially when you're under pressure. There is a close relationship between the *ha-ha* experience of humor and the *aha!* experience of creative discovery. Humor stretches our thinking, and, used in good taste, makes for some great advertising. A classical radio station ran a newspaper ad: "Handel with care." Fila USA got a rave review from *Advertising Age* for its "bizarre, absolutely hilarious, and totally cool" spot of a praying mantis racing up a leaf stem in Fila sneakers to escape his murderous mate.[24]

Blocks to Creativity

Everybody experiences a time when the creative juices just won't flow. There are many causes: information overload, mental or physical fatigue, stress, fear, insecurity. Often, though, the problem is simply the style of thinking being used.

In the Explorer stage, when creatives study reams of marketing data, the facts and figures on sales and share of market may put them in a fact-based frame of mind. But to create effectively, they need to shift gears to a value-based style of thinking.

As von Oech says, "Creative thinking requires an attitude that allows you to search for ideas and manipulate your knowledge and experience."[25] Unfortunately, it is sometimes difficult for creatives to make that mental switch instantaneously. Von Oech recommends some techniques to stimulate integrative thinking. For example: look for the second right answer (there is usually more than one answer to any problem, and the second may be more creative); seek cross-fertilization (TV people could learn a lot from teachers, and vice versa); slay a sacred cow (sacred cows make great steaks); imagine how others would do it (stretch the imagination by role playing); laugh at it (make up jokes about what you're doing); and reverse your viewpoint (open up your thinking and discover things you typically overlook).[26]

George Gier, the creative partner and cofounder of the Leap Partnership, said, "The only thing agencies have left to sell to clients that they can't get anywhere else is creative ideas."[27] Creative blocks can indeed be bad for an agency.

Creative blocking may occur when people in the agency start "thinking like the client," especially if the client is a fact-based thinker. This can also be hazardous to the agency's creative reputation and is one reason agencies sometimes resign accounts over "creative differences." An agency can eliminate a lot of frustration and wasted time and money by evaluating the client's corporate culture, its collective style of thinking, and its creative comfort level in advance.

Creative fatigue sometimes happens when an agency has served an account for a long time and all the fresh ideas have been worked and reworked. It can also happen when a client has rejected a series of concepts. The inspiration is lost and the creatives start trying to force ideas. The creative team suddenly finds it hard to shift its style of thinking or to crank up the creative process again. If this becomes chronic, the only solutions may be to appoint an entirely new creative team or resign the account.

Incubating Concepts: Do Nothing to It

When the brain is overloaded with information about a problem, creatives sometimes find it's best to just walk away from it for a while, do something else, and let the unconscious mind mull it over. This approach yields several benefits. First, it puts the problem back into perspective. It also rests the brain, lets the problem incubate in the subconscious, and enables better ideas to percolate to the top. Upon returning to the task, the creatives frequently discover a whole new set of assumptions.

Once the creatives latch onto the big idea, they have to focus on how to implement it. When Vitro and Robertson suddenly thought "trees" and connected that idea to "guitars" and "music," they then had to translate that concept into a tangible ad. This is where the real art of advertising comes in—writing the exact words, designing the precise layout. To have a sense of how advertising creatives do that, we need to understand what *art* is in advertising, how artistic elements and tools are selected and used, and the difference between good art and bad art.

In advertising, art shapes the message into a complete communication that appeals to the senses as well as the mind. So while **art direction** refers to the act or process of managing the *visual* presentation of the ad, the term **art** actually refers to the *whole* presentation—visual, verbal, and aural—of the commercial or advertisement. For example, the artful selection of words not only communicates information but also stimulates positive feelings for the product. An artfully designed typeface not only makes reading easier, it also evokes a mood. By creatively arranging format elements—surrounding the text with lines, boxes, and colors, and relating them to one another in proportion—the art director can further enhance the ad's message. Art also shapes the style of photography and illustration. An intimate style uses soft focus and close views, a documentary style portrays the scene without pictorial enhancements, and a dramatic style features unusual angles or blurred action images.

In short, if *copy* is the verbal language of an ad, *art* is the body language. TV uses both sight and sound to involve viewers. Radio commercials use sound to create *word pictures* in the minds of listeners. The particular blend of writing, visuals, and sounds makes up an ad's expressive character. So while the quality may vary, every ad uses art.

In advertising, balance, proportion, and movement are guides for uniting images, type, sounds, and colors into a single communication. The art director uses these principles to organize sounds, images, and words so they relate to and enhance one another.

In Chapter 7 we discussed the advertising pyramid as a model for setting advertising objectives based on how people typically behave in a learn-feel-do situation. The **creative pyramid** uses a similar five-step structure (see Exhibit 9–3) to help the creative team convert the advertising strategy and the big idea into the actual physical ad or

THE ARTIST'S ROLE II: IMPLEMENTING THE BIG IDEA

THE CREATIVE PYRAMID: A GUIDE TO FORMULATING COPY AND ART

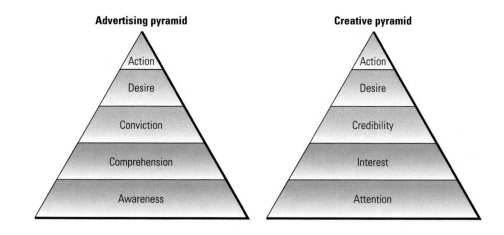

commercial. It is based on the cognitive theory of how people learn new information (discussed in Chapter 4).

The purpose of advertising copy and design is to persuade or remind prospective customers to take some action to satisfy a need or want. But first they need to be made aware of the problem or, if the problem is obvious, of a solution. To create awareness, the creatives must first get prospects' *attention.* Next, the creatives must stimulate the prospect's *interest* in the product and build *credibility* for the product claims. Then they focus on generating *desire,* and finally on stimulating *action.* These five elements should be artistically handled in some way in every ad or commercial.

Ethical Issue Does Sex Appeal?

The use of sexual appeals in advertising is highly controversial. For decades, we've heard the cliché that "sex sells." However, some advertising decisionmakers are reluctant to even acknowledge that sex is used in advertising. They have good reason. Some consumer activist groups charge that ads featuring nudity or strong sexual content are obscene or at least indecent.

This is an important distinction. Obscene material is *illegal;* indecent material is not. Obscenity involves three conditions: it appeals to prurient interests (lustful desires); it is patently offensive; and it lacks any redeeming value. In general, most ads with sexual appeals do not meet these criteria.

However, some ads might indeed be seen as indecent. Indecency is in the eye of the beholder. If enough beholders believe sexually oriented material is indecent, then this belief becomes reflected in community standards. In the case of advertising, the media and various citizen pressure groups become the enforcers of community standards. They won't allow advertising that offends community standards to air.

Sexual appeals can evoke positive reactions as well as negative ones. Where do we draw the line? Print ads for Obsession perfume and cologne by Calvin Klein, which typically feature a nude couple in a suggestive position, are characteristic of the genre. Some people like them. Some don't. Are these ads sexy or sexist? Many advertisers find it increasingly difficult to predict how viewers will perceive that distinction. Most feminists, for example, don't object to sexual appeals in advertising if the woman is in control of her sexuality rather than being shown passively or as a victim.

The real ethical conflict over sexual appeals in advertising takes place between the proponents of *choice enhancement* (which increases consumer choices and encourages individual responsibility) and *consumer protection* (which limits certain choices to promote some good for the community at large). Choice enhancement proponents seek to extend the boundaries of what is permissible; consumer protection proponents seek to restrict these appeals.

There is no simple solution to the dilemma of ad sex. Advertisers need to consider, on a case-by-

case basis, at what point sexual appeals become unethical and therefore counterproductive. Diet Coke raised a few eyebrows with a commercial

---

There is no simple solution to the dilemma of ad sex. Advertisers need to consider, on a case-by-case basis, at what point sexual appeals become unethical and therefore counterproductive.

---

featuring businesswomen gathering at an office window to watch a shirtless male construction worker take a Diet Coke break. With women making up 65 percent of soft-drink buyers, it's no surprise that Nancy Gibson, worldwide brand manager for Diet Coke, says, "Usually, we have made absolutely sure the female appeal is there."

Advertising Age columnist Bob Garfield suggested this ad offers women "psychic benefits" by taking a particular point of view, but it does so at the expense of men. However, it turned out that younger men in the Diet Coke focus groups seemed to appreciate the sentiment, and women loved it.

Attention

An ad or commercial is a stimulus. It must break through consumers' physiological screens to create the kind of attention that leads to perception. *Attention,* therefore, is the first objective of any ad and the fundamental building block in the creative pyramid. The Artist may spend as much time and energy figuring out how to express the big idea in an interesting, attention-getting way as searching for the big idea itself.

Print ads often use the headline as the major attention-getting device. The copywriter's goal is to write a headline that expresses the big idea with verve. Usually designed to appear in the largest and boldest type in the ad, the headline is often the strongest focal point conceptually as well as visually. Many other devices also help gain attention (in print media: dynamic visuals, unusual layout, vibrant color, or dominant ad size; in electronic media: special sound effects, music, animation, or unusual visual techniques).

Some factors are beyond the creatives' control. The budget may determine the size of the ad or length of the commercial. And that may influence how well or quickly it penetrates consumers' screens. Similarly, a TV spot's position in a cluster of commercials between shows or an ad's position in a publication may determine who sees it.

The attention-getting device should create drama, power, impact, and intensity, and it must be appropriate—relate to the product, to the tone of the ad, and to the needs or interests of the intended audience. This is especially true in business-to-business advertising where rational appeals and fact-based thinking dominate.

Headlines that promise something but fail to deliver in a credible manner won't make a sale; in fact, they may alienate a potential customer. Ads that use racy headlines

---

Similarly, an executive on the Valvoline advertising account justified the use of "girlie calendars" for mechanics by noting, "It may offend some groups—but they aren't your customers."

Cultural norms have a strong influence on a society's ethics. And consumer activist groups have successfully changed some cultural norms. Before World War II advertisers portrayed women as managers of the household, but afterward they treated women like little dolls. Ads told women that housework was the way to please a man or to get one. Feminist leader Betty Friedan reports that the move away from "being sold this endless sacrificial housework" by advertising is "real progress" for women.

Ad agencies have sought the advice of women's advocates. Feminist consultants now pass judgment on ads every day to ensure they are not offensive.

Agencies can be stung by not using such consultants. Stroh Brewery now stays away from anything that could be remotely called sexist after getting burned by adverse publicity over a 1991 Swedish Bikini Team campaign for its Old Mil-

waukee beer. The campaign was intended as a parody of both old beer ads and the brand's own old ads, but consumers didn't take it as such.

Research shows that sexual appeals are most effective when the sexuality is related to the product. When it is not, it may distract audiences from the main message. Another consideration is the effect on targeted customers versus the impact on others, such as children, who might be indirectly affected.

Nevertheless, it remains difficult for industry or government policymakers to know how to treat ad sex in a way satisfactory to everyone—or perhaps even to anyone.

Questions

1. How would you explain the "redeeming value" of sexual appeals in advertising?

2. If ad sex is considered okay by audiences that are directly targeted, what responsibility does the advertiser have for any effect on indirect targets, such as children? How can advertisers protect themselves from this problem?

Sources: Adrienne Ward Fawcett, "Friedan Sees Real Progress in Woman's Ads," *Advertising Age Special Report: Marketing to Women,* October 4, 1993, pp. S-1, S-2; John S. Ford and Michael S. LaTour, "Different Reactions to Female Role Portrayals in Advertising," *Journal of Advertising Research,* September/October 1993, p. 43; Stephen J. Gould, "Sexuality and Ethics in Advertising: A Research Agenda and Policy Guideline Perspective," *Journal of Advertising,* September 1994, pp. 73–79; Michael S. LaTour and Tony L. Henthorne, "Ethical Judgments of Sexual Appeals in Print Adver-tising," *Journal of Advertising,* September 1994, pp. 80–90; N. Craig Smith and John A. Quelch, "Ethical Issues in Researching and Targeting Consumers," *Ethics in Marketing* (Homewood, IL: Richard D. Irwin, 1993), pp. 190–92; Daniel Riffe, Patricia C. Place, and Charles M. Mayo, "Game Time, Soap Time and Prime Time TV Ads: Treatment of Women in Sunday Football and Rest-of-Week Advertising," *Journalism Quarterly,* Summer 1993, pp. 437–46; Delia M. Rios, Newhouse News Service, "Provocative Coke Ads Engender Delight, Disgust," *San Diego Union-Tribune,* January 31, 1994, p. E-4; Ira Teinowitz, "Days of 'Beer and Babes' Running Out," *Advertising Age Special Report: Marketing to Women,* October 4, 1993, p. S-8.

or nude figures unrelated to the product often lose sales because prospects can't purchase the item that first attracted their attention.

Interest

Interest, the second step in the creative pyramid, is extremely important. It carries the prospective customer—now paying attention—to the body of the ad. It must keep the prospect excited as the information becomes more detailed. To do this, the copywriter may answer a question asked in the attention step or add facts that relate to the headline. To maintain audience interest, the tone and language should be compatible with the target market's attitude.

The writer and designer must lead prospects from one step to the next. Research shows that people read what interests them and ignore what doesn't, so the writer must maintain prospects' interest at all times.[28] One way to do so is to relate to prospects' psychological screens by talking about their problems, their needs, and how the product or service answers these. Copywriters use the word *you* frequently.

There are many effective ways to stimulate interest: a dramatic situation, a story, cartoons, or charts. In radio, copywriters use sound effects or catchy dialog. Television frequently uses quick cuts to maintain interest. We discuss some of these techniques in later chapters on advertising production.

Credibility

The third step in the creative pyramid is to establish *credibility* for the product or service. Customers today are sophisticated and skeptical. They want claims to be backed up by facts. Comparison ads can build credibility, but they must be relevant to customers' needs—and fair.

Well-known presenters may lend credibility to commercials. For example, TV personality Candice Bergen effectively represents Sprint with her personable, believable, down-to-earth style.

Advertisers often show independent test results to substantiate product claims. To work, such "proofs" must be valid, not just statistical manipulation. Advertisers and agencies must remember that many consumers have extensive product knowledge, even in specialized areas.

● TV commercials stimulate interest with quick cuts from one scene to another. Here subtitles translate as Scandinavian speed skaters confer before a practice session.

So that's the famous Skippy.

Bonnie Blair

SKATER 1: So that's the famous Skippy—the one Bonnie Blair uses? SKATER 2: Yeah. SKATER 1: Do you think it really helps you skate faster? SKATER 2: Well, she's won five gold medals. *The skaters slather Skippy on their skate blades. Camera cuts to* BONNIE BLAIR: Actually, I found Skippy works better if you *eat* it, like I've been doing before every race my entire life.

[Is it OK to make fun of the foreign skaters? Sure. There's plenty of room for good-natured humor about misunderstandings people from different countries have about one another.]

Desire

In the *desire* step, the writer encourages prospects to picture themselves enjoying the benefits of the product or service. Essentially, they are invited to visualize.

In print ads, copywriters initiate visualization by using phrases like "Picture yourself" or "Imagine." In TV, the main character pulls a sparkling clean T-shirt from the washer, smiles, and says "Yeah!" In radio, the announcer says, "You'll look your best."

The desire step hints at the possibilities and lets the consumer's mind take over. If prospects feel they're being led by the nose, they may feel insulted, resent the ad, and lose interest in the product. In some cases, writers maintain this delicate balance by having a secondary character agree with the main character and prattle off a few more product benefits. The secondary character retains the integrity of the main character, the one audiences relate to best.

The desire step is one of the most difficult to write—and that may be why some copywriters omit it.

Action

The final step up the creative pyramid is *action*. The purpose is to motivate people to do something—send in a coupon, call the number on the screen, visit the store—or at least to agree with the advertiser.

This block of the pyramid reaches the smallest audience but those with the most to gain from the product's utility. So the last step is often the easiest. If the copy is clear about what readers need to do and commands them to act, chances are they *will* act. (See Ad Lab 9–B: Applying the Creative Pyramid to Advertising.)

The call to action may be explicit: "Call for additional information"; or implicit: "Fly the friendly skies." Designers cue customers to take action by placing dotted lines around coupons to suggest cutting and by highlighting the company's telephone number with large type or a bright color.

THE JUDGE'S ROLE: DECISION TIME

The next role in the creative process is the **Judge.** This is when the creatives evaluate the practicality of their big idea and decide whether to implement, modify, or discard it.[29]

The Judge's role is delicate. The creatives must be critical enough to ensure that when it's time to play Warrior they have an idea worth fighting for. But they also need to avoid stifling the imagination of the Artist. It's easy to be critical—easier than exploring, conceptualizing, or defending. But the Judge's purpose is to help produce good ideas, not to revel in criticism. Von Oech suggests focusing first on the positive, interesting aspects of a new idea. The negatives will come soon enough.

The Judge needs to ask certain questions when evaluating the big idea: Is this idea an aha! or an uh-oh? (What was my initial reaction?) What's wrong with this idea? (And what's right with it?) What if it fails? (Is it worth the risk?) What is my cultural bias? (Does the audience have the same bias?) What's clouding my thinking? (Am I wearing blinders?)

Risk is an important consideration. When the advertising scores a hit, everybody's happy, sales go up, people get raises, and occasionally there's even positive publicity. But when a campaign flops, all hell breaks loose, especially on high-profile accounts. Sales may flatten or even decline, competitors gain a couple of points in market share, distributors and dealers complain, and the phone rings incessantly with calls from disgruntled client executives. Perhaps worst of all is the ridicule in the trade. Advertising pundits say nasty things about the ads in TV interviews; reviewers write articles in *Ad Age* and *Adweek;* and even the big daily papers get in their licks. In one article, for instance, *The Wall Street Journal* panned the campaigns of four high-profile advertisers: Diet Coke, Subaru, AT&T, and American Express.[30] This is not good for the agency's stock or the client's. And it's how agencies get replaced. So the Judge's role is vital.

Applying the Creative Pyramid to Advertising

Notice how the five objectives of advertising copy apply to the ad shown here.

Attention This headline snares our attention with its large, calligraphy-like type. It tugs at our mental files with humor—dieters diving for a Twinkie before it hits the floor. We suddenly spot the fishing lure and—bang—we take the hook, swallowing the metaphoric cue to a second mental image: hungry fish with open mouths and thrashing tails rushing to hit the lure.

Interest The first line of the body copy suggests that fishing enthusiasts picture a subject of particular interest to them, a starving largemouth hitting the lure with exceptional vigor.

Credibility The credibility step casts specifics, the product name and two features ("one of a kind wiggle" and "irresistible to lunker bass").

Desire The last line begins with the assertion that the reader is on a diet. This lifestyle technique symbolically applies to the target market, identifying them as fishing enthusiasts who suffer from lunker bass deprivation and are in need of the Shore's River Shiner lure to blow their fishless diet!

Action If the reader has taken the bait, then all he or she needs to know is the identity of the product (represented here by the logo) because we assume that it's sold at the closest sporting goods store or tackle shop.

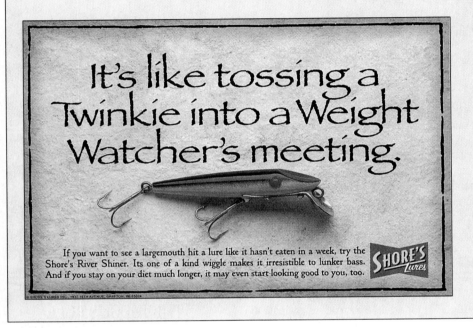

Laboratory Applications

1. Find an ad that exhibits the five elements of the creative pyramid. *(A print ad will be the easiest to find and talk about, but radio or TV commercials also feature the five elements. Beware: The desire step may be hard to find.)*

2. Why do so many good ads lack one or more of the five elements listed here? How do they overcome the omission?

If the Judge does a good job, the next role in the creative process—the Warrior—is easier to perform.

THE WARRIOR'S ROLE

In the final step of the creative process, the **Warrior** wins territory for big new ideas in a world resistant to change. The Warrior carries the concept into action. This means getting the big idea approved, produced, and placed in the media. The Warrior's orders include: be bold, sharpen your sword (skills), strengthen your shield (examine criticism in advance), follow through (overcome obstacles), use your energy wisely, be persistent, savor your victories, and learn from defeat.[31]

To get the big idea approved, the Warrior has to battle people within the agency and often the client, too. So part of the Warrior's role is turning the agency account team into cowarriors for the presentation to the client. At this point, it's imperative that the creatives finish their message strategy document to give their rationale for the copy, art, and production elements incorporated in the concept they're trying to sell. And the message strategy had better mesh with the creative brief, or the valiant Warrior will likely face a wide moat with no drawbridge. (See Ad Lab 9–C: The Creative Gymnasium.)

Part of the Warrior's task may be to help the account managers present the campaign to the client. Bendinger says, "How well you *sell* ideas is as important as how *good* those ideas are." To give a presentation maximum selling power, he suggests five key components:[32]

The Creative Gymnasium   *Ad Lab 9-C*

The Explorer

Here's a visual calisthenics exercise for your Explorer. Find a perfect star in the pattern:

The Artist

The artist uses humor and absurd what-if questions to mentally loosen up. Try these warm-up techniques:

1. Think up a new set of conversion factors:

    10^{12} microphones = 1 megaphone
    10^{12} pins = 1 terrapin
    $3^1/_3$ tridents = 1 decadent
    4 seminaries = 1 binary
    10^{21} piccolos = 1 gigolo
    1 milli-Helen = the amount of beauty
    required to launch 1 ship

2. Another mental muscle stretcher is to change the context of an idea. The roman numeral for 9 shown below can be turned into a 6 by adding only a single line:

    ### IX

    Some people put a horizontal line through the center, turn it upside down, and then cover the bottom. This gives you a roman numeral VI. A more artistic solution might be to put "S" in front of the IX to create "SIX." What we've done here is take the IX out of the context of Roman numerals and put it into the context of "Arabic numerals spelled out in English."

    Or another second right answer might be to add the line "6" after the IX. Then you get IX6, or one times six.

The Judge and the Warrior

As a creative person, what verdict would your Judge give ads that feature creative gymnastics like the ones below? How would your Warrior present these two ads to a client for approval?

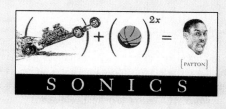

Laboratory Applications

1. Attempt to solve the exercises above. Explain your choices.
2. Create a metaphor for each of these paired concepts:
    a. Boxing + Water.
    b. Magnet + Library.
    c. Rainbow + Clock.

1. **Strategic Precision.** The selling idea must be *on strategy*. The presenting team must be able to prove it, and the strategy should be discussed first, before the big selling idea is presented.

2. **Savvy Psychology.** The presentation, like the advertising, should be receiver-driven. The idea has to meet the client's needs.

3. **Slick Presentation.** The presentation must be prepared and rehearsed; it should use great visuals and emotional appeals. A good presentation makes people want to do the campaign.

4. **Structural Persuasion.** The presentation should be well structured, since clients relate well to organized thinking. The opening is all-important because it sets the tone for the entire presentation.

5. **Solve the Problem.** Clients have needs, and clients frequently report to big shots who ask tough questions about the advertising. Solve the client's problem and you'll sell the big idea—and do it with style.

For clients, recognizing a big idea and evaluating it are almost as difficult as coming up with one. When the agency (or the in-house advertising department) presents the concepts, the client is suddenly in the role of the Judge, without having gone through the other roles first. Ogilvy recommends that clients ask themselves five questions: Did it make me gasp when I first saw it? Do I wish I had thought of it myself? Is it unique? Does it fit the strategy to perfection? Could it be used for 30 years?[33]

As Ogilvy points out, campaigns that run five years or more are the superstars: Dove soap (33 percent cleansing cream), Ivory soap (99 44/100 percent pure), Perdue chickens ("It takes a tough man to make a tender chicken"), the U.S. Army ("Be all you can be"). These campaigns are still running today, and some have run for as long as 30 years. Those are big ideas!

When the client approves the campaign, the creative person's role as a Warrior is only half over. Now the campaign has to be executed. That means the Warrior shepherds it through the intricate details of design and production to see that it is completed on time, under budget, and with the highest quality possible. At the same time, the creatives revert to their Artist roles to design, write, and produce the ads.

The next step in the process, therefore, is to implement the big idea—to produce the ads for print and electronic media—the subject of our next two chapters.

Summary

In the marketing communications process, the creative team is responsible for encoding advertising messages. It is the author of the communications. The creative team typically comprises an art director and a copywriter who report to a creative director.

Behind the visuals and the text of every ad is an advertising strategy. Typically written by the account management team, the advertising (or creative) strategy includes four elements: the target audience, the product concept, the communications media, and the advertising message. Once the general parameters of the plan have been developed, the account managers prepare a creative brief that outlines the key strategic decisions. The creative brief should contain at least three elements: an objective statement, a support statement, and either a tone statement or a brand character statement. The brief gives strategic guidance to the art director and copywriter, but it is their responsibility to develop a message strategy that lays out the specifics of how the advertising will be executed. The three elements of message strategy are copy, art, and production.

Copy is the verbal and art the nonverbal, or visual, presentation of the message strategy. Production refers to the mechanical details of how the ads and commercials will be produced.

To create means to originate, and creativity involves combining two or more previously unconnected elements, objects, or ideas to make something new. Creativity helps advertising inform, persuade, and remind customers and prospects by making the advertising more vivid. All people have creativity; they just differ in degree.

Scholars believe certain styles of thinking are more conducive to creativity than others. The two basic thinking styles are fact-based and value-based. People who prefer the fact-based style tend to be linear thinkers, analytical and rational. Value-based thinkers tend to be less structured, more intuitive, and more willing to use their imagination. They are good at synthesizing divergent viewpoints to arrive at a new one. And, with their ability to think metaphorically, they tend to be more creative.

In one model of the creative process, the creative person must play four roles along the way to acceptance of a new idea: the Explorer, Artist, Judge, and Warrior. The Explorer searches for new information, paying attention to unusual patterns. The Artist experiments with a variety of approaches looking for the big idea. The Artist also determines how to implement it. For this, the creative pyramid may help. The pyramid models the formation of an ad after the way people learn new information, using five steps: attention, interest, credibility, desire, and action.

The Judge evaluates the results of experimentation and decides which approach is most practical. The Warrior overcomes excuses, idea killers, setbacks, and obstacles to bring a creative concept to realization. Each role has unique characteristics, and there are many techniques for improving performance in each role. In some cases it's better for the creative person to use a fact-based style of thinking; in others a value-based style is more effective.

One of the worst blocks to creativity is getting stuck in the wrong mindset—the wrong style of thinking—for the task at hand. However, there are numerous techniques for escaping these mental blocks.

Questions for Review and Discussion

1. Select an ad in this chapter. What do you believe is the sponsor's advertising and message strategy?

2. What are the most important elements of a creative brief?

3. What are the elements of message strategy and how does it differ from advertising (or creative) strategy?

4. In what ways have you exercised your personal creativity in the last week?

5. What characterizes the two main styles of thinking? Which style do you usually prefer? Why?

6. What are the four roles of the creative process? Have you played those roles in preparing a term paper? How?

7. What is the difference between a strategy statement and a big idea?

8. Select five creative ads from a magazine. What techniques of the Artist can you recognize in those ads?

9. In those same ads, can you identify each step of the creative pyramid?

10. What are the important things to remember about making a presentation?

10

Creative Execution
Art and Copy

Objective: To present the role of art and copy—the nonverbal and verbal elements of message strategy—in print, radio, and television advertising. Artists and copywriters include a variety of specialists who follow specific procedures for conceptualizing, designing, writing, and producing advertising materials. To be successful, advertising people must be conversant with the copywriting and commercial art terms and formats used in the business. They must also develop an esthetic sensitivity to be able to recognize, create, evaluate, or recommend quality work.

After studying this chapter, you will be able to:

- Describe the roles of the various types of artists in the advertising business.

- Explain the use of advertising layouts and the steps in creating them.

- Explain the creative approval process.

- Explain the role of the copywriter in relation to other members of the creative team.

- Describe the format elements of an ad and discuss how they relate to the objectives of advertising copywriting.

- Explain the art director's role in radio commercials.

- Discuss the advantages of the major types of television commercials.

For all those who commute to work in the dead of winter.

Many companies have testing labs in their factories, but Timberland's is too large to fit indoors. You see, we test our boots and clothing on a stretch of Alaskan tundra 1,049 miles long. Once a year this blizzard-whipped trail becomes the arena for the Iditarod, a race in which huskies get hot meals every sixty miles and humans snack on dried moose meat.

Although the Iditarod has been called the Last Great Race on Earth, we view it as merely the world's longest commute. For the mushers are only performing, in panoramic scale, a ritual familiar to us all.

They are facing wind, water, earth and sky to get from one place to another in an appointed time. To do this, they

steel themselves in Timberland Pac Boots.

This assures them polar bear warmth in arctic environments—but you can get equally good results on a frozen shore in Chicago or a bitter avenue in New York. Whether you're commuting to the office or the trading post, look to Timberland. For extreme comfort under all extremes.

Boots, shoes, clothing, wind, water, earth and sky.

For 17 years, Timberland Co.'s award-winning ads featured witty copy and beautifully lit studio shots of its all-weather gear. One ad pictured a column of water rolling out of a spigot onto the golden-rough, natural leather toe of a Timberland boot. The headline: "For long wear and rugged good looks, just add water." But Timberland wanted a new direction for the 90s.

John Doyle, an art director for Boston-based Mullen Advertising, was assigned to the job. Doyle chose to break with the studio look and take the client's products outdoors into nature's expansive settings and full spectrum of light. "We wanted people to be visually transported to a different place," says Doyle, "where they could feel the environment and the elements."

The big idea was Timber Land, an imaginary place that played off the company's name. Timber Land would be a utopian setting of extraordinary landscapes and crystalline waters where the mountains dramatically disappeared into the clouds. Great creativity, as well as photographic skill, would be needed to express such a wondrous place.

Noted New York photographer Eric Meola is a master at capturing the look and feel of monumental subject matter. He is also known for his work in portraits and architecture. Doyle hired him,

noting that Meola's "shots are so intriguing, a viewer is compelled to spend time with them—which is just what we needed for this campaign."

They spent 44 days shooting in Alaska, Arizona, and Scotland. They auditioned over 200 models, struggled through blinding snow gusts, and rented six planes to stage shots at the 7,000-foot level of Mount McKinley. After all this effort, Meola and Doyle captured only nine shots of Timber Land that they deemed usable—just enough to start the campaign.

With the photos in hand, Doyle had to finalize the ads. Brainstorming with copywriter Paul Silverman produced a lot of ideas but only a few real winners.

Finally it all came together. Meola's stunning wide-angle shots across lakes, plains, and mountainous landscapes with a lone person in the foreground were capped by Silverman's headlines: "Timberland. Because the earth is two-thirds water," and "Timberland. Where the elements of design are the elements themselves." Doyle's design included a special typeface whose character added elegance.

This was the look and concept that expressed the mystique of Timber Land, the place. And the image that would carry Timberland, the company, successfully into the new decade.[1] ●

CREATING ADS FOR PRINT MEDIA

The Timberland campaign was hailed worldwide in a variety of competitions and set the tone for its unprecedented growth in the 90s. What characterized the Timberland campaign was the nonverbal message strategy, created by Doyle's thoughtful design and execution and Meola's magnificent photography.

The nonverbal aspect of an ad or commercial carries half the burden of encoding the message, determining the way it *feels* to the viewer. That mood flavors the verbal message. In this chapter, we discuss the execution of advertising concepts from the standpoint of both visual and verbal details: the art and copy of print advertising first and then electronic media.

THE ROLE OF ART IN CREATING PRINT ADVERTISING

Timberland's ad campaign stands out because of its vivid presentation of the big idea, which demanded rare artistic vision. But to be relevant to the audience and the company's objectives, Doyle had to execute the design with brilliance and precision.

Designing the Print Ad

Design refers to how the art director and graphic artist (or graphic designer) choose and structure the artistic elements of an ad. A designer sets a *style*—the manner in which a thought or image is expressed—by choosing particular artistic elements and blending them in a unique way.

The Timberland designs enhance the message through a feeling of spaciousness. First, the sheer size of the photograph captures attention. Sparse text gives the ad breathability. The copy is set in a neat, easy-to-read format with lots of *white space*. This space gives the ad unity and balance in spite of the diversity of elements.

A number of artists, working under the art director, may produce initial layouts of the ad concept. In collaboration with copywriters, artists draw on their expertise in graphic design—including photography, typography, and illustration—to create the most effective ad or brochure.

Timberland. Where the elements of design are the elements themselves.

Unlike some designers who slavishly follow the winds of change, we Timberland people take our inspiration from the winds that never change. Be they the mighty gales that hammer the Carolina coast, the sandstorms that parch the Southwestern canyons, or the tropical murmurs that dance across the Pacific, calling you to points unknown. And although you may admire our boots, shoes and cloth-ing in the setting of a fine store, it may take a different setting for you to see their deeper worth. A setting shaped by their true elements.

Wind, water, earth and sky.

Timberland ⏚

Boots, shoes, clothing, wind, water, earth and sky.

• This elegant ad uses the natural elements of ancient sandstone, flowing water, and spacious caverns to enhance our awareness that the elements of design (shape, texture, color, line, etc.) are truly grand. And that these same design elements are used to create Timberland boots.

The Role of the Advertising Artist   *Ad Lab 10-A*

All the people employed in commercial art are called artists, but they may perform entirely different tasks. Surprisingly, some can't even draw well; instead, they're trained for different artistic specialties.

Art Directors

Art directors are responsible for the visual presentation of the ad. Along with a copywriter, they develop the initial concept. They may do initial sketches or layouts, but after that they may not touch the ad again. Their primary responsibility is to supervise the ad's progress to completion.

The best art directors are good at presenting ideas in both words and pictures. They are usually experienced graphic designers with a good understanding of consumers. They may have a large or small staff, depending on the organization. Or they may be freelancers (independent contractors) and do more of the work themselves.

Graphic Designers

Graphic designers are precision specialists preoccupied with shape and form. In advertising they arrange the various graphic elements (type, illustrations, photos, white space) in the most attractive and effective way possible. While they may work on ads, they usually design and produce collateral materials, such as posters, brochures, and annual reports.

In an agency, the art director often acts as the designer. Sometimes, however, a separate designer is used to offer a unique touch to a particular ad.

Illustrators

Illustrators paint or draw the visuals in an ad. Illustrators frequently specialize in one type of illustrating, such as automotive, fashion, or furniture. Very few agencies or advertisers retain full-time illustrators; most advertising illustrators freelance. Typically, agencies hire different illustrators for different jobs, depending on an ad's particular needs, look, and feel.

Photographers

Like the illustrator, the advertising photographer creates a nonverbal expression that reinforces the verbal message. Photographers use the tools of photography—cameras, lenses, and lights—to create images. They select interesting angles, arrange subjects in new ways, carefully control the lighting, and use many other techniques to enhance the subject's image quality. A studio photographer uses high-powered lights to photograph products in front of a background or as part of an arranged setting. A location photographer generally shoots in real-life settings like those in the Timberland ads. Many photographers specialize—in cars, celebrities, fashion, food, equipment, or architecture. Agencies and

advertisers rarely employ staff photographers. They generally hire freelancers by the hour or pay a fee for the assignment. Photographers also sell stock photography, photos on file from prior shootings.

Production Artists

Production (or pasteup) artists assemble the various elements of an ad and mechanically put them together the way the art director or designer indicates. Good production artists are fast, precise, and knowledgeable about the whole production process. Production artists today must be computer literate; they use a variety of software programs for page making, drawing, painting, and photo scanning. Most designers and art directors start their careers as production artists and work their way up. It's very difficult work, but it is also very important, for this is where an ad actually comes together in its finished form.

Laboratory Applications

1. Select an ad in the Creative Director's Portfolio (pp. 290–93). Explain which advertising artists were probably involved in its creation and what the responsibility of each artist was.

2. Which ad in the Creative Director's Portfolio do you think needed the fewest artists? How many?

The Use of Layouts

A **layout** is an overall orderly arrangement of all the format elements of an ad: headline, subheads, visual(s), copy, captions, trademarks, slogans, and signature.

The layout serves several purposes. First, it helps both the agency and the client develop and evaluate the ad's final look and feel. It gives the client (usually not an artist) a tangible item to correct, change, comment on, and approve.

Second, the layout helps the creative team develop the ad's psychological elements—the nonverbal and symbolic components. The "look" of the ad should elicit an image or mood that reflects and enhances the advertiser and the product. Therefore, when designing the initial ad layout, the creative team must be very sensitive to the desired image of the product or business. In the Timberland ads, image was the primary reason for combining a dominant, spacious photograph with sparse, elegant copy. The ad makes a credible instant impression on its target audience, and that adds value to the brand.

Third, once the best design is chosen, the layout serves as a blueprint. It shows the size and placement of each element in the ad. Once the production manager knows the dimensions of the ad, the number of photos, the amount of typesetting, and the use of art elements such as color and illustrations, he or she can determine the cost of producing the ad (see Ad Lab 10–A: "The Role of the Advertising Artist").

The Advertising Design Process: Creative and Approval

The design process serves as both a creative and an approval process. In the creative phase, the designer uses thumbnails, roughs, dummies, and comprehensives—in other words, nonfinal art—to establish the ad's look and feel. Then in the prepress (or production art) phase, the artist prepares a mechanical—the final artwork with the actual type in place along with all the visuals the printer will need to reproduce the ad. The approval process takes place throughout the entire design process.

Thumbnail sketches

The thumbnail sketch, or **thumbnail,** is a small, rough, rapidly produced drawing the artist uses to visualize layout approaches without wasting time on details. Thumbnails are very basic. Blocks of straight or squiggly lines indicate text placement, and boxes show placement of visuals. The best sketches are then developed further.

Rough layout

In a **rough,** the artist draws to the actual size of the ad. Headlines and subheads suggest the final type style, illustrations and photographs are sketched in, and body copy is simulated with lines. The agency may present roughs to clients—particularly cost-conscious ones.

Comprehensive

The **comprehensive layout, or comp,** is a highly refined facsimile of the finished ad. A comp is generally quite elaborate, with colored photos, press-on lettering, photostats of subvisuals, and a glossy spray coat. Today, copy for the comp is typeset on computer and positioned with the visuals, and the ad is printed as a full-color proof. At this stage, all visuals should be final.

Dummy

A **dummy** presents the handheld look and feel of brochures, multipage materials, or point-of-purchase displays. The artist assembles the dummy by hand, using color markers and computer proofs, mounting them on sturdy paper, and then cutting and folding them to size. A dummy for a brochure, for example, is put together, page by page, to look exactly like the finished product.

Mechanical (pasteup)

The type and visuals must be placed into their exact position for reproduction by a printer. Today, most designers do this work on the computer, completely bypassing the need for a mechanical. Some agencies, however, still make traditional **mechanicals** where black type and line art are pasted in place on a piece of white artboard—called a **pasteup**—with overlay sheets indicating the hue and positioning of color. Printers refer to the mechanical or pasteup as **camera-ready art** because they photograph it using a large production camera before starting the reproduction process—creating color keys, prints, and films of the finished ad.

At any time during the design process—until the printing press lays ink on paper—changes can be made on the art. However, the expense may grow tenfold with each step from roughs to mechanicals to printing.

Approval

The work of the copywriter and art director is always subject to approval. The larger the agency and the larger the client, the more formidable this process becomes (see Exhibit 10–1). A new ad concept is first approved by the agency's creative director.

● Thumbnails and a rough layout of an ad by the Muse Cordero Chen agency celebrate the firm's philosophy and "out-of-the-box" approach to advertising. The final sketch humorously shows the firm's cultural diversity. The body copy emanating from the pipe proclaims: *advertising. bold. culturally hip. t.v. radio. print. out-of-the-box. award winning. on target. fresh. impactful. relevant. generation x. latino. black. asian. diverse. the new america. dare to be different. challenge the status quo.*

Then the account management team reviews it. Next, the client's product managers and marketing staff review it, often changing a word or two or sometimes rejecting the whole approach. Both the agency's and client's legal departments scrutinize the copy and art for potential problems. Finally, the company's top executives review the final concept and text.

The biggest challenge in approval is keeping approvers from corrupting the style of the ad. The creative team works hard to achieve a cohesive style. Then a group of non-

Exhibit • 10–1

The copy approval process begins within the agency and ends with approval by key executives of the client company. Each review usually requires some rewrite and a presentation to the next level of approvers. When the agency and the advertiser are large companies, the process can require long lead times.

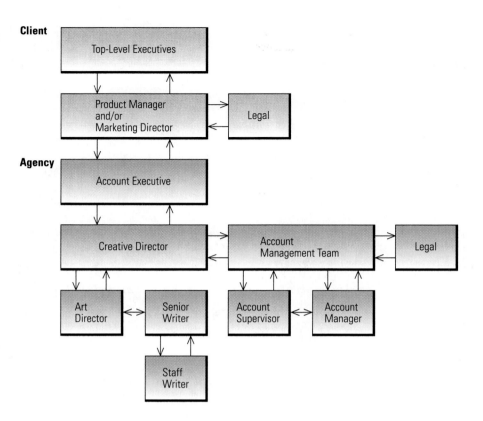

Ethical Issue — Manipulating Morphing's Magic

Digital photographer Laurence Gartel was thumbing through a copy of *Byte* magazine when a computer-rendered illustration of a man with a clock face caught his eye. It looked amazingly similar to an illustration he had once created. Certain details convinced him his illustration had been digitally copied from a book of published photographs and then edited and distorted. He immediately called the magazine. The editor apologized and printed a clarification.

To morph or not to morph is a big ethical question in computer-generated art and design these days. Only recently has it become possible to *metamorphose*—change something in form or character—with a few computer keystrokes. The effect is usually dramatic. Take a television spot for Chanel No. 5, in which a mousy moviegoer transforms magically into Marilyn Monroe.

The dowdily dressed young woman is eating popcorn and watching Marilyn on a large movie

screen when suddenly a button pops open on the viewer's dress, and, to her shock, out bursts . . . cleavage! Next, her moussed-back hair begins to grow and the black-and-white scene turns to Technicolor. Her dark hair becomes blonde and, thanks to digital metamorphosis, she becomes the ravishing Monroe. The popcorn container turns into a 2-quart bottle of Chanel No. 5 and Marilyn coos, "You know what I mean? No. 5!" Then, in the blink of a heavy-lidded eye, Marilyn reverts to the moviegoer, hugging her $15,000 bottle of perfume as she settles in her seat for more movie magic.

Blame computers and photo manipulation technology for defying the adage, "Seeing is believing." Image manipulation can be obvious, as in *TV Guide*'s cover photo of Oprah Winfrey's head on the body of Ann Margret. Or it can be subtle, as when *National Geographic* moved one of the great pyramids closer to the others for a more esthetic cover shot.

According to Fred Ritchin, professor of photography and interactive telecommunications at New York University, the news media jeopardize

---

> **Blame computers and photo manipulation technology for defying the adage, "Seeing is believing."**

---

their integrity with each doctored photo. While readers have always accepted that text is rewritten and sometimes edited with a point of view, they have relied on photos to represent the unvarnished truth.

So vital is the question of news integrity that the American Society of Media Photographers has adopted a policy that a photo used in a *news* context may not be altered in any fashion. Major news organizations have adopted the same hands-off policy. For other kinds of photography, writers and nonartists have the opportunity to change it all. Maintaining artistic purity is extremely difficult and requires patience, flexibility, maturity, and the ability to articulate an important point of view.

Impact of Computers on Graphic Design

By using graphics or imaging programs on computers, today's graphic artist or designer can do much of the work previously performed by staff artists. On the screen, the artist can see an entire page layout, complete with illustrations and photos, and easily alter any of them in a few minutes. With manual design, designing a variety of layouts could take days, and final art was not so detailed or complete as designs created on the computer.

Small IBM PC and Macintosh-based systems are ideal for computer design, and sophisticated PC graphics software is now available for page making (QuarkXPress® and PageMaker®), painting and drawing (CorelDraw!®, FreeHand®, Adobe Illustrator®), and image manipulation (ColorStudio®, PhotoStyler®, Adobe Photoshop®). For word processing the most popular programs include Microsoft Word®, WordPerfect®, Claris MacWrite®.[2] Moderate cost makes such software accessible to freelancers, small businesses, and agency creative departments. Today's graphic artist, illustrator, and retoucher must be computer literate in addition to having a thorough knowledge of esthetics, rendering, and design.

The Advertising Visual

The artists who paint, sketch, and draw in advertising are called **illustrators.** The artists who produce pictures with a camera are **photographers.** Together they are responsible for all the visuals, or pictures, we see in advertising.

---

such as advertising and creative work, the rule is no alteration without permission.

Skilled photographers with razor blades and airbrushes have moved objects and people in and out of photographs for decades, but the issue today is the sheer number of people who can do this. Making composites and doctoring photos is easy, thanks to the myriad digital scanners and software available.

Morphing also poses the question: Who owns the final product? If one photographer takes the shot of a head, another provides the body, and a third party actually makes the composite, are they all entitled to ownership? FCL/Colorspace, the New York City–based studio that designs *Spy's* covers, addresses the question case by case. "If we shoot all the photography and do all the photo manipulation, then the image is ours," explains Phil Heffernan, creative director.

But what about manipulating an image of a cloud to create steam coming out of an engine? Is it ethical to take a picture of a tree and use the bark as background texture in another image? "The line between photography and illustration is blurring," says Heffernan.

To help educate digital artists about the integrity of published images, the Center for Creative Imaging published *Ethics, Copyright and the Bottom Line.* Director Ray DeMoulin notes that changing images is becoming more acceptable. "This is the most talked-about issue in graphics today," he says.

Until copyright laws address this gray area, the advertising industry will have to rely on its own code of ethics and the integrity of its people.

Questions

1. What ethical issues should an advertiser be aware of when considering alteration of an existing photograph or illustration? Enumerate and explain them.

2. Should photos and illustrations in ads carry some small-type disclaimer when the visual has been changed or computer enhanced? Why or why not?

Sources: Bob Garfield, "Wondrous Chanel No. 5 Spot Deftly Nurtures the Product," *Advertising Age,* December 12, 1994, p. 3; Jean Marie Angelo, "Photo Manipulation, Retouching Stirs Legal, Ethical Questions," *Computer Pictures,* March/April 1993, pp. 20–25; "FPG Wins Digital Plagiarism Suit," *New Media,* January 1995, p. 28; Christopher R. Harris and Don E. Tomlinson, "The Lanham Act and Copyright: Application vis-à-vis Computer Manipulation of Photographic Imagery," paper presented to the annual conference of the Association for Education in Journalism and Mass Communication, Montreal, Quebec, August 8, 1992.

Purpose of the visual

Most prospects spot the picture, read the headline, and then peruse the body copy, in that order. Since the visual carries so much responsibility for an ad's success, it should:

- Capture the reader's attention.
- Identify the subject of the ad.
- Qualify readers by stopping those who are legitimate prospects.
- Arouse the reader's interest in the headline.
- Create a favorable impression of the product or advertiser.

- Clarify claims made by the copy.
- Show the product actually being used.
- Help convince the reader of the truth of copy claims.
- Emphasize the product's unique features.
- Provide continuity for the campaign by using a unified visual technique in each ad.[3]

Determining the chief focus for visuals

The Timberland ads are dominated by a large, single visual that demonstrates the environment in which the product is used rather than the product itself. The visuals capture a mood and create a feeling—a context for the consumer's perception of the product.

Selecting the focus for advertising visuals is a major step in the creative process. It often determines how well the big idea is executed. Print advertising uses many standard subjects for ad visuals, including:

1. **The package containing the product.** Especially important for packaged goods, it helps the consumer identify the product on the grocery shelf.
2. **The product alone.** This doesn't work well for nonpackaged goods.
3. **The product in use.** Automobile ads typically show a car in use while talking about its ride, luxury, handling, or economy. Cosmetic ads usually show the product in use with a close-up photo of a beautiful woman or a virile man.
4. **How to use the product.** Recipe ads featuring a new way to use food products historically pull very high readership scores.
5. **Product features.** Computer software ads frequently show the monitor screen so the prospect can see how the software features are displayed.
6. **Comparison of products.** The advertiser shows its product next to a competitor's and compares the important features of the two.
7. **User benefit.** It's often difficult to illustrate intangible user benefits. However, marketers know that the best way to get customers' attention is to show how the product will benefit them. So it's worth the extra creative effort.

• This business-to-business ad uses a negative headline to stir attention and reinforce the idea that the agency can create media attention. Over time, customers may forget the point of the message and continue to associate a negative feeling with the product or service, which can hurt sales over the long haul.

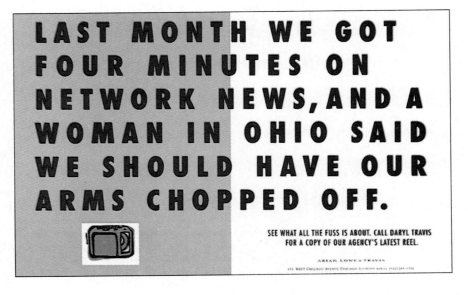

LAST MONTH WE GOT FOUR MINUTES ON NETWORK NEWS, AND A WOMAN IN OHIO SAID WE SHOULD HAVE OUR ARMS CHOPPED OFF.

SEE WHAT ALL THE FUSS IS ABOUT. CALL DARYL TRAVIS FOR A COPY OF OUR AGENCY'S LATEST REEL.

ARIAN, LOWE & TRAVIS

8. **Humor.** If used well, a humorous visual can make an entertaining and lasting impression, but it can destroy credibility if used incorrectly.

9. **Testimonial.** Before and after endorsements are very effective for weight-loss products, skin-care lotions, and body-building courses.

10. **Negative appeal.** Sometimes, visuals point out what happens if you don't use the product. If done well, that can spark interest.

Selecting the visual

The kind of picture used is often determined during the visualization process. (See RL 10–1: Techniques for Creating Advertising Visuals, and RL 10–2: Checklist of Design Principles in the Reference Library.) But frequently the visual is not determined until the art director or designer actually lays out the ad.

Selecting an appropriate photo or visual is a difficult creative task. (See the Creative Director's Portfolio on pages 290–93 for several examples of dynamic, creative ads.) Art directors deal with several basic issues:

• Is a visual needed for effective communication?

• Should the visual be black-and-white or color? Is this a budgetary decision?

• What should the subject of the picture be? Is that subject relevant to the advertiser's creative strategy?

• Should the ad use an illustration or a photograph?

• What technical and budgetary issues must be considered?

Now let's examine the formats copywriters use to link art and copy.

In print advertising, the key format elements are the *headlines,* the *visuals, subheads, body copy, slogans, seals, logotypes (logos),* and *signatures.* As Exhibit 10–2 shows, copywriters can correlate the headline, visual, and subhead to the attention step of the creative pyramid. The interest step typically corresponds to the subheadline and the first

COPYWRITING AND FORMATS FOR PRINT ADVERTISING

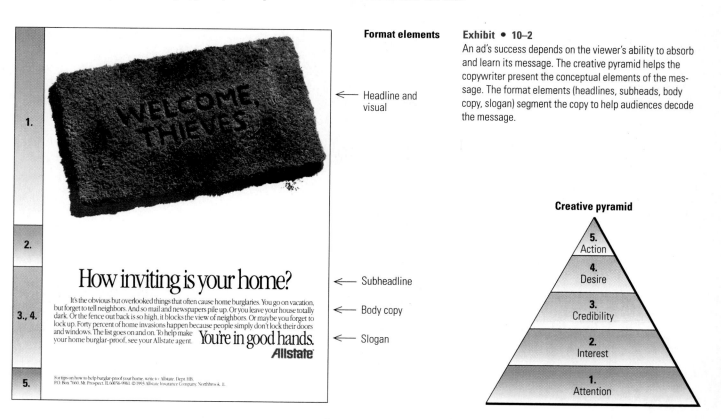

Format elements

← Headline and visual

← Subheadline

← Body copy

← Slogan

How inviting is your home?

It's the obvious but overlooked things that often cause home burglaries. You go on vacation, but forget to tell neighbors. And so mail and newspapers pile up. Or you leave your house totally dark. Or the fence out back is so high, it blocks the view of neighbors. Or maybe you forget to lock up. Forty percent of home invasions happen because people simply don't lock their doors and windows. The list goes on and on. To help make your home burglar-proof, see your Allstate agent. **You're in good hands.**

Allstate

For tips on how to help burglar-proof your home, write to: Allstate, Dept. HB, P.O. Box 7660, Mt. Prospect, IL 60056-9961. © 1993 Allstate Insurance Company, Northbrook, IL.

Exhibit • 10–2

An ad's success depends on the viewer's ability to absorb and learn its message. The creative pyramid helps the copywriter present the conceptual elements of the message. The format elements (headlines, subheads, body copy, slogan) segment the copy to help audiences decode the message.

Creative pyramid

5. Action
4. Desire
3. Credibility
2. Interest
1. Attention

paragraph of body copy. Body copy handles credibility and desire, and the action step takes place with the logo, slogan, and signature block. We discuss these elements first and then look at the formats for radio and television commercials.

Headlines

The **headline** is the words in the leading position in the advertisement—the words that will be read first and are situated to draw the most attention. That's why headlines usually appear in larger type than other parts of the ad.

Role of headlines

Effective headlines attract attention, engage the audience, explain the visual, lead the audience into the body of the ad, and present the selling message.

One popular way to attract attention is to occupy the entire top half of the ad with a headline written in large letters. This technique can be just as eye-catching as a dramatic photograph or illustration.

Another goal of a headline is to engage the reader—fast—and give a reason to read the rest of the ad. If the headline lacks immediacy, prospects turn their attention to another subject and pass the ad's message by.[4]

An ad for Esser's wine store is a good example of a headline leading the reader into the body copy.

Headline: "Esser's Knows."

Body copy: "Manfred Esser's nose knows a good wine . . ."

The headline is the most important thing an advertiser says to the prospect. It explains or gives greater meaning to the visual and then immediately dictates the ad-

● Unlike most ads that feature very bold, large-sized headlines, this headline links the dramatic imagery of the angry, snarling dog with the power of government to collect taxes. It engages the audience with the concept, explains the visual (from some small business owners' perspective, at least!), and leads the audience into the body copy. Notice how the headline poses the problem; the subhead points the way to the solution.

GOVERNMENT
IN YOUR
FACE ABOUT
TAXES?

WE CAN HELP.

COUNT
ON IT.

Count on Comprehensive to attack your payroll returns. Ditto for income and sales tax returns. We get our teeth into the regulations to make sure you get every advantage. We won't dog the deadlines, either. So you avoid the risk of big penalties for late filing. But tax planning and on-time preparation are only part of our service. We also do monthly accounting and financial statements, business consulting, and payroll. We'll help you bite back.

COMPREHENSIVE®
Financial Intelligence For Small Business.®

There are over 200 independently owned Comprehensive offices.
For the office near you, call 1-800-773-9880 from 8 A.M. to 5 P.M.

© 1994 Comprehensive Business Services, Inc.

vertiser's position in that person's mind, whether or not the prospect chooses to read on.[5]

Ideally, headlines present the complete selling idea. Research shows that, on average, three to five times as many people read the headline as read the body copy. So if the ad doesn't sell in the headline, the advertiser is wasting money.[6] Nike uses beautiful magazine and outdoor ads featuring just an athlete, the logo, and the memorable headline: "Just do it." Working off the visual, the headline creates the mood and tells the reader to take action (through implication, buy Nikes). Headlines help trigger a recognition response, which reinforces brand recognition and brand preference.

The traditional notion is that short headlines with one line are best but a second line is acceptable. Many experts believe that headlines with ten words or more gain greater readership. And in one study of over 2,000 ads, most headlines averaged eight words in length.[8] David Ogilvy says his best headline contained 18 words: "At 60 miles an hour, the loudest noise in the new Rolls-Royce comes from the electric clock."[9]

Headlines should offer a benefit that is apparent to the reader and easy to grasp. For example: "When it absolutely, positively has to be there overnight" (Federal Express) or "Folds flat for easy storage" (Honda Civic Wagon).[10]

Finally, headlines should present product news. Consumers look for new products, new uses for old products, or improvements on old products. If they haven't been overused in a category, "power" words that imply newness can increase readership and should be employed whenever honestly applicable.[11] Examples include *free, now, amazing, suddenly, announcing, introducing, it's here, improved, at last, revolutionary, just arrived,* and *important development.*

Types of headlines

Copywriters use many variations of headlines depending on the advertising strategy. Typically, they use the headline that presents the big idea most successfully. Headlines may be classified by the type of information they carry: *benefit, news/information, provocative, question,* and *command.*

Benefit headlines promise the audience that experiencing the utility of the product or service will be rewarding. Benefit headlines shouldn't be too cute or clever, just simple statements of the product's most important benefit.[12] Two good examples are

Gore-Tex® Fabrics
Keep you warm and dry.   and   Speak a foreign language in 30 days
Regardless of what falls   or your money back.
Out of the sky.

Note that both of these headlines focus on the benefit of using the product, not the features of the product itself.[13]

News/information headlines announce news or promise information. Sea World began its television announcement of a new baby whale with the headline "It's a Girl." The information must be believable, though. A claim that a razor "shaves 200% smoother" isn't.[14]

Copywriters use **provocative headlines** to provoke the reader's curiosity—to stimulate questions and thoughts. For example: "My chickens eat better than you do" (Perdue Chickens). To learn more, the reader must read the body copy. The danger, of course, is that the reader won't read on. To avoid this, the creative team designs visuals to clarify the message or provide some story appeal.

A **question headline** asks a question, encouraging readers to search for the answer in the body of the ad. An ad for 4day Tire Stores asks: "What makes our tire customers smarter & richer than others?" A good question headline piques the reader's curiosity and imagination. But if a headline asks a question the reader can answer quickly (or even worse, negatively) the rest of the ad may not get read. Imagine a headline that reads: "Do you want to buy insurance?" The reader answers, "No," and turns the page.[15]

A **command headline** orders the reader to do something, so it might seem negative. But readers pay attention to such headlines. Ocean Spray targets youth with the

Last year, the U.S. Department of Transportation reported more traffic fatalities on normal weather days than on rainy and snowy days combined. Unfortunately, the sun's glare and haze can create a blind spot right where a driver needs visibility most: the front wind-shield. Ordinary sunglasses give drivers only partial protection from the sun's distractions. After all, they were designed more for viewing the curves on the beach than the ones on the road. That's exactly why we've developed Ray-Ban Sunglasses for Driving, sunglasses created specifically to help you keep your eyes on the road. With brown B-15 Top Gradient Mirror lenses and 100% UV protection, they're highly effective at screening out blue light. Which simply means they clear up road haze and sharpen detail without any color distortion. What's more, the top portion of the lens is mirrored to

help reduce overhead glare, while the uncoated lower lens still gives you a crisp and clear view of the instrument panel. And unlike photochromic lenses that require ultra-violet sunlight to darken fully, Ray-Ban B-15 lenses always stay dark enough to reduce dangerous glare. All of which help make Ray-Ban Sunglasses for Driving the safest thing you could wear in your car next to a seat belt. Of course it doesn't hurt if the car you're driving is also designed for safety — like the Volvo 740, the Grand Prize in our Test-Drive Sweepstakes. To enter, just pick up an official entry form at your Ray-Ban dealer. And while you're there, test-wear a pair of Ray-Ban Sunglasses for Driving. They can turn 78° and sunny back into what it was always meant to be: a beautiful day for a drive.

78° And Not A Cloud In The Sky. What A Hazardous Day For A Drive.

Ray-Ban **Sunglasses For Driving.**

● This ad uses a provocative headline to get attention. The visual clarifies the headline and draws the reader into the body copy, which gives the rationale for using the product and credibility for the headline.

hip headline: "Crave the Wave."[16] Some command headlines make a request: "Please don't squeeze the Charmin" (bathroom tissue).

Many headline types are easily combined. But the type of headline used is less important than the way it's used. Copywriters must always write with style—for the receiver's pleasure, not their own.[17]

Subheads

The **subhead,** an additional smaller headline, may appear above the headline or below it. A subhead above the headline, called a **kicker** (or *overline*), is often underlined. Subheads may also appear in body copy.

Subheads are usually set smaller than the headline but larger than the body copy or text. Subheads generally appear in **boldface** (heavier) type or a different color. Like a headline, the subhead transmits key sales points fast. But it usually carries less impor-

● Subheads reinforce the headline and transmit key sales points. In this poster campaign for General Accident, the headline is embedded in the jarring visual. In contrast, the subhead, *Fortunately, it's covered by Accident,* is calm and reassuring and includes a play on the company name. The headline and subhead effectively carry the entire message without needing body copy.

Fortunately, it's covered by Accident   GA

General Accident

Writing Effective Copy — *Checklist*

- **Get to the main point—fast.**
- **Emphasize one major idea simply and clearly.**
- **Be single-minded.** Don't try to do too much. If you chase more than one rabbit at a time, you'll catch none.
- **Position the product clearly.**
- **Keep the brand name up front and reinforce it.**
- **Write with the consumer's ultimate benefit in mind.**
- **Write short sentences.** Use easy, familiar words and themes people understand.
- **Don't waste words.** Say what you have to say—nothing more, nothing less. Don't pad, but don't skimp.

- **Avoid bragging and boasting.** Write from the reader's point of view, not your own. Avoid "we," "us," "our."
- **Avoid clichés.** They're crutches; learn to get along without them. Bright, surprising words and phrases perk up readers, keep them reading.
- **Write with flair.** Drum up excitement. Make sure your own enthusiasm comes through in the copy.
- **Use vivid language** with lots of verbs and adverbs.
- **Stick to the present tense, active voice.** It's crisper. Avoid the past tense and passive voice. Exceptions should be deliberate, for special effect.

- **Use personal pronouns.** Remember, you're talking to just one person, so talk as you would to a friend. Use "you" and "your."
- **Use contractions.** They're fast, personal, natural. People talk in contractions. (Listen to yourself.)
- **Don't overpunctuate.** It kills copy flow. Excessive commas are the chief culprits. Don't give readers any excuse to jump ship.
- **Read the copy aloud.** Hear how it sounds; catch errors. The written word is considerably different from the spoken word.
- **Rewrite and write tight.** Edit mercilessly. Tell the whole story and no more. When finished, stop.

tant information than the headline. Subheads are important for two reasons: most individuals read only the headline and subheads, and subheads usually support the interest step best.

Subheads are longer and more like sentences. They serve as stepping stones from the headline to the body copy, telegraphing what's to come.[18]

Body Copy

The advertiser tells the complete sales story in the **body copy, or text.** The body copy comprises the interest, credibility, desire, and often even the action steps. It is a logical continuation of the headline and subheads, set in smaller type. Body copy covers the features, benefits, and utility of the product or service.

The body copy is typically read by only one out of ten readers, so the writer must speak to the reader's self-interest, explaining how the product or service satisfies the customer's need.[19] The best ads focus on one big idea or one clear benefit. Copywriters often read their copy aloud to hear how it sounds, even if it's intended for print media. The ear is a powerful copywriting tool.[20]

Experts tout the techniques in the Checklist for Writing Effective Copy.

Body copy styles

Experienced copywriters look for the technique and style with the greatest sales appeal for the idea being presented. Common copy styles include *straight sell, institutional, narrative, dialog/monolog, picture caption,* and *device.*

In **straight-sell copy,** writers immediately explain or develop the headline and visual—or the pictures on the screen—in a straightforward, factual presentation. The straight-sell approach appeals to the prospect's reason. Since it ticks off the product's sales points in order of importance, straight-sell copy is particularly good for high think-involvement products or products that are difficult to use. It's especially effective in direct-mail advertising and industrial or high-tech situations. Advertisers use the straight-sell approach more than all other techniques combined.[21]

Advertisers use **institutional copy** to promote a philosophy or extol the merits of an organization rather than product features. The Timberland ad at the beginning of this chapter uses an institutional copy style to explain the company's design philosophy. Institutional copy is intended to lend warmth and credibility to the organization's image. Banks, insurance companies, public corporations, and large manufacturing firms use institutional copy in both print and electronic media. However, David Ogilvy warns against the "self-serving, flatulent pomposity" that characterizes the copy in many corporate ads.[22]

Copywriters use **narrative copy** to tell a story. Ideal for the creative writer, narrative copy sets up a situation and then resolves it at the last minute by having the product or service come to the rescue. Narrative copy offers good opportunities for emotional appeals. Insurance companies, for example, tell the poignant story of the man who died unexpectedly but, fortunately, had just renewed his policy.[23]

By using **dialog/monolog copy,** the advertiser can add the believability that narrative copy sometimes lacks. The characters portrayed in a print ad do the selling in their own words. A caution—poorly written dialog copy can come off as dull or, even worse, hokey and unreal.

Sometimes it's easier to tell a story with illustrations and captions. A photo with **picture-caption copy** is particularly useful for products that have a number of different uses or come in a variety of styles or designs.

With any copy style, the copywriter may use some device copy to enhance attention, interest, and memorability. **Device copy** uses figures of speech (like puns, alliteration, assonance, and rhymes) as well as humor and exaggeration. Verbal devices help people remember the brand and tend to affect attitude favorably.[24] The Timberland headline ("Where the elements of design are the elements themselves") plays off the double meaning of the word *element*.

Humor can be effective when the advertiser needs high memorability in a short time, wants to dispel preconceived negative images, or needs to create a distinct personality for an undifferentiated product. However, humor should always be used carefully and never be in questionable taste. Some researchers believe humor distracts from the selling message and can even be detrimental when used poorly or for serious services like finance, insurance, and crematoriums.[25]

• Device copy enhances an ad's attention-getting quality, sustains interest, and contributes to its memorability. This ad for Carolina Allergy & Asthma Research Group uses well-known *Snow White* images and a play on words to send out a call for participants in a paid research program. The subhead—*Better see Doc*—continues the humorous but sympathetic approach to an unfunny subject.

Formatting body copy

The keys to good body copy are simplicity, order, credibility, and clarity. Or, as John O'Toole says, prose should be "written clearly, informatively, interestingly, powerfully, persuasively, dramatically, memorably, and with effortless grace. That's all."[26] (Study the Creative Director's Portfolio on pages 290–93 for some good examples.)

Four basic format elements are used to construct long copy ads: the *lead-in paragraph, interior paragraphs, trial close,* and *close.*

Lead-in paragraph   The **lead-in paragraph** is a bridge between the headline and the sales ideas presented in the text. Like a subhead, the lead-in paragraph is part of the *interest* step. It must be engaging and able to convert a prospect's reading interest to product interest.

Interior paragraphs   **Interior paragraphs** develop *credibility*—by providing proof for claims and promises—and build *desire* by using language that stirs the imagination. Advertisers should rely on research data, testimonials, and warranties to support their product promises. Such proofs help avoid costly lawsuits, convince customers of the validity of the product, improve goodwill toward the advertiser, and stimulate sales.

Trial close   Interspersed in the interior paragraphs should be suggestions to act now. Good copy asks for the order more than once; mail-order ads ask several times. Consumers often make the buying decision without reading all the body copy. The **trial close** gives them the opportunity to make the buying decision early.

Close   The **close** is the *action* step. A good close asks consumers to do something and tells them how. The close should simplify the audience's response, making it easy for them to order the merchandise, send for information, or visit a showroom. A business reply card or a toll-free phone number may be included. Of course, not all ads sell products or services. Advertisers may want to change attitudes, explain their viewpoints, or ask for someone's vote.

The close can be direct or indirect. A *direct close* seeks immediate response in the form of a purchase, a store visit, or a request for further information.

Slogans

Many **slogans** (also called **themelines** or **taglines**) begin as successful headlines, like AT&T's "Reach out and touch someone." Through continuous use, they become standard statements, not just in advertising but for salespeople and company employees.

Slogans have two basic purposes: to provide continuity to a series of ads in a campaign and to reduce an advertising message strategy to a brief, repeatable, and memorable positioning statement. DeBeers' ads, for example, still use the famous slogan "Diamonds are forever." But Miller Lite's corny "It's It and That's That" was "major league pathetic," according to one *Wall Street Journal* article. Lacking the creativity, freshness, and power to become a full-fledged slogan, it was short-lived.[27]

Seals, Logos, and Signatures

A **seal** is awarded only when a product meets standards established by a particular organization such as the Good Housekeeping Institute, Underwriters Laboratories, and Parents Institute. Since these organizations are recognized authorities, their seals provide an independent, valued endorsement for the advertiser's product.

Logotypes and **signature cuts** (sig cuts) are special designs of the advertiser's company or product name. They appear in all company ads and, like trademarks, give the product individuality and provide quick recognition at the point of purchase.

(continued on page 294)

Creative Director's Portfolio

The art director plans and then pulls together all elements of a print ad or a commercial so the finished product meets the advertiser's needs. This includes planning the ad's artistic elements to make the message understandable, believable, and appealing—and then combining them with simple, orderly, credible, and clear body copy. Not as easy as it sounds!

Photography captures details so accurately that it is the ideal medium for building credible images, particularly when high-think purchase decisions are involved. The road-handling benefit of the Audi 80 Estate featured in this photo-dominant ad is dramatized by the many hats swirling in the air—an image easily created by digital enhancement. If carried too far, though, computerized imagery can damage a photo's (and therefore an ad's) inherent credibility.

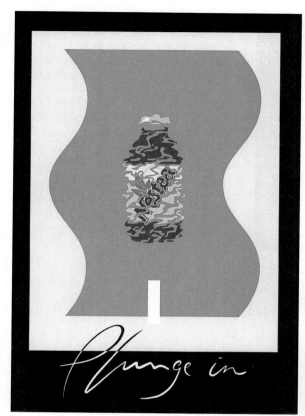

The use of style can improve the power of advertising messages. However, the word *style* pertains to a number of different concepts in advertising. For example, it may pertain to the overall flavor or mood of an image. In this Canadian ad for lemon-flavored Nestea, the wavy form of the abstract pool enveloping the Nestea bottle and the sweep of the headline create an overall relaxing appearance.

Artists often borrow styles from other periods to enhance an ad's appearance. Here the ad's typeface and layout create an *artistic style* popular in the late 1950s. This ad also uses a type style similar to calligraphy that is dramatically more romantic than the clinical feeling of a typeface such as Helvetica.

Illustration is the technique for expressing concepts that do not exist in real life. This light-hearted illustration shows one of Oneida's more decoratively patterned spoons dressed up like a woman and starring as the center of attention—with the tag, "Well, no wonder." Although manipulated photography is sometimes used to present creative ideas, its detailed nature makes it more difficult to control, and therefore often more expensive than illustration.

Because this illustration bleeds off the page, the lines of the floor pattern converging in the distance emphasize the feeling of motion as the dish and spoon run out of the picture.

The artistic use of visual space can create a sense of dimension and a feeling of movement in ads. Because the eye tends to perceive darkness as receding, the doorknob appears to jump out even farther from the dark background. Also, the relative blankness of the right half of the ad provides the visual space needed for the handle to fly across it, enhancing the feeling of movement.

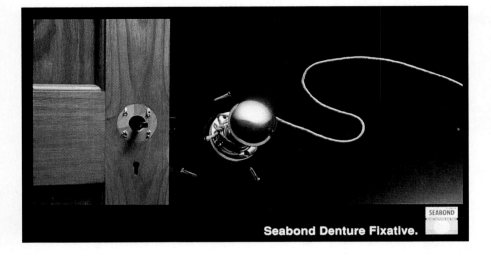

Thank God There Are People Who Stayed In The Science Club.

The overall flatness and linear qualities of this ad for S-Works FSR mountain bikes suggest we're looking at a scientific diagram. Like a diagram or blueprint, the bicycle is structurally very linear, there are no broad areas, and every element has a direction and is line-like. Similarly, the letter forms of the type and the handwritten math formulas are very linear.

Also like a diagram, this print ad is not deep in appearance; the elements seem to rest close to the plane of the picture. The picture plane is like the glass of a window—we look through it as well as see things on it. The bike is situated flat to our view, not receding in space. The headline type appears to rest on the picture plane, and the reversed body copy at the bottom of the ad seems to float in front of the dark background as though rising up to the picture plane.

In radio, sound is everything. In this spot for Plochman's mustard, the Bronx cheer (also known as a raspberry)—a high-pitched sputtering sound made by blowing air between the tongue and lips—is the mnemonic device that makes the ad a success. Used early in the ad, the sound captures attention by its very rudeness (its association with bodily functions usually implies disrespect). At the conclusion of the commercial, it stimulates our memory to buy the product, lest we embarrass ourselves by running out of Plochman's.

Mom & Son :50

SON: You're in the living room watching TV, waiting for mom to finish making dinner. When all of a sudden you hear a noise in the kitchen.

SFX: Bronx cheer.

SON: Was that what you thought it was? No, you dismiss it as something else. Until that is, you hear it again.

SFX: Bronx cheer.

SON: And again.

SFX: Bronx cheer.

SON: You can't ignore it any longer. So you ask, am I hearing what I think I'm hearing? To which your mom replies, Steven, come into the kitchen this instant. Worried, you rush in only to have your worst fears confirmed. Your mom's hands are clutching an empty squeeze barrel of Plochman's Mustard over her world-famous potato salad. With her culinary reputation on the line, she hands you the bottle. Naturally you show her the value of having a man around the house.

SFX: Bronx cheer.

SON: The last of the Plochman's shoots out. You grin triumphantly. Don't embarrass yourself. Don't . . .

SFX: Bronx cheer.

SON: . . . run out of Plochman's.

(Music under throughout.)
SINGER: Oh, well I'm the kind of light that likes to bend around. You can point me left or right, or hang me upside down.

But I'm not the kind of light you have to hang on to. Just use me when you need three hands, but you've only got two.

'Cause I'm the Snakelight.
They call me the Snakelight.
I get around, around, around, around, around.

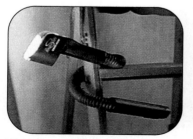

VO: It's the hands-free flexible flashlight, new from Black & Decker.

SINGER: Yeah, we're the Snakelights, from Black & Decker.

We get around, around, around, around, around. (Music out.)

TV commercials are most effective when every scene is artistically crafted to be a complete visual and audio experience. In this commercial, Black & Decker introduces its new Snakelight flexible flashlight in a series of situations and uses. The Snakelight brightens a series of darkened scenes as it wraps around a fisherman's neck, helping him tie a lure, drapes over a pipe under the kitchen sink, helps a woman change a tire, and in the finale, struts its stuff in a chorus line and lights up the inside of a tent. The audio is appropriately sung to the tune and beat of *The Wanderer*, with its refrain of *around, around, around, around* (try singing it). The only "straight" audio is one voiceover announcement: *It's the hands-free flexible flashlight, new from Black & Decker*—all the more effective because of its contrast to the catchy tune in the rest of the spot.

COPYWRITING FOR ELECTRONIC MEDIA

For electronic media, the fundamental elements—the five steps of the creative pyramid—remain the primary guides, but the copywriting formats differ. Radio and television writers prepare scripts and storyboards.

Writing Radio Copy

A **script** resembles a two-column list. On the left side, speakers' names are arranged vertically along with descriptions of any sound effects and music. The right column contains the dialog, called the **audio.**

Copywriters first need to understand radio as a medium. Radio provides entertainment or news to listeners who are busy doing something else—driving, washing dishes, reading the paper, or even studying. To be heard, an advertising message must be catchy, interesting, and unforgettable. Radio listeners usually decide within five to eight seconds if they're going to pay attention. To attract and hold listeners' attention, particularly those not attracted to a product category, radio copy must be intrusive.

Intrusive, yes; offensive, no. An insensitive choice of words, overzealous effort to attract listeners with irritating everyday sounds (car horn, alarm clock, screeching tires), or characters that sound too exotic, odd, or dumb can cause listener resentment and ultimately lose sales. Tom Bodett's ads for Motel 6 show how effective a personal, re-

• A radio script format resembles a two-column list, with speakers' names and sound effects on the left and the dialog in a wider column on the right. The quality of radio commercials depends on the actor/announcer's delivery of the message and the background music and sound effects.

McCANN-ERICKSON

RADIO SCRIPT

Client:	United Nations	**Date:**	4/95
Product:	50th Anniversary	**Length:**	:30
Title:	Health/Disease		

As Produced....

SFX - V/O	**Audio**
SFX: Small girl coughing	
AVO	Darjhi has whooping cough. And without medical care she might die. But today, in a United Nations' mobile health clinic, she's on the road to recovery.
SFX: Background sounds of doctor's office	
Doctor's voice	Take a deep breath.
AVO	For 50 years, the UN has developed initiatives like mobile medical units. So while 80% of the world's children *are* vaccinated against whooping cough, the UN also ensures that patients like Darjhi can receive treatment.
SFX: Background sounds of doctor's office.	
Doctor's voice	All better.
AVO	The United Nations proudly celebrates 50 years of work for better medical care. And proudly continues nursing the world back to health.

Creating Effective Radio Commercials   *Checklist*

□ **Make the big idea crystal clear.** Concentrate on one main selling point. Radio is a good medium for building brand awareness, but not for making long lists of copy points or complex arguments.

□ **Mention the advertiser's name early and often.** If the product or company name is tricky, consider spelling it out.

□ **Take time to set the scene and establish the premise.** A 30-second commercial that nobody remembers is a waste of money. Fight for 60-second spots.

□ **Use familiar sound effects.** Ice tinkling in a glass, birds chirping, or a door shutting can create a visual image. Music also works if its meaning is clear.

□ **Paint pictures with your words.** Use descriptive language to make the ad more memorable.

□ **Make every word count.** Use active voice and more verbs than adjectives. Be conversational. Use pronounceable words and short sentences.

□ **Be outrageous.** The best comic commercials begin with a totally absurd premise from which all developments follow logically. But remember, if you can't write humor really well, go for drama.

□ **Ask for the order.** Try to get listeners to take action.

□ **Radio is a local medium.** Adjust your commercials to the language of your listeners and the time of day they'll run.

□ **Presentation counts a lot.** Even the best scripts look boring on paper. Acting, timing, vocal quirks, and sound effects bring them to life.

---

laxed, and cheerful style can be. Other guidelines are given in the Checklist for Creating Effective Radio Commercials.

One of the most challenging aspects is making the script fit the time slot. The delivery changes for different types of commercials, so writers should read the script out loud for timing. With electronic compression, recorded radio ads can now include 10 to 30 percent more copy than text read live. Still, the following is a good rule of thumb:

10 seconds: 20–25 words.   30 seconds: 60–70 words.
20 seconds: 40–45 words.   60 seconds: 130–150 words.[28]

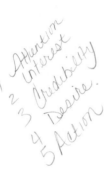

Radio writing has to be clearer than any other kind of copywriting. For example, the listener can't refer back, as in print, to find an antecedent for a pronoun. Likewise, the English language is so full of homonyms (words that sound like other words) that one can easily confuse the meaning of a sentence ("who's who is whose").[29]

Writing Television Copy

Radio's basic two-column script format also works for television. But in a TV script, the left side is titled "Video" and the right side "Audio." The video column describes the visuals and production—camera angles, action, scenery, and stage directions. The audio column lists the spoken copy, sound effects, and music.

Broadcast commercials must be believable and relevant. And even zany commercials must exude quality in their creation and production to imply the product's quality.

Wake Up Male

Wake up, hit the snooze, attempt to kiss wife. Get out of bed, step on the dog, brush teeth, gargle, kiss wife again. Shower, dry hair, put on boxers, shirt, pants, socks, shoes, tie, jacket. Pour a cup of coffee, trip over toy truck, spill coffee, change tie. Kiss wife, baby, wave at neighbor Ernie. Start car, drive to work. Notice woman staring at me at stoplight. Turn on defrost. Park. Walk to work. Sit at desk, work, work, work. Meet with boss. Promise to kill boss. Eat lunch, work, work, work. Meet with boss again. Boss gives you bonus, promotion. Put plans to kill boss on hold. Drive home, run over toy truck. Park. Kiss wife, baby, step on dog. Eat dinner, play with baby, feed baby, burp baby, change baby, put baby to bed. Talk to wife; celebrate promotion, bonus. Pick up remote, turn on TV, read paper, fall asleep on sofa, wake up to national anthem. Get up, step on dog, take off pants, shirt, socks. Brush teeth, gargle, climb in bed, kiss wife, sleep. Dream of stepping on dog.

ANNCR: You have a lot to do in a day, so we make it easy for you to talk to a Signet banker. Call our telephone banking center any time, 24 hours a day, seven days a week. It's as easy as 1-800-2-SIGNET. All Signet banks are equal opportunity lenders. Members FDIC.

● This award-winning 60-second radio spot features a fast-talking man describing his busy day in excruciating detail. The actor crammed 182 words into 45 seconds, leaving just 15 seconds for the announcer to explain that the sponsor, Signet Bank, offered telephone banking around the clock, seven days a week, for such busy people.

• A script for a TV commercial is set up in a two-column format, with the video column on the left describing the visuals and giving production information. The audio column on the right lists spoken copy, sound effects, and music. The copywriter sets the tone of the commercial, establishes the language that determines which visuals to use, and pinpoints when they should appear.

McCANN-ERICKSON

BLACK & DECKER SNAKELIGHT FLASHLIGHT
:30 COMMERCIAL
"THE WANDERER"
PREPARED BY MCCANN-ERICKSON

VIDEO	AUDIO
WE OPEN ON TOOL BOX. SNAKELIGHT FLASHLIGHT POPS OUT AND SHINES AROUND.	MUSIC THROUGHOUT, TO THE TUNE OF THE 60'S CLASSIC, "THE WANDERER". <u>SINGER:</u> "Oh, well I'm the kind of light that likes to bend around.
SNAKELIGHT IS SEEN WRAPPED AROUND FISHERMAN'S NECK HELPING HIM TIE A LURE.	You can point me left or right,
SNAKELIGHT IS SEEN UNDER KITCHEN SINK LIGHTING A PIPE.	or hang me upside down.
SNAKELIGHT IS SEEN UNDERNEATH CAR HOOD.	But I'm not the kind of light,
SNAKELIGHT IS SEEN WRAPPED AROUND CLOSET POLE.	you have to hang on to.
SNAKELIGHT IS SEEN HELPING ELECTRICIAN REPAIR OUTLET.	Just use me when you need three hands,
SNAKELIGHT IS SEEN HELPING A WOMAN FIX A FLAT TIRE.	but you've got only two. 'Cause I'm the Snakelight.
SNAKELIGHT FLASHLIGHT COMES OUT OF TOOL BOX AGAIN.	They call me the Snakelight. I get around, around, around, around, around.
SNAKELIGHT IS SEEN WRAPPING AROUND A LADDER.	<u>ANNOUNCER VOICE OVER</u>: It's the hands free flexible flashlight, new from Black & Decker.
THREE SNAKELIGHT'S POP OUT OF KITCHEN DRAWER.	<u>SINGER</u>: Yeah, we're the Snakelights, from Black & Decker.
SNAKELIGHT IS SEEN LIGHTING UP THE INSIDE OF A TENT.	We get around, around, around, around, around.

While the art director's work is very important, the copywriter typically sets the tone of the commercial, establishes the language that determines which visuals to use, and pinpoints when the visuals should appear. Research shows the techniques given in the Checklist for Creating Effective TV Commercials work best.

To illustrate these principles, let's look at a commercial. Many people want smooth, soft skin and consider a patch of rough, flaky skin anywhere on their body a disap-

---

Checklist — Creating Effective TV Commercials

☐ **Begin at the finish.** Concentrate on the final impression the commercial will make.

☐ **Create an attention-getting opening.** An opening that is visually surprising or full of action, drama, humor, or human interest sets the context and allows a smooth transition to the rest of the commercial.

☐ **Use a situation that grows naturally out of the sales story.** Avoid distracting gimmicks. Make it easy for viewers to identify with the characters.

☐ **Characters are the living symbol of the product.** They should be appealing, believable, nondistracting, and most of all, relevant.

☐ **Keep it simple.** The sequence of ideas should be easy to follow. Keep the number of elements in the commercial to a minimum.

☐ **Write concise audio copy.** The video should carry most of the weight. Fewer than two words per second is effective for demonstrations. For a 60-second commercial, 101 to 110 words is most effective; more than 170 words is too talky.

☐ **Make demonstrations dramatic but believable.** They should always be true to life and avoid the appearance of camera tricks.

☐ **Let the words interpret the picture** and prepare viewers for the next scene. Use conversational language; avoid "ad talk."

☐ **Run scenes five or six seconds on average.** Rarely should a scene run less than three seconds. Offer a variety of movement-filled scenes without "jumping."

☐ **Keep the look of the video fresh and new.**

• This commercial for Lubriderm Lotion is a well-crafted example of copywriting and creativity. The woman and setting are metaphors for smooth, feminine skin while the alligator represents dry, scaly skin. The announcer's copy is understated, a modest approach that melds well with the visual and the music.

SFX: Music.
VO: A quick reminder. Lubriderm Lotion

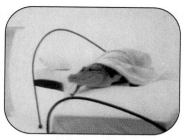

restores lost moisture to heal your dry skin and protect it. Remember, the one created

for dermatologists is the one that heals and protects. Lubriderm. See you later, alligator.

pointment. If you were the copywriter for Lubriderm skin lotion, how would you approach this somewhat touchy, negative subject?

The creative staff of J. Walter Thompson crafted an artistic solution for Lubriderm. An alligator was the big idea. The gator's scaly sheath was a metaphor for rough, flaky skin. Its appearance ignited people's survival instincts—they paid attention, fast. A beautiful, sophisticated woman with smooth, feminine skin was seated in a lounge chair, completely unruffled by the passing gator. The swing of the animal's back and tail echoed the graceful curves of the two simple pieces of furniture on the set, and its slow stride kept the beat of a light jazz tune.

This commercial opened with an attention-getting big idea that was visually surprising, compelling, dramatic, and interesting. It was also a quasi-demonstration: we saw the alligator's scaly, prickly skin, and the woman's confidence and willingness to touch the alligator as it passed by symbolized the confidence Lubriderm can bring.

This ad follows the creative pyramid. The alligator captures attention visually while the announcer's first words serve as an attention-getting headline: "A quick reminder." The ad commands us to listen and sets up the interest step that offers this claim: "Lubriderm restores lost moisture to heal your dry skin and protect it." Now for the credibility step: "Remember, the one created for dermatologists is the one that heals and protects." Then a quick trial close (action), "Lubriderm." And then the desire step recaps the primary product benefit and adds a touch of humor: "See you later, alligator."

THE ROLE OF ART IN RADIO AND TV ADVERTISING

When they received a flood of calls from amputees, the executives at Du Pont knew their new commercial was a success.

Created by BBDO Worldwide from an inspiration by a Du Pont department head, the ad featured Bill Demby, a Vietnam veteran who had lost his legs in a rocket attack. In the TV spot, Demby is on his way to play basketball in an urban neighborhood. As he pulls off his sweatpants, attention focuses on his two artificial legs. As Demby freely dashes, jumps, scrambles, and shoots, the voice-over explains that he is wearing the "Seattle Foot," a prosthesis designed by the Prosthetics Research Study in Seattle, Washington. Suddenly, Demby falls. Play stops. He's offered a helping hand but jumps right up, and the rapid-fire action begins again. As the spot ends, an out-of-breath player calls out: "Hey, Bill, you've been practicing!"

Developing the Artistic Concept for Commercials

Creating the concept for a radio or TV commercial is similar to creating the concept for print ads. The first step is to determine the big idea. Then, the art director and copywriter must decide what commercial format to use. Should a celebrity present the message? Or should the ad dramatize the product's benefits with a semifictional story? The next step is to write a script containing the necessary copy or dialog plus a basic description of any music, sound effects, and/or camera views.

• In this ad, the story line is a framework within which to portray the value of the product and demonstrate its ruggedness. The story itself began without a specific person in mind, but Bill Demby—a real-life beneficiary of the product—helped make its utility come alive.

(Music under.)
ANNCR: When Bill Demby was in Vietnam, he dreamed of coming home and playing a little basketball.

MAN: Hey, Bill!
ANNCR: A dream that all but died when he lost both legs to a Vietcong rocket. But

then researchers discovered that a Du Pont plastic could help make truly lifelike artificial limbs.

(SFX: Sounds of game in progress.)
ANNCR: Now Bill's back, and some say he

hasn't lost a step. At Du Pont, we make things that make a difference.

MAN: Hey, Bill, you've been practicing!
ANNCR: Better things for better living.

In both radio and TV, the art director assists the copywriter in script development. But in television, artistic development is much more extensive. Using the TV script, the art director creates a series of **storyboard roughs** to present the artistic approach, the action sequences, and the style of the commercial. When the storyboard is approved, it serves as a guide for the final production phase.

Getting through these first phases, though, can be tough. For BBDO, the biggest challenge for the Du Pont commercial was finding the main "actor." BBDO staff wanted the credibility of a real Vietnam veteran with his own Seattle Foot. But he also had to be telegenic, physically strong, and able to display athletic skills. Cathy Mendel, BBDO account supervisor, said, "After exhausting all the traditional casting sources, we finally looked at participants in the Disabled Games. That's where we found Bill Demby."

In casting, the most important consideration is relevance to the product; agencies don't use a comic to sell financial products—or cremation services. And in spite of Michael Jordan's success for Nike, Gatorade, and McDonald's, some experts don't believe in using celebrities. David Ogilvy, for example, thinks viewers remember the celebrity more than the product.[30] As the concept evolves, the creative team defines the characters' personalities in a detailed, written **casting brief.** These descriptions serve as guides in casting sessions when actors audition for the roles. Sometimes, agencies discover a Tony and Sharon (of Taster's Choice fame)—solid, memorable characters who go beyond a simple role and actually create a personality or image for the product.

Formats for Radio and TV Commercials

Similar to print advertising, the format for a broadcast ad serves as a template for arranging message elements into a pattern. Once the art director and copywriter establish the big idea, they must determine the commercial's format.

Many radio and TV commercial styles have been successful. Some of these are listed in Ad Lab 10–B, "Creative Ways to Sell on Radio." Hank Seiden, the former chair of

Ketchum Advertising, developed the Execution Spectrum—24 basic formats that range from frivolous to serious (see Exhibit 10–3). Here we consider eight common commercial formats that can be used in either radio or television: *straight announcement, presenter, testimonial, demonstration, musical, slice of life, lifestyle,* and *animation*.

Straight announcement

The **straight announcement** is the oldest and simplest type of radio or TV commercial and probably the easiest to write. One person, usually a radio or TV announcer, delivers the sales message. Music may play in the background. Straight announcements are popular because they are adaptable to almost any product or situation. In radio, a straight announcement can also be designed as an **integrated commercial**—that is, it can be woven into a show or tailored to a given program.

For TV, an announcer may deliver the sales message **on camera** or off screen, as a **voice-over,** while a demonstration, slide, or film shows on screen. If the script is well written and the announcer convincing, straight announcements can be very effective. Since they don't require elaborate production facilities, they save money, too.

Straight announcements are commonly used on late-night TV programs, by local advertisers, and by nonprofit or political organizations.

Presenter

The **presenter commercial** uses one person or character to present the product and carry the sales message. Some presenters are celebrities, like Lindsay Wagner for Ford. Others are corporate officers of the sponsor, like Dave Thomas, the president of Wendy's, or actors playing a role (the lonely Maytag repairman). However, a presenter doesn't have to be a real person. Remember Tony the Tiger?

A **radio personality**—like Rush Limbaugh or Larry King—may ad lib an ad message live in his or her own style. Done well, such commercials can be very successful, as evidenced by Snapple. However, the advertiser surrenders control to the personality. The main risk, outside of occasional blunders, is that the personality may criticize the product. Even so, this sometimes lends an appealing realism. The personality gets a highlight sheet listing the product's features, the main points to stress, and the phrases or company slogans to repeat. But he or she can choose the specific wording and mode of delivery.

Testimonial

The true **testimonial**—where a satisfied user tells how effective the product is—can be highly credible in both TV and radio advertising. Celebrities may gain attention, but they must be believable and not distract from the product. Actually, people from all walks of life endorse products, from known personalities to unknowns and nonprofessionals. Which type of person to use depends on the product and the strategy. Satisfied customers are the best sources for testimonials because their sincerity is usually persuasive. Ogilvy suggests shooting candid testimonials when the subjects don't know they're being filmed.[31] But advertisers must be sure to get their permission before use.

Demonstration

Television is uniquely suited to visual demonstration. And a **demonstration** convinces an audience better and faster than an oral message. So don't say it, show it.[32] Naturally, it's easier to demonstrate the product on TV than on radio, but some advertisers have used radio to create humorous, tongue-in-cheek demonstrations.

Products may be demonstrated in use, in competition, or before and after. These techniques help viewers visualize how the product will perform for them.

Musical

The **musical commercials,** or **jingles,** we hear on radio and TV are among the best—and worst—ad messages produced. Done well, they can bring enormous success, well beyond the average nonmusical commercial. Done poorly, they can waste the advertising budget and annoy audiences beyond belief.

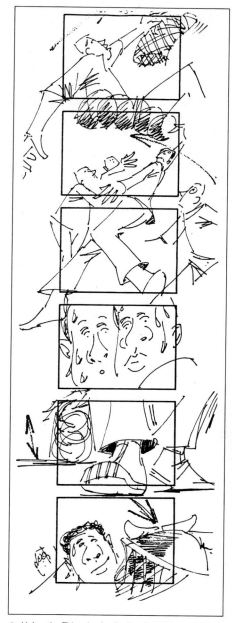

• Using the TV script for Du Pont's Bill Demby commercial, the art director created a storyboard depicting the artistic approach, action sequences, and style of the commercial.

Ad Lab 10-B   Creative Ways to Sell on Radio

Product demo The commercial tells how a product is used or the purposes it serves.

Voice power A unique voice gives the ad power.

Electronic sound Synthetic sound-making machines create a memorable product-sound association.

Customer interview A spokesperson and customer discuss the product advantages spontaneously.

Humorous fake interview The customer interview is done in a lighter vein.

Hyperbole (exaggeration) statement Overstatement arouses interest in legitimate product claims that might otherwise pass unnoticed; often a spoof.

Fourth dimension Time and events are compressed into a brief spot involving the listener in future projections.

Hot property Commercial adapts a current sensation—a hit show, performer, or song.

Comedian power Established comedians do commercials in their own unique style, implying celebrity endorsement.

Historical fantasy Situation with revived historical characters is used to convey product message.

Sound picture Recognizable sounds involve the listener by stimulating imagination.

Demographics Music or references appeal to a particular segment of the population, such as an age or interest group.

Imagery transfer Musical logo or other sound reinforces the memory of a television campaign.

Celebrity interview Famous person endorses the product in an informal manner.

Product song Music and words combine to create a musical logo, selling the product in the style of popular music.

Editing genius Many different situations, voices, types of music, and sounds are combined in a series of quick cuts.

Improvisation Performers work out the dialog extemporaneously for an assigned situation; may be postedited.

Laboratory Applications

1. Select three familiar radio commercials and discuss which creative techniques they use.

2. Select a familiar radio commercial and discuss how a different creative technique would increase its effectiveness.

Musical commercials have several variations. The entire message may be sung; jingles may be written with a **donut** in the middle (a hole for spoken copy); or orchestras may play symphonic or popular arrangements. Many producers use consistent musical themes for background color or to close the commercial. This is called a **musical logo.** After many repetitions of the advertiser's theme, the listener begins to associate the musical logo with the product. To achieve this, the jingle should have a **hook**—that part of the song that sticks in your memory.[33]

Advertisers have three sources of music. They can buy the right to use a tune from the copyright owner, which is usually expensive. They can use a melody in the public domain, which is free. Or they can hire a composer to write an original tune. Some original tunes, including Coke's famous "I'd like to teach the world to sing," have become popular hits.

Slice of life (problem solution)

The **slice-of-life** commercial is a dramatization of a real-life situation. It usually starts with just plain folks, played by professional actors, discussing some problem. Often, the situation deals with a problem of a personal nature—bad breath, loose dentures, dandruff, body odor, or yellow laundry. A relative or a co-worker drops the hint, the product is tried, and the next scene shows the result—a happier, cleaner, more fragrant

Exhibit • 10–3
The Execution Spectrum, developed by Hank Seiden for use with clients, shows 24 execution formats, ranging in style from frivolous to serious, for both print and electronic advertising.

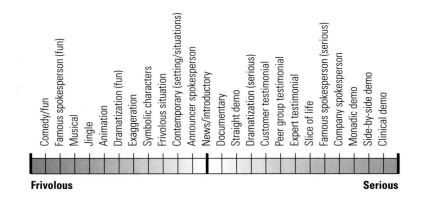

person off with a new date. The drama always concludes with a successful trial. Such commercials can get attention and create interest even though they are often irritating to viewers and hated by copywriters.

The key to effective slice-of-life commercials is simplicity. The ad should concentrate on one product benefit and make it memorable. Often, a **mnemonic device** can dramatize the product benefit and trigger instant recall. Users of Imperial margarine suddenly discover crowns on their heads, for example.

Believability in slice commercials is difficult to achieve. People don't really talk about "the sophisticated taste of Taster's Choice," so the actors must be highly credible to put the fantasy across. That's why most *local* advertisers don't use the slice-of-life technique. Creating that believability takes very professional talent and money. (Chapter 11 presents an artful slice-of-life commercial in the Creative Department, pp. 318–22.) In all cases, the story should be relevant to the product and simply told.

Lifestyle

To present the user rather than the product, advertisers may use the **lifestyle** technique. For example, Levi's targets its 501 Jeans messages to young, contemporary men by showing characters working in various occupations and participating in many pastimes. Likewise, beer and soft-drink advertisers frequently target their messages to active, outdoorsy young people, focusing on who drinks the brand rather than on specific product advantages.

Animation

Cartoons, puppet characters, and demonstrations with computer-generated graphics are very effective **animation** techniques for communicating difficult messages and reaching specialized markets, such as children. The way aspirin or other medications affect the human system is difficult to explain. Animated pictures of headaches and stomachs can simplify the subject and make a demonstration understandable.

Computer animation requires a great deal of faith on the part of advertisers. Since most of this very expensive work is done on the computer, there's nothing to see until the animation is well developed. (This is more fully discussed in Chapter 11.)

Basic Mechanics of Storyboard Development

After the creative team selects the big idea and the format for a TV commercial, the art director and the writer develop the script. Television is so visually powerful and expressive that the art director's role is particularly important. Art directors must be able to work with a variety of professionals—producers, directors, lighting technicians, and set designers—to develop and produce a commercial successfully.

Storyboard design

Once the basic script is completed, the art director must turn the video portion of the script into real images. This is done with a storyboard, a sheet preprinted with a series of 8 to 20 blank windows (frames) in the shape of TV screens. Below each frame is room to place the text of the commercial, including the sound effects and camera views as abbreviated in Exhibit 10–4.

Through a process similar to laying out a print ad—thumbnail, rough, comp—the artist carefully designs how each scene should appear, arranging actors, scenery, props, lighting, and camera angles to maximize impact, beauty, and mood. The storyboard helps the creatives visualize the commercial's tone and sequence of action, discover any conceptual weaknesses, and make presentations for management approval. It also serves as a guide for filming.

Even when designed to the level of a comp, though, the storyboard is only an approximation. Actual production often results in many changes in lighting, camera angle, focal point, and emphasis. The camera sees many things that the artist couldn't visualize, and vice versa (see Chapter 11 for more details on working with storyboards).

Exhibit • 10–4

Cut, zoom, and wipe, please! (Common abbreviations used in TV scripts.)

CU: Close-up. Very close shot of person or object.

ECU: Extreme close-up. A more extreme version of the above. Sometimes designated BCU (big close-up) or TCU (tight close-up).

MCU: Medium close-up. Emphasizes the subject but includes other objects nearby.

MS: Medium shot. Wide-angle shot of subject but not whole set.

FS: Full shot. Entire set or object.

LS: Long shot. Full view of scene to give effect of distance.

DOLLY: Move camera toward or away from subject. Dolly in (DI), dolly out (DO), or dolly back (DB).

PAN: Scan from one side to the other.

ZOOM: Move in or out from the subject without blurring.

SUPER: Superimpose one image on another—as showing lettering over a scene.

DISS: Dissolve (also DSS). Fade out one scene while fading in another.

CUT: Instantly change one picture to another.

WIPE: Gradually erase picture from screen. (Many varied effects are possible.)

VO: Voice-over. An off-screen voice, usually the announcer's.

SFX: Sound effects.

DAU: Down and under. Sound effects fade as voice comes on.

UAO: Up and over. Voice fades as sound effects come on.

Animatic: The video comp

To supplement the storyboard or pretest a concept, a commercial may be taped in rough form using the writers and artists as actors. Or an **animatic** may be shot—a film strip of the sketches in the storyboard accompanied by the audio portion of the commercial synchronized on tape. Even a standard animatic now costs more than $10,000 to produce. But computers are cutting costs. Peter Farago of Farago Advertising, for example, developed a Macintosh-based editing system that lets the agency create moving pictures on the screen, lay sound behind them, and transfer the entire package onto videotape to send to the client. This system cuts the cost to produce testable material from about $11,000 to $1,100.[34] This kind of technology is being adopted by more agencies as they look for ways to serve clients' creative needs better for less money.

Upon approval of the storyboard and/or the animatic, the commercial is ready for production, a subject we cover in detail in Chapter 11.

CREATING ADS FOR INTERNATIONAL MARKETS

When Galleries Lafayette tried to market fake furs in the United States, the company took out a two-page ad in *Elle* magazine and pitched the product as it would have in France—as an up-market, haute couture garment. But U.S. consumers don't think of fake furs in those terms, so the campaign was not a success. This example points out a basic rule: Advertisers must base foreign appeals on the foreign consumer's purchasing abilities, habits, and motivations.

Foreign Audiences May Have Different Purchasing Habits

Advertising messages—foreign or domestic—must address markets that can afford to buy the product. In low-income countries, housing ads that talk about luxury qualities will draw only a small audience.

How and when consumers normally make purchases are also important considerations. Most important, though, is *who* makes the buying decision. In North America and Europe, spouses usually exercise about equal control over purchasing decisions. In Latin American countries, the husband often controls major decisions. In the U.S., even children may have a strong influence (especially in the choice of breakfast cereals, snacks, toothpastes, and fast-food chains), but this is much less common in foreign markets.

Factors vary from country to country and product to product. Advertisers must consider these issues carefully before creating ads or buying media.

Consumer Motives and Appeals

Advertisers also need to understand the personal motivations, national pride, social roles, and differences in taste and attitude among markets.

Foreign marketing environments may place greater emphasis on social or political issues than domestic markets do. In Europe, for example, *green marketing* is much bigger than in the U.S. To be a good corporate citizen in those markets, companies may choose to focus a portion of their advertising on local issues of importance. Timberland became a signatory to the CERES Principles, a set of ethics that guide environmental conduct. It also developed its own magazine, called *Elements: The Journal of Outdoor Experience,* which effectively positions the company as a conservationist. To speak out against hatred and intolerance globally, the company launched a campaign called "Give Racism the Boot" in Germany, France, the U.K., and the U.S.[35]

Some lower-income, less-developed nations desire U.S. products but resent the national influence and power these products represent. Global advertisers must be careful to avoid irritating national sensitivities.

Social roles play an important part in determining whom the ads should address. In Saudi Arabia, for example, shopping is a social affair, and Saudi Arabians almost always shop in groups. So an ad campaign stressing peer approval might be more effective than one emphasizing individual growth or self-indulgence.

Differences in taste and attitude aren't such a problem in business-to-business advertising. Businesspeople's problems are fairly universal, as are the advertising appeals to solve them. Differences in approach come down to a region's economics.

• Timberland launched a campaign against hatred and intolerance called "Give Racism the Boot" with print ads that ran in Germany, France, the U.K., and the U.S.

The Question of Language and Campaign Transfer

The most important consideration for copywriters and creative directors is language. In Western Europe, people speak at least 15 different languages and more than twice as many dialects. A similar problem exists in Asia, Africa, and, to a lesser extent, South America.

International advertisers have debated the transferability of campaigns for years. One side believes it's too expensive to create a unique campaign for each national group. They simply translate one campaign into the necessary language. Timberland thinks globally but acts locally. It creates ads for various language groups in those languages, but the overall themes are consistent globally. Other advertisers believe the only way to ensure success is to create a special campaign for each market. Still others find both solutions expensive and unnecessary. They run their ads in English worldwide.

Advertisers must look at each situation individually. Moreover, they have to weigh the economics of various promotional strategies.

Regardless of strategy, translation remains a basic issue. Classic examples of mistranslations and faulty word choices abound in international advertising. A faulty Spanish translation for Perdue chickens read, "It takes a sexually excited man to make a chick affectionate."[36]

A poorly chosen or badly translated product name can undercut advertising credibility in foreign markets. Coke's product name was once widely translated into Chinese characters that sounded like "Coca-Cola" but meant "bite the wax tadpole."[37]

People in the U.S., Canada, England, Australia, and South Africa all speak English, but with wide variations in vocabulary, word usage, and syntax. Similarly, the French spoken in France, Canada, Vietnam, and Belgium may differ as much as the English spoken by a British aristocrat and a Tennessee mountaineer. Language variations exist even within countries. The Japanese use five lingual "gears," ranging from haughty to servile, depending on the speaker's and the listener's respective stations in life. Japanese translators must know when to change gears.

• Global advertisers often use a single basic ad, translating it into the languages of the various countries where it will run.

Advertisers should follow some basic rules in using translators:

- The translator *must* be an effective copywriter. In the United States and Canada, most people speak English, yet relatively few are good writers and even fewer are good copywriters. Too often advertisers simply let a translation service rewrite their ads in a foreign language. That's not good enough.

- The translator must understand the product, its features, and its market. It is always better to use a translator who is a product or market specialist rather than a generalist.

- Translators should be translating into their native tongue, and they should live in the country where the ad will appear. This way the advertiser can be sure the translator has a current understanding of the country's social attitudes, culture, and idioms.

- The advertiser should give the translator easily translatable English copy. The double meanings and idiomatic expressions that make English such a rich language for advertising rarely translate well. They only make the translator's job more difficult.

There is no greater insult to a national market than to misuse its language. The translation must be accurate, *and* it must also be good copy.

English is rapidly becoming the universal language for corporate ad campaigns directed to international businesspeople. However, some firms still also print their instructional literature and brochures in English. This approach can incite nationalistic feelings against the company. Worse yet, it automatically limits a product's use to people who understand technical English.[38]

Art Direction for International Markets

Philosophers often refer to the arts as a kind of international language whose nonverbal elements translate freely regardless of culture. A nice idea but, in advertising, a very costly one. People ascribe different meanings to color depending on their culture. When designing ads for use in other countries, the art director must be familiar with each country's artistic preferences and peculiarities.

Some consider color to indicate emotion: someone "has the blues" or is "green with envy." (Refer back to Ad Lab 9–A, "The Psychological Impact of Color.") National flags—the Canadian maple leaf, the red-white-and-blue of the United States, the tricolor of France—are nonverbal signals that stir patriotic emotions, thoughts, and actions. However, these same symbols could hurt sales. For example, a promotion using the colors in the U.S. and French flags could easily fail in Southeast Asia, where some people still have painful memories of wars fought against the U.S. and France.

An **icon,** a visual image representing some idea or thing, can have a meaning that cuts across national boundaries and reflects the tastes and attitudes of a group of cultures. An ad with a snake—an icon for the devil and eroticism in many Western cultures—could easily lose sales in North American markets. But in the Far East, where the snake represents renewal (by shedding its skin), the same visual might work as a dynamic expression of a product's staying power.

On a more personal level, a culture's icons can express social roles. When an agency calls a casting company or talent agent in search of a model, the agency, in essence, seeks an icon. It hopes the model will effectively symbolize the product's benefits or help the target market relate better to the ad. A model considered attractive in one culture is not necessarily seen that way in another, however.

Catchy phrases popular in a local culture are often used for advertising. But even if the idea translates verbally into another language, which is rarely the case, the art director may still have difficulty using the same imagery. Advertisers working in global markets must pretest art and design concepts with natives of each country.

Legal Restraints on International Advertisers

Finally, all advertising creativity, including what the ads say, show, or do, is at the mercy of foreign governments and cultures. As we discussed in Chapter 2, many countries strongly regulate advertising claims and the use of particular media.

Summary

The nonverbal aspect of an ad or commercial carries half the burden of encoding the message. In fact, the nonverbal message is inseparable from the verbal. Either one can enhance the other or destroy it.

Design refers to how the art director and graphic artist conceptually choose and structure the artistic elements that make up an ad's appearance or set its tone. For print advertising, the first work from the art department is a simple, undeveloped design of the ad's layout. The layout has several purposes: it shows where the parts of the ad are to be placed; it is an inexpensive way to explore creative ideas; it helps the creative team check the ad's psychological or symbolic function; and it serves as a blueprint for the production process.

As advertising copy goes through the editing process, copywriters must be prepared for an inevitable—and sometimes lengthy—succession of edits and reedits from agency and client managers and legal departments. Copywriters must be more than creative; they must be patient, flexible, mature, and able to exercise great self-control.

Several steps are used to develop an ad's design: thumbnail sketch, rough layout, and comprehensive layout. The mechanical is the final art ready for reproduction. Brochures and other multipage materials use a three-dimensional rough called a dummy.

The computer has dramatically affected graphic design. Inexpensive PC software programs allow artists to paint and draw, make up pages, and manipulate images in ways that would not be possible manually. Every graphic designer must now be computer literate.

In print advertising, the visual has a great deal of responsibility for an ad's success. The picture may be used to capture the reader's attention, identify the subject of the ad, create a favorable impression, or serve a host of other functions.

The two basic devices for illustrating an ad are photography and drawings. Photography can contribute realism; a feeling of immediacy; a feeling of live action; the special enhancement of mood, beauty, and sensitivity; and speed, flexibility, and economy. Drawn illustrations do many of these things, too, and may be used if the artist feels they can achieve greater impact than photos. The chief focus for visuals may be the product in a variety of settings, a user benefit, a humorous situation, a testimonial, or even some negative appeal.

The key format elements for writing print ads are headlines, subheads, body copy, slogans, seals, logos, and signatures. Many headline types and copy styles are used in print advertising. There are five basic types of advertising headlines: benefit, provocative, news/information, question, and command. Copy styles also fall into several categories: straight sell, institutional, narrative, dialog/monolog, picture caption, and device.

The creative pyramid and the format elements come together in creating effective print ads. The headline carries the attention step, the subhead and lead-in paragraph hold the interest step, and the interior paragraphs, trial close, and close of body copy contain the credibility, desire, and action steps.

In electronic media, copy is normally spoken dialog that is prepared using a script; it is referred to as the audio portion of the commercial. The copy may be delivered as a voice-over by an unseen announcer or on camera by an announcer, spokesperson, or actor.

Radio commercials must be intrusive to catch and hold the attention of people who are usually doing something else. Radio copy must be more conversational than print copy and should paint word pictures for listeners to see in their mind's eye.

Television copywriters use scripts and storyboards to communicate the verbal and nonverbal ideas of a commercial. When writing TV ads, the creative team must strive for credibility, relevance, and consistency in tone. While TV commercials should be entertaining, the entertainment should not interfere with the selling message.

In radio and TV advertising, art plays an important role. Art includes concept development, character definition, set and scene design, costuming, lighting, scripting, and camera angles—everything having to do with the visual value of the commercial.

Common formats for radio and TV commercials include straight announcement, presenter, testimonial, demonstration, musical, slice of life, lifestyle, and animation. The art director works with a writer to develop the artistic qualities of the big idea, the format, and the storyboard. The storyboard, the basic rough design of a TV commercial, contains sketches of the scenes along with the script. To supplement the storyboard and pretest a commercial, an animatic may be used.

When creating ads for international markets, advertisers must consider the different purchasing habits of foreign consumers, the variations in language, and the legal restrictions imposed by foreign governments or cultures. Art direction for international markets requires an in-depth knowledge of the foreign culture. Even if the verbal message translates well, the icons and images may not.

Questions for Review and Discussion

1. What is a layout? What is its purpose?
2. What are the steps in the design process for a print ad?
3. What color is white space?
4. From any chapter in the book, select an ad that contains a visual. What is the visual's purpose? How would you improve the visual if you were the art director?
5. What kind of headline does the ad from question 4 have? How well has the creative team followed the steps up the creative pyramid? Explain.
6. Choose an ad you don't like. Rewrite the headline using three different styles.
7. What is a storyboard, and what is its role?
8. Give examples of television spots that typify the eight major types of television commercials.
9. Find an international ad or commercial you like. What is its message strategy? Can you discern the copy style? Do you think the copy and headline reflect the strategy? What do you like about the ad? Why?
10. What guidelines can you cite for preparing an ad in a foreign language?

Chapter

11

Producing Ads for Print, Electronic, and Digital Media

Objective: To present an overview of how ads and commercials are produced for print, electronic, and digital media. With their dynamic effect on the production process, computers now give advertisers many more options for saving money and time and enhancing production quality. But to control cost and quality, advertisers still need a basic knowledge of the processes and methods used in printing and broadcasting as well as in the new digital media.

After studying this chapter, you will be able to:

- Discuss the role of computers in the print production process.

- Explain the process ads and brochures go through from concept through final production.

- Discuss how materials for printing are prepared for the press.

- Explain the process TV and radio commercials go through from concept through final production.

- Describe the major types of radio and TV commercials.

- Understand how to save money in television production.

- Discuss the opportunities for special effects in television.

- Explain how the major types of digital media are useful to advertisers.

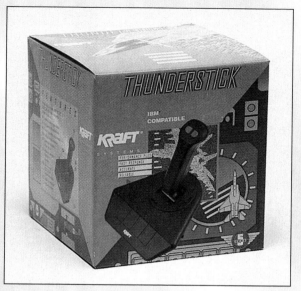

raft Systems was on the move. Since the 60s, when its only product was a radio flight controller for model aircraft, it had grown to a family of 12 computer products—computer joysticks, mice, and game boards for Mac and DOS computers. The company's reputation for quality products had grown as well; *PC/Computing* magazine placed four of the company's products on its top-12 list, and two received first and second place honors.

June Tahoma, Kraft's director for purchasing and special project development, knew it was time to enhance the company's advertising and packaging to match its rising-star reputation. She liked the highly graphic quality of the advertising created by Market Design and awarded it the Kraft image program.

The challenge was clear. Market Design had six weeks to conceptualize, design, and produce a series of print ads and packaging for a family of 12 products.

The creative team went to work immediately. Tom Michael, president and senior creative director for Market Design, served as the project's art director, accompanied by Jonathan Hulsh, the team's copywriter, and Mark Watkins, the designer and production manager. Their big idea—instrumentation for flying—was the catalyst for Hulsh's headline based on Kraft's historic rise:

30 Years Ago We Flew Our First Plane.
Today We're Flying This Entire Squadron.

Tahoma was pleased by the concept and approved it. Now Watkins had to turn creative roughs into the final ad.

As production manager, Watkins has one of the most demanding positions in the advertising business, because to achieve great advertising, every technical detail of production must be resolved precisely and correctly. A simple mistake like a misspelled word or a blemish on the visual can ruin a job, damage the agency's reputation, and lose huge amounts of time and money.

Once Watkins was handed the approved layout and text, he visualized how the ad's various components would be produced. The ad called for a photo of eight packages next to the Kraft products. But the packaging hadn't even been printed yet! Watkins would have to create dummies for the photo session. He immediately put the production artists to work on the computers to produce the artwork for all eight boxes.

Once the dummy packages were ready for the photo shoot, Watkins and Michael took them to the studio. Getting the boxes arranged, adjusting the lights to control the shadows, and shooting Polaroid proof prints took four hours.

Watkins initiated the artwork for the first ad. The serif type on the computer screen matched the positioning on the approved comprehensive layout, but somehow it didn't seem to be very attention-getting. Michael suggested kerning the characters in the headline so that the serifs on some letters would just touch. He then asked the production artist to move each line of type more snugly under the line above. These changes turned the headline into a visual magnet.

Watkins then scanned the new photos of the dummy packages and imported them into the page-making software. As the various images appeared on the page, the artist moved them into position and sized them to fit. Once all the elements—photos, type, logo, etc.—looked good on the screen, he saved the file and copied it onto a cartridge for Headline Graphics, a local reprographics service bureau, to output. The next morning, Michael presented a proof of the finished ad to Tahoma for approval. At lunch, Headline Graphics generated a set of negatives and a color proof destined for each publication. By 5:00 P.M., the negatives were being expressed overnight to each publication.

Market Design had just completed another routine job—on time and under budget. •

• Kraft Systems ad as it appeared in targeted publications.

MANAGING THE ADVERTISING PRODUCTION PROCESS

The average reader of ads has little idea of the intricate, technical stages ads go through from start to finish. But experienced advertising people do—especially art directors, designers, print production managers, and producers. They know the details give an ad added impact and completeness. Since careful management is the key to success in producing advertising, we'll discuss the management issues before examining the details of the production processes.

The Changing Role of the Production Manager and Producer

Every ad or commercial represents the completion of a highly complex process that includes many steps, such as the reproduction of visuals in full color, the shooting and editing of scenes, the precise specification and placement of type, and the checking, approving, duplicating, and shipping of final art, negatives, tape, or film to various communication media (newspapers, magazines, radio and television stations, and sometimes even computer stores).

These tasks are usually the responsibility of a print **production manager** or, for electronic media, a **producer.** The overall responsibility of the manager is to keep the project moving smoothly and under budget, while maintaining the required level of quality through every step of the production process.

Essentially, production managers and producers perform the four classic functions of management: *planning, organizing, directing*, and *controlling*. Mark Watkins at Market Design, for example, had to review the conceptual art and then *plan* which production process would resolve each requirement. Next he *organized* the tasks and established priorities. He then *directed* the production staff in completing each section of the art. Finally, to perform the *control* function—essential for optimizing quality, economy, and speed—he carefully reviewed the work of each subcontractor and solicited feedback from the art director to be sure they were all on the same track.

Planning and organizing

In the computer age, the *allocation of time* is an important facet of management. Every phase of a project comprises many tasks, so the production manager must anticipate where irregularities will occur within each phase. For example, five phases are needed to complete one animated commercial, but the amount of time required for each varies from spot to spot (see Exhibit 11–1).[1]

Directing and controlling

The supervision of the production staff is another important management challenge. If artists fail to follow the art director's design correctly, they can kill an ad's power, beauty, and effectiveness. Improper printing processes, papers, or inks can also weaken the impact of the image, increase costs, and even lead to reprinting. Print production managers can lose tens of thousands of their client's or agency's dollars (and sometimes their jobs) by forgetting to double-check the details of print production and the work of the production staff.

The production manager has to keep up with the technological changes occurring in print and electronic production, including the emerging forms of **digital media** (multimedia, interactive media, and online networks). The manager must also understand how computers can serve the production process, because virtually all advertising agency employees now use computers (see Exhibit 11–2).[2]

Managing Production Costs

When Market Design began working with Kraft, Mark Watkins submitted an estimate for anticipated production costs, including computer artwork and subcontracted work like photography, reproduction services, and delivery. When he received the approved art concepts a couple of weeks later, it was understood that he would keep the actual costs below his estimate.

A good production manager continually monitors the time spent on a job and the charges submitted by outside suppliers so as to not exceed the budget. The big effort is to control *unplanned costs*.

Common budget busters

Advertising managers should be aware of five things that commonly break budgets. First, cost overruns occur most frequently because of *inadequate planning* and lack of preparation. Another insidious culprit is *production luxuries*. When the creative director wants to reward the staff by taking everyone to lunch at the company's expense, the first question should be: "Was money budgeted for this?" The third budget buster is *overtime:* night and weekend work. Whenever possible, managers should develop alternative plans to avoid overtime hours. *Special equipment* for unusual production effects can also wreak havoc on budgets. An exotic computer gizmo is often far more expensive than standard equipment. Finally, a complex *hierarchy* of decision makers, approvers, and lawyers can stall decision making, cause negative debate, and stop progress.

Some other budget issues are peculiar to each medium.

Managing the cost of print production

The term **print production** refers to the systematic process an approved design goes through from concept to final publication in a printed medium such as magazines, newspapers, or collateral materials like brochures and direct-mail packages.

For print media, production managers can choose from more than 60 techniques to execute the creative team's design and get it printed on any of a variety of materials (usually paper).[3] They must translate the rough or comprehensive design into a final

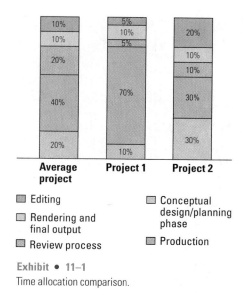

Editing

Rendering and final output

Review process

Conceptual design/planning phase

Production

Exhibit • 11–1
Time allocation comparison.

Exhibit • 11–2
Percentage of ad agency employees with their own personal computer.

Creative	75%
Account management	77
Media	90
Research	91
Business/finance/administration	75
Secretarial (all departments)	90

Ethics, Ergonomics, and Economics

Who is likely to be injured at work? Half of all workplace injuries are caused by cumulative trauma disorders (CTDs), also known as repetitive-motion injuries—the kind that affect advertising agency staffs: computer operators (administrative and creative), graphic artists, audiovisual specialists, and anyone who performs the same set of motions many times daily. These disorders cost business $20 billion annually just in workers' compensation expenses, according to Dr. Barbara Silverstein, special assistant for ergonomics at the Occupational Safety & Health Administration (OSHA).

A few decades ago, relatively few ad agency managers were aware of CTDs. Occasionally artists and typists reported back and neck problems, but managers took little action because there was no proof that these problems were caused by the office environment. The problems seemed minor and were certainly not considered related to ethics.

It gradually became clear that business managers were not meeting their ethical obligation to protect workers and workplaces. The government moved in to fill the ethical void; workplace safety is now protected by federal and state OSHA regulations. And these regulations are becoming stricter—requiring, among other things, an ergonomics risk factor checklist. Key risk factors are force, the repetitive nature or frequency of a task, awkward postures, the time spent on a task, and the pace of work. "The human body is simply not designed to sit," says Rajendra Paul, corporate ergonomist at Haworth Inc. in Michigan. "Yet between 70 and 75 percent of today's workforce is sitting and working on computers."

Other regulations affect equipment. If choosing a monitor based on something as ephemeral as ergonomics sounds like a big headache, consider that using the wrong monitor can give you migraines and even worse. According to one estimate, as many as 10 million people may suffer from an ailment known as CVS (computer vision syndrome), which has an array of symptoms including eyestrain, fatigue, blurred vision, double vision, and headaches. Cal OSHA, for example, wants those who work at video display terminals (VDTs) or computers to be positioned so that the screen's entire primary viewing area is less than 60 degrees below the horizontal plane passing through the eyes of the operator. And after two hours of repetitive work, each operator must get a 15-minute break or be assigned to 15 minutes of alternative work.

Even the quality of an agency's equipment has ethical implications. Some poorly designed computer monitors, for example, generate high levels of low-frequency electromagnetic fields, which some studies have associated with miscarriages and cancer. Although there is no conclusive proof that emissions from computers or monitors cause adverse health effects, standards for measuring emissions have been set. When dealing with a gray area like this, ethics are often our only guide.

Materials can also require ethical review. For years, advertising artists have used marker pens

assembly of black-and-white artwork. Then they make sure the mechanical is converted into a correct set of negatives for the printer to use to make printing plates. We'll discuss this process in detail shortly.

A big cost factor in the production of Kraft's ads was the reprographic service bureau that provided all the proofs and negatives. Packaging incurred additional printing and assembly charges by the package manufacturer.

Many production managers prefer using printers to provide all the prepress graphic services (such as processing negatives from artwork or disk). Printers know exactly which processing specifications yield the most suitable negatives for their platemaking equipment and printing presses, and they often charge less than outside service bureaus. Other production managers feel safer ordering the negatives from a reprographics service bureau because they get to proof the negatives before the printer mounts them for platemaking (a process called *stripping*). A 1994 survey revealed that only 14 percent of printers offered digital graphic services in-house, but 54 percent of those without such services said they planned to do so in the next five years.[4]

Paper costs affect budgets. When agencies place ads in print media, the cost of paper is included in the charge for the ad. This pass-along cost is not noticed by advertisers. However, when an agency prints collateral materials such as data sheets, brochures, or packaging for a client, the cost of paper is noticeable. For example, on a full-color job, a short run of 2,000 units would require only a few thousand sheets of paper (a variable cost), while the prepress and press set-up charges (fixed costs) would comprise the bulk of the final selling price. But if the same job were to have a long run of 100,000 or more units, the prepress and press set-up charges would remain the same, while the cost for paper would rise according to the volume used—a cost increase of 700 to 1,000 percent. Thus, paper would greatly outweigh the press costs.

For *sheetfed* printing jobs (where individual sheets are fed into the press), the cost of paper averages about 22 percent of the selling price of the job. Huge *web presses,*

and spray glues (that use vaporous chemicals as solvents) to create and mount artwork. Once trade publications began reporting a link between spray

---

Agency managers are now better informed that offices (in contrast to manufacturing work sites) have some unique and potentially harmful elements . . . that must be considered when work areas are designed.

---

glue and tingling and numbing in the fingers, agencies set up spray booths for capturing floating solvent and glue particles. They also adopted the OSHA standards for good ventilation to disperse toxic fumes.

Agency managers are now better informed that offices (in contrast to manufacturing work sites) have some unique and potentially harmful elements—distinct types of lighting, furniture,

and tools such as computers, keyboards, and telephones—that must be considered when work areas are designed. Orincon, a think tank, hired an ergonomic consultant while setting up its in-house agency and graphics department at its San Diego headquarters. The consultant helped select the chairs, proposed the layout for the computer stations, and consulted with employees about their individual needs.

Agencies can learn from other types of companies. At IDS Financial Services—which has 6,000 employees, two-thirds of them in five office buildings in Minneapolis—each individual gets a choice of chairs, footrests, and options for computer location. And anyone at IDS with an ergonomics complaint gets a personal evaluation of his or her workstation.

While all this may seem like coddling, nonbelievers should remember that one bout of monitor migraine, carpal tunnel syndrome, or incapacitating backache—not to mention the stress of a resultant lawsuit stemming from such an injury—

could debilitate the smooth operation of any agency. Ethical behavior can pay big dividends when workplace safety is the issue.

Questions

1. Would the possibility of being called a troublemaker by your company's managers stop you from telling your employer that the company was not meeting its ethical ergonomic responsibilities? Describe your reasoning.

2. If you owned your own company and had 15 employees, do you think an ergonomic evaluation of each person's workstation would be important? Explain your answer by informally estimating the cost of the survey and the potential savings (from work loss, hiring replacement workers, and legal damages).

Sources: Michael A. Verespej, "Ergonomics: An Unfounded Fear?" *Industry Week,* December 5, 1995, pp. 36–42; Winn L. Rosch, "In Search of the Safest Monitor," *Mac User,* February 1994, pp. 92–105.

---

frequently used by catalog publishers and magazines, require rapid printing, so they use rolls of paper and inks that dry instantly when heated (*heat set*). The paper cost for this process averages about 35 percent of the printer's selling price.[5]

Managing the cost of electronic production

The term **electronic production** refers to the process of converting a script or storyboard to a finished commercial for use on radio, TV, or digital media. While the overall process is similar to print production, the technical details and the costs of electronic production are quite different. And the end result, rather than print film or negatives, may be audio or videotape, motion picture film, or some digital format like CD-ROM or floppy disk.

Radio Radio is the least expensive electronic medium to produce because it deals only with the dimension of sound. Equipment and labor costs are less than for, say, TV production—there's no need for hairstylists, makeup artists, or cue card holders. And commercials are duplicated on inexpensive audiotape.

The primary control factors in producing radio spots, therefore, are the costs of talent and music. Celebrity talent especially can be very expensive. But even standard union talent, paid at **scale** (the regular charge agreed to in the union contract), can mount rapidly if there are multiple voices or if the commercial is aired in many markets or for an extended period of time. The advertiser, for example, may initially contract for a four-week or a thirteen-week run. If the commercial is extended beyond that time, the advertiser will have to pay a **residual fee** to the talent again.

Likewise, the cost of original music (composing, scoring, and orchestration) can range from very inexpensive to frightful, depending on the talent and scope of use. For this reason, many clients—especially small local and regional advertisers—prefer to use prerecorded music available for commercial use from the studio or radio station.

Exhibit • 11–4

Exhibit • 11–3
Average cost to produce a TV commercial ($000).

Commercial type	1993 National advertisers
Special effects	$254
Interview/testimonial	249
Multistory line/vignettes	246
Single situation—voiceover	233
Single situation—dialog	217
Animation	210
Large-scale product performance	208
Song and dance	187
Monolog	172
Tabletop/products, food	111

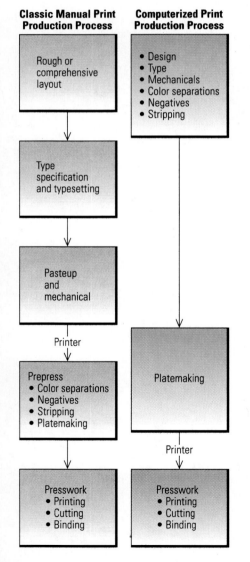

Television Many companies require the coverage offered by television. However, the television industry is susceptible to prohibitive costs of equipment and labor. In 1993, for example, the average cost of producing a national television spot soared to over $220,000, a 13 percent increase over the year before.[6] With costs like that, clients become very picky very quickly (see Exhibit 11–3).

There is a belief in the industry that high-priced celebrity talent and extravagant effects get attention and increase memorability. Not true. A recent study showed that advertising that features a brand differentiation message along with a demonstration of the product is actually more effective and costs on average 28 percent less. The study further indicated that advertisers sometimes use lavish production values to compensate for having nothing to say.[7]

Numerous factors can torture TV production budgets. They include the use of children and animals, superstar talent and directors, large casts, animation, involved opticals, special effects, stop-motion photography, using both location and studio shooting for one commercial, expensive set decoration or construction, additional shooting days, and major script changes during a shoot.[8] Commercial producers have to be aware of all these factors and plan for them very carefully.

Digital media The computer has engendered a whole new class of digital media. This has dramatically increased the importance of the tasks performed by the agency producer and creative staff and made it critical for them to stay current with new recording and duplicating processes as well as special effects technology.

In the past, to dramatically display their portfolios, agencies created *multimedia presentations*—fast-paced slide shows using multiple projectors and synchronized, recorded sound. Today's **multimedia** presenter aims a laser beam at the screen, and a sensor signals a portable computer to fade the slide machine and brighten the RGB projector. Then it runs a short animated video, complete with computer graphics and special effects. The creative team may write these multimedia sales presentations, but the production managers and producers are typically responsible for actually creating them.[9] Doing this in a cost-effective manner can be a challenge.

Although Market Design used computers to design the Kraft advertising, Watkins did not order digital media as a final product. However, if Kraft had needed a multimedia presentation, he could easily have used the existing digitized art to electronically make 35-millimeter slides, overhead projector cells, a self-running computer presentation on disk, or a CD-ROM.

One of the new media created by the computer is the stand-alone electronic kiosk. There are currently 70,000 kiosks in the U.S., and this number is expected to explode to over 600,000 by 1998. Featuring a computerized interactive touch screen, a printer, and in some cases, a credit card reader, kiosks will soon have agencies busy preparing storyboards, electronic images, and presentations. Advertising production managers now have to be knowledgeable in presentation and image software and know reliable suppliers for cabinet fabrication and computer hardware installation.[10]

Finally, some ads are totally created by computer for use on computers—electronic images and text designed for transmission around the world via the Internet or some online database service such as CompuServe, Prodigy, or America Online. The production manager can construct ads using off-the-shelf image and text development software. But to go onto the Net, the completed files have to be combined with some simple computer programming. For this service, most production managers will subcontract the work—but they'll have to know the suppliers, and charges can range from $30 to $100 per hour.[11]

The overall production process for creating images, graphic design, texts, and interactive digital programs for various electronic media is similar to working in print. Final output, though, is to a medium suitable for storage and transmission: CD-ROM, diskette, cartridge, or a computer file easily transmitted via telephone.

With digital media, costs rise dramatically when multiple copies are made. CD-ROMs can cost as little as $3 each if you purchase 1,000 copies or more. This is because of the up-front, fixed cost of making a master.[12] Computer diskettes can cost less

• Music store customers can use the iStation touch-screen kiosk to preview selections from more than 35,000 albums. iStations also collect data such as what customers preview, for how long, how they rate the albums, and how frequently they shop the store.

than $1 each to duplicate, but they hold only a few hundred pages of information. Cartridges hold up to 1,200 pages, but at $40 dollars or more each, they are not yet suitable for mass marketing.

Once Kraft's ads were produced and off to the media, Mark Watkins turned his attention to the series of packages that needed to be printed in full color. This involved the same process used for collateral materials such as brochures and direct-mail packages.

The **print production process** consists of four major phases: *preproduction, production, prepress,* and *printing and distribution.* For a simple model of this process, see Exhibit 11–4. (A detailed version appears as RL 11–1 in the Reference Library.)

The Preproduction Phase: Planning the Project

The first step, **preproduction,** begins when the creative department submits the approved creative concepts—rough or comprehensive layout and copy—to the production department. The production manager's first task is to log the project into the department's *traffic system* and open a **job jacket** for storing the various pieces of artwork and ideas that will be generated throughout the process. The next task is to examine the general nature of the job and consider several questions pertinent to managing it efficiently. For example:

- What equipment will be needed?
- How will we get it? (Will we have to lease another machine or use a freelancer?)
- What materials are necessary? (If this is a packaging job, what material will we be printing on: tin, paper, cardboard?)
- What human resources are needed? (Do we need to hire any freelancers?)
- How many production artists will be needed? (Is the deadline so near that we'll have to call up the reserves?)

THE PRINT PRODUCTION
PROCESS

Ad Lab 11-A   The Characteristics of Type

Readability

The most important consideration in selecting a typeface is readability. As David Ogilvy says, good typography helps people read; bad typography prevents them from doing so. General factors that contribute to readability include the type's style, boldness, and size; the length of the line; and the spacing between words, lines, and paragraphs. An ad is meant to be read, and reduced readability kills interest. Difficult-to-read typefaces should be used infrequently and only to create special effects.

Large, bold, simply designed typefaces are the easiest to read. However, the amount of space in the ad and the amount of copy that must be written limit the use of these type forms. The length of the line of copy can also affect the readability. Newspaper columns are usually less than 2 inches wide; magazine columns slightly wider. For ads, columns of copy should be less than 3 inches (18 picas) wide.

Spacing between lines also influences an ad's readability. Space between lines of type allows for descenders (the part of the letter that extends downward, as in the letters j, g, p) and ascenders (the part of the letter that extends upward, as in the letters b, d, k). When this is the only space between lines, type is said to be "set solid." Sometimes an art director adds extra space between lines (called leading, pronounced ledding) to give a more "airy" feeling to the copy. The name comes from the thin lead strips that used to be inserted between lines of metal type.

Kerning—spreading or narrowing the spaces between letters—also improves an ad's appearance and readability. The narrower the kerning, the more type can fit into the available space. Narrow kerning is effective in headlines because people read large type faster when the letters are close together. But narrow kerning is hard to read if overdone or in smaller type sizes.

Appropriateness

A typeface must be appropriate to the product being advertised. Each typeface and size conveys a mood and feeling quite apart from the meanings of the words themselves. One typeface whispers "luxury," another screams "bargain!" A typeface that looks old-fashioned would generally be inappropriate for an electronic watch.

Harmony/Appearance

Advertising novices often mix too many typefaces, creating disharmony and clutter. Type should harmonize with the other elements of an ad, including the illustration and layout. Skilled artists choose typefaces in the same family or faces that are closely related in appearance.

Emphasis

Contrast creates emphasis. Artists often use more than one type style or mix italic and roman, small and large type, lowercase and uppercase. But they must be careful not to emphasize all elements or they won't emphasize any.

Classes of Type

There are two classes of type used in advertising. Display type is larger and heavier than text type; useful in headlines, subheads, logos, addresses, and for emphasis. Text type is smaller and finer, used in body copy.

Type Groups

Serif (roman) type is the most popular type group due to its readability and warm personality. It is distinguished by small lines or tails called serifs that finish the ends of the main strokes and by variations in the thickness of the strokes. It comes in a wide variety of designs and sizes.

Sans serif (gothic) type is the second most popular type group; also referred to as block or contemporary. Characterized by lack of serifs (hence the name sans serif) and relatively uniform thickness of the strokes, it is not as readable as roman but widely used because the simple, clean lines give a slick, modern appearance. (See **a**.)

Square serif type combines sans serif and serif typefaces. It has serifs, but letter strokes have uniform thickness.

Cursive or script type resembles handwriting; letters often connect and may convey a feeling of femininity, formality, classicism, or beauty. It is difficult to read and is used primarily in headlines, formal announcements, and cosmetic and fashion ads.

Ornamental type uses novel designs with a high level of embellishment and decorativeness. It adds a "special effects" quality but is often difficult to read.

a.

Working backward from publication **closing dates** (deadlines), the production manager decides when each step of the work must be completed. Deadlines can vary from months to hours. The manager tries to build extra time into each step because every word, art element, and aesthetic choice may need some last-minute change.

Once these general questions are answered, the production manager can look more closely at the specific needs of the project.

Typography and copy casting

Art directors select type styles to enhance the desired personality of the product and complement the tone of the ad. Typefaces affect an ad's appearance, design, and readability. Good type selection can't compensate for a weak headline, poor body copy, or an inappropriate illustration, but it can create interest and attract readers.

Type Families

A type family is made up of related typefaces. The sans serif typeface you are reading now is called Univers. Within a family, the basic design remains the same but varies in the proportion, weight, and slant of the characters. The type may be light, medium, bold, extra bold, condensed, extended, and italic. Variations enable the typographer to provide contrast and emphasis without changing the family. (See **b.**)

A font is a complete assortment of capitals, small capitals, lowercase letters, numerals, and punctuation marks for a particular typeface and size.

Measuring Type

Type characters have height, width, weight and, for some ornamental typefaces, depth. They also come in shapes called a case. And with the advent of computers, type comes in a variety of resolutions.

Size is the height of a character (or letter) measured in points (72 points to the inch) from the bottom of the descenders to the top of the ascenders. (See **c.**)

The set width of a letter, known as an em space, is usually based on the maximum width and proportions of the capital letter "M" for that particular typeface. Set width of the letter "N" is called an en space.

Capital letters are uppercase, small letters lowercase (in the hot type era, compositors stacked the case containing the capital letters above the one with the small letters). It's easiest to read a combination of uppercase and lowercase. Type may be set in all caps (for emphasis) or in commoncase (caps and small caps).

Resolution refers to the fineness of the type. The goals of fine typesetting are readability, clarity, and smoothness of appearance. Type on a

computer screen is usually 72 to 78 dots per inch (dpi). A dot-matrix printer outputs type at 144 dpi, a laser printer at 300 dpi. The preferred level of quality for magazines and brochures begins at 1,000 dpi; advertisers often use resolutions of 2,400 to 3,750 dpi.

Laboratory Applications

Use the various figures and terms in this Ad Lab to answer the following:

1. Describe the class, group, family, and size of the type used in the title, "Producing

Garamond Book
Garamond Book Italic
Garamond Bold
Garamond Bold Italic
Garamond Light
Garamond Light Italic
Garamond Ultra
Garamond Ultra Italic
Garamond Condensed Book
Garamond Condensed Book Italic
Garamond Condensed Bold
Garamond Condensed Bold Italic
Garamond Condensed Light
Garamond Condensed Light Italic
Garamond Condensed Ultra
Garamond Condensed Ultra Italic

b.

Text type
6 pt. Type size
8 pt. Type size
9 pt. Type size
10 pt. Type size
12 pt. Type size
14 pt. Type size

Display type
16 pt. Type size
18 pt. Type size
20 pt. Type size
24 pt. Type size
30 pt. Type size
36 pt. Type size

c.

Ads for Print, Electronic, and Digital Media," that appears on the first page of this chapter.

2. Do the same for the captions that appear with the exhibits in this book.

It's imperative that production managers as well as graphic artists understand **typography,** the art of selecting and setting type. Advertising artists have to know the five major type groups, the artistic variations within a type family, and the structure of type. They should consider four important concepts when selecting type: *readability, appropriateness, harmony or appearance,* and *emphasis.* Ad Lab 11–A, "The Characteristics of Type," describes these and other type-related topics.

Artists who plan to buy type outside must **copy cast** (or *copyfit*) to forecast the total block of space the type will occupy in relation to the typeface's letter size and proportions. This is an important task because type is expensive to buy and costly to change. There are two ways to fit copy: the word-count method and the character-count method.

With the **word-count method,** the words in the copy are counted and divided by the number of words per square inch that can be set in a particular type style and size, as given in a standard table. The **character-count method** is more accurate. Someone counts the number of characters (letters, word spaces, and punctuation marks) in the copy, finds the average number of characters per pica for each typeface and size, and determines how much space the copy will fill.

Copyfitting ability was essential for all artists less than a decade ago, but now type can be manipulated in minutes on most computers. Copyfitting is still useful in the preproduction phase for avoiding typesetting problems downstream. When clients provide the agency with text for printed materials, they expect the artist to make the type "look good," even though there is far too much or too little text to fit properly in the space available. By measuring the copy early in the process, the artist has enough time to suggest that the text be rewritten to fit. Once production begins, deadlines may be missed waiting for text rewrites.

To make their ads unique and exclusive, some advertisers even commission a new type design. Other companies tailor their typography to blend with the magazines or newspapers their advertising appears in. This gives the ad an editorial look and, the advertiser hopes, enhanced credibility (or at least interest).

Planning the job

The overall purpose of preproduction is to plan the job thoroughly, which usually entails making a number of strategic choices before launching into full production. For example, since the conceptual rough layouts are made with marker colors that do not match printing inks well, the production manager should consult with the art director to formally select a color palette in advance, using a color guide like the PANTONE® system.

There is also the question of which printing process and which type of printing press to use for the job (see RL 11–2: Choosing the Best Method of Printing in the Reference Library). This will affect the budget and dictate how art is prepared in the production and prepress phases.

The art director and production manager will also consult on the paper to be used. Advertisers use three categories of paper: *writing, text,* and *cover stock.* Letters and fliers commonly use **writing paper**. Bond writing paper is the most durable and most frequently used. There are many types of **text papers,** such as news stock, antique finish, machine finish, English finish, and coated. These range from the inexpensive, coarse, porous papers (*newsprint*) used by newspapers to the smooth, expensive, coated stocks used in upscale magazines, industrial brochures, and fine-quality annual reports. **Cover paper** is thicker, tougher, and more durable. It comes in many finishes and textures for use on soft book covers, direct-mail pieces, and brochure covers.

Finally, the production manager must decide early which is most important for a particular project: speed, quality, or economy. Typically, the manager must sacrifice one in favor of the other two. The answer determines the production methods used and the personnel employed. Once all these decisions are made, the manager can begin the production phase.

The Production Phase: Creating the Artwork

Following the preproduction phase of the Kraft project, Mark Watkins faced the daunting task of producing the actual art for the 12 packages in a few weeks. Essentially, the **production phase** involves setting up the artwork and typesetting, completing ancillary functions such as illustration or photography, and then melding all these components into a final tangible form for the printer or publisher.

Preparing mechanicals

● In a multicolor piece of art, the printer needs layers that can be reproduced individually. This is done by computer or assembled by hand with plastic overlays. The total image is then reconstructed as each layer is printed over the other.

To create the art for an ad, brochure, or package, the production artist normally begins by marking out a grid on which to lay the type and art. In traditional handcrafted pasteup, the artist draws the grid on a piece of artboard in light blue pencil. The grid provides an underlying consistency to the spacing and design of the piece. Page-making computer software does this with commands for setting up columns and guides.

The production artist then specifies the style and size of the typefaces for the text and inputs this information, along with the copy, into the computer. If the company doesn't have its own typesetting machines or computer systems, the artist must still specify the type so the typesetting company can understand the data. The type may be positioned electronically or output onto paper and glued onto the artboard within the image area.

The Kraft package designs were quite complex, featuring photography, airbrushed art, and a patchwork of solid colors. Watkins studied the comps to visualize how the various art and copy elements could be isolated in individual layers in the mechanical art and the page-making software.

Whenever an additional color is to be printed, a second artboard marked to the same dimensions is used for the second image. The second image may be glued onto a clear plastic **overlay** that lies on top of the first image (called the **base art**). The production artist places crossmarks in the corners of the base art and then superimposes crossmarks on the transparent overlay precisely over those on the base art. This registers the exact position of the two layers of art to one another.

The art elements must be properly positioned in the artwork—whether mechanical or computer generated—because the printer needs to have layers of art that can be reproduced individually. The total image is then constructed as each layer is printed over the other. Since the printer must photograph each layer to make separate plates, this kind of artwork is called **camera-ready art**.

This procedure is easily performed in the computer. The various elements of art are assigned to a layer the operator names and can be run out as separate film negatives or paper positive images as needed.

Camera-ready art and halftones

Production art for the printing process is like an on/off switch: where the art is black, ink will stick; where the art is white, ink won't stick. The production artist adheres to this printing principle by using black-and-white artwork that is called *line art* and by converting gray images to a form of line art called *halftones*.

Line art Normal photographic paper (like snapshots made with a camera) produces images in **continuous tones**—black and white with shades of gray in between. But printing presses cannot print gray. So printers use special **orthographic film**, a high-contrast film yielding only black-and-white images with no gray tones. The artwork is simply photographed as is, and the result is called a **line film**. From that a **line plate** is produced for printing.

A continuous-tone photograph or other illustration requiring gradations in tone cannot be reproduced on orthographic film or a plate without an additional process, the *halftone screen*.

Halftone screens While line plates print lines and solid areas (like type), **halftone plates** print dots. The key element is the **halftone screen**, which breaks up continuous-tone artwork into tiny dots. The combination of dots, when printed, produces an optical illusion of shading, as in a photograph. In the dark areas of the image, the dots bump into each other and make the paper appear nearly black. In the gray areas, the size of the black dots equals the amount of white paper showing through, and in the white areas, the black dots are surrounded by a lot of white or are almost completely missing. The human eye perceives the dots as gradations of tone.

The fineness of the halftone screen determines the quality of the illusion. Fine magazine ads are printed with halftone screens as fine as 200 lines to the inch (lpi), while newspaper photos appear very coarse at 80 to 100 lpi. Coarser screens are used to

● A halftone screen breaks up continuous tone artwork into tiny dots. The combination of printed dots produces an optical illusion of shading, as in a photograph. The color dots show the separation for the color photo above. The other set of dots show the range that would appear in a black and white photo.

(continued on page 323)

From Concept through Production of a Magazine Ad and Television Commerical

Marketing Considerations

In 1993, Nike and Reebok held over 25 percent of the U.S. athletic footwear market. The next six brands held 25 percent, with the remainder divided among many tiny competitors. Adidas America was the number-eight brand at this time, but it saw an unprecedented opportunity approaching.

The situation

The U.S. would host the World Cup of Soccer in 1994, and Adidas was the leading brand in soccer shoes. Moreover, the company was ready to introduce its new Predator model, a technological breakthrough in soccer shoe design. Adidas hoped the World Cup competition would help raise soccer's profile in the U.S., increase market size, and offer an excellent showcase for the Predator. Adidas turned to its agency, Team One Advertising, for help.

Marketing and advertising objectives

Adidas and Team One set specific objectives for the Predator campaign: to maintain the company's soccer shoe leadership position in the minds of the target market and to increase Adidas' overall revenues by 12 percent. To accomplish this, Team One proposed positioning Adidas as "the real player's brand," and the Predator as the best offensive weapon a player can have.

Target markets

The primary target market was soccer-playing boys aged 13 to 18. The secondary market was all boys aged 13 to 18 who might take up soccer. Team One considered athletic shoe retailers an ancillary market, driven by consumer preferences.

Creative Strategy

The creative strategy included a mix of product concept, target audience, communications media, and advertising message:

1. **Product concept.** Predator featured innovative fins and jets on the toe and heel that enabled a player to control the ball and made the shoe a mighty offensive weapon and a nightmare for goalies.

2. **Target audience.** The campaign would focus on boys aged 13 to 18 who play soccer and are typically rebellious and individualistic by nature.

3. **Communications media.** Team One proposed a mixed-media campaign of soccer enthusiast magazines and TV. Plus, Adidas was the only soccer-related sponsor of the World Cup broadcasts, among credit card companies, soft drinks, cars, and candy bars.

4. **Advertising message.** The message strategy was to avoid slick presentations and to make the shoe the hero by looking at it from the soccer goalie's perspective. The copy concept was a sophisticated, minimalist approach, with U.S. Team goalie Tony Meola describing why he hated this shoe, and product features relegated to small type in parenthetical asides. The artistic concept in both print and TV was a hip, gritty, urban street tone—understated, honest, and straight. Print ads would show the shoe in detail; the TV commercials would show how the shoe affected the goalie's life. The big idea was embodied in the goalie's words: "This shoe sucks!"

Production Planning

Once the creative roughs were approved, the production supervisors prepared the schedule for both TV and print production. Considerations included the Adidas marketing deadlines; the World Cup Soccer schedule; international concerns such as filming rights and cultural taboos or customs; seasonal conditions; and production factors such as equipment needs, production support people, and facilities. The production department also prepared cost estimates for approval by agency and client managers.

Print Production Process

The print ad would show the Predator close up so the reader could clearly see the fins and jets on the toe and heel. The black shoe would be suspended toe down, pointing to the first line of copy against a bright yellow background that bled off the page. Nothing should detract from the stark photo of the shoe.

Predator ad

Shoe with red background

Stan Toyama, Team One's art director, did the initial layouts using a photo supplied by Adidas. The photo was well shot but showed the shoe against a red background, so Toyama scanned it into his computer and changed the background into a bright yellow.

Copy approval form

Print production and distribution

The production team assembled the approved copy and photography and opened a computer graphics file featuring guide-marked pages based on the specs provided by the magazines in which the ads would appear. The photo was rescanned larger and with higher resolution.

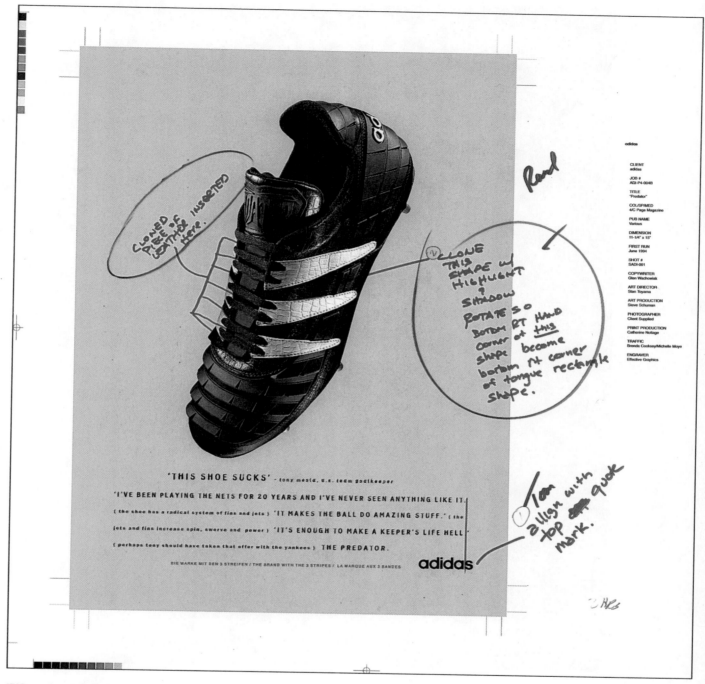

IRIS proof with Team One's comments

The computer operator initiated the production phase, entering the percentages of yellow and magenta ink that would print a golden yellow background bleeding beyond the overall size of the ad. The high-resolution scan of the Predator was dropped into the image and flipped. The operator added the digitized text, resizing portions of it, converting it into a unique type font, and giving it a distressed look. Each letter of the headline was individually sized and placed. The operator then produced a low-resolution print for internal review and after it was checked, copied the file and sent it to Effective Graphics, the graphics service bureau. There technicians ran a high-resolution IRIS color proof for Team One's review. Then Effective Graphics produced a set of negatives and a Chromalin four-color proof.

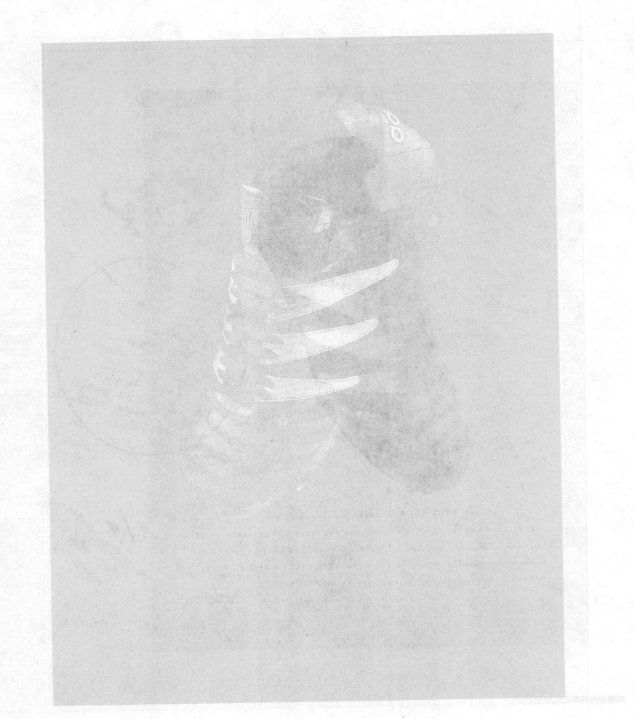

Yellow